SHY 2

Bukimi Miki

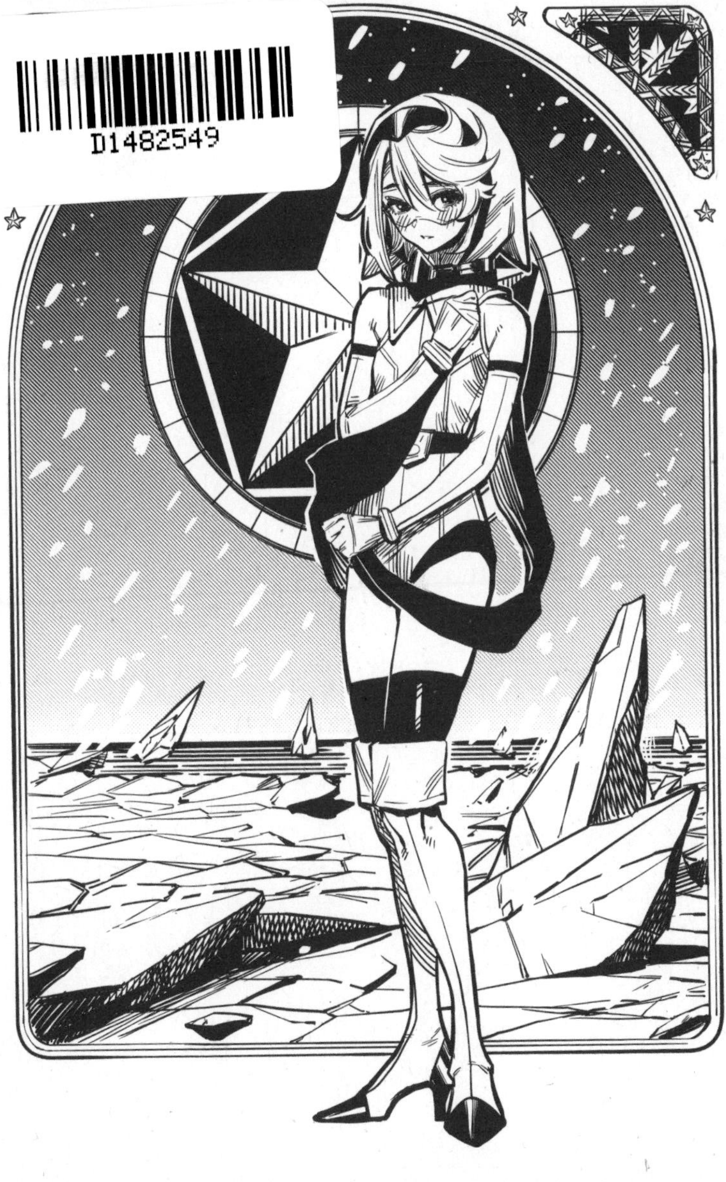

CHARACTERS

HEROES

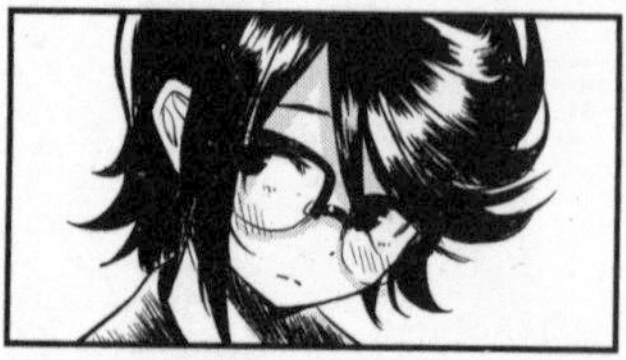

HEART-SHIFT ⟷

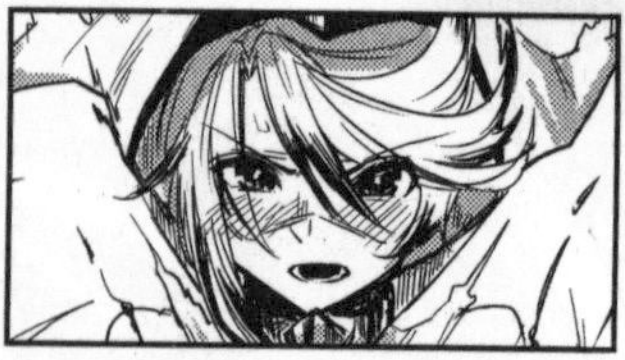

Teru Momijiyama

A kind-hearted girl in her second year of middle school. She's deathly shy and afraid of people.

Shy

Japan's hero. Teru Momijiyama after undergoing heart-shift. Iko is the only civilian who knows her true identity.

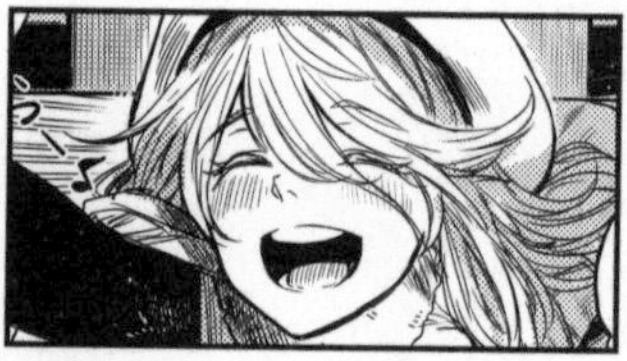

Spirit

Russia's hero. A boozehound who tends to show up when least expected. She often appears in Teru's room.

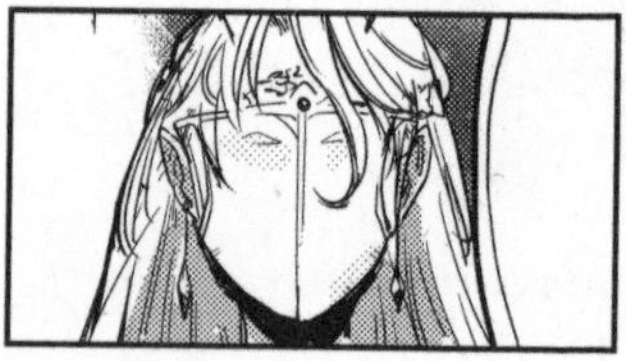

Unilord

She acts as a coordinator for all of Earth's heroes. No one knows what her real face looks like under her mask. Her nickname is "Eunnie."

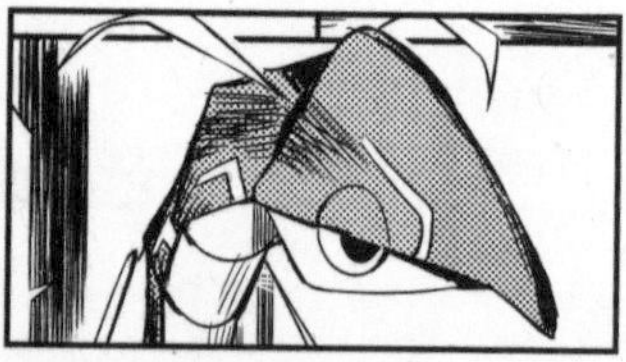

N. Vilio

Shy's partner. Its nickname is "Shrimpy." There are many organisms that look like it.

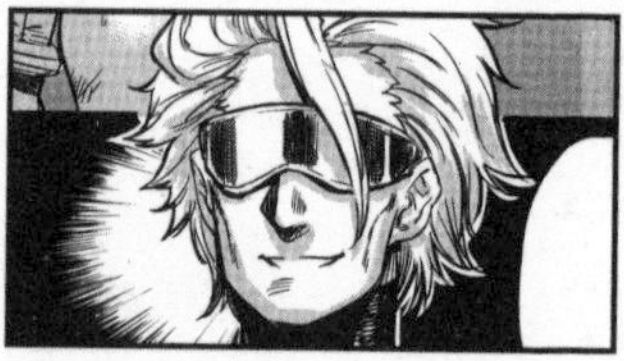

Stardust

The United Kingdom's hero. In his everyday life, he's a charismatic rock star.

VILLAINS

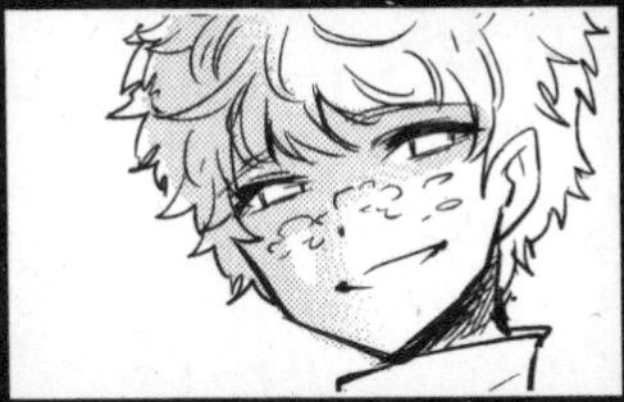

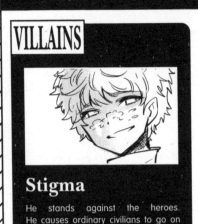

Stigma

He stands against the heroes. He causes ordinary civilians to go on violent rampages by having them wear a ring that is similar to the heart-shift bracelets.

CIVILIANS

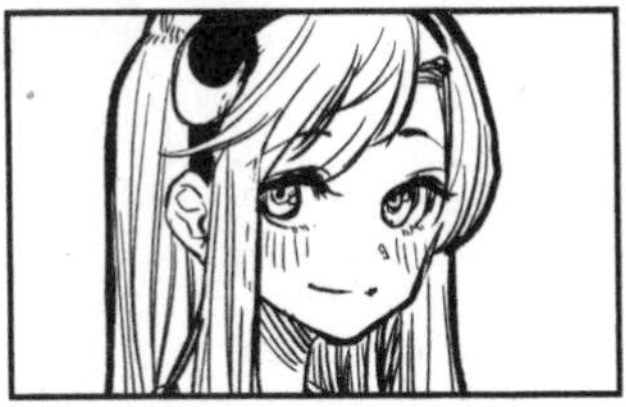

Iko Koishikawa

The girl who Shy previously failed to save. After that, she was attacked by a mysterious boy, but she was rescued by Shy. She's in the same class as Teru.

HEART-SHIFT BRACELETS

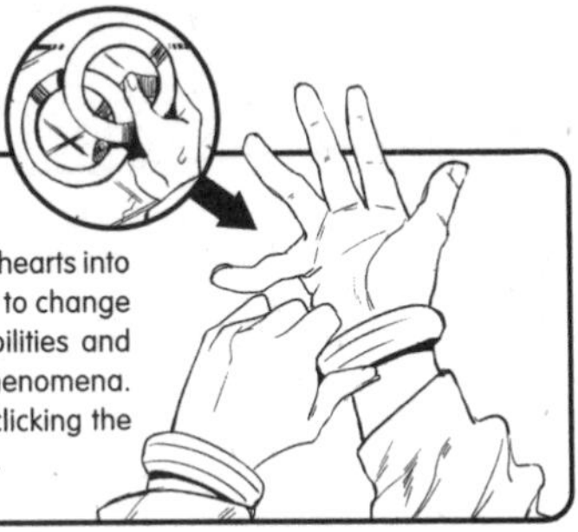

A device worn by heroes that converts the energy of their hearts into various powers and abilities. "Heart-shift" allows heroes to change into a form that gives them access to superhuman abilities and allows them to produce flames and other physical phenomena. The heart-shift bracelets are worn on both wrists, and clicking the bracelets together twice initiates the heart-shift process.

STORY

In the mid-twenty-first century, daring and stylish heroes from around the globe are actively working in the name of world peace. Among these noble defenders and their dashing efforts is Japan's hero—a bashful girl named Shy. One day, a boy named "Stigma" appears in front of Shy while she is suffering under the weighty responsibility of being a hero. Before her own eyes, Shy witnesses the boy's cruel and inhumane ability to utilize the hearts of others to turn them into rampaging monsters. And now, in order to learn the skills she needs to stand against Stigma, it has been decided that Shy will battle with the United Kingdom's hero, Stardust.

2
CONTENTS

Chapter 7

I'll Give It All I've Got

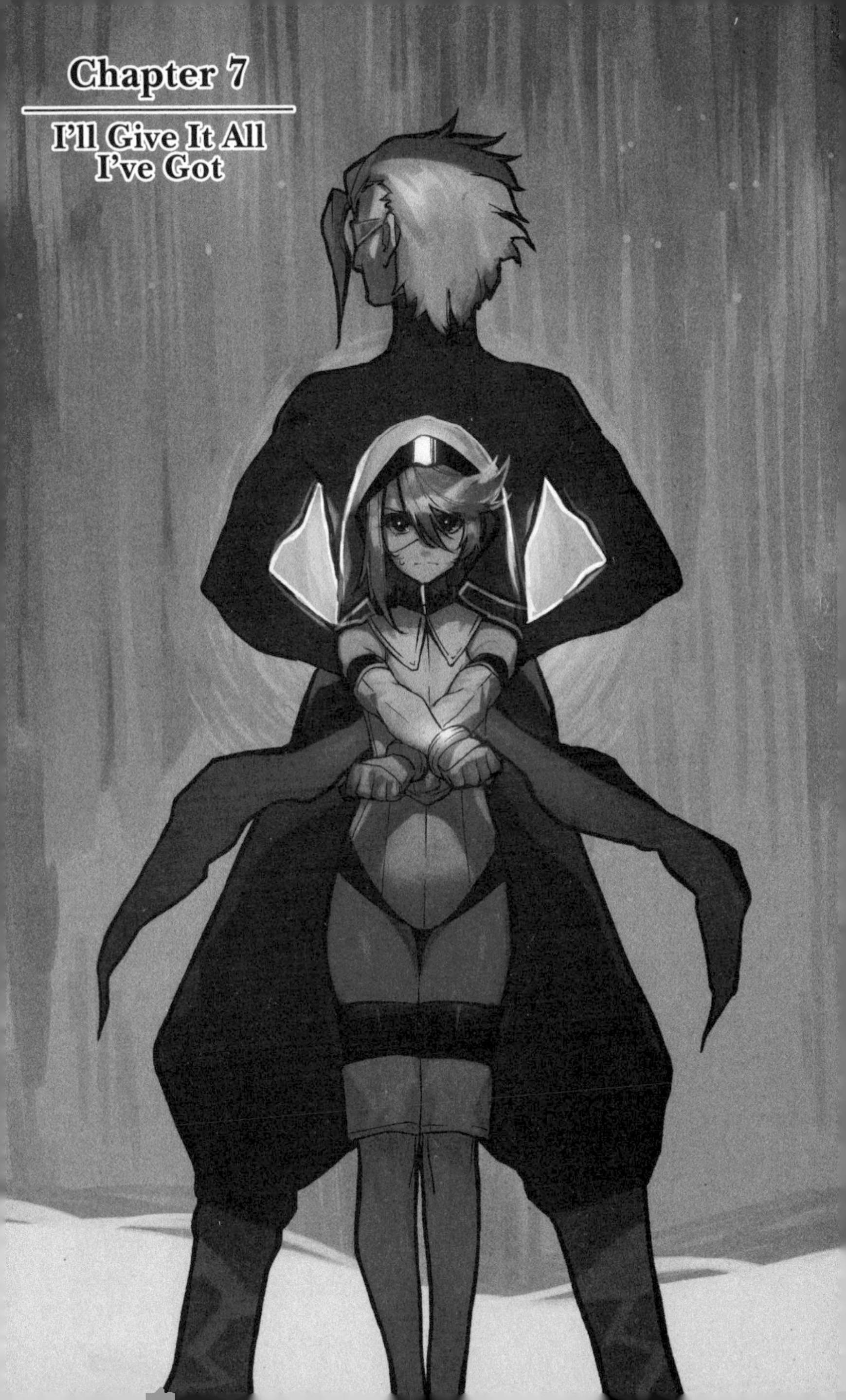

SHY

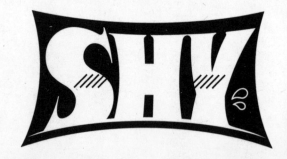

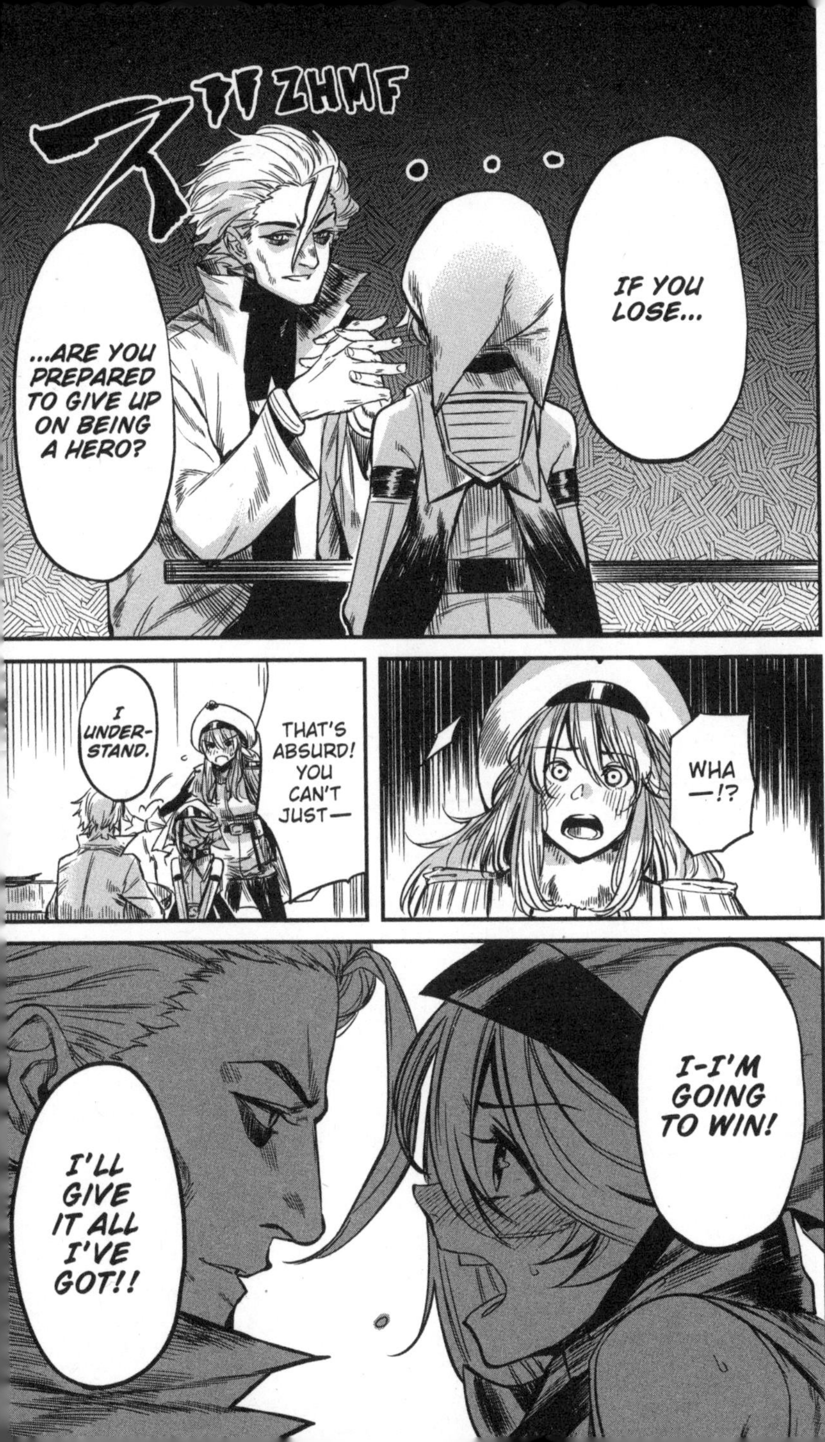
IF YOU LOSE...
ZHMF
...ARE YOU PREPARED TO GIVE UP ON BEING A HERO?
WHA—!?
THAT'S ABSURD! YOU CAN'T JUST—
I UNDER-STAND.
I-I'M GOING TO WIN!
I'LL GIVE IT ALL I'VE GOT!!

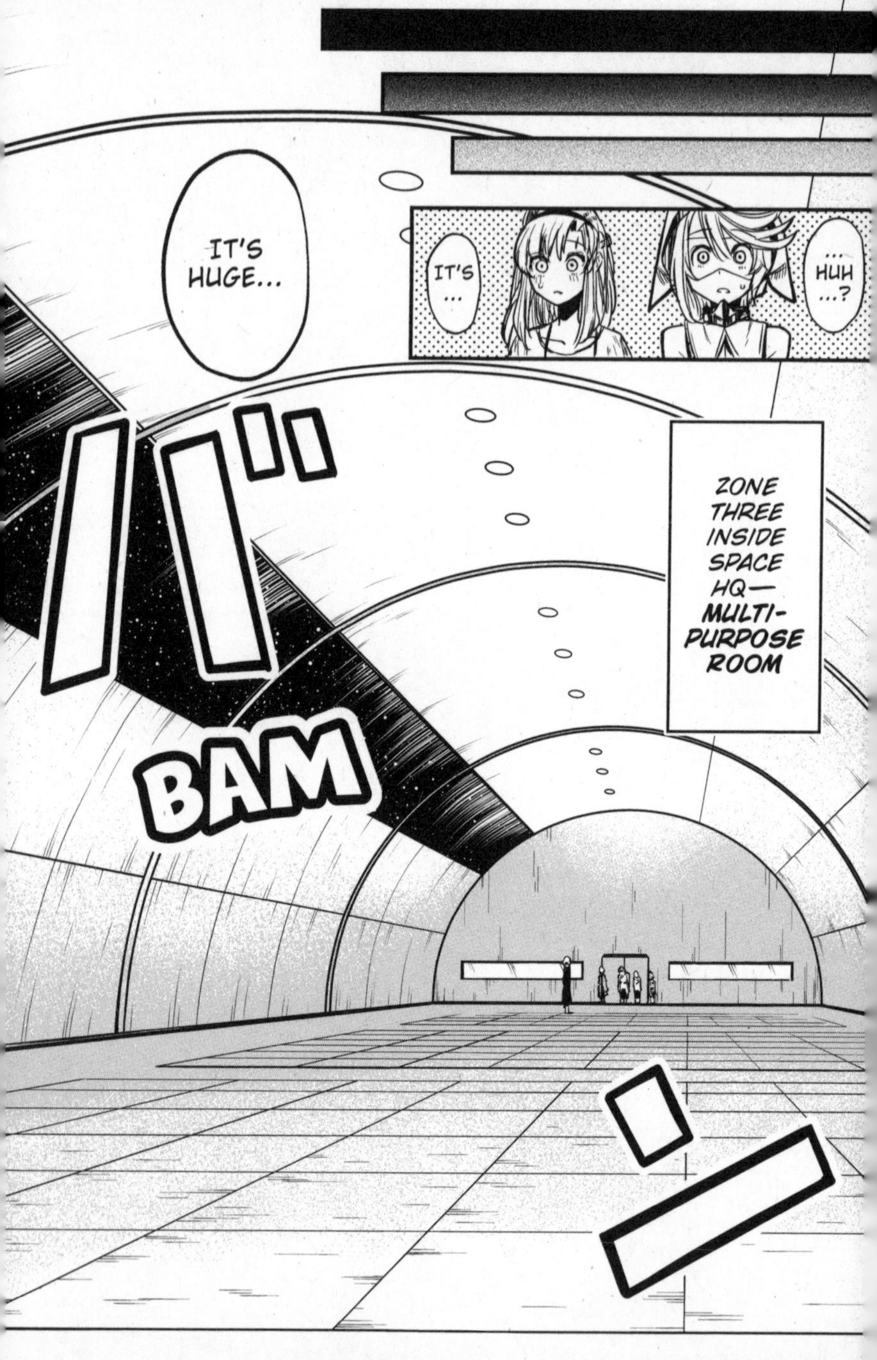
...HUH...?
IT'S...
IT'S HUGE...
ZONE THREE INSIDE SPACE HQ—MULTI-PURPOSE ROOM
BAM

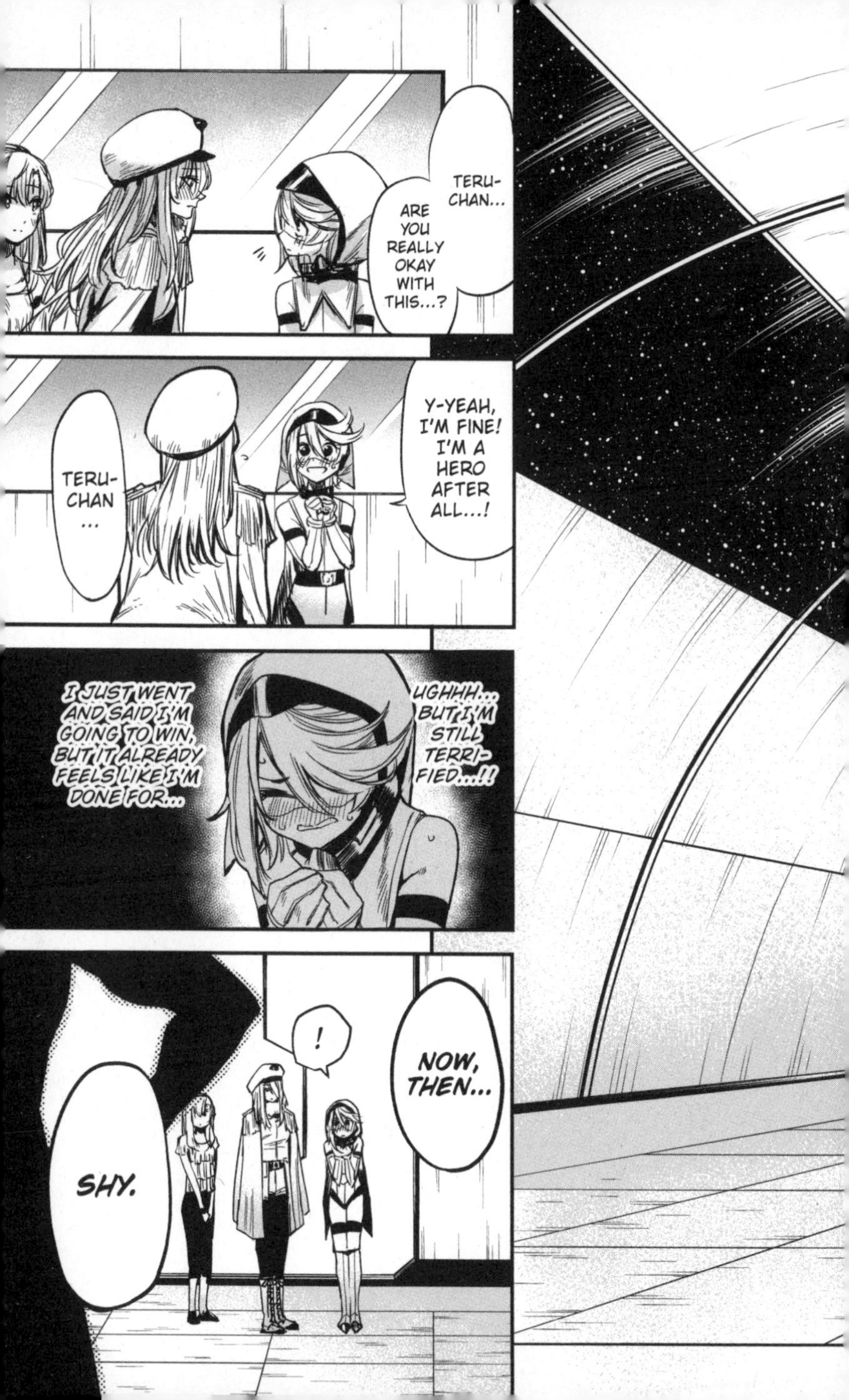
TERU-CHAN...
ARE YOU REALLY OKAY WITH THIS...?
Y-YEAH, I'M FINE! I'M A HERO AFTER ALL...!
TERU-CHAN...
UGHHH... BUT I'M STILL TERRI-FIED...!!
I JUST WENT AND SAID I'M GOING TO WIN, BUT IT ALREADY FEELS LIKE I'M DONE FOR...
NOW, THEN...
!
SHY.

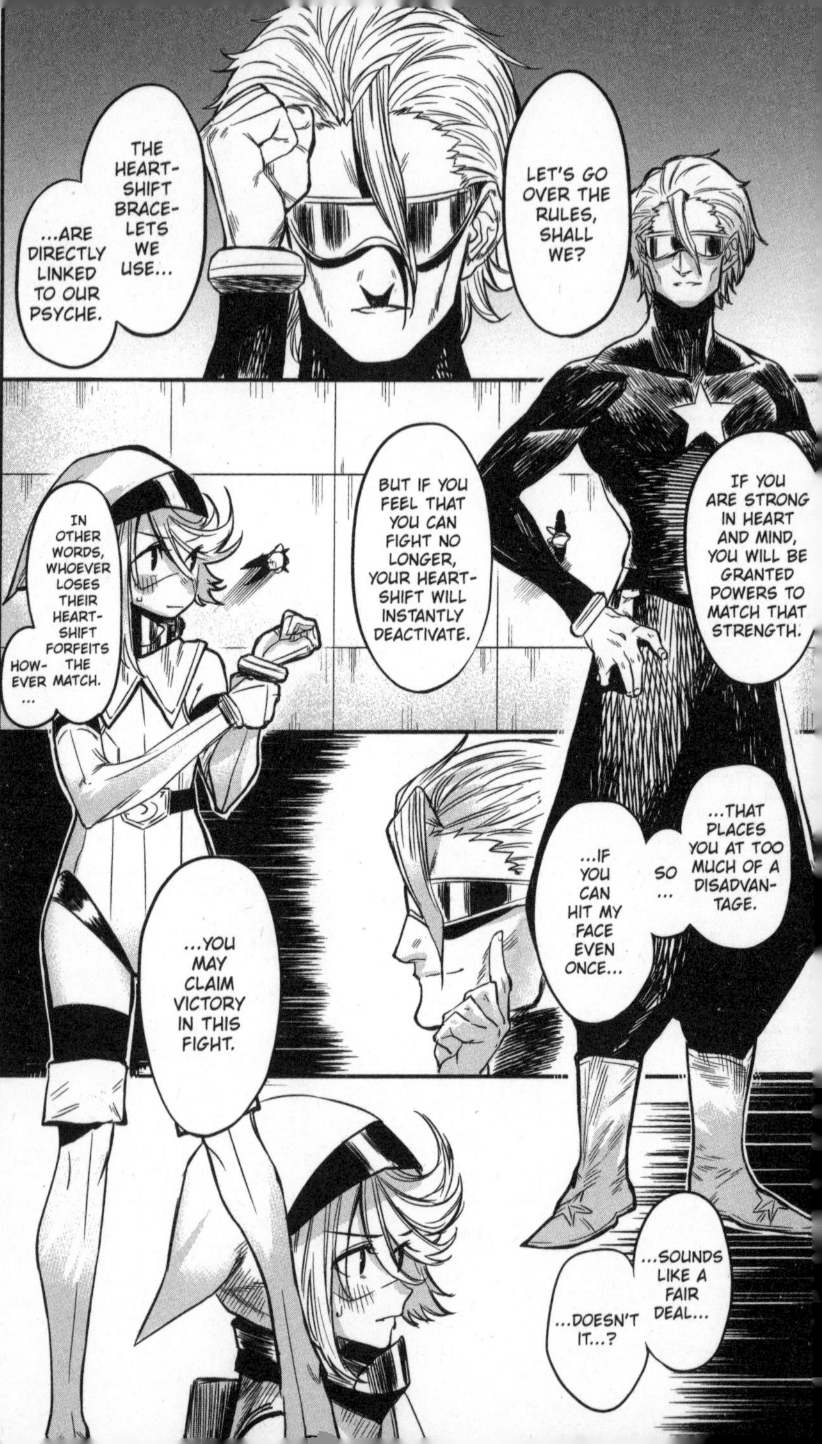
LET'S GO OVER THE RULES, SHALL WE?
THE HEART-SHIFT BRACELETS WE USE...
...ARE DIRECTLY LINKED TO OUR PSYCHE.
IF YOU ARE STRONG IN HEART AND MIND, YOU WILL BE GRANTED POWERS TO MATCH THAT STRENGTH.
BUT IF YOU FEEL THAT YOU CAN FIGHT NO LONGER, YOUR HEART-SHIFT WILL INSTANTLY DEACTIVATE.
IN OTHER WORDS, WHOEVER LOSES THEIR HEART-SHIFT FORFEITS THE MATCH.
HOWEVER...
...THAT PLACES YOU AT TOO MUCH OF A DISADVANTAGE.
SO...
...IF YOU CAN HIT MY FACE EVEN ONCE...
...YOU MAY CLAIM VICTORY IN THIS FIGHT.
...SOUNDS LIKE A FAIR DEAL...
...DOESN'T IT...?

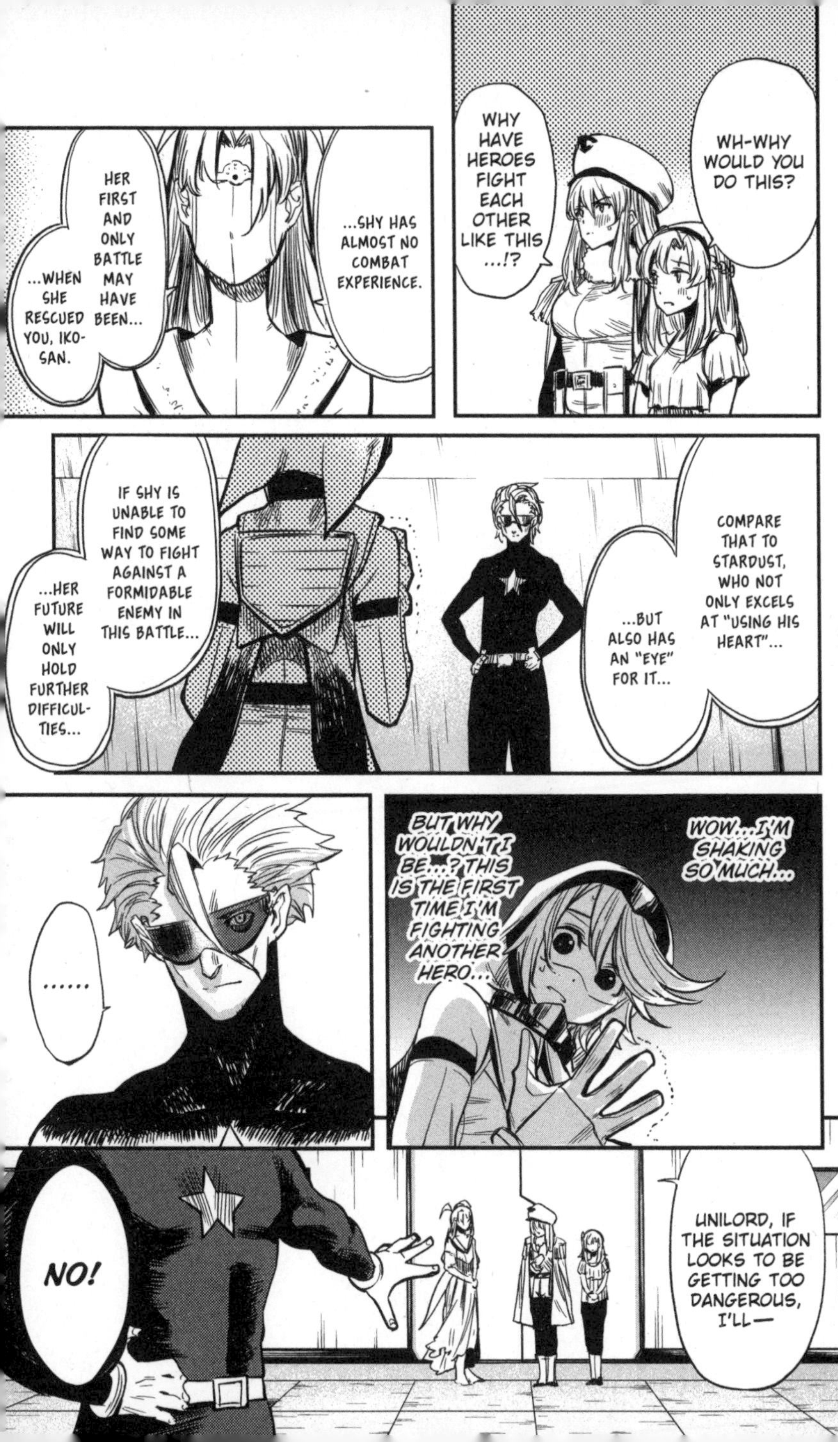
WH-WHY WOULD YOU DO THIS?
WHY HAVE HEROES FIGHT EACH OTHER LIKE THIS ...!?
...SHY HAS ALMOST NO COMBAT EXPERIENCE.
HER FIRST AND ONLY BATTLE MAY HAVE BEEN...
...WHEN SHE RESCUED YOU, IKO-SAN.
COMPARE THAT TO STARDUST, WHO NOT ONLY EXCELS AT "USING HIS HEART"...
...BUT ALSO HAS AN "EYE" FOR IT...
IF SHY IS UNABLE TO FIND SOME WAY TO FIGHT AGAINST A FORMIDABLE ENEMY IN THIS BATTLE...
...HER FUTURE WILL ONLY HOLD FURTHER DIFFICUL-TIES...
WOW...I'M SHAKING SO MUCH...
BUT WHY WOULDN'T I BE...? THIS IS THE FIRST TIME I'M FIGHTING ANOTHER HERO...
......
UNILORD, IF THE SITUATION LOOKS TO BE GETTING TOO DANGEROUS, I'LL—
NO!

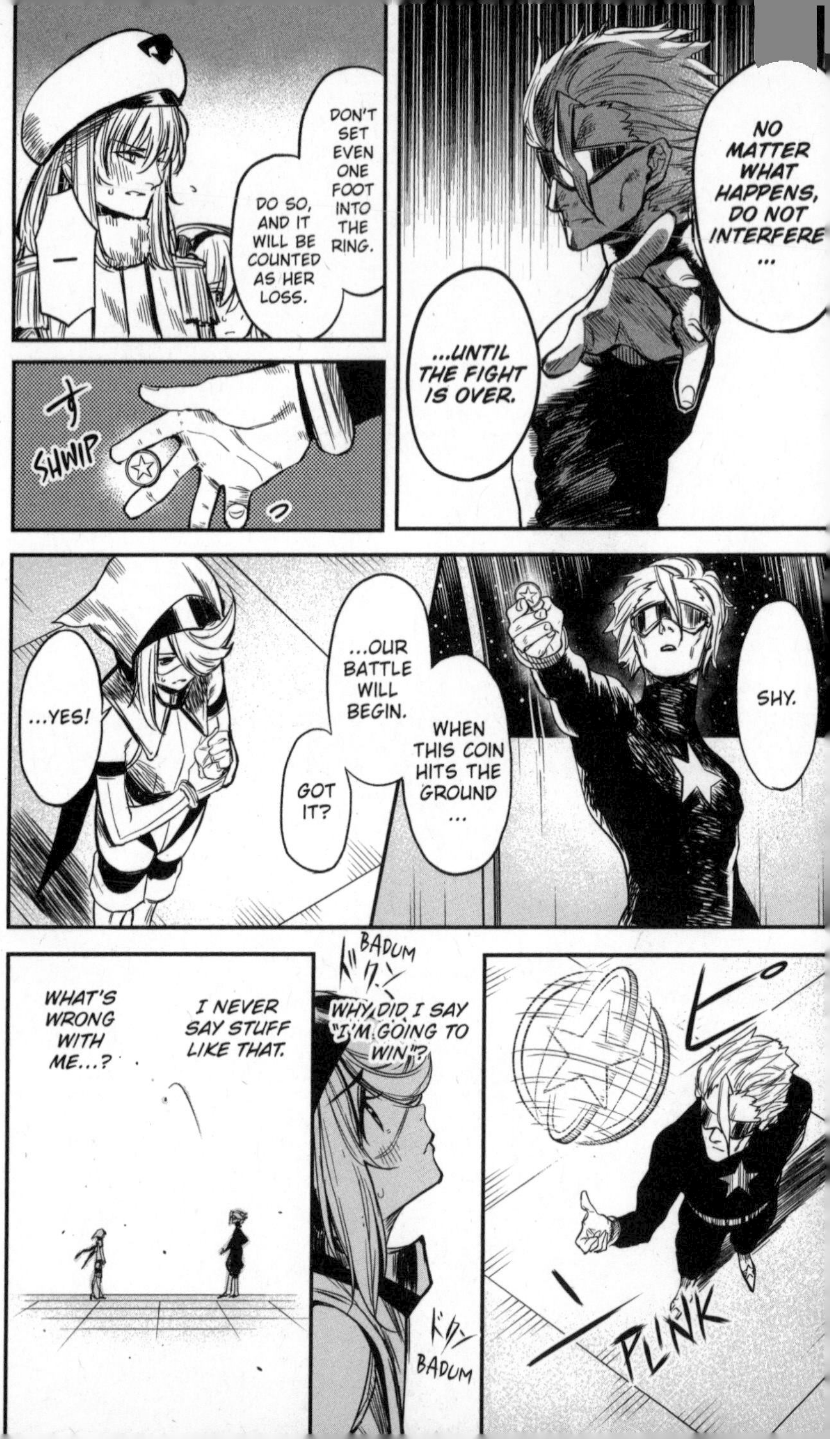
NO MATTER WHAT HAPPENS, DO NOT INTERFERE...
...UNTIL THE FIGHT IS OVER.
DON'T SET EVEN ONE FOOT INTO THE RING.
DO SO, AND IT WILL BE COUNTED AS HER LOSS.
す
SHWIP
SHY.
WHEN THIS COIN HITS THE GROUND...
...OUR BATTLE WILL BEGIN.
GOT IT?
...YES!
PLINK
BADUM
WHY DID I SAY "I'M GOING TO WIN"?
BADUM
I NEVER SAY STUFF LIKE THAT.
WHAT'S WRONG WITH ME...?

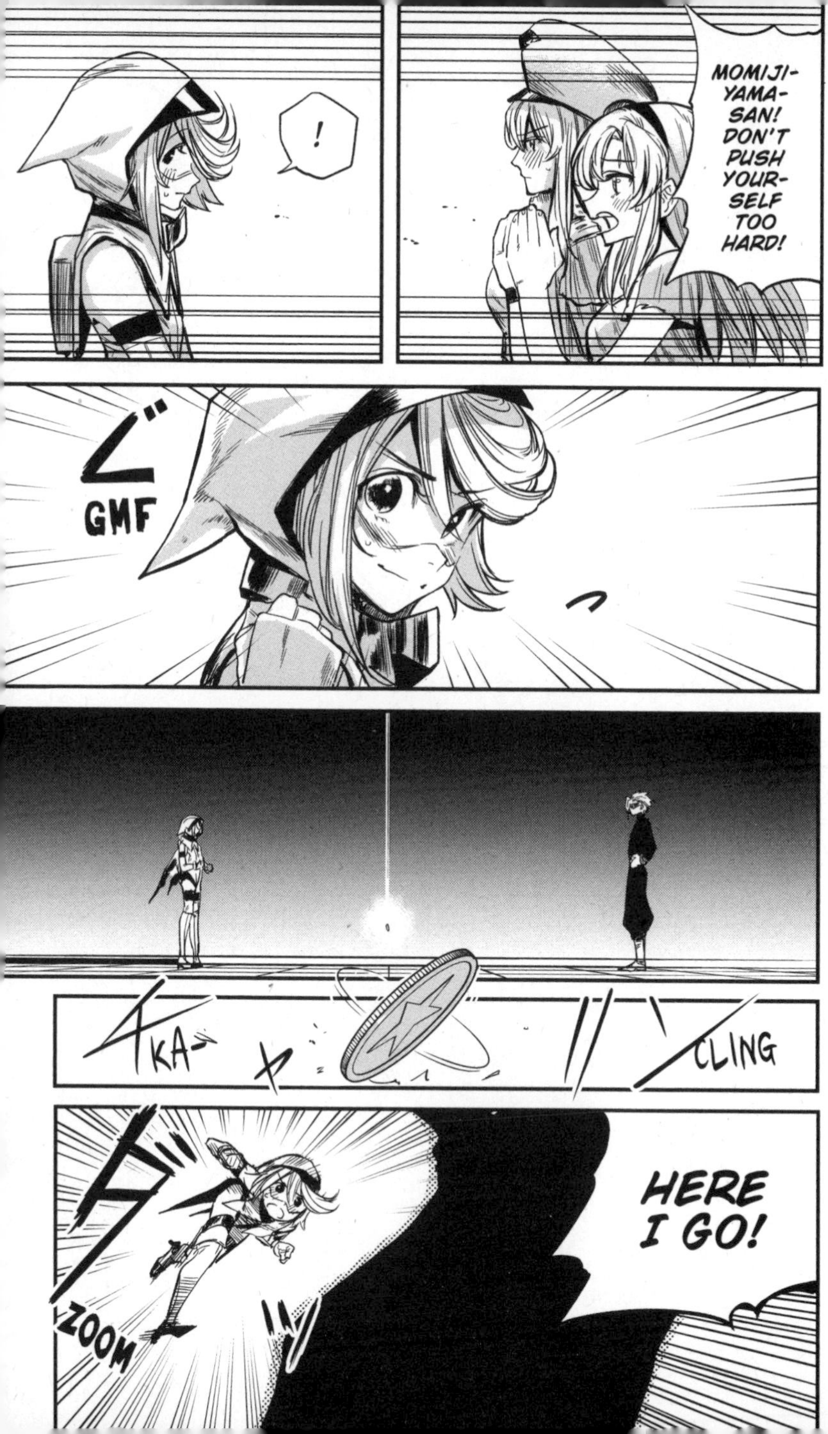
MOMIJI-YAMA-SAN! DON'T PUSH YOURSELF TOO HARD!
!
GMF
CLING
KA-
HERE I GO!
ZOOM

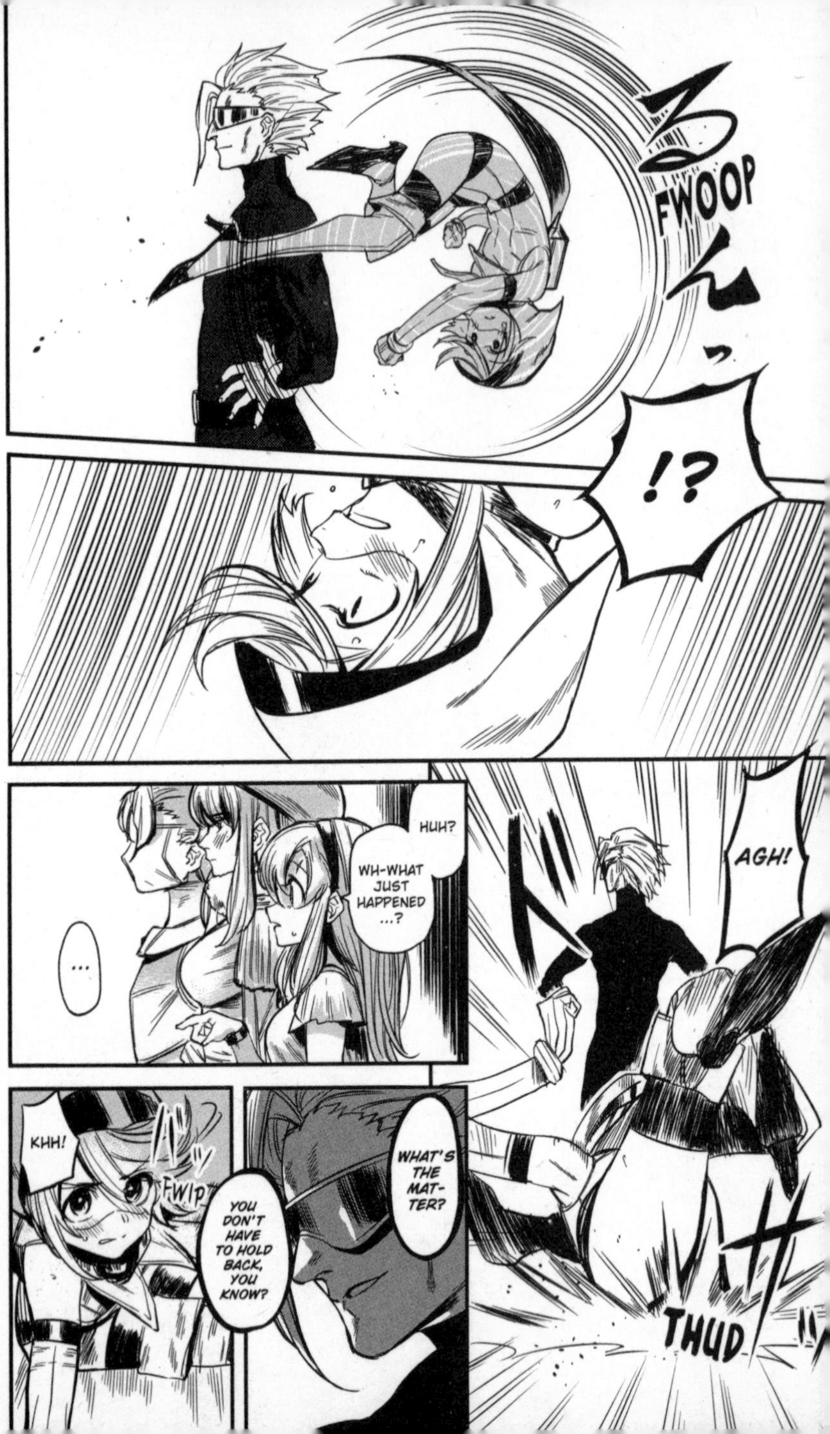
FWOOP
!?
AGH!
THUD
HUH?
WH-WHAT JUST HAPPENED ...?
...
WHAT'S THE MAT-TER?
YOU DON'T HAVE TO HOLD BACK, YOU KNOW?
KHH!
FWIP

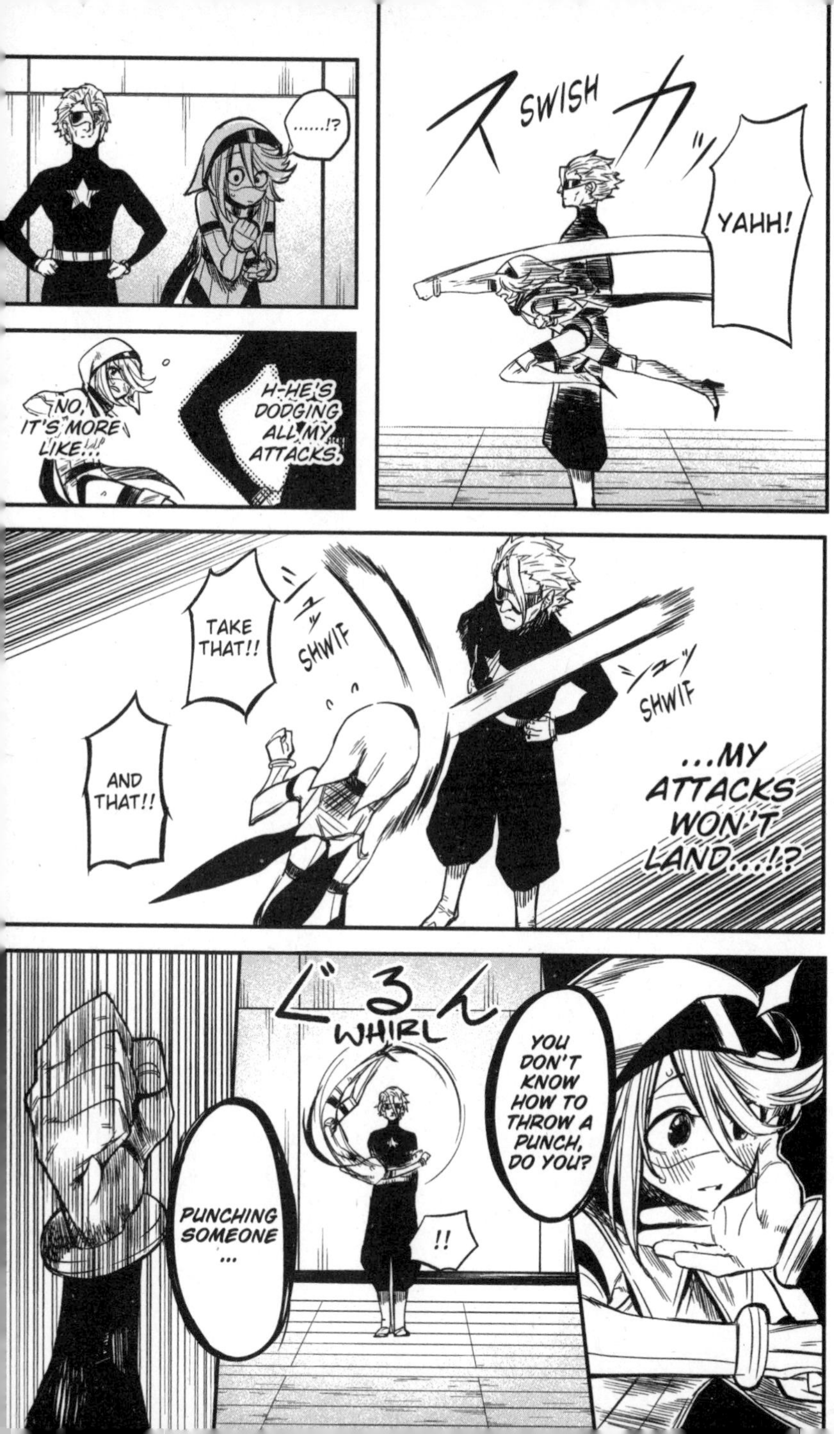
SWISH
YAHH!
......!?
H-HE'S DODGING ALL MY ATTACKS.
NO, IT'S MORE LIKE...
SHWIF
...MY ATTACKS WON'T LAND...!?
TAKE THAT!!
SHWIF
AND THAT!!
YOU DON'T KNOW HOW TO THROW A PUNCH, DO YOU?
ぐるん
WHIRL
!!
PUNCHING SOMEONE ...

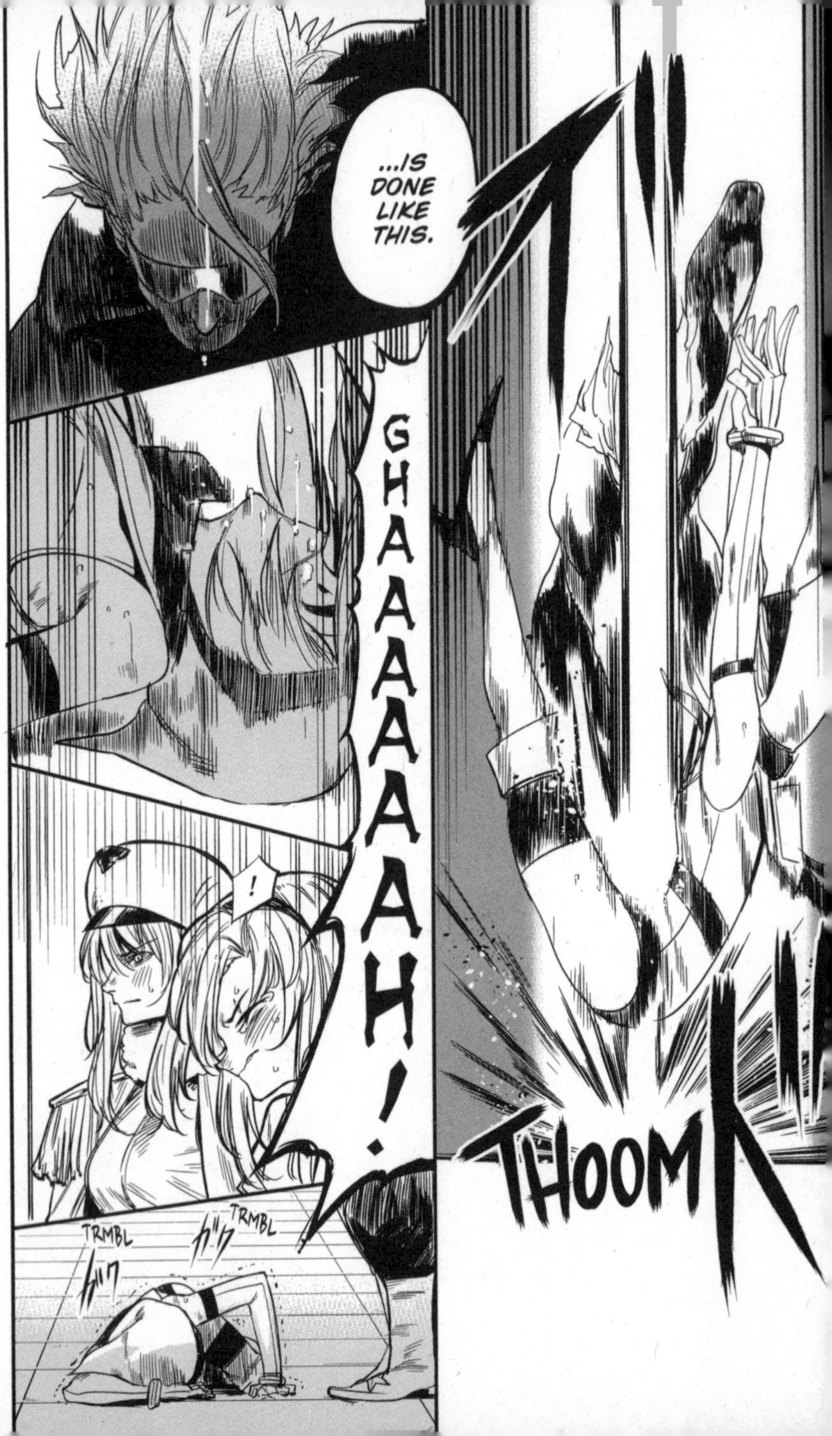
THOOM
...IS DONE LIKE THIS.
GHAAAAAAH!!
!
TRMBL
TRMBL

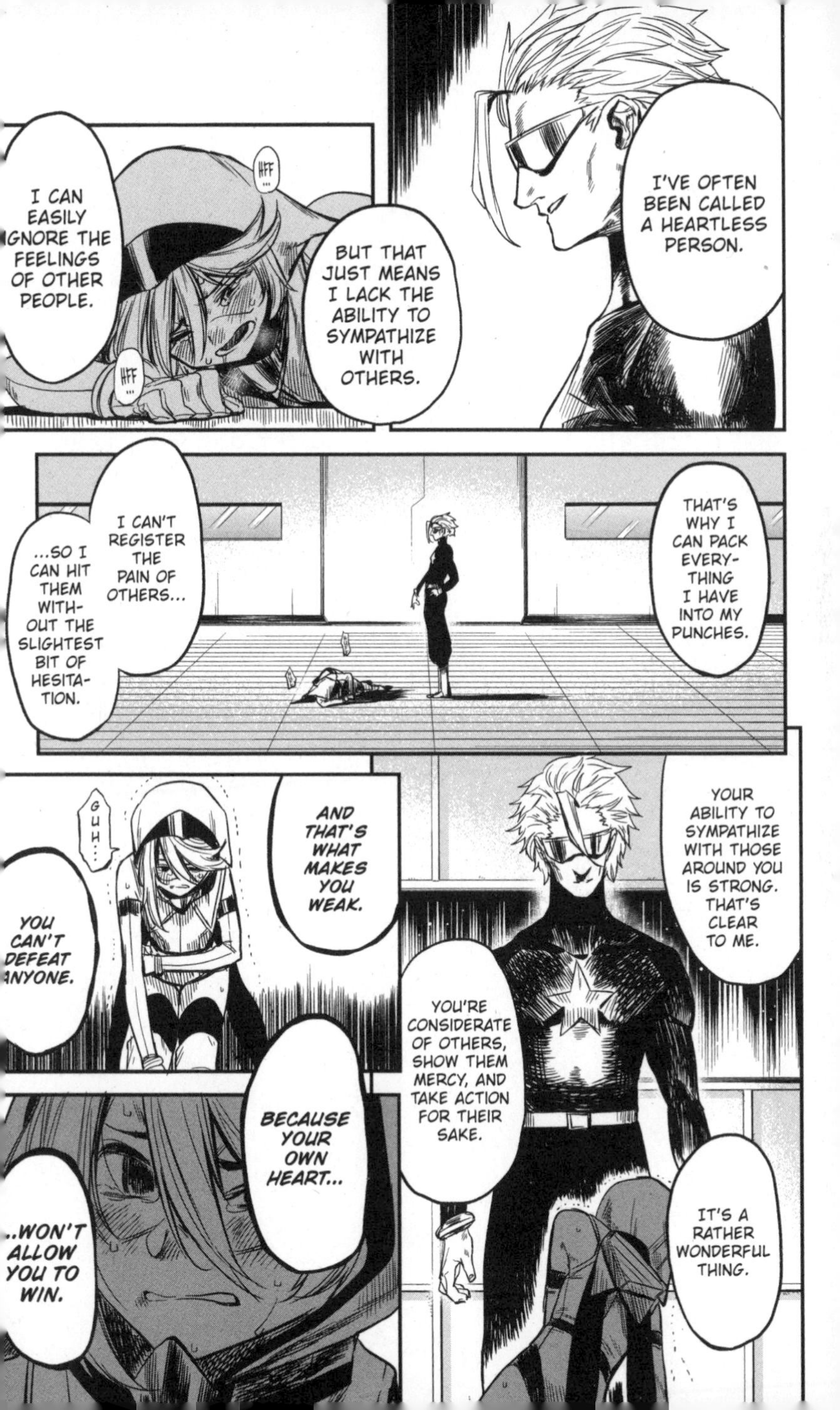
I'VE OFTEN BEEN CALLED A HEARTLESS PERSON.
BUT THAT JUST MEANS I LACK THE ABILITY TO SYMPATHIZE WITH OTHERS.
HFF...
I CAN EASILY IGNORE THE FEELINGS OF OTHER PEOPLE.
HFF...
THAT'S WHY I CAN PACK EVERYTHING I HAVE INTO MY PUNCHES.
I CAN'T REGISTER THE PAIN OF OTHERS...
...SO I CAN HIT THEM WITHOUT THE SLIGHTEST BIT OF HESITATION.
YOUR ABILITY TO SYMPATHIZE WITH THOSE AROUND YOU IS STRONG. THAT'S CLEAR TO ME.
YOU'RE CONSIDERATE OF OTHERS, SHOW THEM MERCY, AND TAKE ACTION FOR THEIR SAKE.
IT'S A RATHER WONDERFUL THING.
AND THAT'S WHAT MAKES YOU WEAK.
GUH...
YOU CAN'T DEFEAT ANYONE.
BECAUSE YOUR OWN HEART...
...WON'T ALLOW YOU TO WIN.

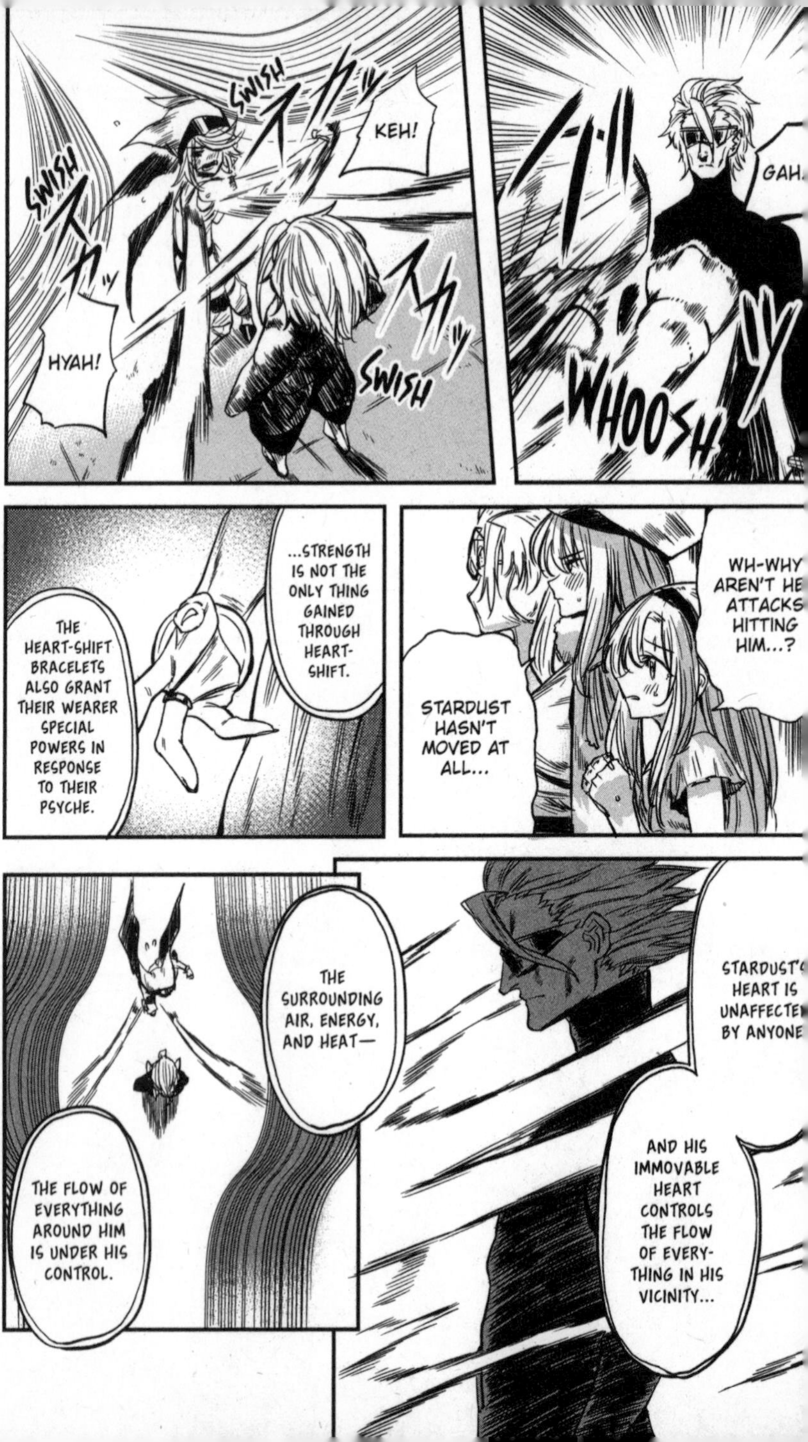
GAH.
WHOOSH
KEH!
SWISH
SWISH
HYAH!
SWISH
WH-WHY AREN'T HE ATTACKS HITTING HIM...?
STARDUST HASN'T MOVED AT ALL...
...STRENGTH IS NOT THE ONLY THING GAINED THROUGH HEART-SHIFT.
THE HEART-SHIFT BRACELETS ALSO GRANT THEIR WEARER SPECIAL POWERS IN RESPONSE TO THEIR PSYCHE.
STARDUST'S HEART IS UNAFFECTE BY ANYONE
AND HIS IMMOVABLE HEART CONTROLS THE FLOW OF EVERY-THING IN HIS VICINITY...
THE SURROUNDING AIR, ENERGY, AND HEAT—
THE FLOW OF EVERYTHING AROUND HIM IS UNDER HIS CONTROL.

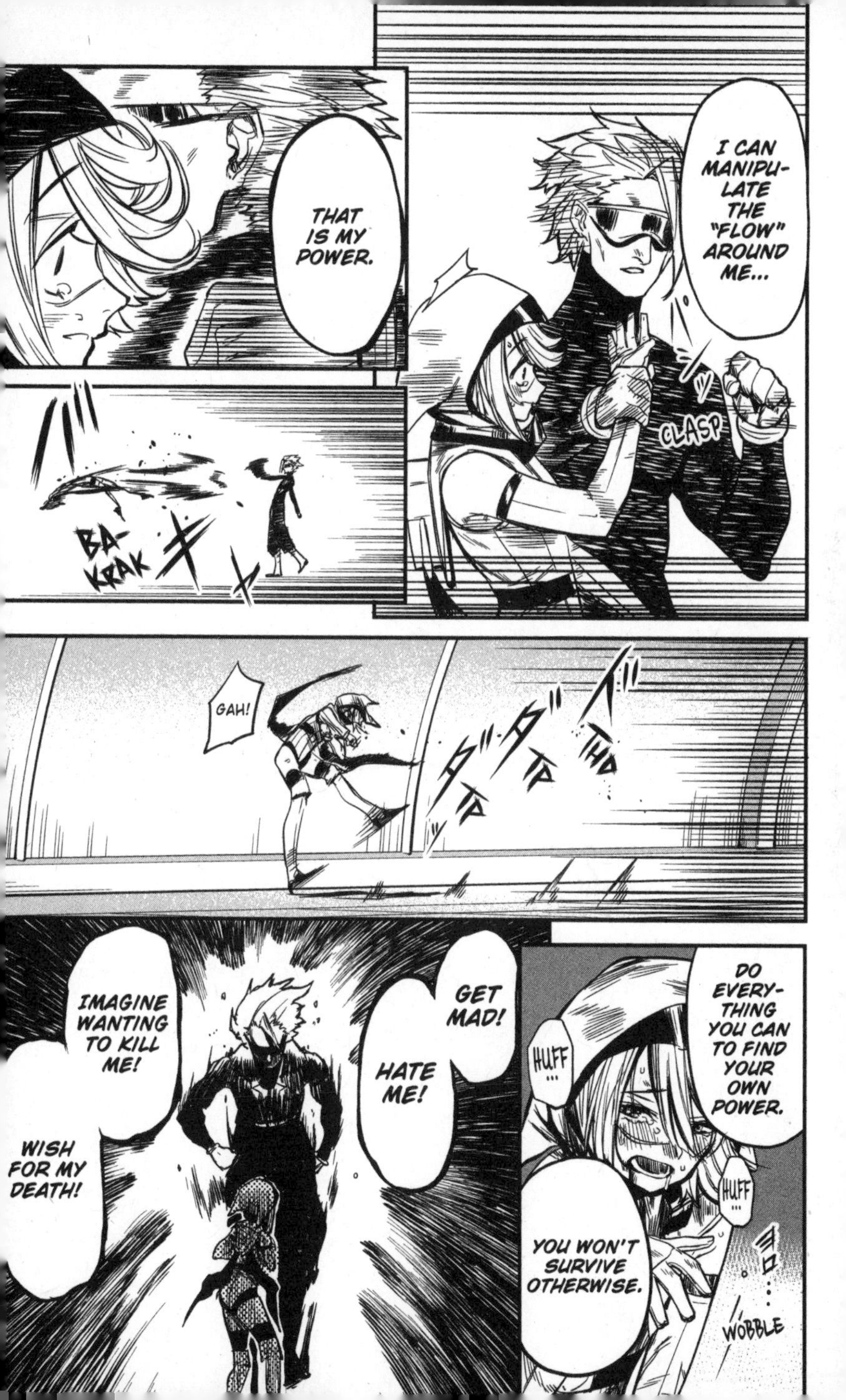
I CAN MANIPULATE THE "FLOW" AROUND ME...
CLASP
THAT IS MY POWER.
BA-KRAK
GAH!
DO EVERYTHING YOU CAN TO FIND YOUR OWN POWER.
HUFF...
HUFF...
YOU WON'T SURVIVE OTHERWISE.
WOBBLE
GET MAD!
HATE ME!
IMAGINE WANTING TO KILL ME!
WISH FOR MY DEATH!

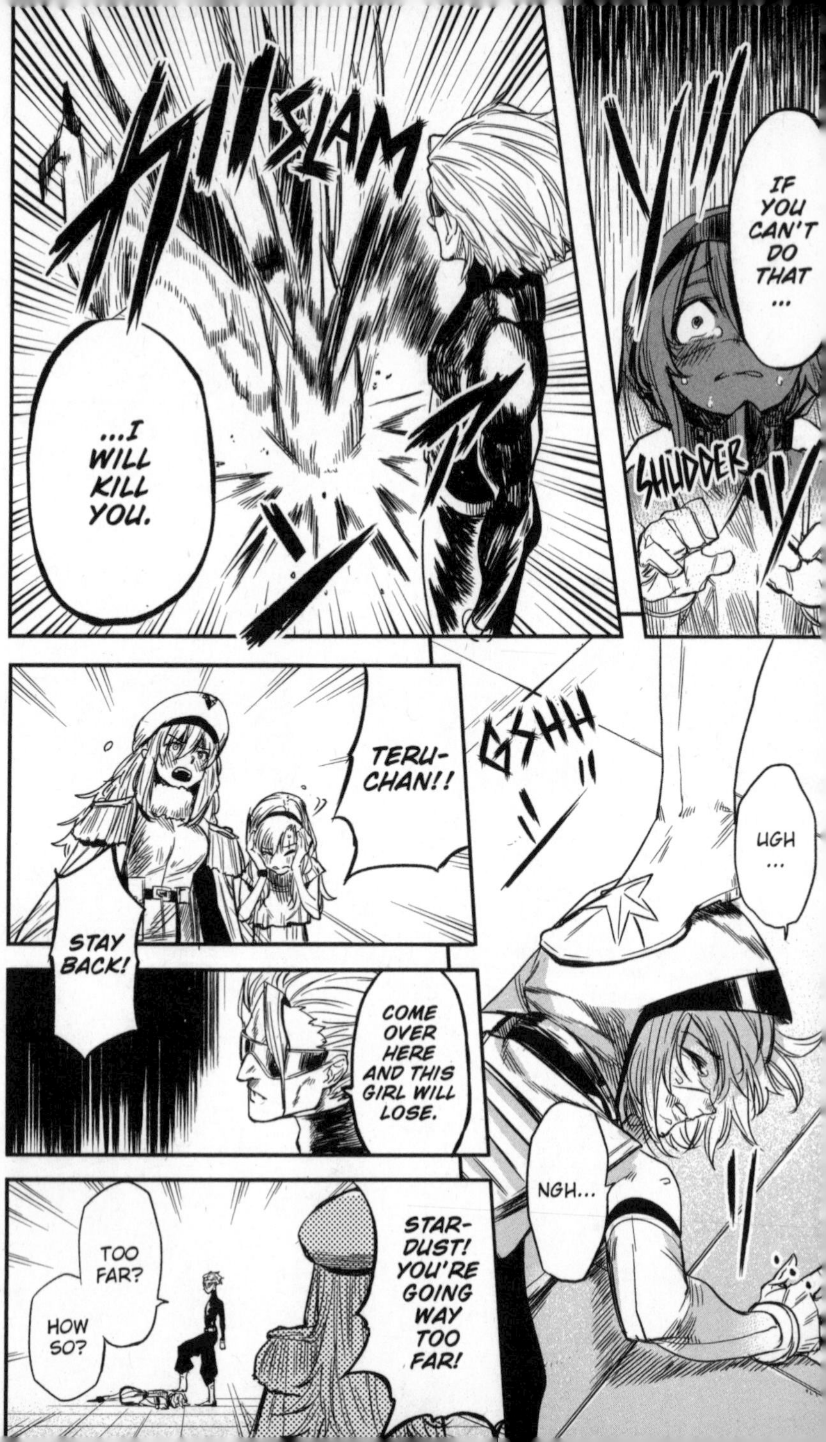
IF YOU CAN'T DO THAT...
SHUDDER
SLAM
...I WILL KILL YOU.
GSHH
UGH...
NGH...
TERU-CHAN!!
STAY BACK!
COME OVER HERE AND THIS GIRL WILL LOSE.
STAR-DUST! YOU'RE GOING WAY TOO FAR!
TOO FAR?
HOW SO?

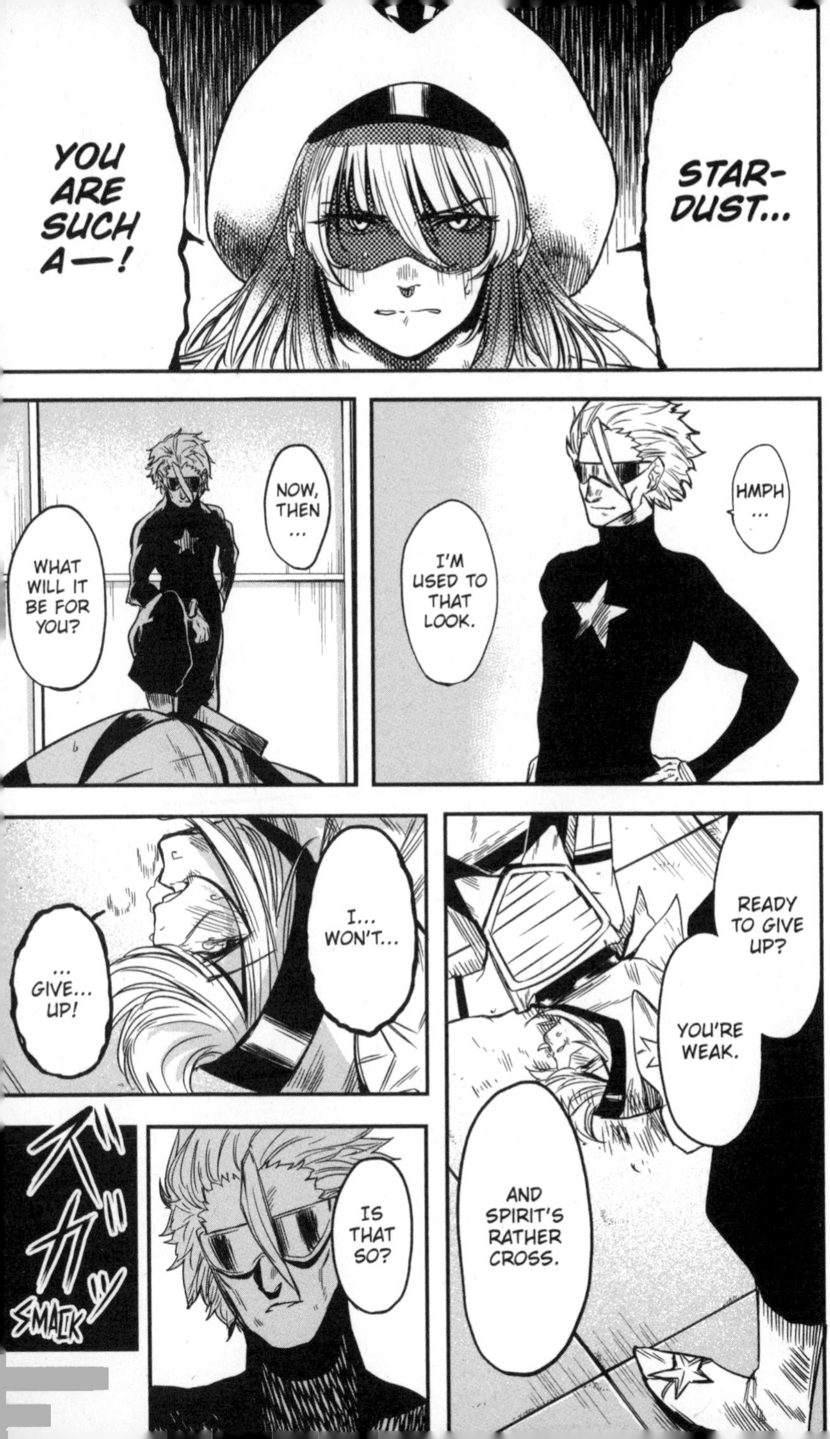
STAR-DUST...
YOU ARE SUCH A—!
HMPH...
I'M USED TO THAT LOOK.
NOW, THEN...
WHAT WILL IT BE FOR YOU?
READY TO GIVE UP?
YOU'RE WEAK.
AND SPIRIT'S RATHER CROSS.
I... WON'T...
...GIVE... UP!
IS THAT SO?
SMACK

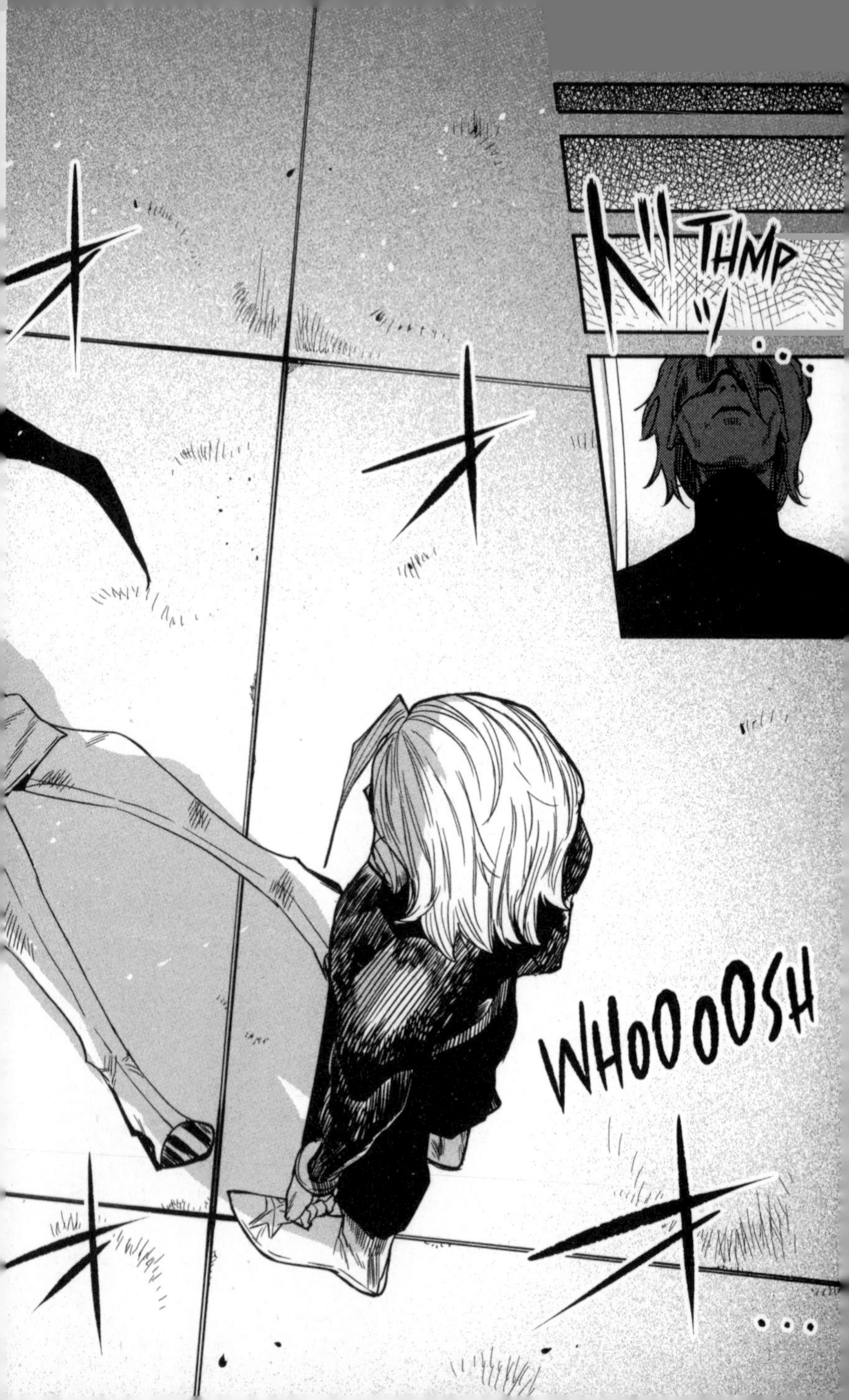
THMP
...
WHOOOOSH
...

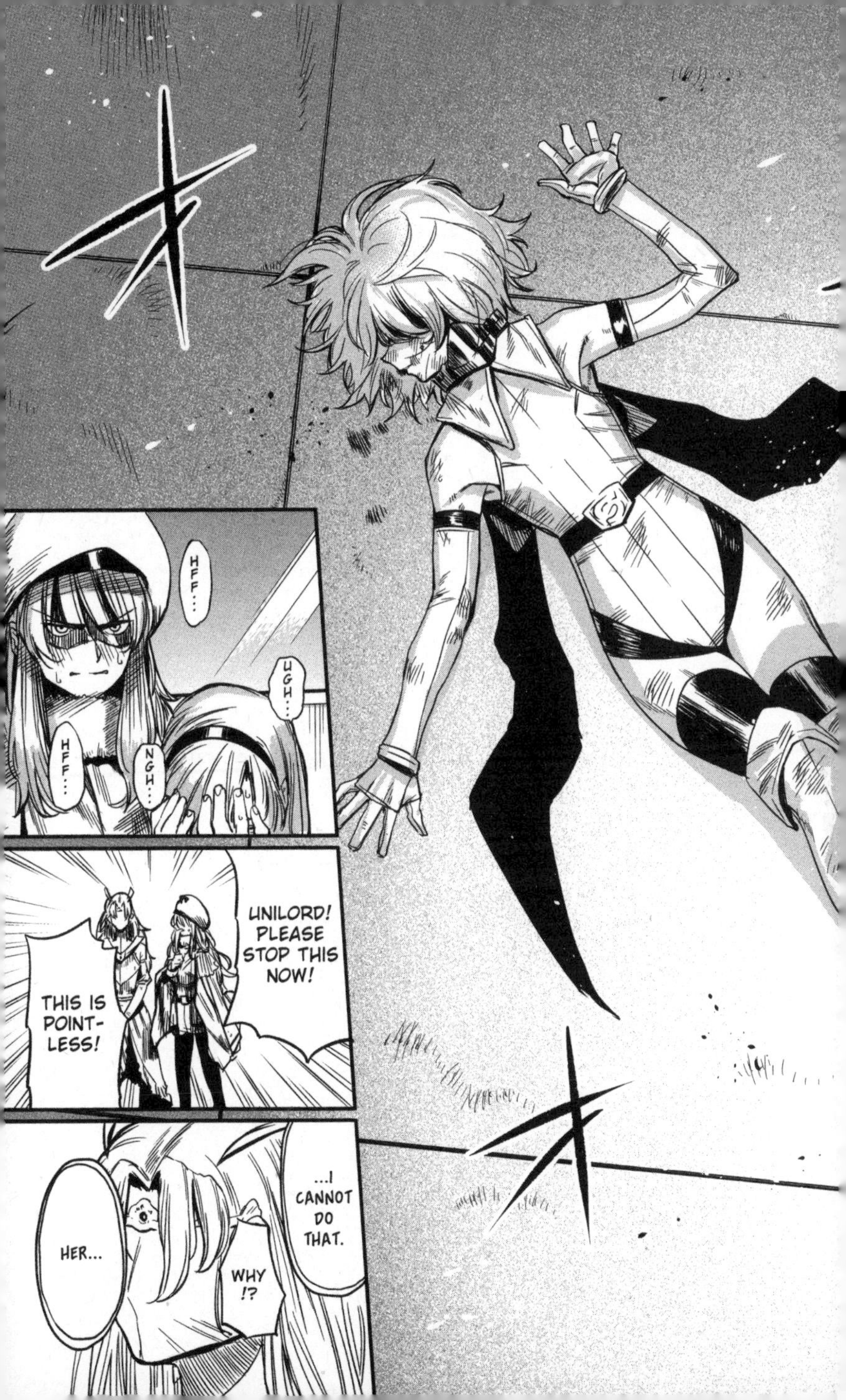
HFF...
UGH...
NGH...
HFF...
UNILORD! PLEASE STOP THIS NOW!
THIS IS POINTLESS!
...I CANNOT DO THAT.
WHY!?
HER...

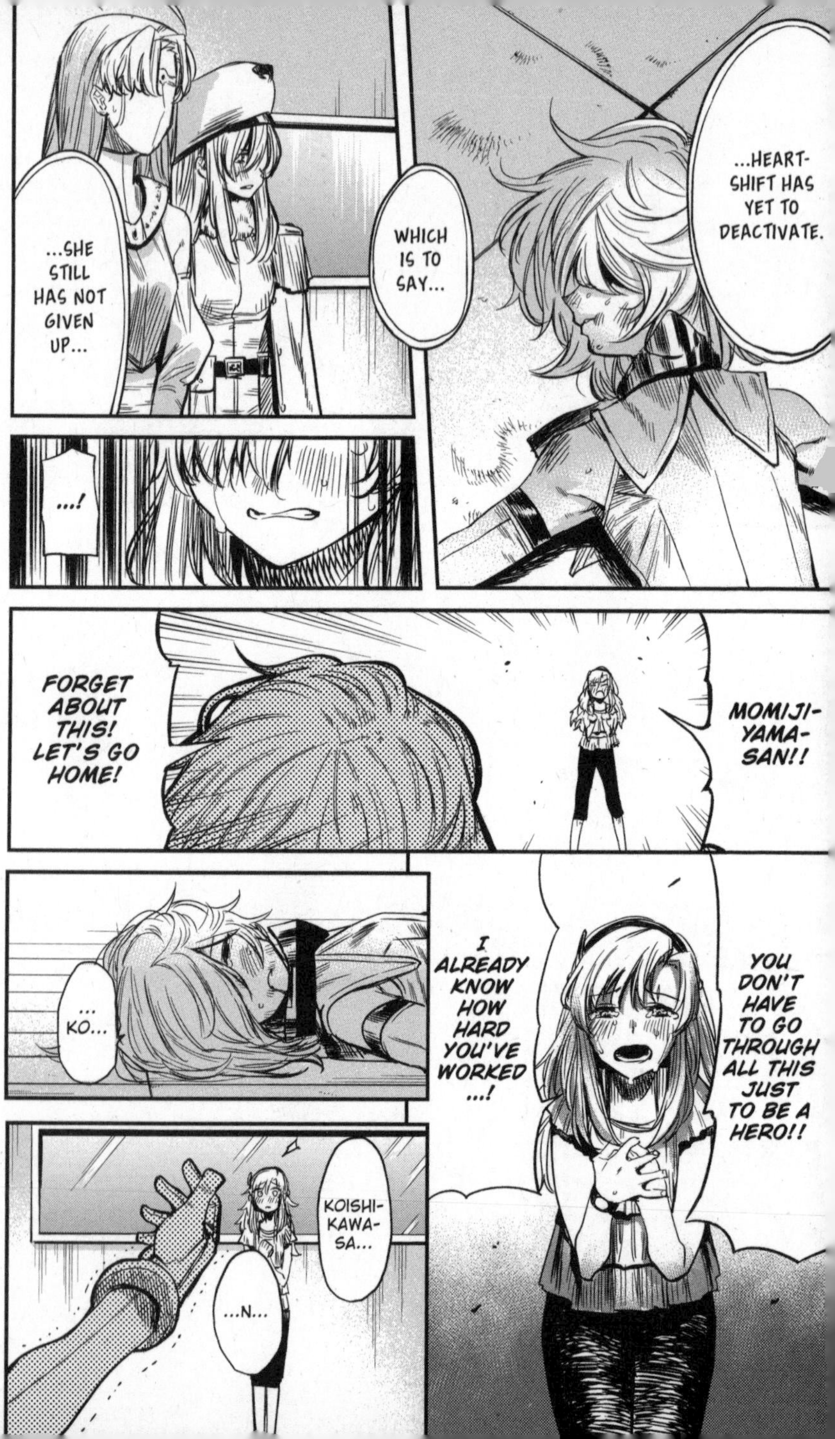
...HEART-SHIFT HAS YET TO DEACTIVATE.
WHICH IS TO SAY...
...SHE STILL HAS NOT GIVEN UP...
...!
MOMIJI-YAMA-SAN!!
FORGET ABOUT THIS! LET'S GO HOME!
YOU DON'T HAVE TO GO THROUGH ALL THIS JUST TO BE A HERO!!
I ALREADY KNOW HOW HARD YOU'VE WORKED...!
...KO...
KOISHI-KAWA-SA...
...N...

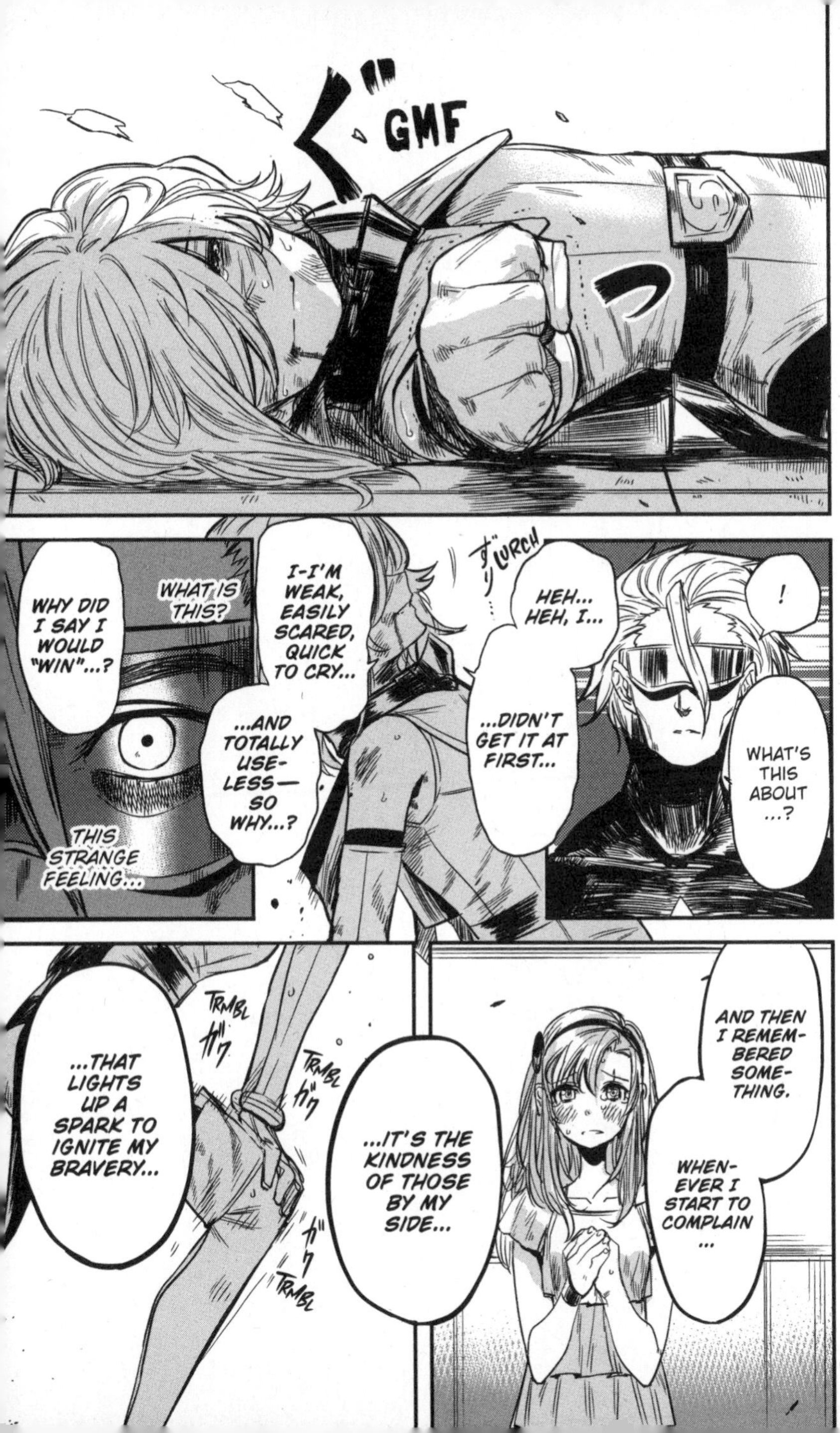
GMF
!
WHAT'S THIS ABOUT ...?
LURCH
HEH... HEH, I...
...DIDN'T GET IT AT FIRST...
I-I'M WEAK, EASILY SCARED, QUICK TO CRY...
...AND TOTALLY USELESS— SO WHY...?
WHAT IS THIS?
WHY DID I SAY I WOULD "WIN"...?
THIS STRANGE FEELING...
AND THEN I REMEMBERED SOMETHING.
WHENEVER I START TO COMPLAIN ...
...IT'S THE KINDNESS OF THOSE BY MY SIDE...
TRMBL
TRMBL
TRMBL
...THAT LIGHTS UP A SPARK TO IGNITE MY BRAVERY...

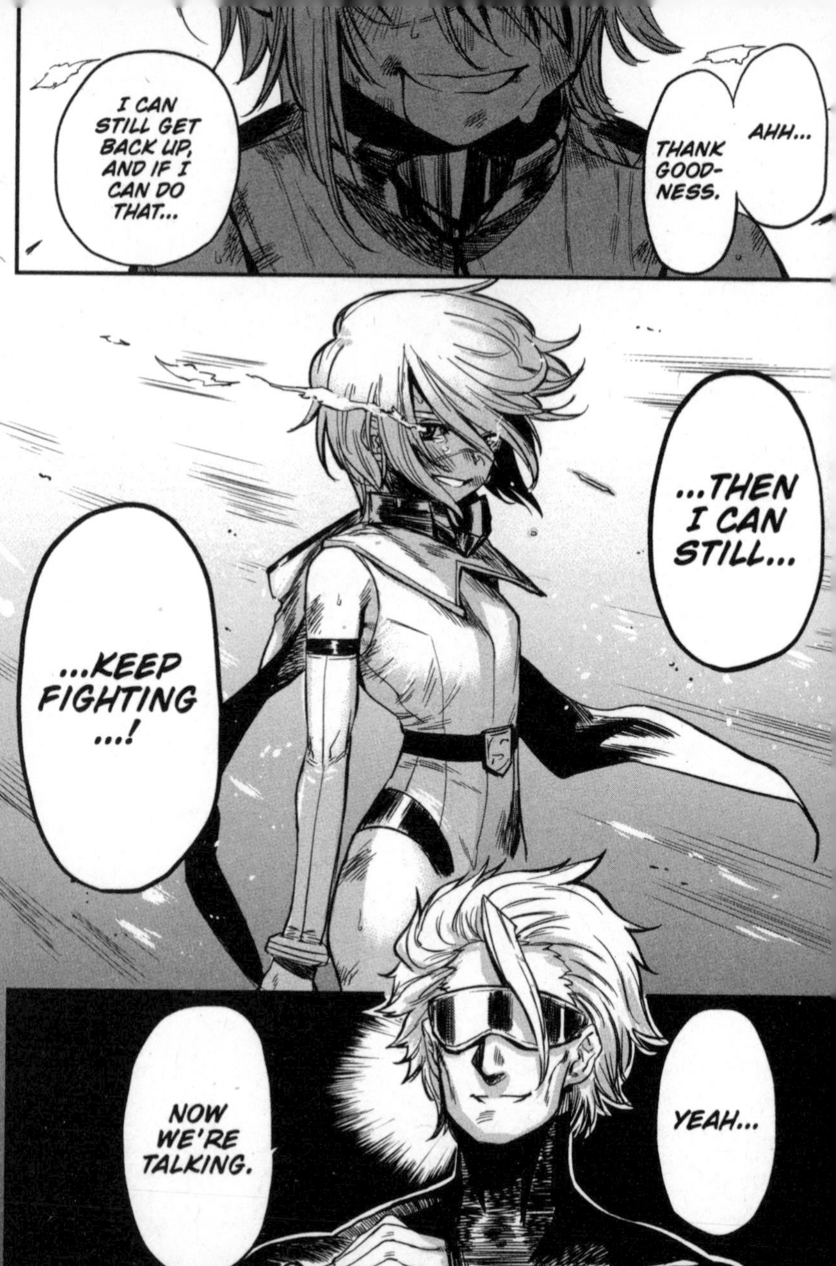
AHH...
THANK GOODNESS.
I CAN STILL GET BACK UP, AND IF I CAN DO THAT...
...THEN I CAN STILL...
...KEEP FIGHTING ...!
YEAH...
NOW WE'RE TALKING.

SHY

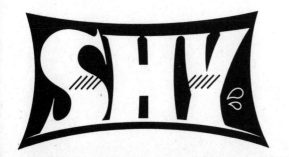

Chapter 8

Heartless Person

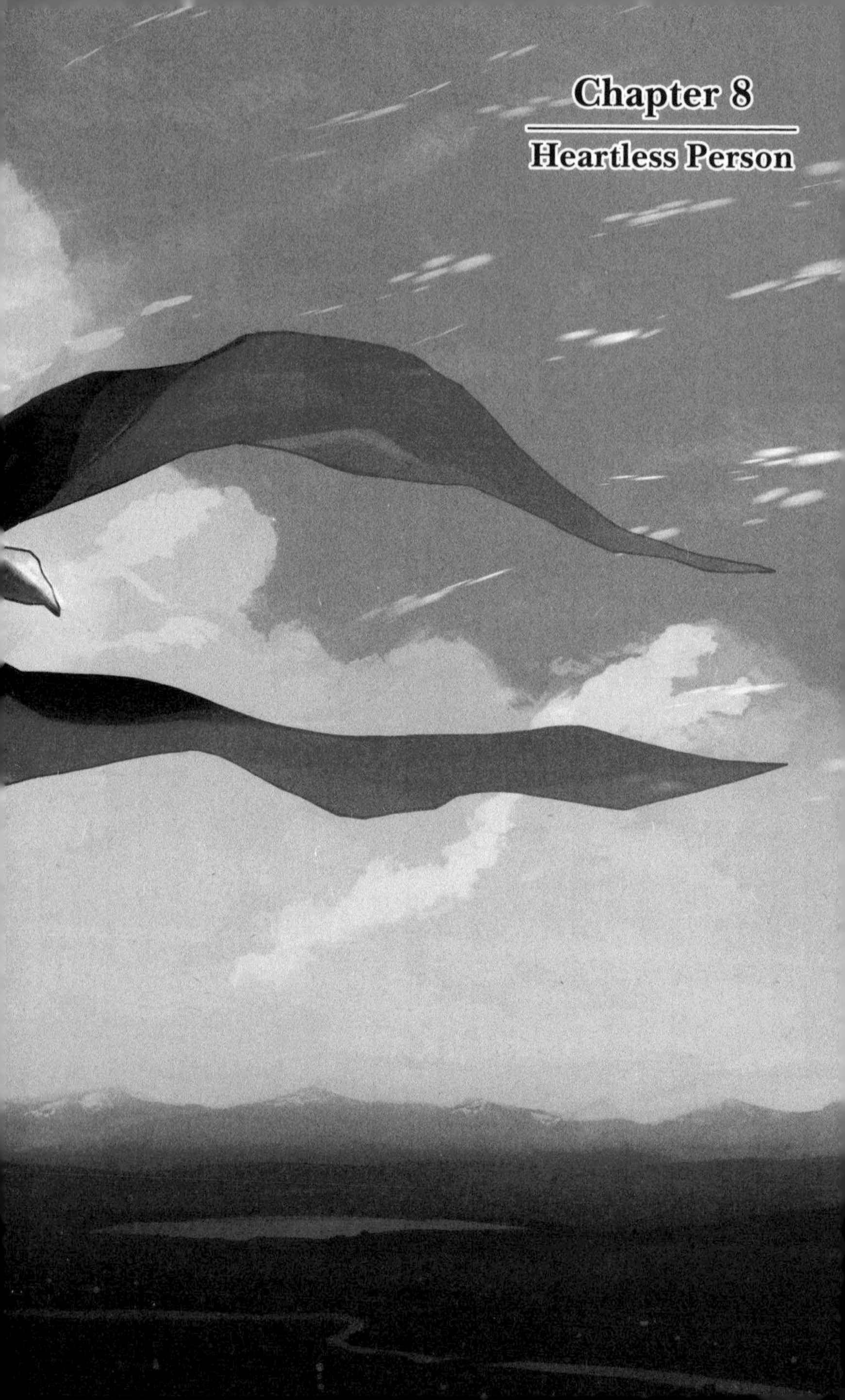

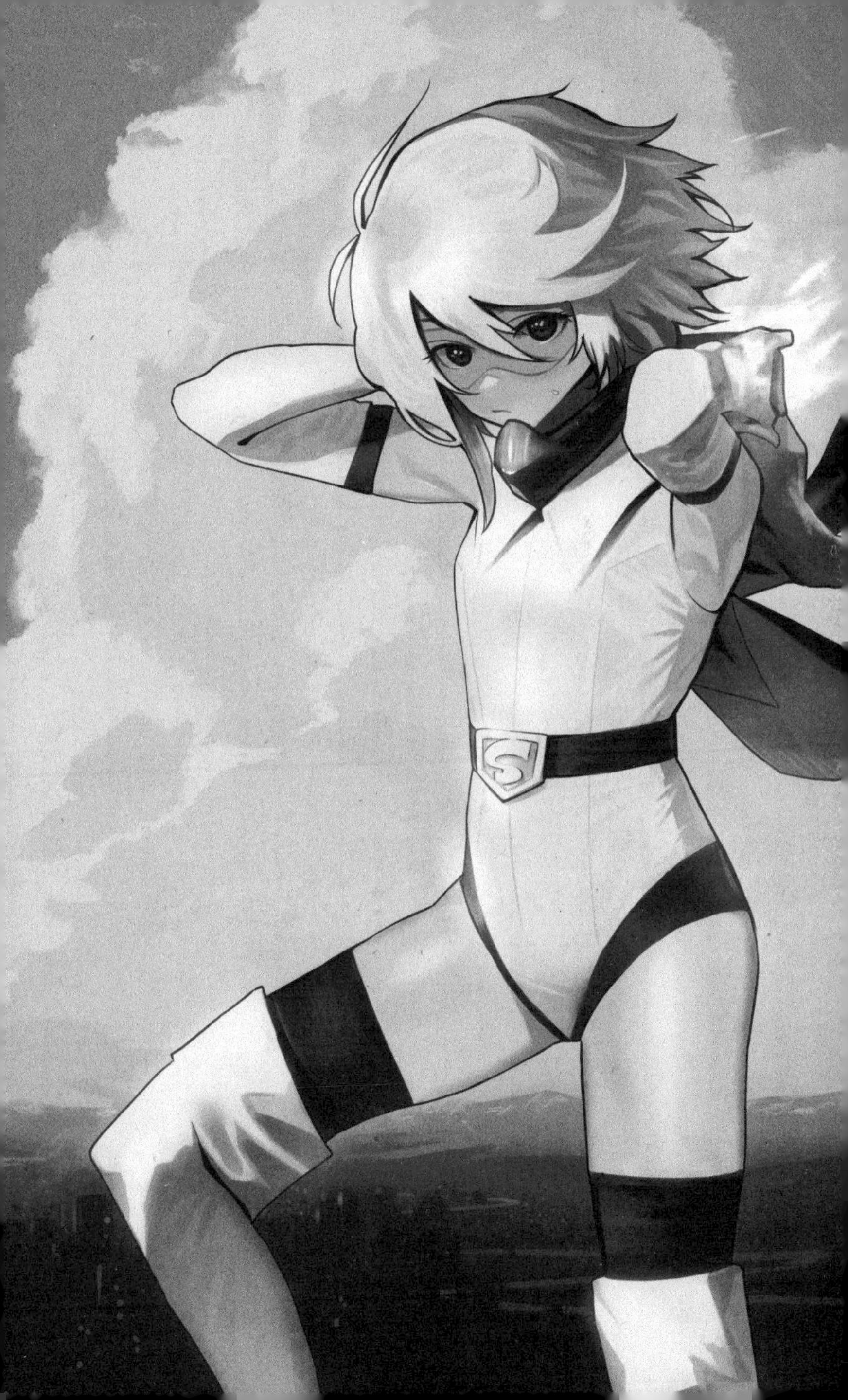

SHY

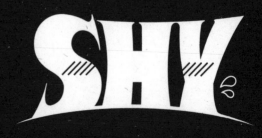

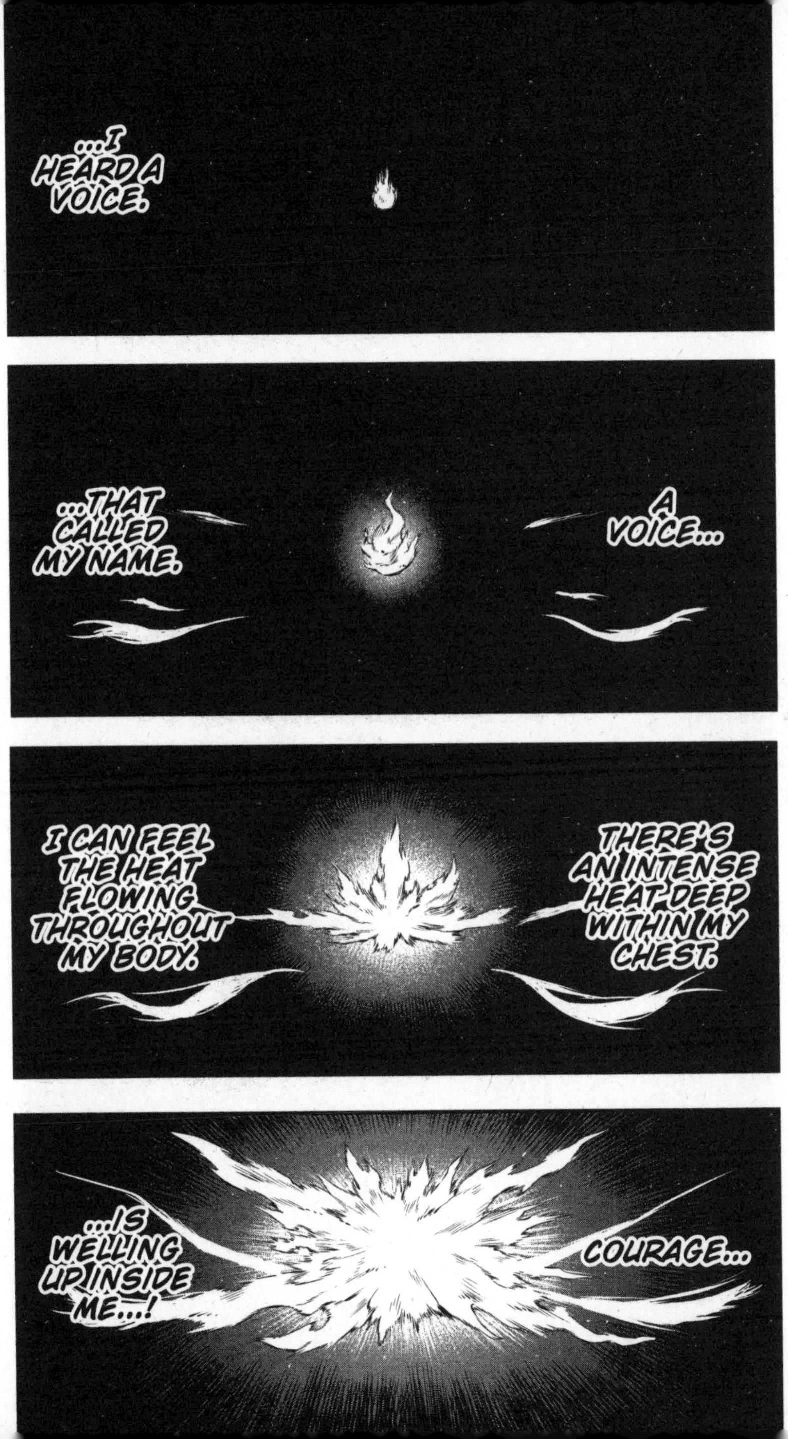
...I HEARD A VOICE.
A VOICE...
...THAT CALLED MY NAME.
THERE'S AN INTENSE HEAT DEEP WITHIN MY CHEST.
I CAN FEEL THE HEAT FLOWING THROUGHOUT MY BODY.
COURAGE...
...IS WELLING UP INSIDE ME...!

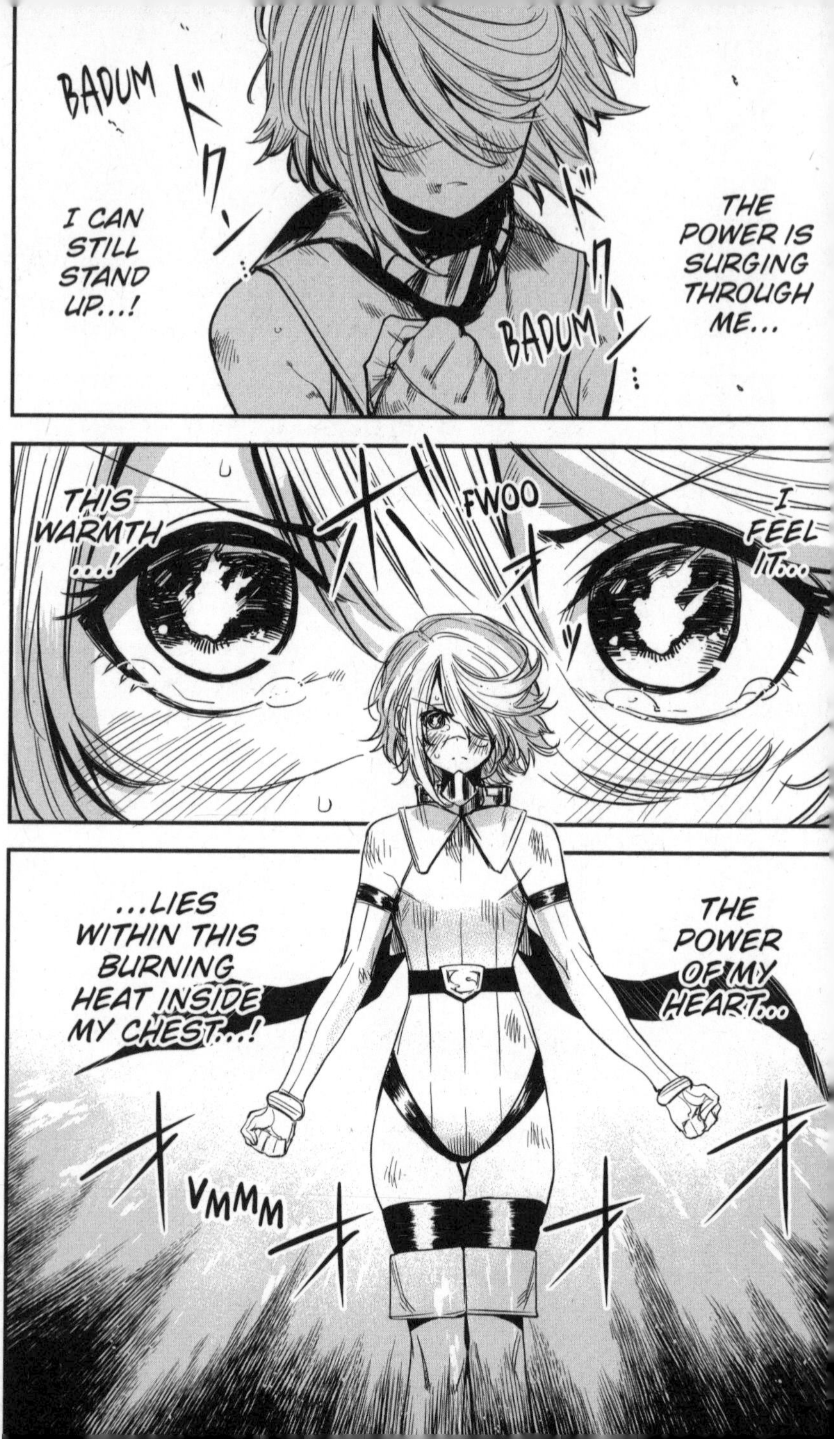
THE POWER IS SURGING THROUGH ME...
BADUM
ドクン
BADUM
ドクン
I CAN STILL STAND UP...!
I FEEL IT...
FWOO
THIS WARMTH...!
THE POWER OF MY HEART...
...LIES WITHIN THIS BURNING HEAT INSIDE MY CHEST...!
VMMM

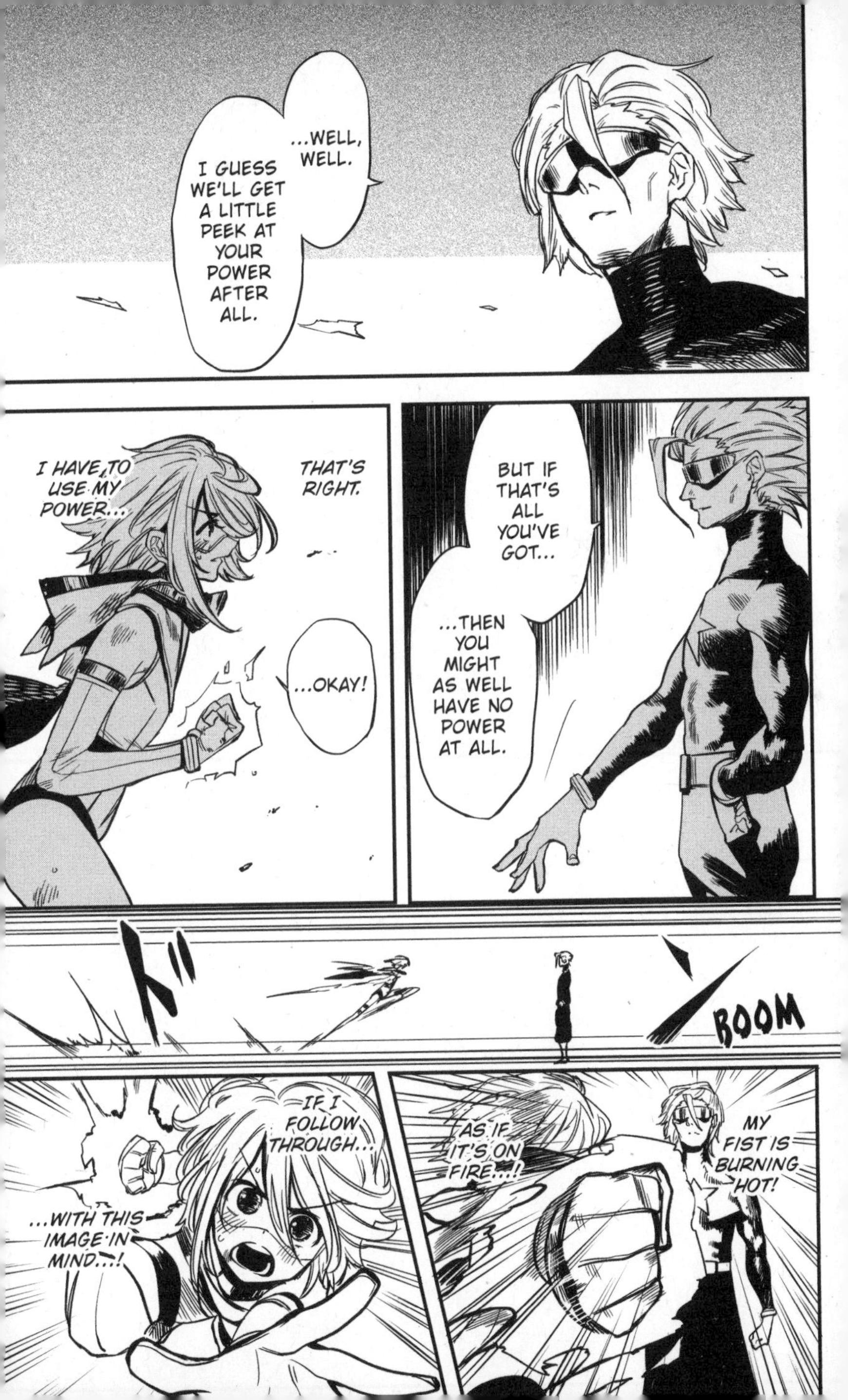
...WELL, WELL.
I GUESS WE'LL GET A LITTLE PEEK AT YOUR POWER AFTER ALL.
BUT IF THAT'S ALL YOU'VE GOT...
...THEN YOU MIGHT AS WELL HAVE NO POWER AT ALL.
THAT'S RIGHT.
I HAVE TO USE MY POWER...
...OKAY!
BOOM
MY FIST IS BURNING HOT!
AS IF IT'S ON FIRE...!
IF I FOLLOW THROUGH...
...WITH THIS IMAGE IN MIND...!

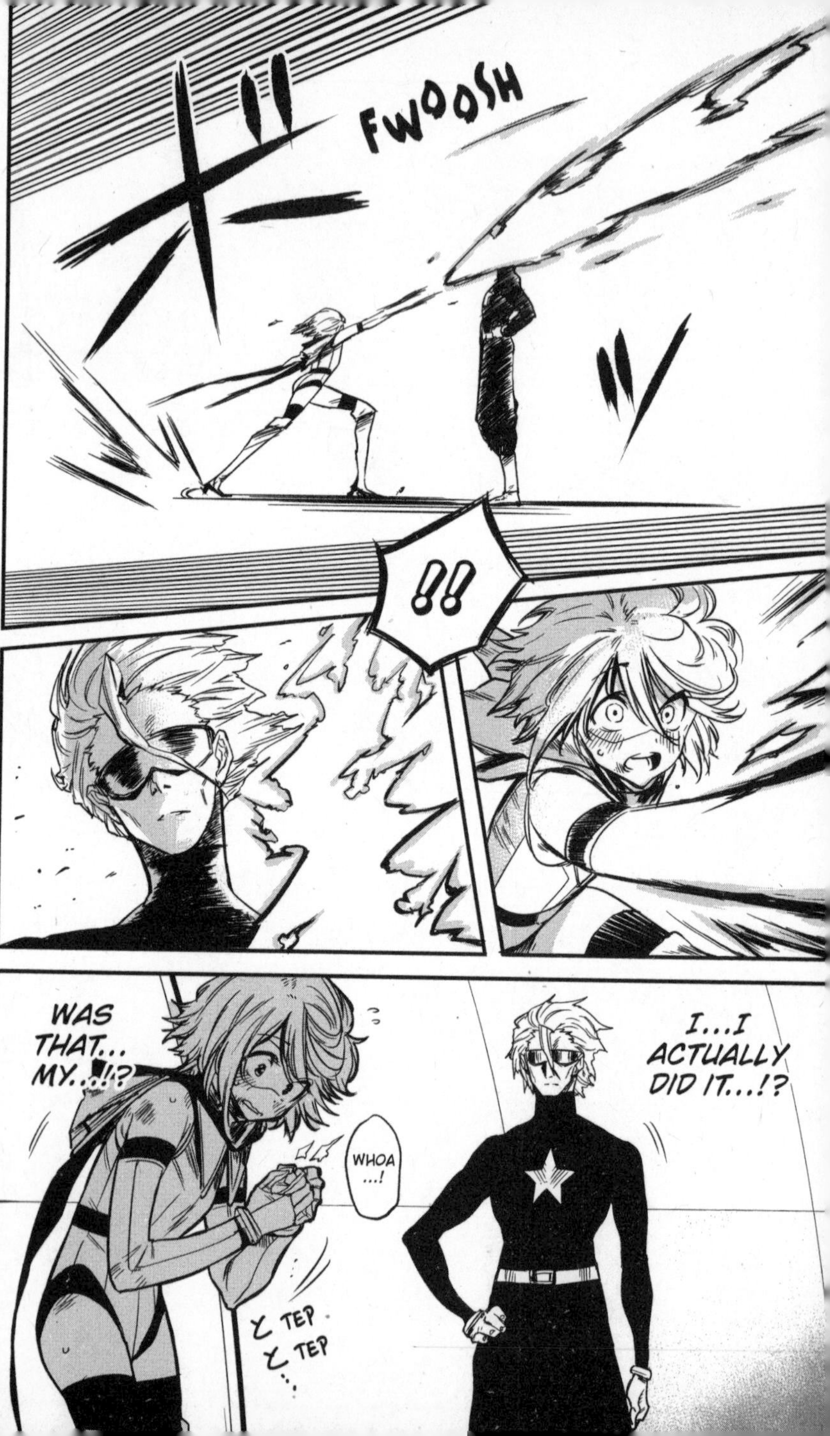
FWOOSH
!!
I...I ACTUALLY DID IT...!?
WHOA...!
WAS THAT... MY...!!?
TEP TEP

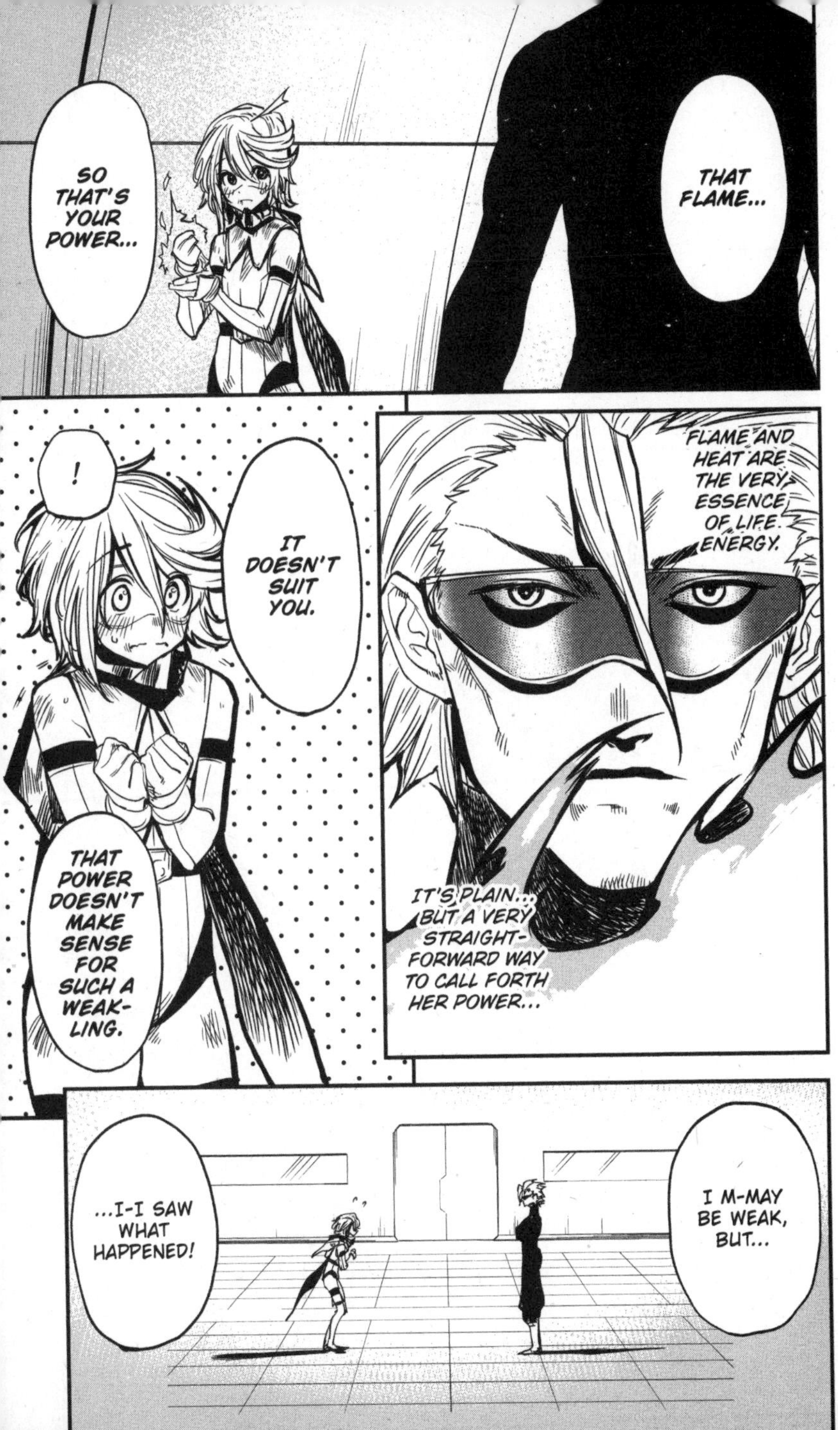
THAT FLAME...
SO THAT'S YOUR POWER...
FLAME AND HEAT ARE THE VERY ESSENCE OF LIFE ENERGY.
IT'S PLAIN... BUT A VERY STRAIGHT-FORWARD WAY TO CALL FORTH HER POWER...
!
IT DOESN'T SUIT YOU.
THAT POWER DOESN'T MAKE SENSE FOR SUCH A WEAK-LING.
I M-MAY BE WEAK, BUT...
...I-I SAW WHAT HAPPENED!

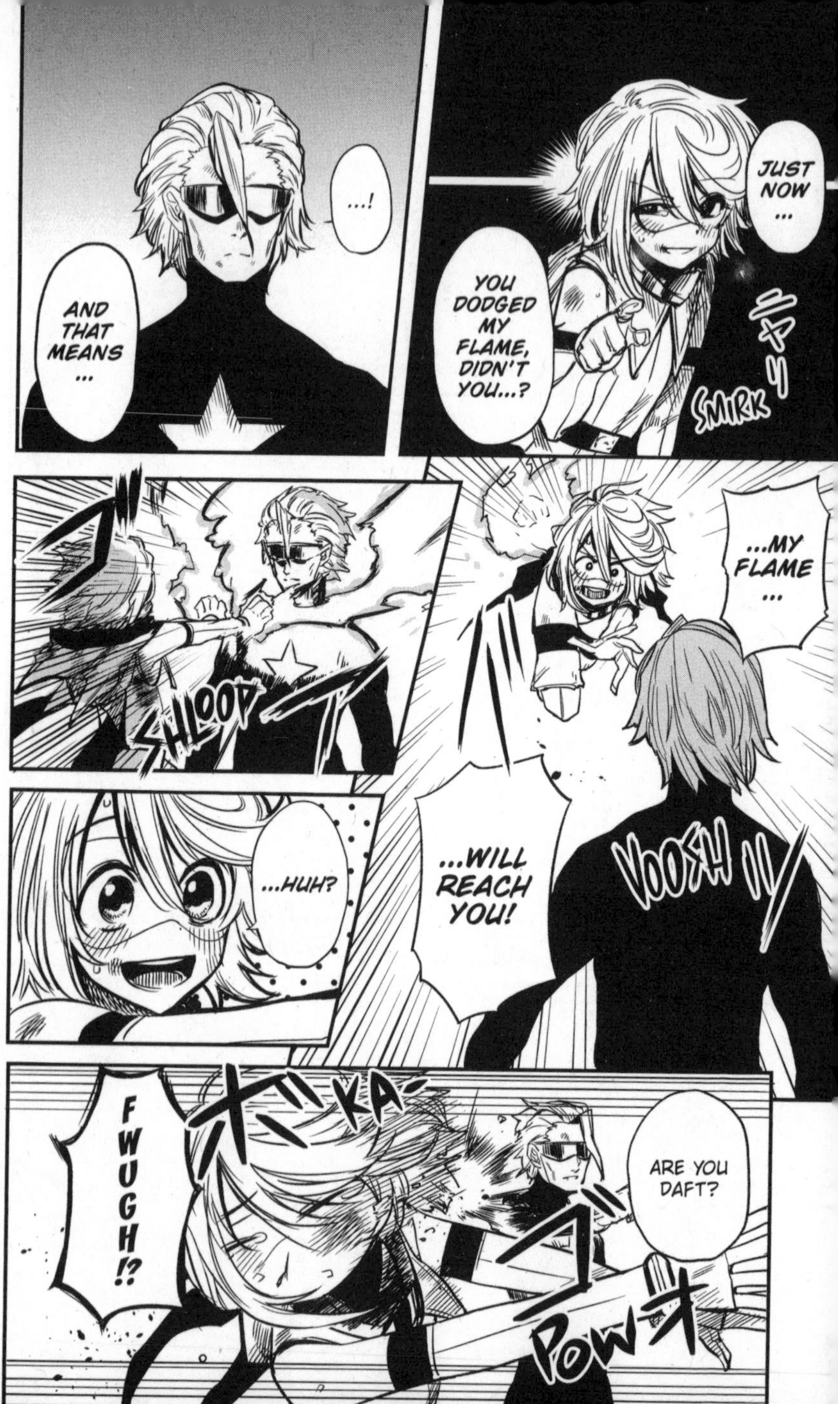
JUST NOW ...
YOU DODGED MY FLAME, DIDN'T YOU...?
ニヤリ
SMIRK
...!
AND THAT MEANS ...
...MY FLAME ...
...WILL REACH YOU!
VOOSH
SHLOOP
...HUH?
ARE YOU DAFT?
KA
POW
FWUGH!?

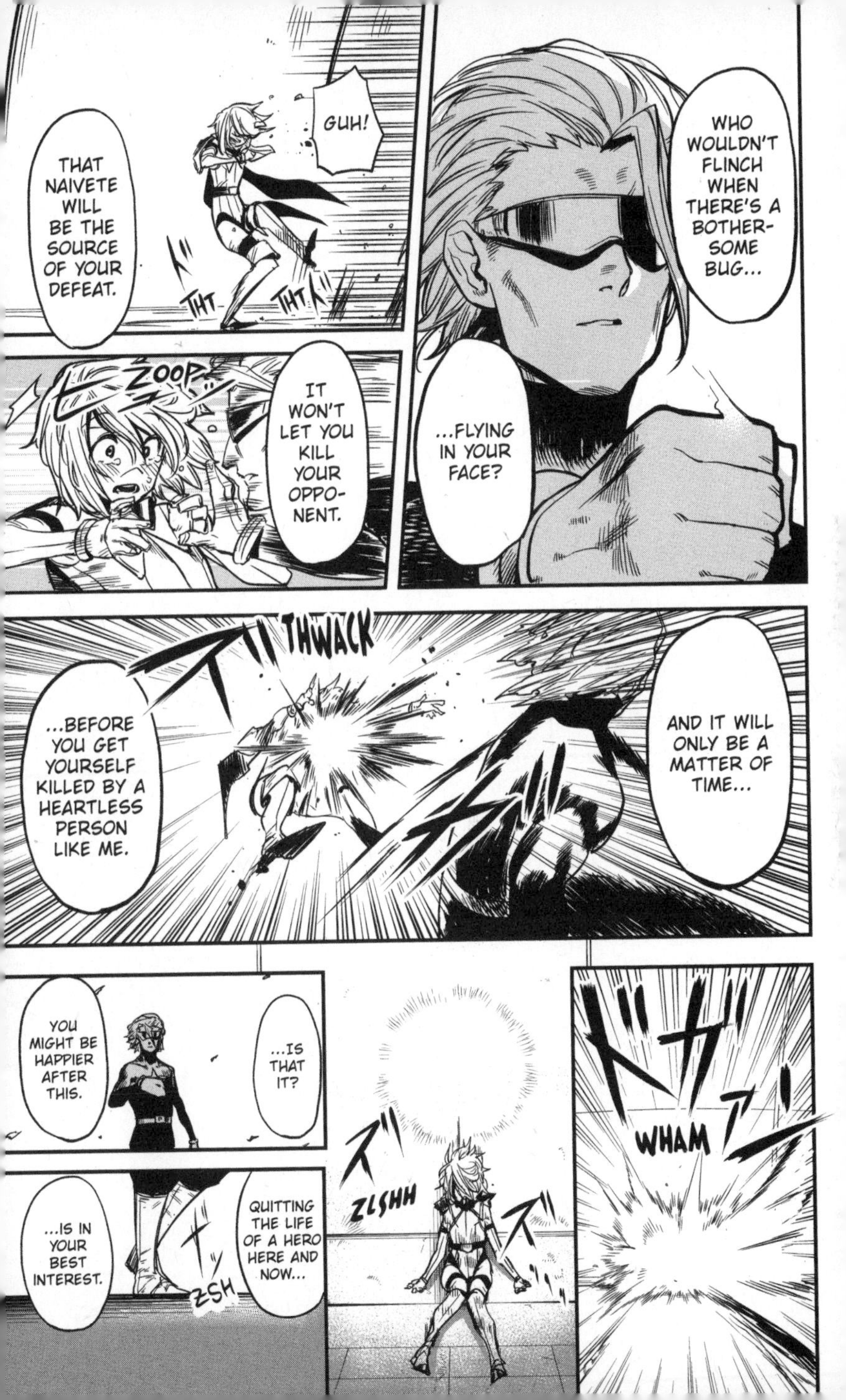
WHO WOULDN'T FLINCH WHEN THERE'S A BOTHER-SOME BUG...
...FLYING IN YOUR FACE?
GUH!
THAT NAIVETE WILL BE THE SOURCE OF YOUR DEFEAT.
THT
THT
ZOOP
IT WON'T LET YOU KILL YOUR OPPONENT.
THWACK
AND IT WILL ONLY BE A MATTER OF TIME...
...BEFORE YOU GET YOURSELF KILLED BY A HEARTLESS PERSON LIKE ME.
WHAM
ZLSHH
...IS THAT IT?
YOU MIGHT BE HAPPIER AFTER THIS.
QUITTING THE LIFE OF A HERO HERE AND NOW...
...IS IN YOUR BEST INTEREST.
ZSH

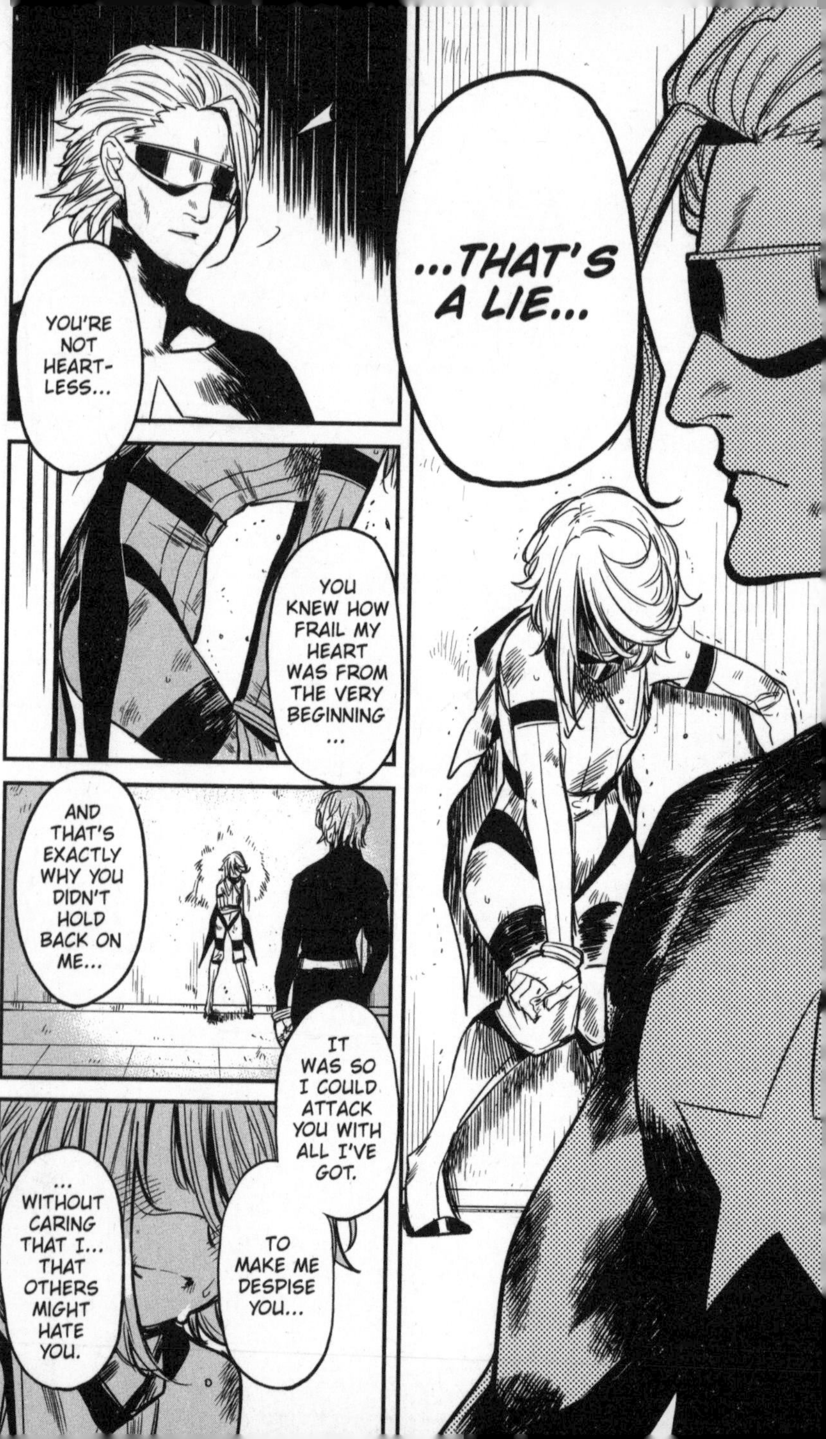
...THAT'S A LIE...
YOU'RE NOT HEARTLESS...
YOU KNEW HOW FRAIL MY HEART WAS FROM THE VERY BEGINNING...
AND THAT'S EXACTLY WHY YOU DIDN'T HOLD BACK ON ME...
IT WAS SO I COULD ATTACK YOU WITH ALL I'VE GOT.
TO MAKE ME DESPISE YOU...
...WITHOUT CARING THAT I... THAT OTHERS MIGHT HATE YOU.

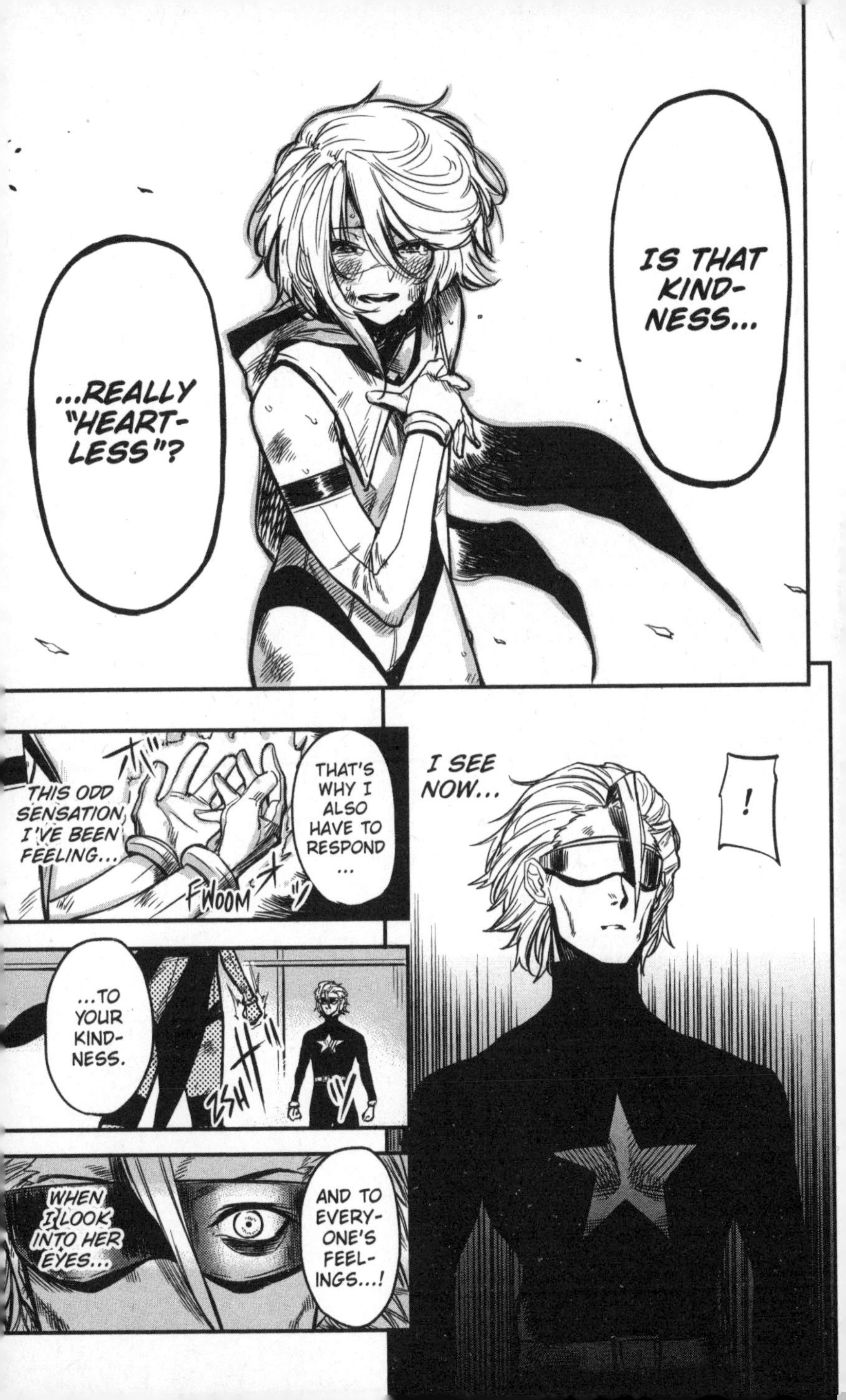
IS THAT KIND-NESS...
...REALLY "HEART-LESS"?
!
I SEE NOW...
THAT'S WHY I ALSO HAVE TO RESPOND ...
THIS ODD SENSATION I'VE BEEN FEELING...
FWOOM
...TO YOUR KIND-NESS.
ZSH
AND TO EVERY-ONE'S FEEL-INGS...!
WHEN I LOOK INTO HER EYES...

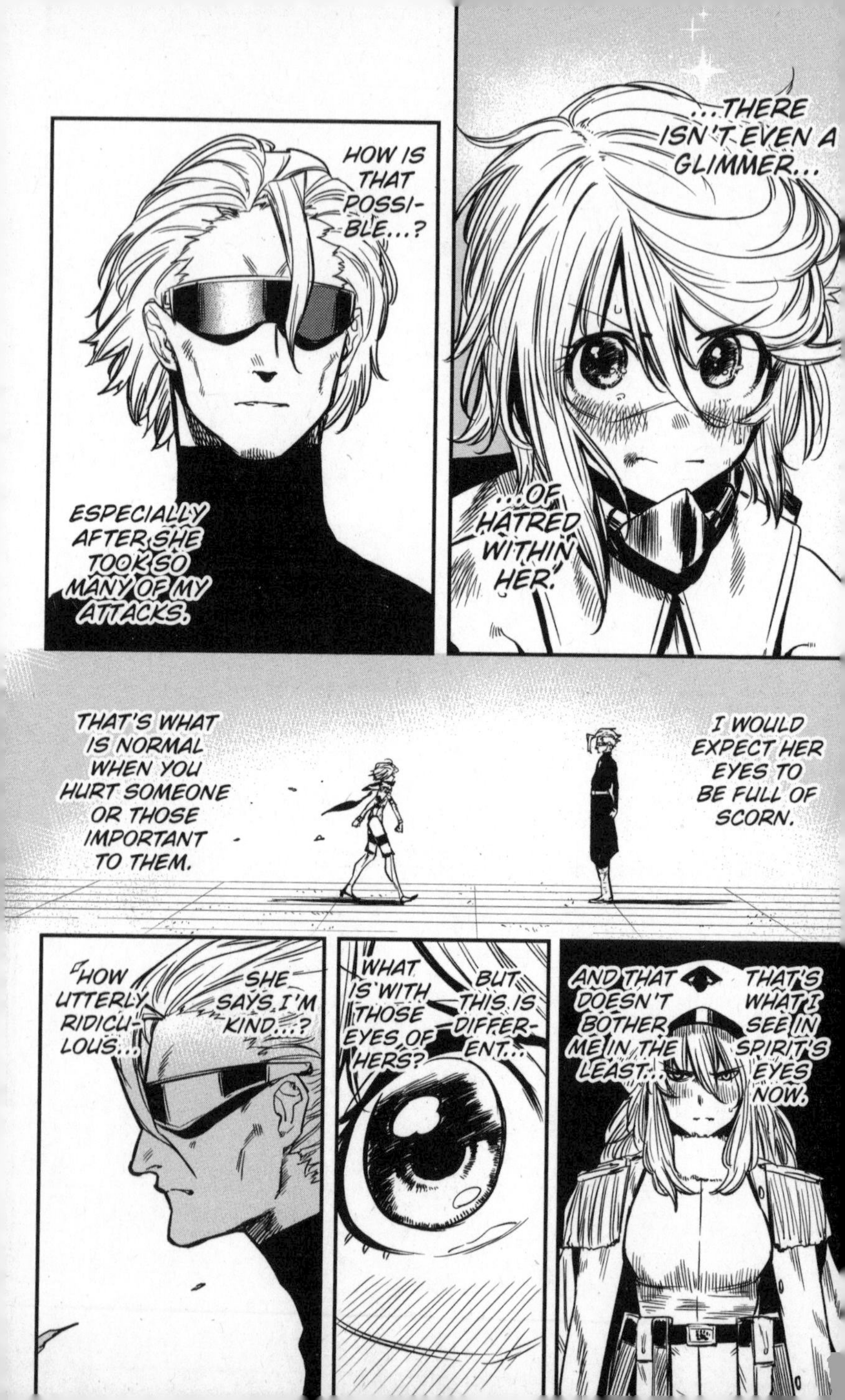
...THERE ISN'T EVEN A GLIMMER...
...OF HATRED WITHIN HER.
HOW IS THAT POSSI-BLE...?
ESPECIALLY AFTER SHE TOOK SO MANY OF MY ATTACKS.
I WOULD EXPECT HER EYES TO BE FULL OF SCORN.
THAT'S WHAT IS NORMAL WHEN YOU HURT SOMEONE OR THOSE IMPORTANT TO THEM.
THAT'S WHAT I SEE IN SPIRIT'S EYES NOW.
AND THAT DOESN'T BOTHER ME IN THE LEAST...
BUT THIS IS DIFFER-ENT...
WHAT IS WITH THOSE EYES OF HERS?
SHE SAYS I'M KIND...?
HOW UTTERLY RIDICU-LOUS...

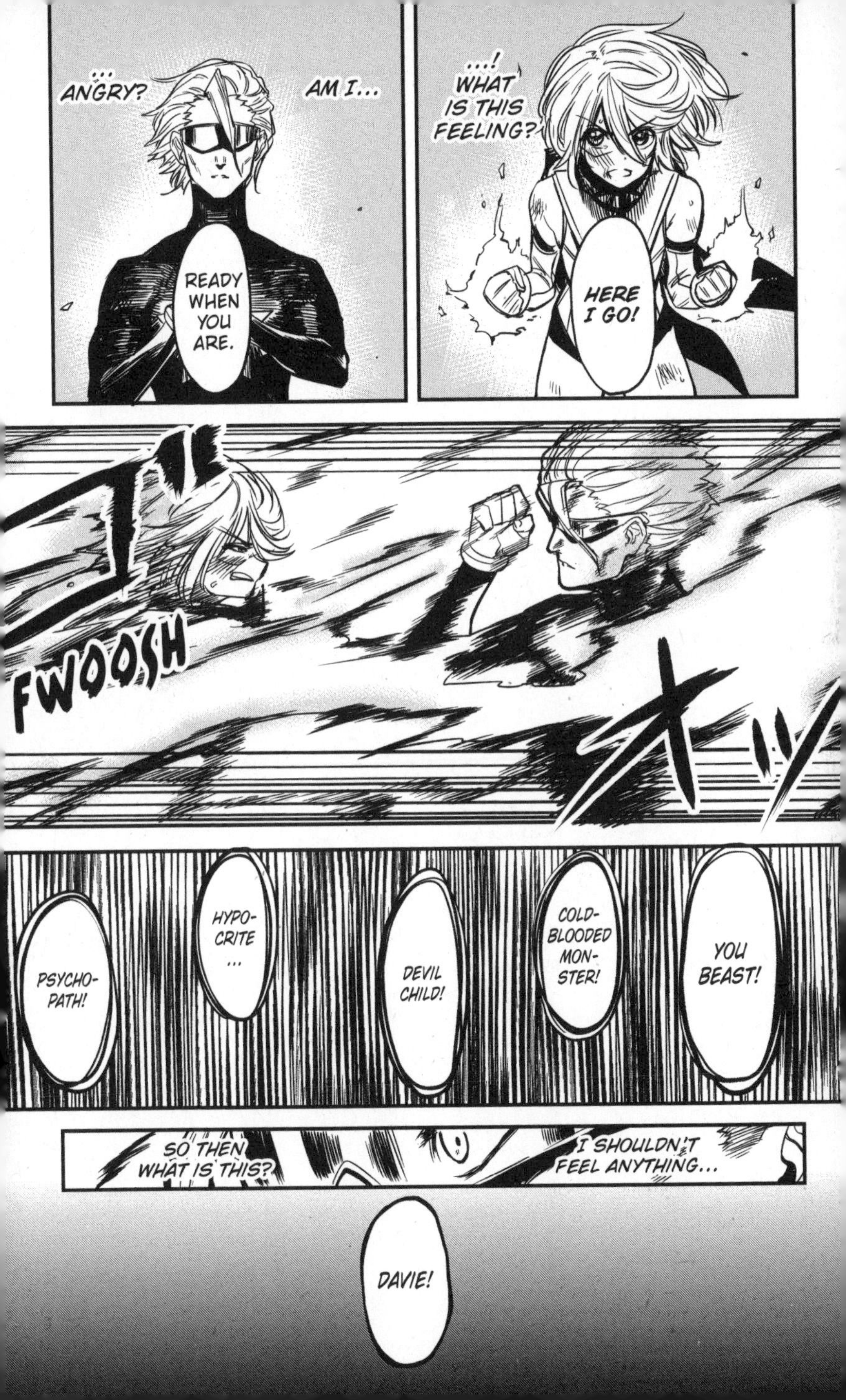
...! WHAT IS THIS FEELING?
HERE I GO!
AM I...
... ANGRY?
READY WHEN YOU ARE.
FWOOSH
YOU BEAST!
COLD-BLOODED MON-STER!
DEVIL CHILD!
HYPO-CRITE ...
PSYCHO-PATH!
I SHOULDN'T FEEL ANYTHING...
SO THEN WHAT IS THIS?
DAVIE!

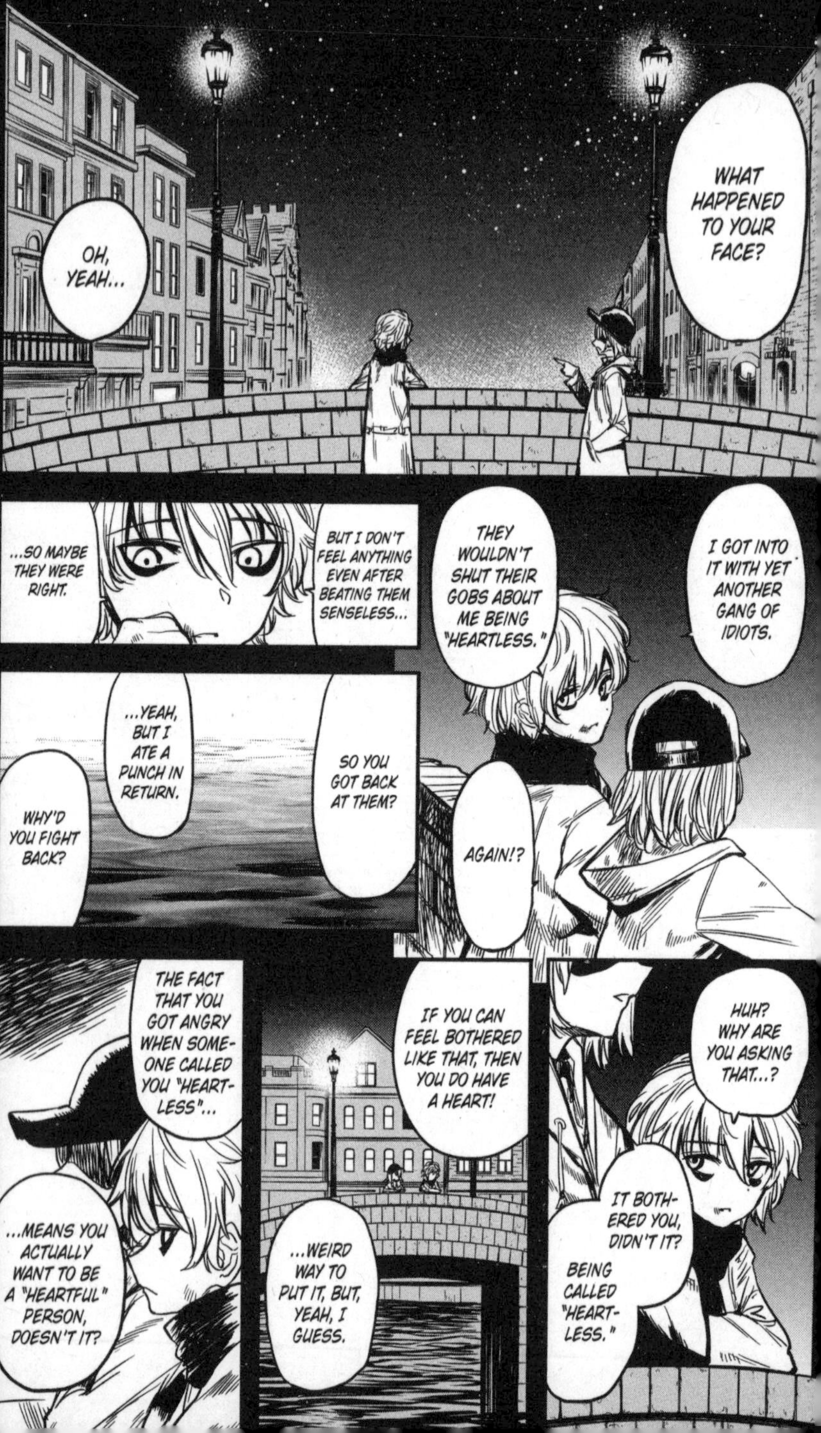
WHAT HAPPENED TO YOUR FACE?
OH, YEAH...
I GOT INTO IT WITH YET ANOTHER GANG OF IDIOTS.
THEY WOULDN'T SHUT THEIR GOBS ABOUT ME BEING "HEARTLESS."
AGAIN!?
BUT I DON'T FEEL ANYTHING EVEN AFTER BEATING THEM SENSELESS...
...SO MAYBE THEY WERE RIGHT.
SO YOU GOT BACK AT THEM?
...YEAH, BUT I ATE A PUNCH IN RETURN.
WHY'D YOU FIGHT BACK?
HUH? WHY ARE YOU ASKING THAT...?
IT BOTHERED YOU, DIDN'T IT?
BEING CALLED "HEARTLESS."
IF YOU CAN FEEL BOTHERED LIKE THAT, THEN YOU DO HAVE A HEART!
...WEIRD WAY TO PUT IT, BUT, YEAH, I GUESS.
THE FACT THAT YOU GOT ANGRY WHEN SOMEONE CALLED YOU "HEARTLESS"...
...MEANS YOU ACTUALLY WANT TO BE A "HEARTFUL" PERSON, DOESN'T IT?

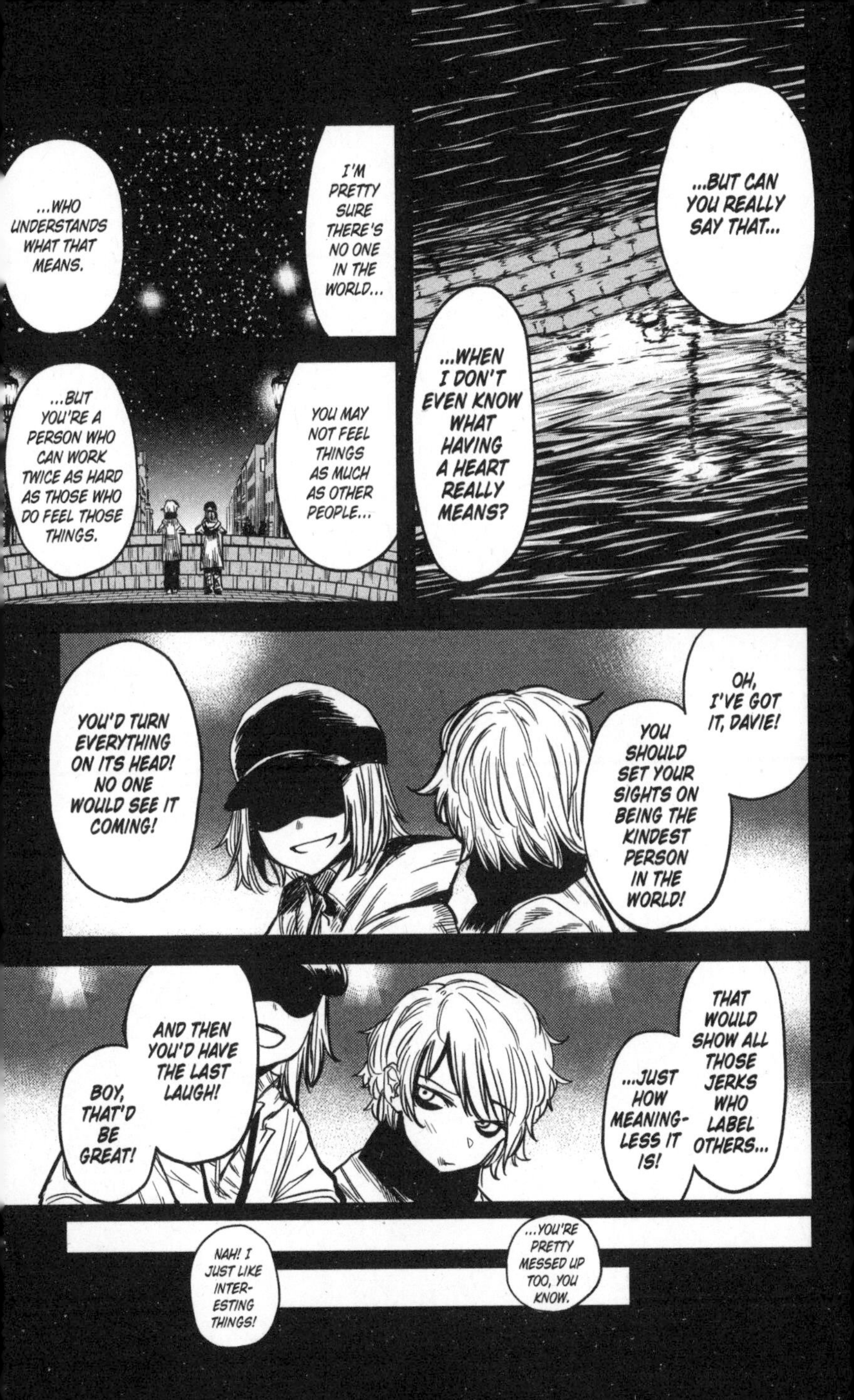
...BUT CAN YOU REALLY SAY THAT...
...WHEN I DON'T EVEN KNOW WHAT HAVING A HEART REALLY MEANS?
I'M PRETTY SURE THERE'S NO ONE IN THE WORLD...
...WHO UNDERSTANDS WHAT THAT MEANS.
YOU MAY NOT FEEL THINGS AS MUCH AS OTHER PEOPLE...
...BUT YOU'RE A PERSON WHO CAN WORK TWICE AS HARD AS THOSE WHO DO FEEL THOSE THINGS.
OH, I'VE GOT IT, DAVIE!
YOU SHOULD SET YOUR SIGHTS ON BEING THE KINDEST PERSON IN THE WORLD!
YOU'D TURN EVERYTHING ON ITS HEAD! NO ONE WOULD SEE IT COMING!
THAT WOULD SHOW ALL THOSE JERKS WHO LABEL OTHERS...
...JUST HOW MEANING-LESS IT IS!
AND THEN YOU'D HAVE THE LAST LAUGH!
BOY, THAT'D BE GREAT!
...YOU'RE PRETTY MESSED UP TOO, YOU KNOW.
NAH! I JUST LIKE INTER-ESTING THINGS!

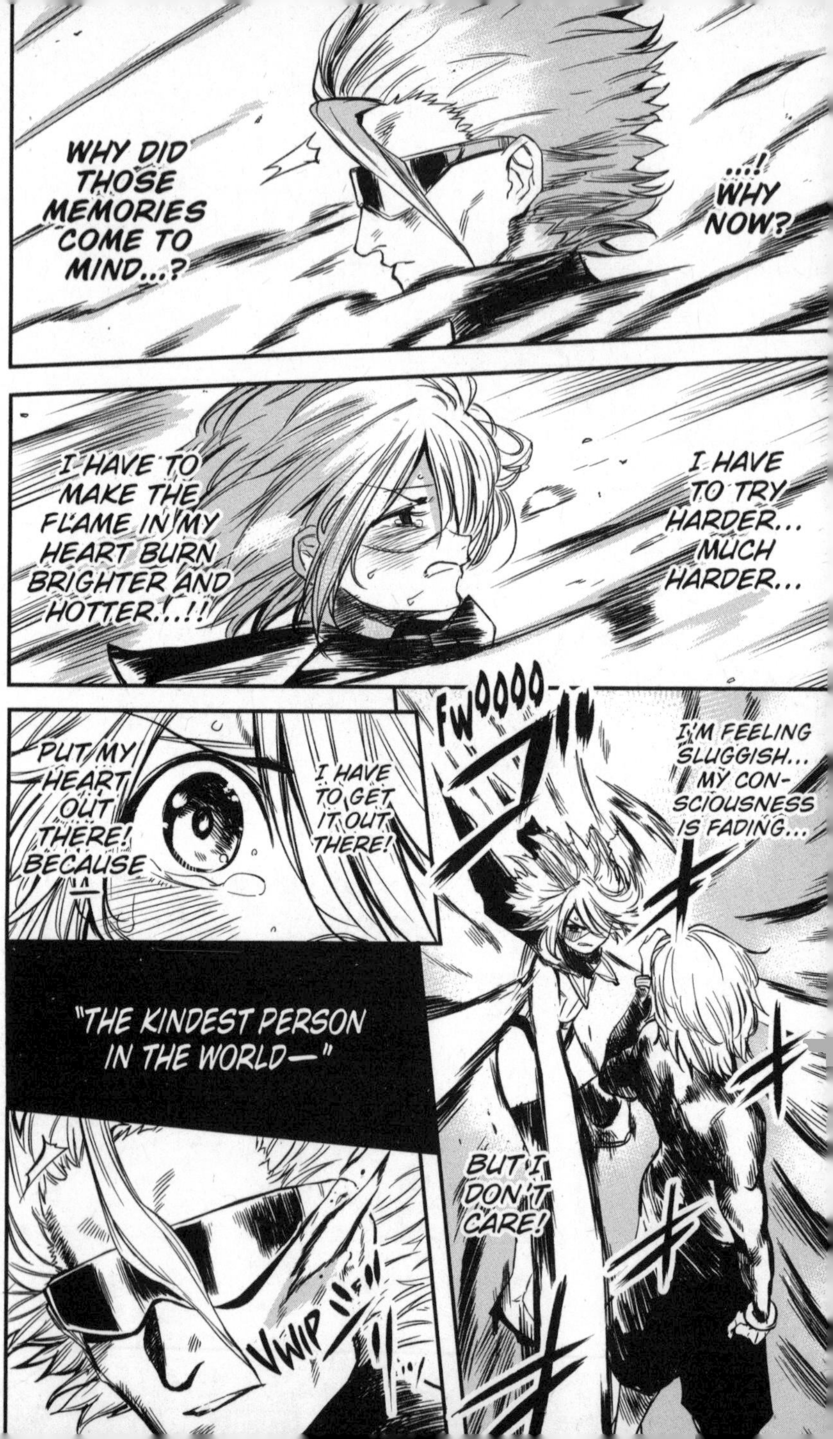
...! WHY NOW?
WHY DID THOSE MEMORIES COME TO MIND...?
I HAVE TO TRY HARDER... MUCH HARDER...
I HAVE TO MAKE THE FLAME IN MY HEART BURN BRIGHTER AND HOTTER...!!
FWOOOO-
I'M FEELING SLUGGISH... MY CONSCIOUSNESS IS FADING...
BUT I DON'T CARE!
I HAVE TO GET IT OUT THERE!
PUT MY HEART OUT THERE! BECAUSE—
"THE KINDEST PERSON IN THE WORLD—"
VWIP

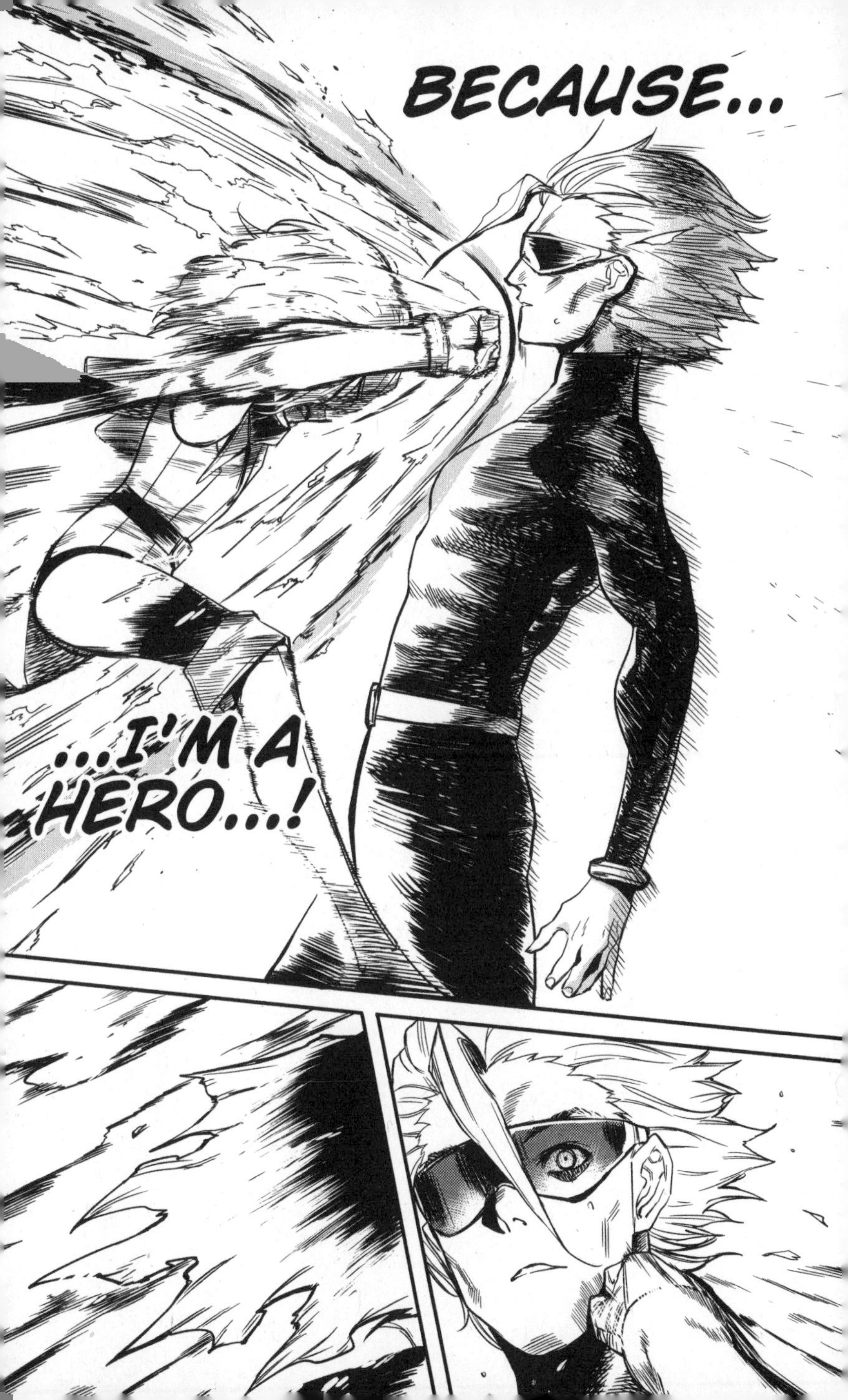
BECAUSE...
...I'M A HERO...!

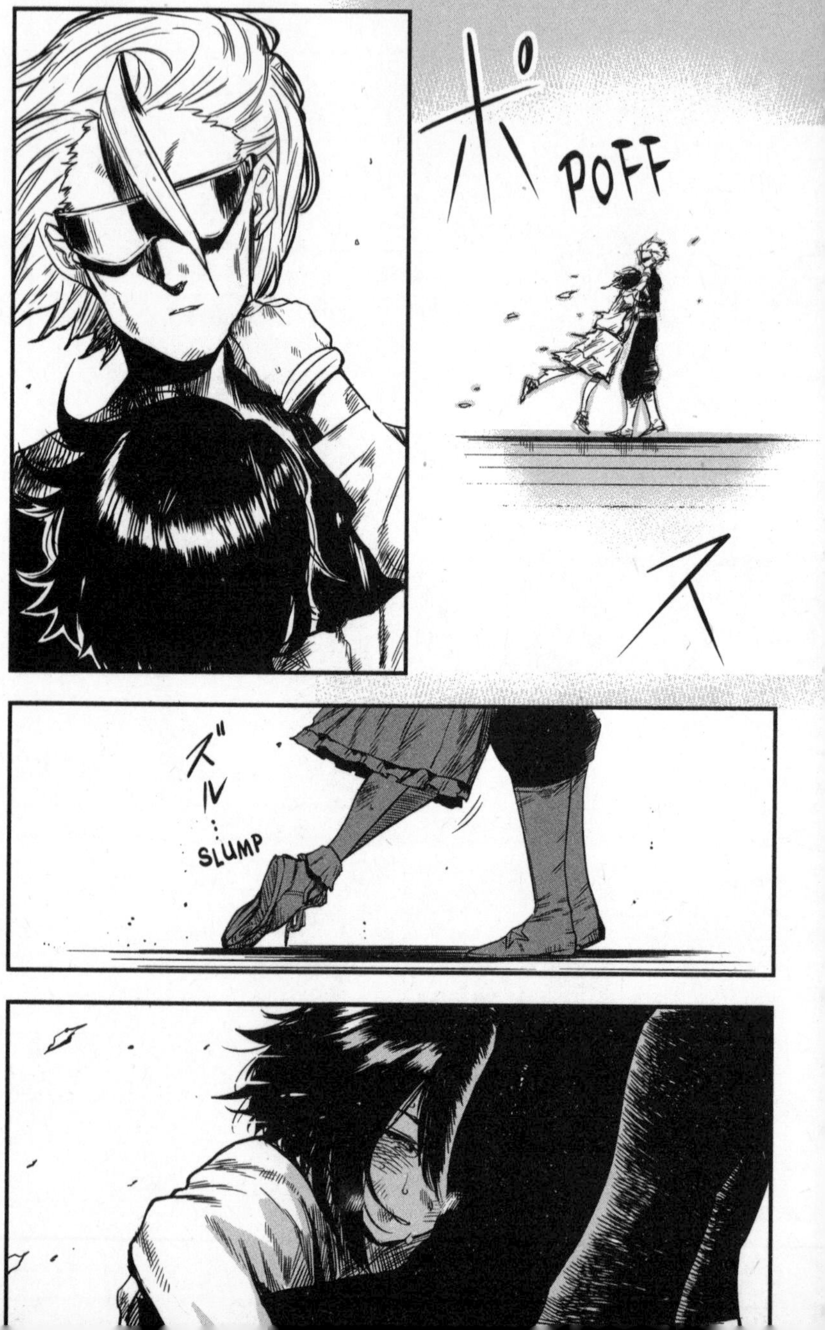
ポ
POFF
ス
ズル…
SLUMP

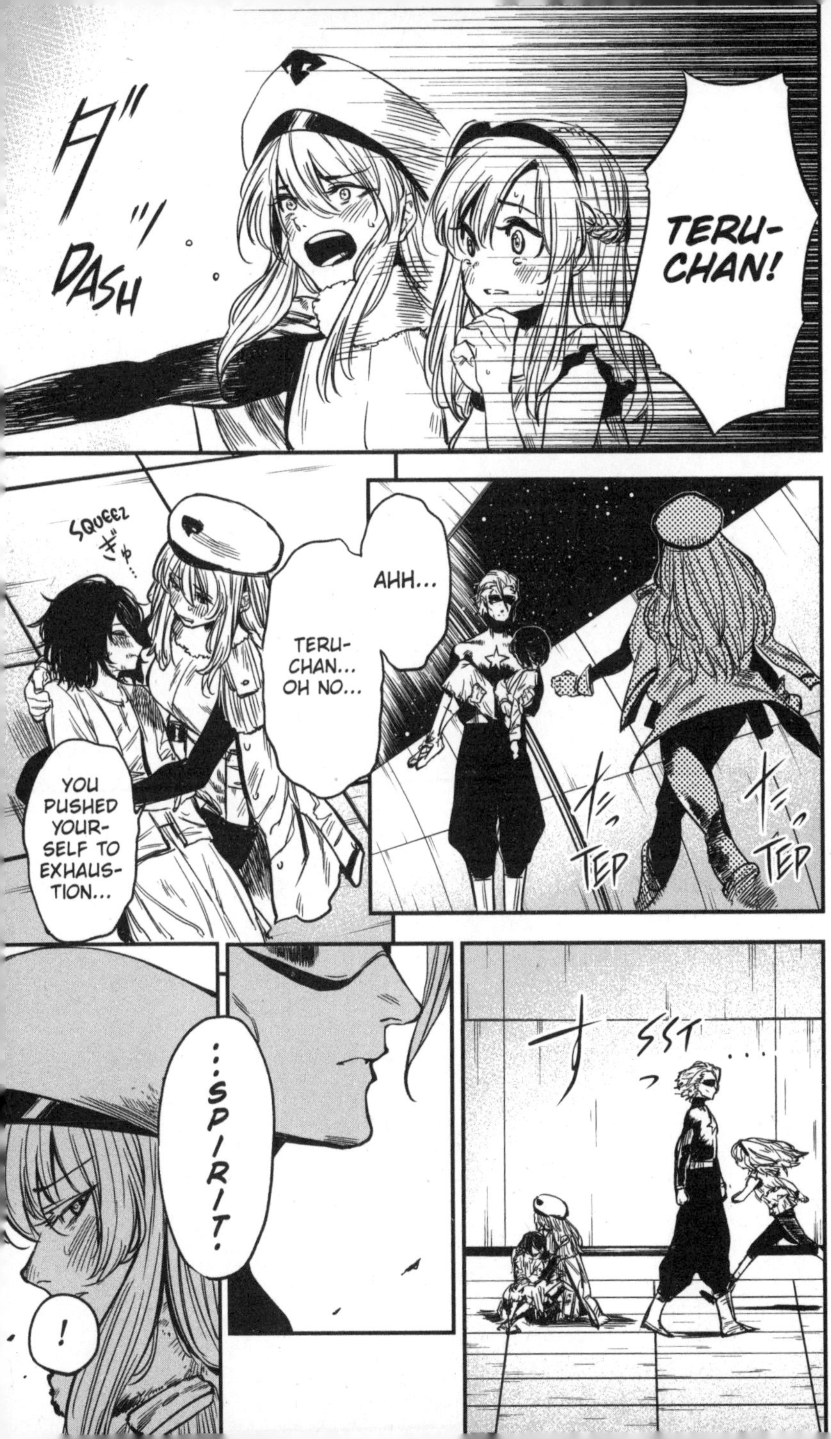
TERU-CHAN!
DASH
TEP
TEP
AHH...
TERU-CHAN... OH NO...
SQUEEZ
YOU PUSHED YOUR-SELF TO EXHAUS-TION...
SST
...
...SPIRIT.
!

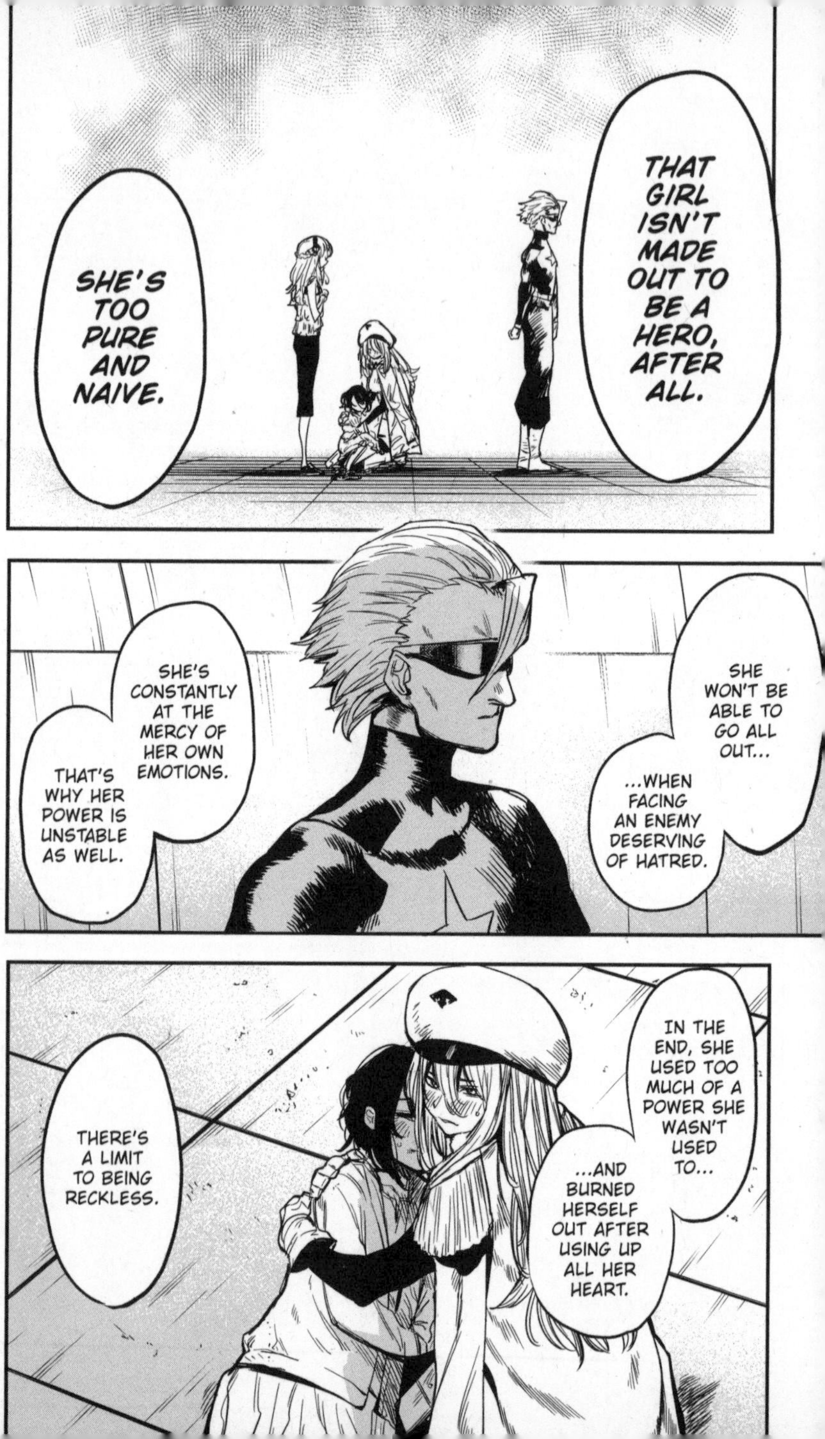
THAT GIRL ISN'T MADE OUT TO BE A HERO, AFTER ALL.
SHE'S TOO PURE AND NAIVE.
SHE WON'T BE ABLE TO GO ALL OUT...
...WHEN FACING AN ENEMY DESERVING OF HATRED.
SHE'S CONSTANTLY AT THE MERCY OF HER OWN EMOTIONS.
THAT'S WHY HER POWER IS UNSTABLE AS WELL.
IN THE END, SHE USED TOO MUCH OF A POWER SHE WASN'T USED TO...
...AND BURNED HERSELF OUT AFTER USING UP ALL HER HEART.
THERE'S A LIMIT TO BEING RECKLESS.

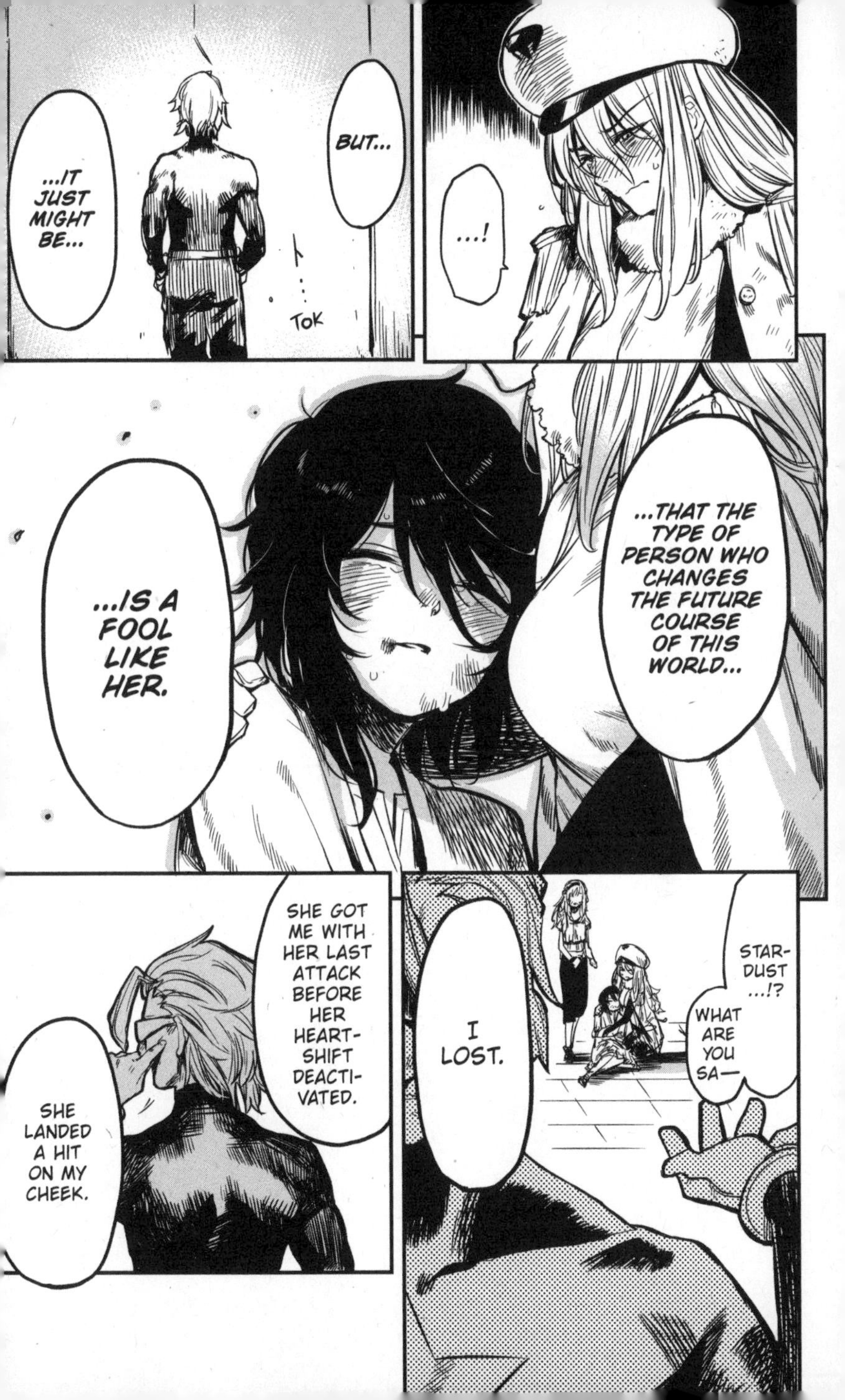
...!
BUT...
...IT JUST MIGHT BE...
TOK
...THAT THE TYPE OF PERSON WHO CHANGES THE FUTURE COURSE OF THIS WORLD...
...IS A FOOL LIKE HER.
STARDUST ...!?
WHAT ARE YOU SA—
I LOST.
SHE GOT ME WITH HER LAST ATTACK BEFORE HER HEART-SHIFT DEACTIVATED.
SHE LANDED A HIT ON MY CHEEK.

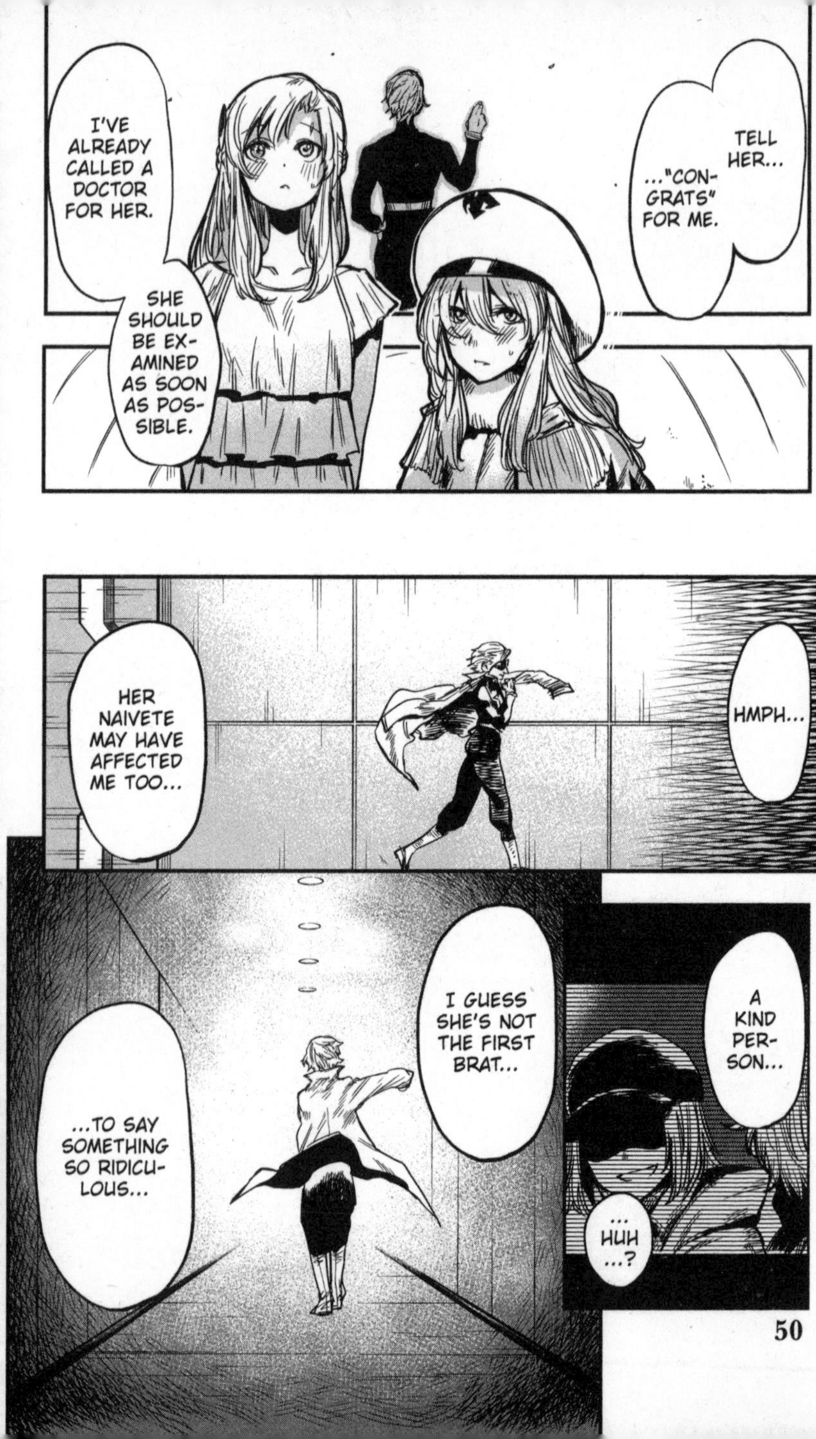
TELL HER...
..."CONGRATS" FOR ME.
I'VE ALREADY CALLED A DOCTOR FOR HER.
SHE SHOULD BE EXAMINED AS SOON AS POSSIBLE.
HMPH...
HER NAIVETE MAY HAVE AFFECTED ME TOO...
A KIND PERSON...
...HUH...?
I GUESS SHE'S NOT THE FIRST BRAT...
...TO SAY SOMETHING SO RIDICULOUS...

Chapter 9
Get Stronger

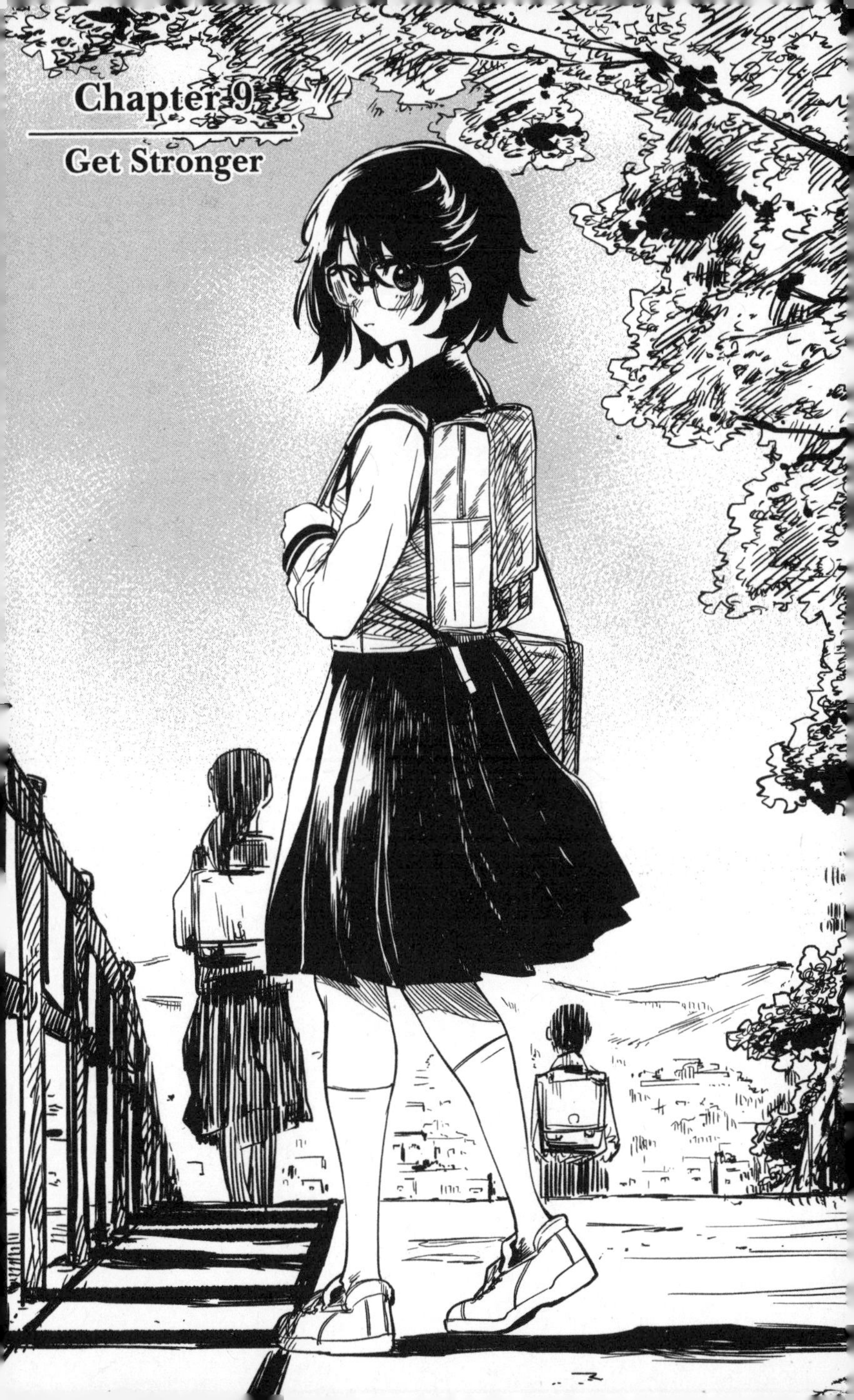

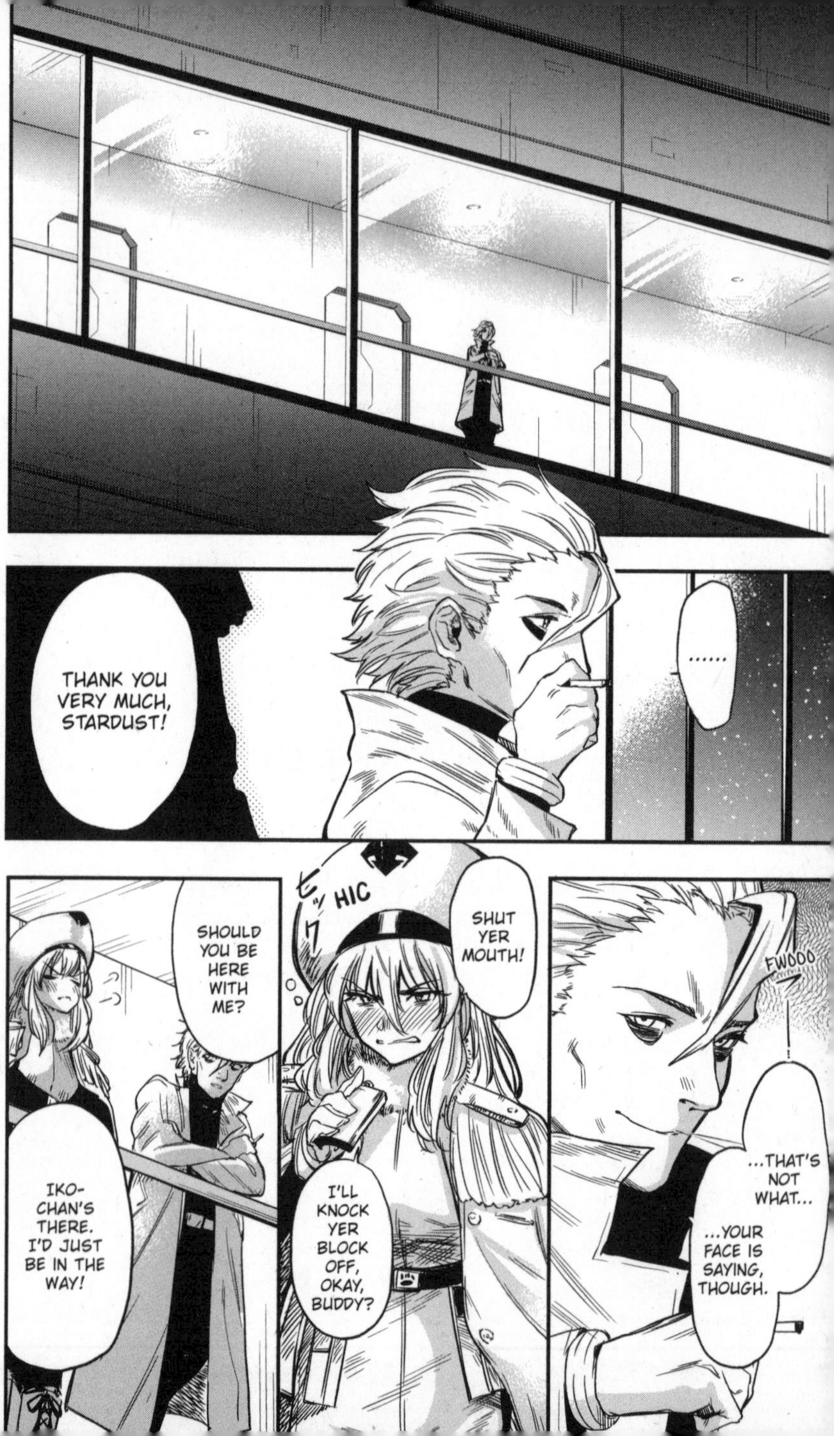
......
THANK YOU VERY MUCH, STARDUST!
FWOOO
!
...THAT'S NOT WHAT...
...YOUR FACE IS SAYING, THOUGH.
SHUT YER MOUTH!
HIC
I'LL KNOCK YER BLOCK OFF, OKAY, BUDDY?
SHOULD YOU BE HERE WITH ME?
IKO-CHAN'S THERE. I'D JUST BE IN THE WAY!

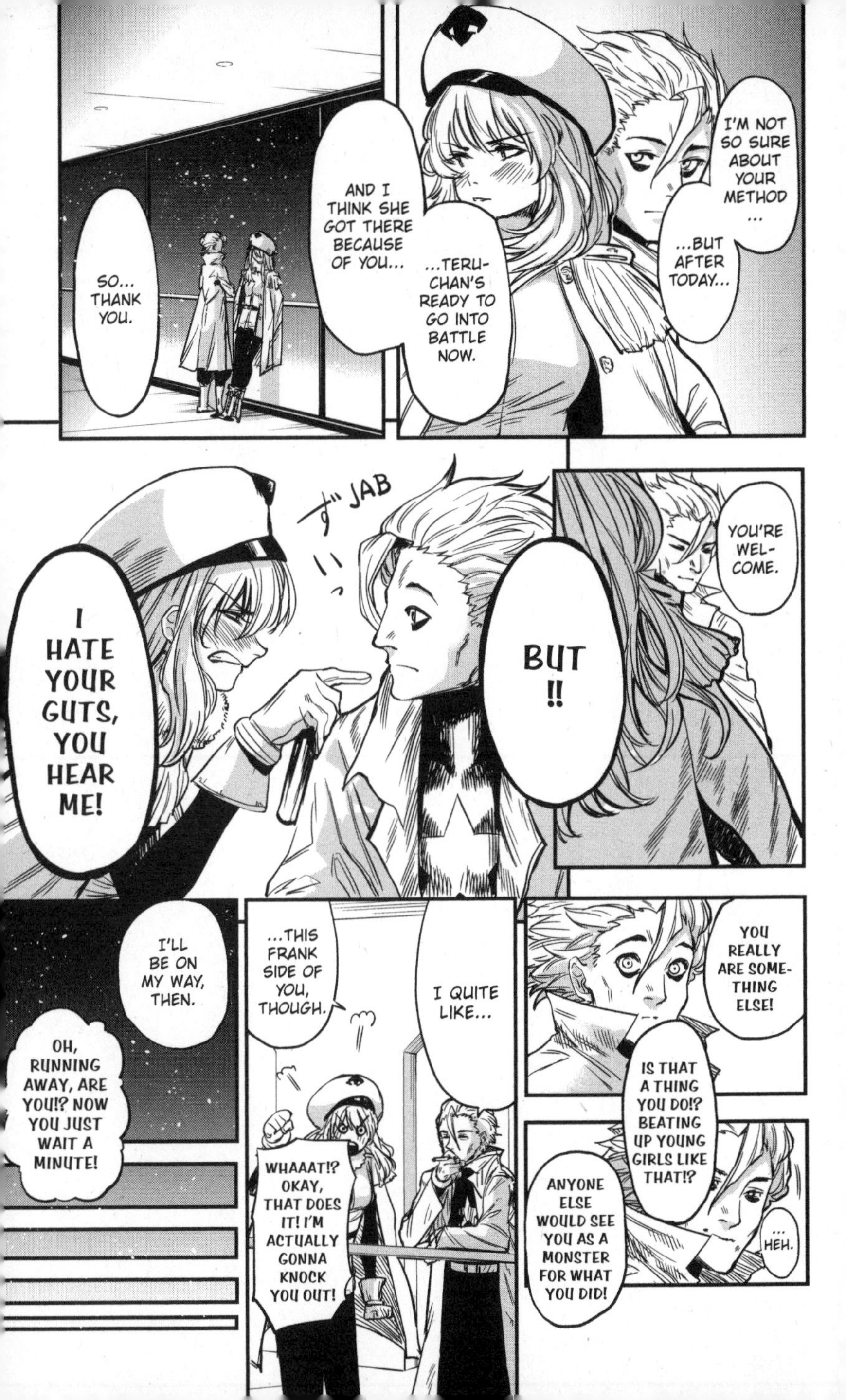
I'M NOT SO SURE ABOUT YOUR METHOD...
...BUT AFTER TODAY...
...TERU-CHAN'S READY TO GO INTO BATTLE NOW.
AND I THINK SHE GOT THERE BECAUSE OF YOU...
SO... THANK YOU.
YOU'RE WEL-COME.
BUT!!
JAB
I HATE YOUR GUTS, YOU HEAR ME!
YOU REALLY ARE SOME-THING ELSE!
IS THAT A THING YOU DO!? BEATING UP YOUNG GIRLS LIKE THAT!?
ANYONE ELSE WOULD SEE YOU AS A MONSTER FOR WHAT YOU DID!
...HEH.
I QUITE LIKE...
...THIS FRANK SIDE OF YOU, THOUGH.
WHAAAT!? OKAY, THAT DOES IT! I'M ACTUALLY GONNA KNOCK YOU OUT!
I'LL BE ON MY WAY, THEN.
OH, RUNNING AWAY, ARE YOU!? NOW YOU JUST WAIT A MINUTE!

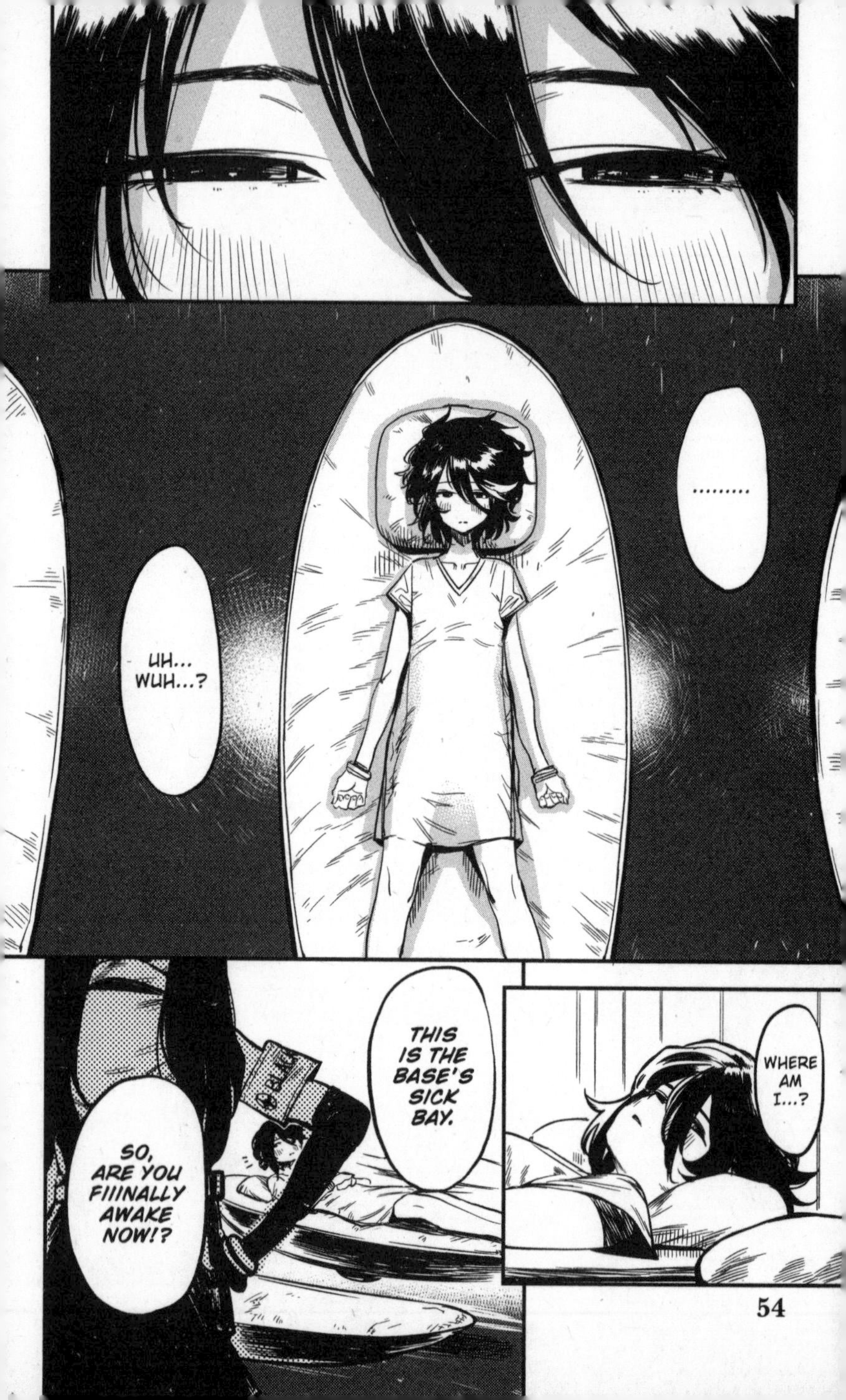
....
UH... WUH...?
WHERE AM I...?
THIS IS THE BASE'S SICK BAY.
SO, ARE YOU FIIINALLY AWAKE NOW!?

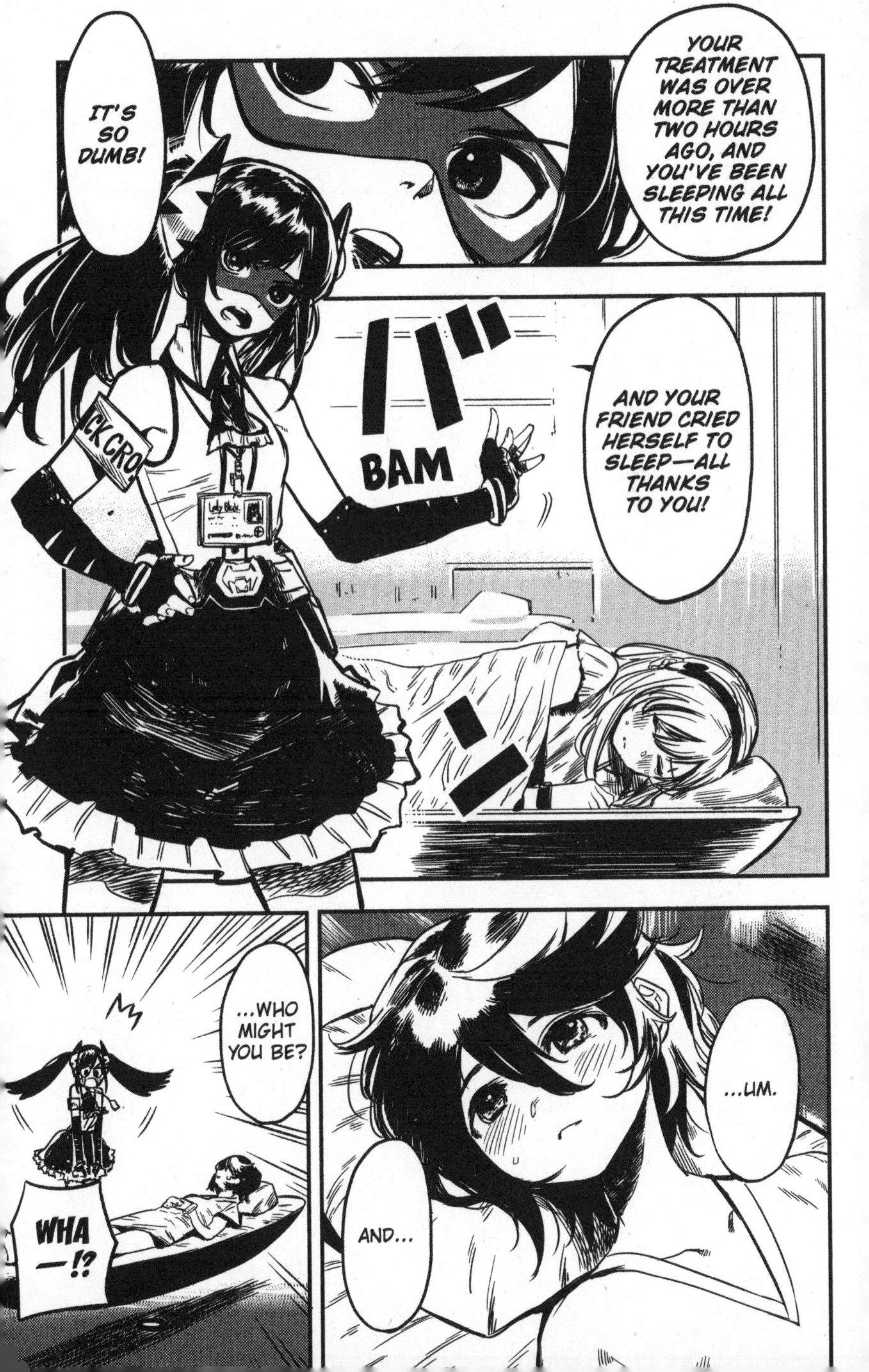
YOUR TREATMENT WAS OVER MORE THAN TWO HOURS AGO, AND YOU'VE BEEN SLEEPING ALL THIS TIME!
IT'S SO DUMB!
AND YOUR FRIEND CRIED HERSELF TO SLEEP—ALL THANKS TO YOU!
BAM
...UM.
AND...
...WHO MIGHT YOU BE?
WHA—!?

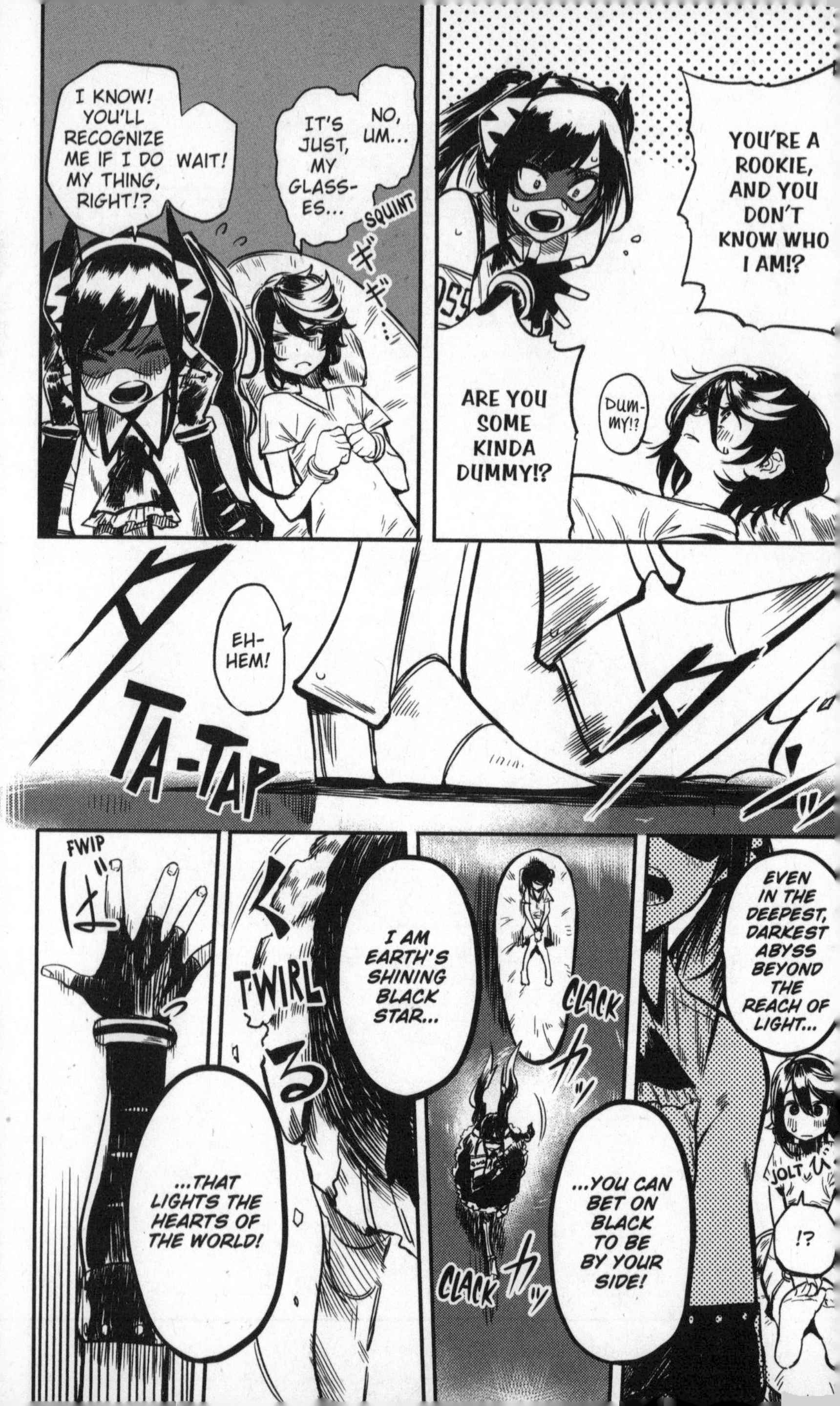
YOU'RE A ROOKIE, AND YOU DON'T KNOW WHO I AM!?
ARE YOU SOME KINDA DUMMY!?
DUM-MY!?
NO, UM... IT'S JUST, MY GLASSES...
SQUINT
WAIT!
I KNOW! YOU'LL RECOGNIZE ME IF I DO MY THING, RIGHT!?
EH-HEM!
TA-TAP
EVEN IN THE DEEPEST, DARKEST ABYSS BEYOND THE REACH OF LIGHT...
JOLT
!?
CLACK
...YOU CAN BET ON BLACK TO BE BY YOUR SIDE!
CLACK
I AM EARTH'S SHINING BLACK STAR...
TWIRL
...THAT LIGHTS THE HEARTS OF THE WORLD!
FWIP

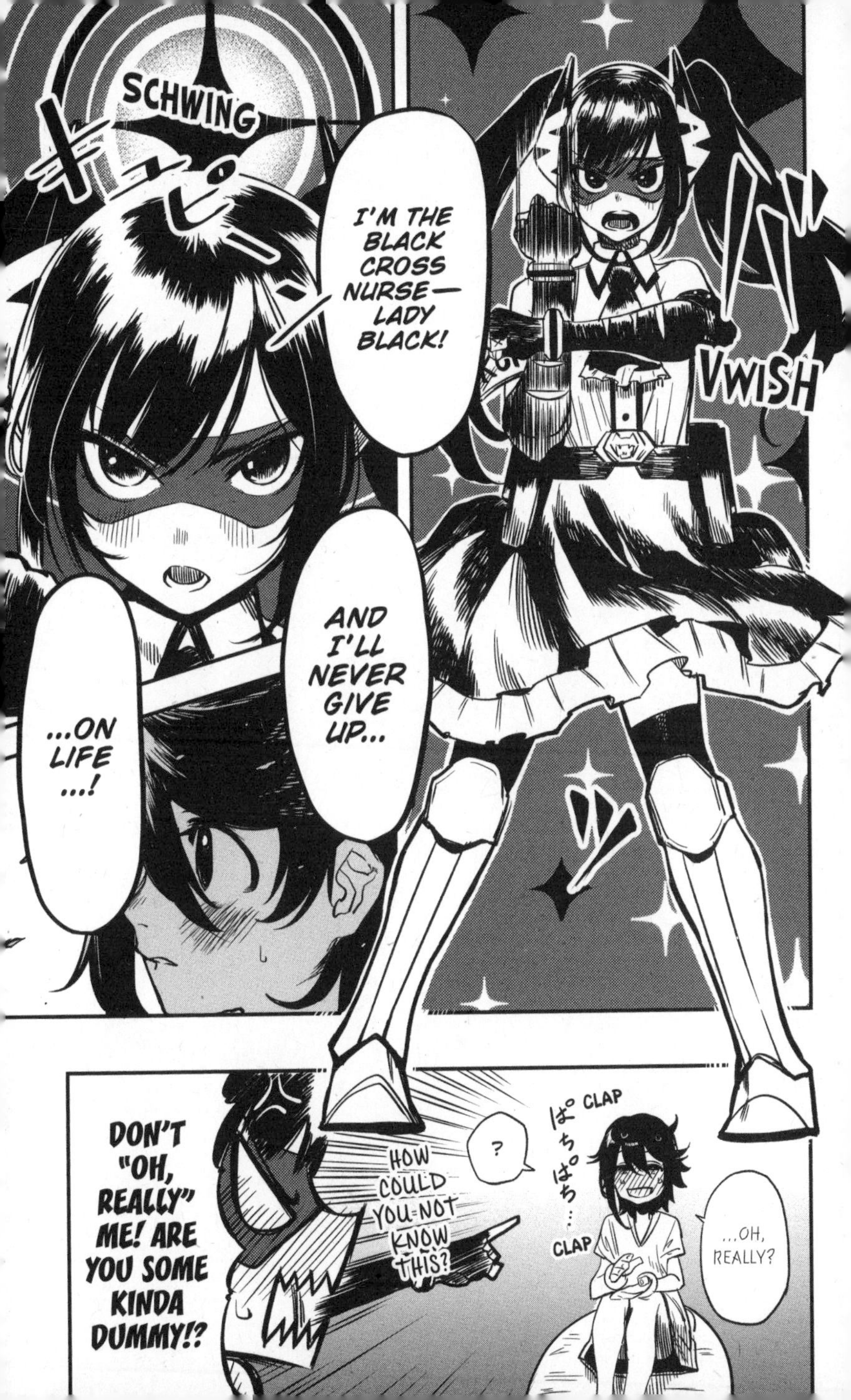
VWISH
SCHWING
I'M THE BLACK CROSS NURSE—LADY BLACK!
AND I'LL NEVER GIVE UP...
...ON LIFE ...!
ぱちぱち… CLAP CLAP
...OH, REALLY?
?
HOW COULD YOU NOT KNOW THIS?
DON'T "OH, REALLY" ME! ARE YOU SOME KINDA DUMMY!?

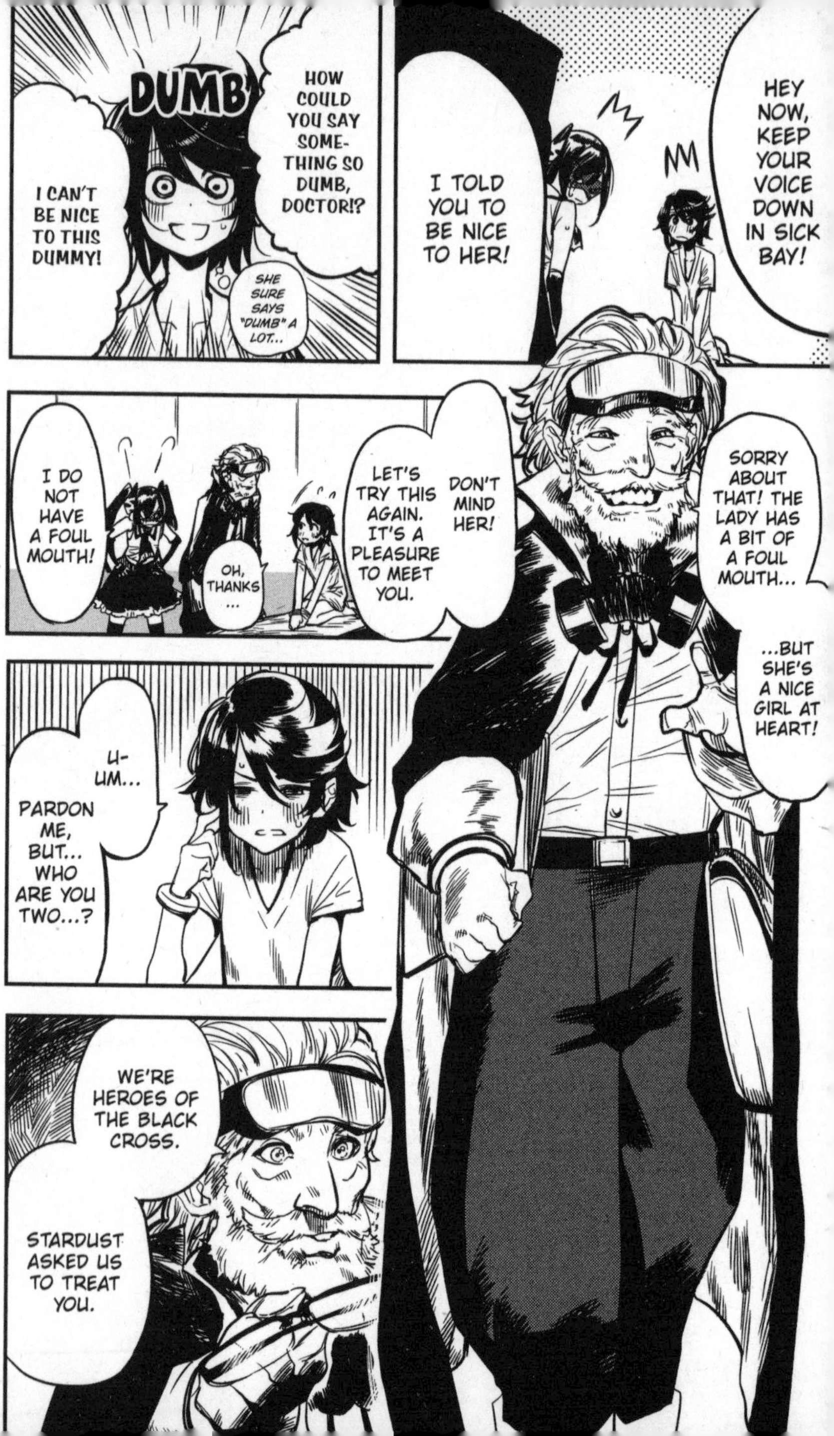
HEY NOW, KEEP YOUR VOICE DOWN IN SICK BAY!
I TOLD YOU TO BE NICE TO HER!
HOW COULD YOU SAY SOME-THING SO DUMB, DOCTOR!?
DUMB
I CAN'T BE NICE TO THIS DUMMY!
SHE SURE SAYS "DUMB" A LOT...
SORRY ABOUT THAT! THE LADY HAS A BIT OF A FOUL MOUTH...
...BUT SHE'S A NICE GIRL AT HEART!
DON'T MIND HER!
LET'S TRY THIS AGAIN. IT'S A PLEASURE TO MEET YOU.
OH, THANKS...
I DO NOT HAVE A FOUL MOUTH!
U-UM...
PARDON ME, BUT... WHO ARE YOU TWO...?
WE'RE HEROES OF THE BLACK CROSS.
STARDUST ASKED US TO TREAT YOU.

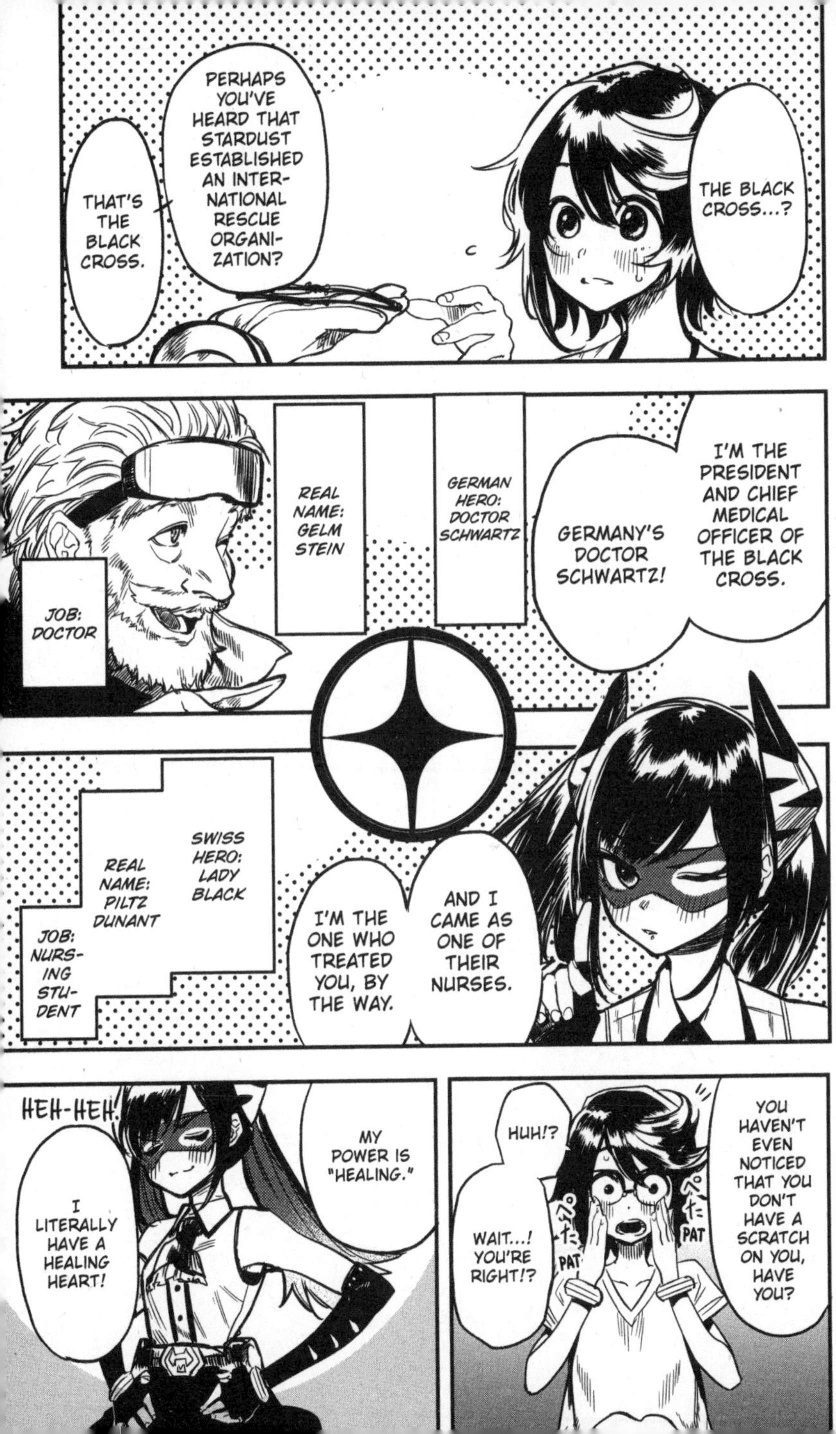
THE BLACK CROSS...?
PERHAPS YOU'VE HEARD THAT STARDUST ESTABLISHED AN INTERNATIONAL RESCUE ORGANIZATION?
THAT'S THE BLACK CROSS.
I'M THE PRESIDENT AND CHIEF MEDICAL OFFICER OF THE BLACK CROSS.
GERMANY'S DOCTOR SCHWARTZ!
GERMAN HERO: DOCTOR SCHWARTZ
REAL NAME: GELM STEIN
JOB: DOCTOR
AND I CAME AS ONE OF THEIR NURSES.
I'M THE ONE WHO TREATED YOU, BY THE WAY.
SWISS HERO: LADY BLACK
REAL NAME: PILTZ DUNANT
JOB: NURSING STUDENT
YOU HAVEN'T EVEN NOTICED THAT YOU DON'T HAVE A SCRATCH ON YOU, HAVE YOU?
HUH!?
PAT
PAT
WAIT...! YOU'RE RIGHT!?
MY POWER IS "HEALING."
HEH-HEH
I LITERALLY HAVE A HEALING HEART!

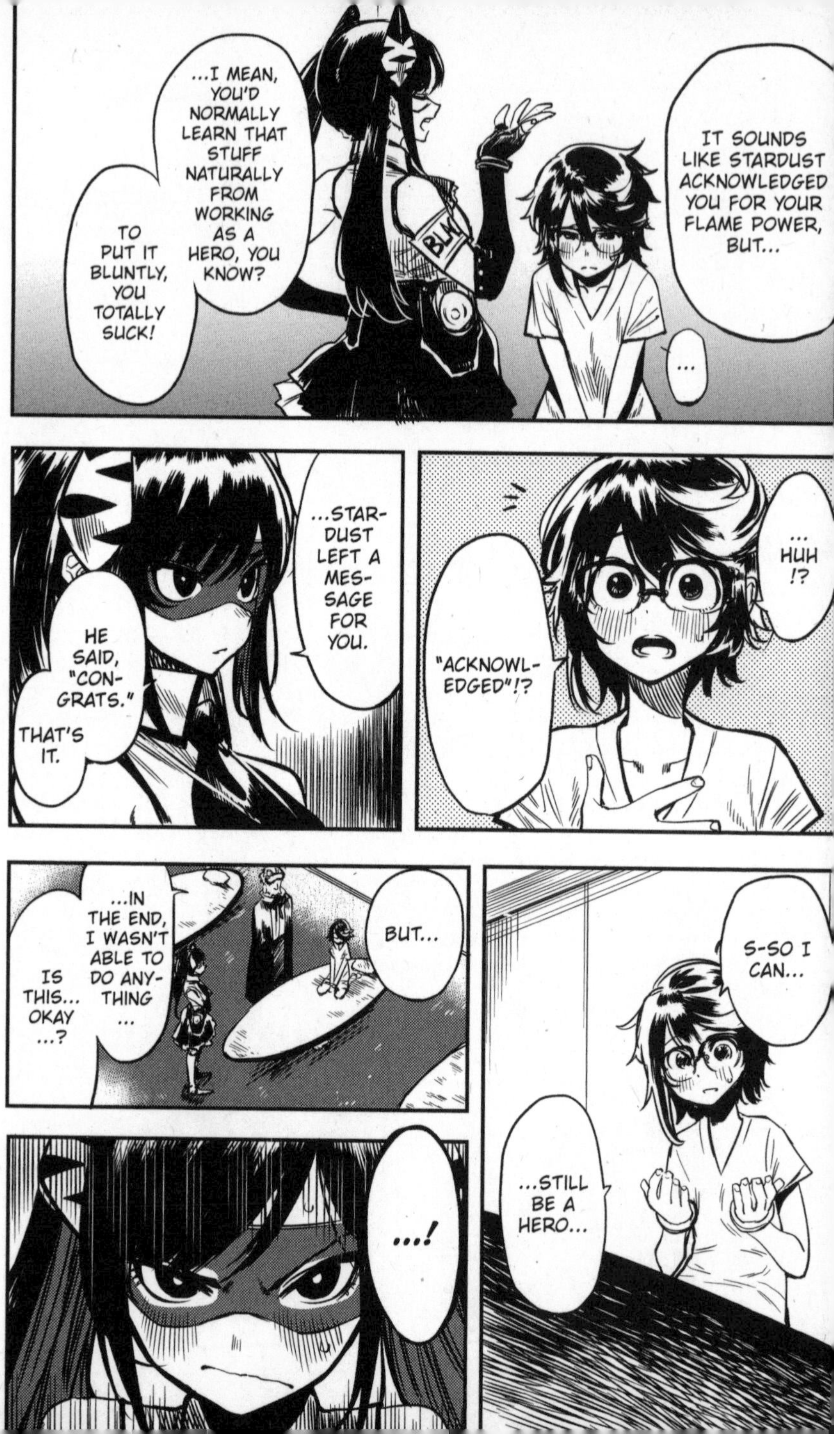
IT SOUNDS LIKE STARDUST ACKNOWLEDGED YOU FOR YOUR FLAME POWER, BUT...
...
...I MEAN, YOU'D NORMALLY LEARN THAT STUFF NATURALLY FROM WORKING AS A HERO, YOU KNOW?
TO PUT IT BLUNTLY, YOU TOTALLY SUCK!
...HUH!?
"ACKNOWLEDGED"!?
...STARDUST LEFT A MESSAGE FOR YOU.
HE SAID, "CONGRATS."
THAT'S IT.
S-SO I CAN...
...STILL BE A HERO...
BUT...
...IN THE END, I WASN'T ABLE TO DO ANYTHING...
IS THIS... OKAY...?
...!

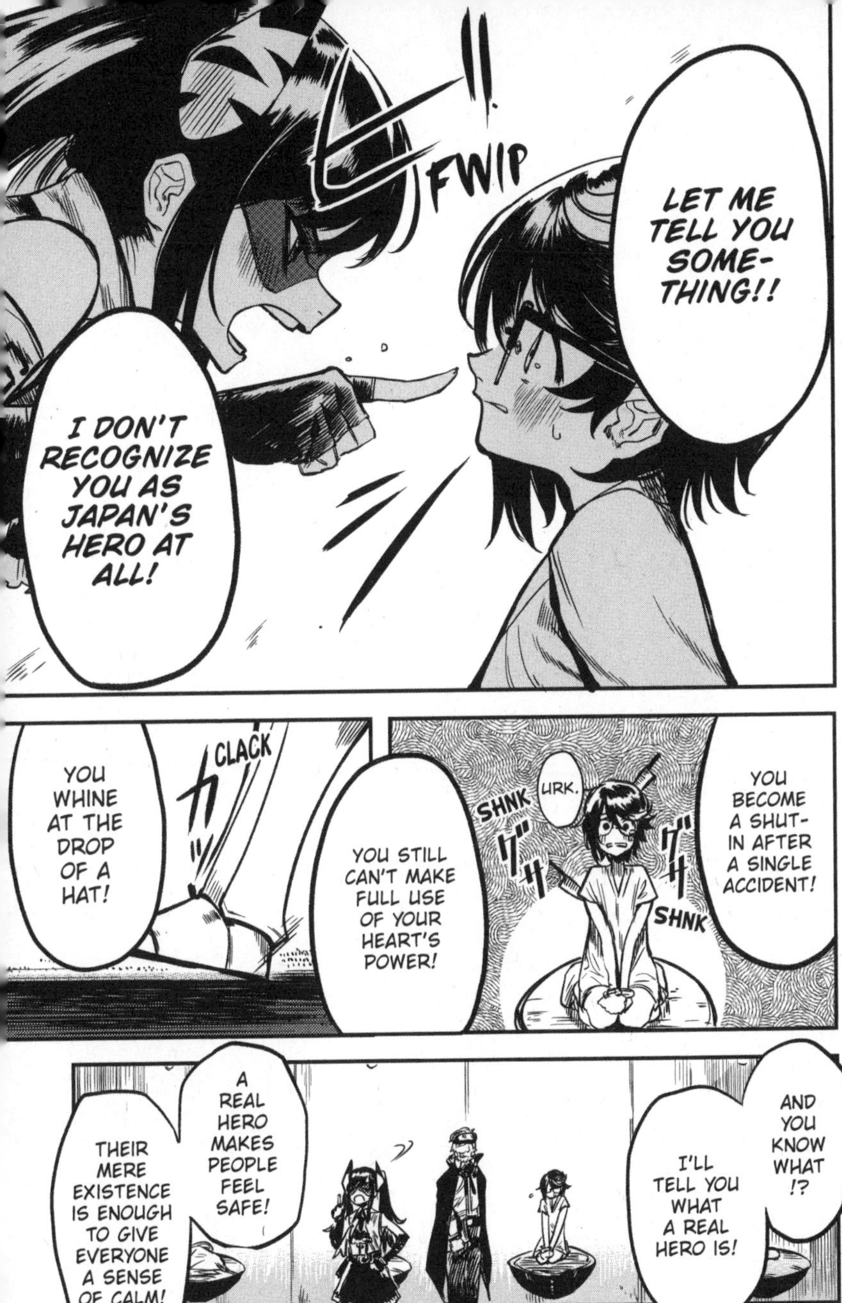
LET ME TELL YOU SOME-THING!!
FWIP
I DON'T RECOGNIZE YOU AS JAPAN'S HERO AT ALL!
YOU BECOME A SHUT-IN AFTER A SINGLE ACCIDENT!
URK.
SHNK
SHNK
YOU STILL CAN'T MAKE FULL USE OF YOUR HEART'S POWER!
CLACK
YOU WHINE AT THE DROP OF A HAT!
AND YOU KNOW WHAT!?
I'LL TELL YOU WHAT A REAL HERO IS!
A REAL HERO MAKES PEOPLE FEEL SAFE!
THEIR MERE EXISTENCE IS ENOUGH TO GIVE EVERYONE A SENSE OF CALM!

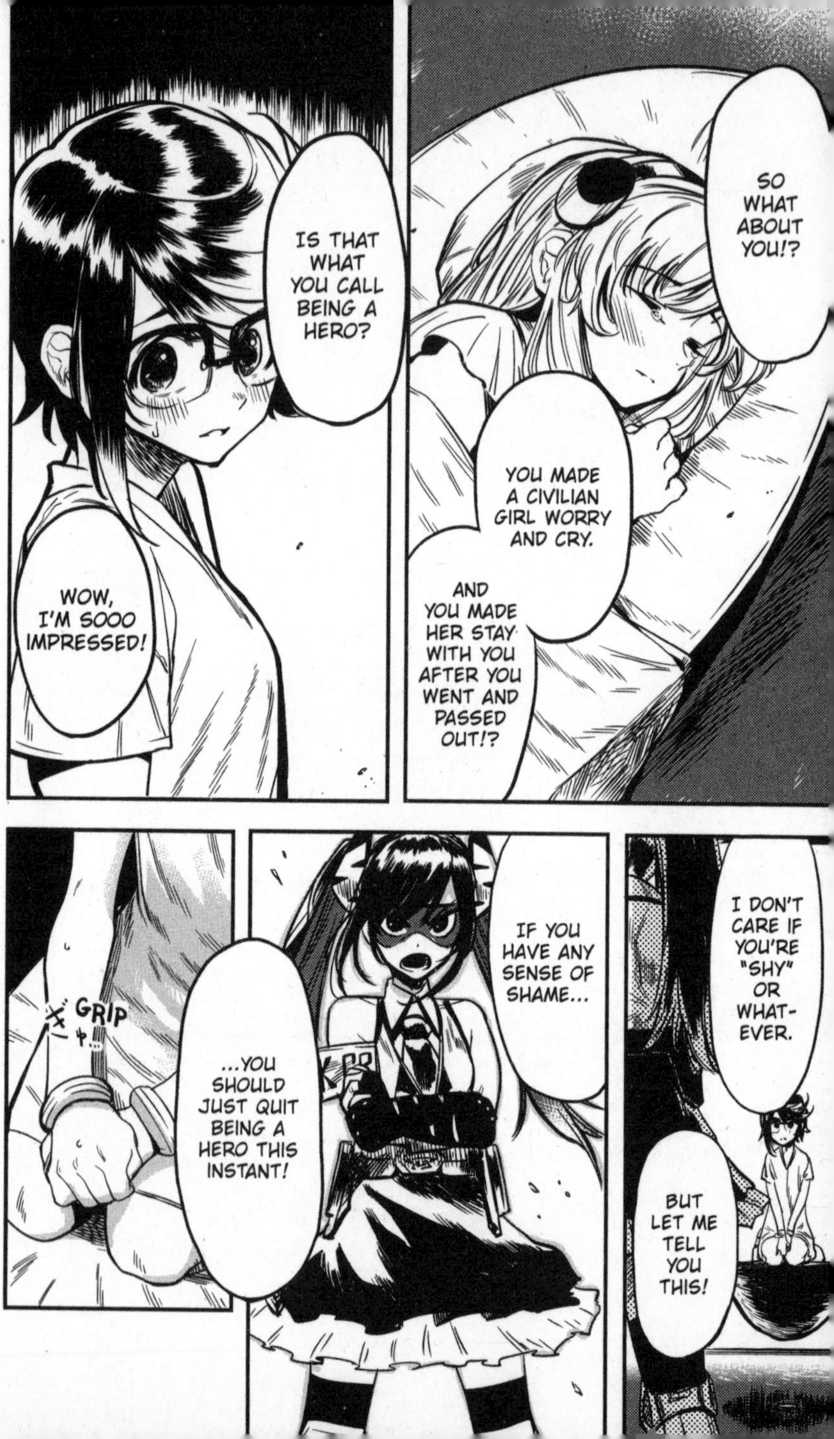
SO WHAT ABOUT YOU!?
YOU MADE A CIVILIAN GIRL WORRY AND CRY.
AND YOU MADE HER STAY WITH YOU AFTER YOU WENT AND PASSED OUT!?
IS THAT WHAT YOU CALL BEING A HERO?
WOW, I'M SOOO IMPRESSED!
I DON'T CARE IF YOU'RE "SHY" OR WHATEVER.
BUT LET ME TELL YOU THIS!
IF YOU HAVE ANY SENSE OF SHAME...
...YOU SHOULD JUST QUIT BEING A HERO THIS INSTANT!
GRIP

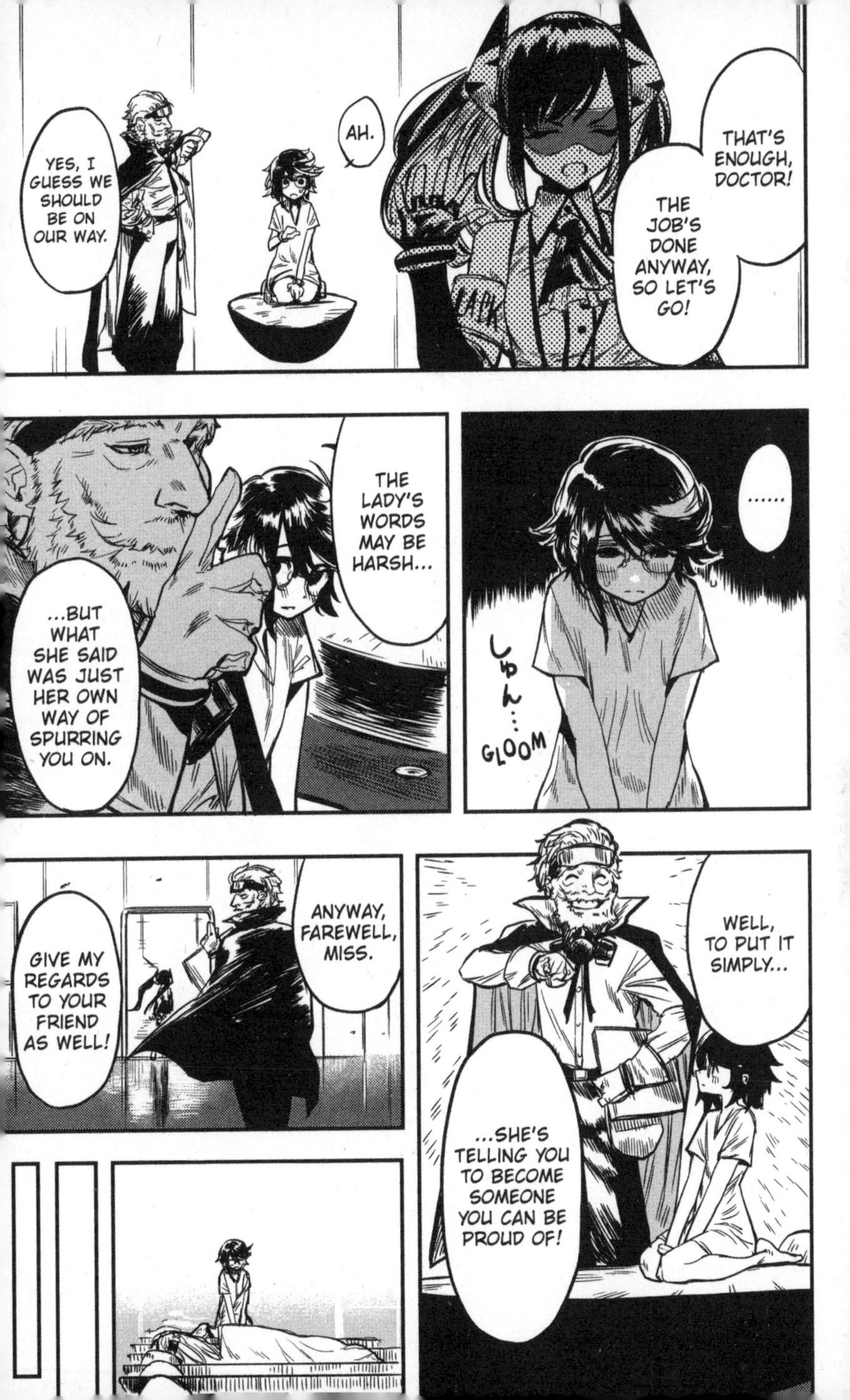
THAT'S ENOUGH, DOCTOR!
THE JOB'S DONE ANYWAY, SO LET'S GO!
AH.
YES, I GUESS WE SHOULD BE ON OUR WAY.
......
しゅん…
GLOOM
THE LADY'S WORDS MAY BE HARSH...
...BUT WHAT SHE SAID WAS JUST HER OWN WAY OF SPURRING YOU ON.
WELL, TO PUT IT SIMPLY...
...SHE'S TELLING YOU TO BECOME SOMEONE YOU CAN BE PROUD OF!
ANYWAY, FAREWELL, MISS.
GIVE MY REGARDS TO YOUR FRIEND AS WELL!

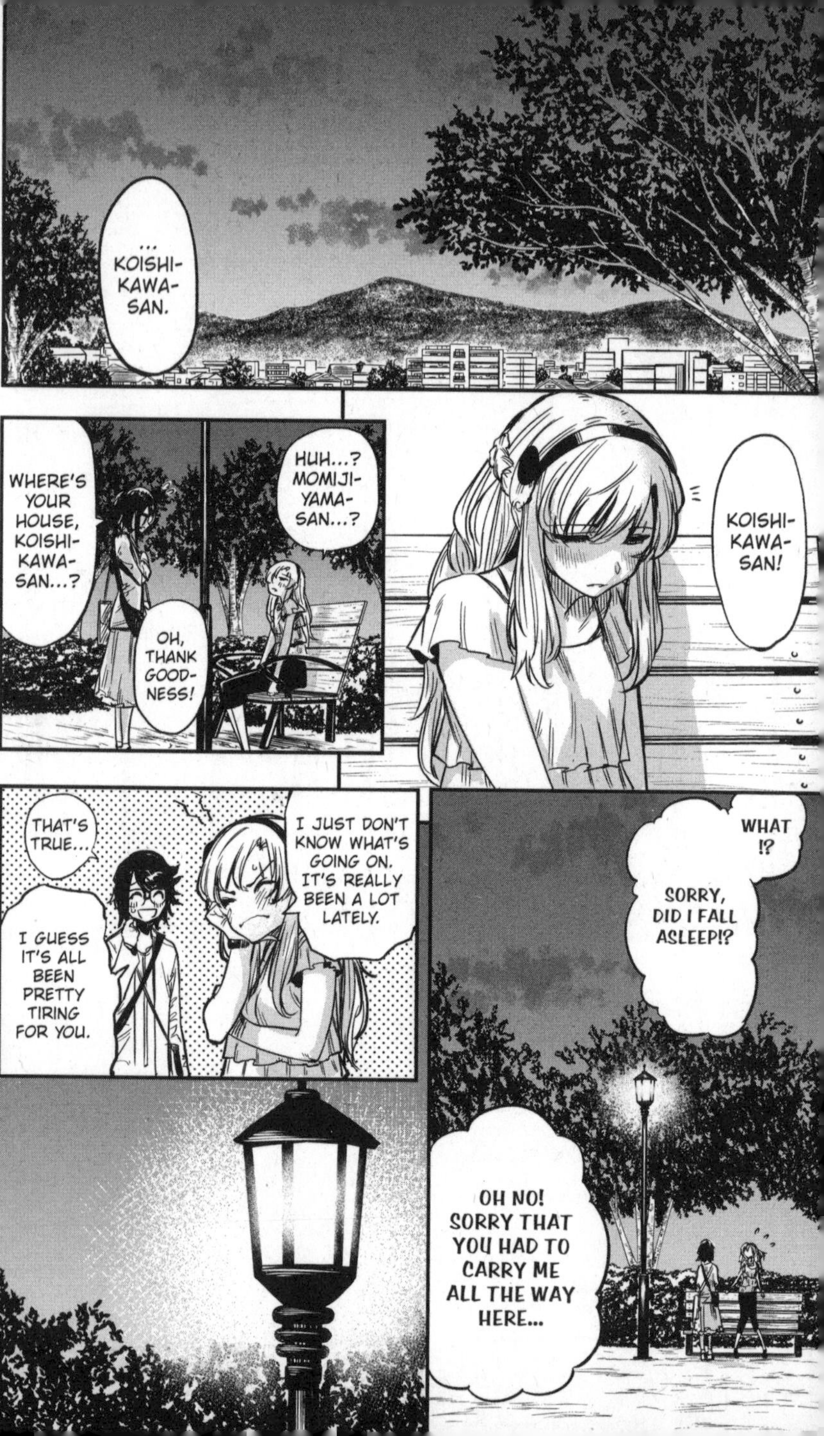

... KOISHI-KAWA-SAN.
KOISHI-KAWA-SAN!
HUH...? MOMIJI-YAMA-SAN...?
WHERE'S YOUR HOUSE, KOISHI-KAWA-SAN...?
OH, THANK GOODNESS!
WHAT!?
SORRY, DID I FALL ASLEEP!?
OH NO! SORRY THAT YOU HAD TO CARRY ME ALL THE WAY HERE...
I JUST DON'T KNOW WHAT'S GOING ON. IT'S REALLY BEEN A LOT LATELY.
THAT'S TRUE...
I GUESS IT'S ALL BEEN PRETTY TIRING FOR YOU.

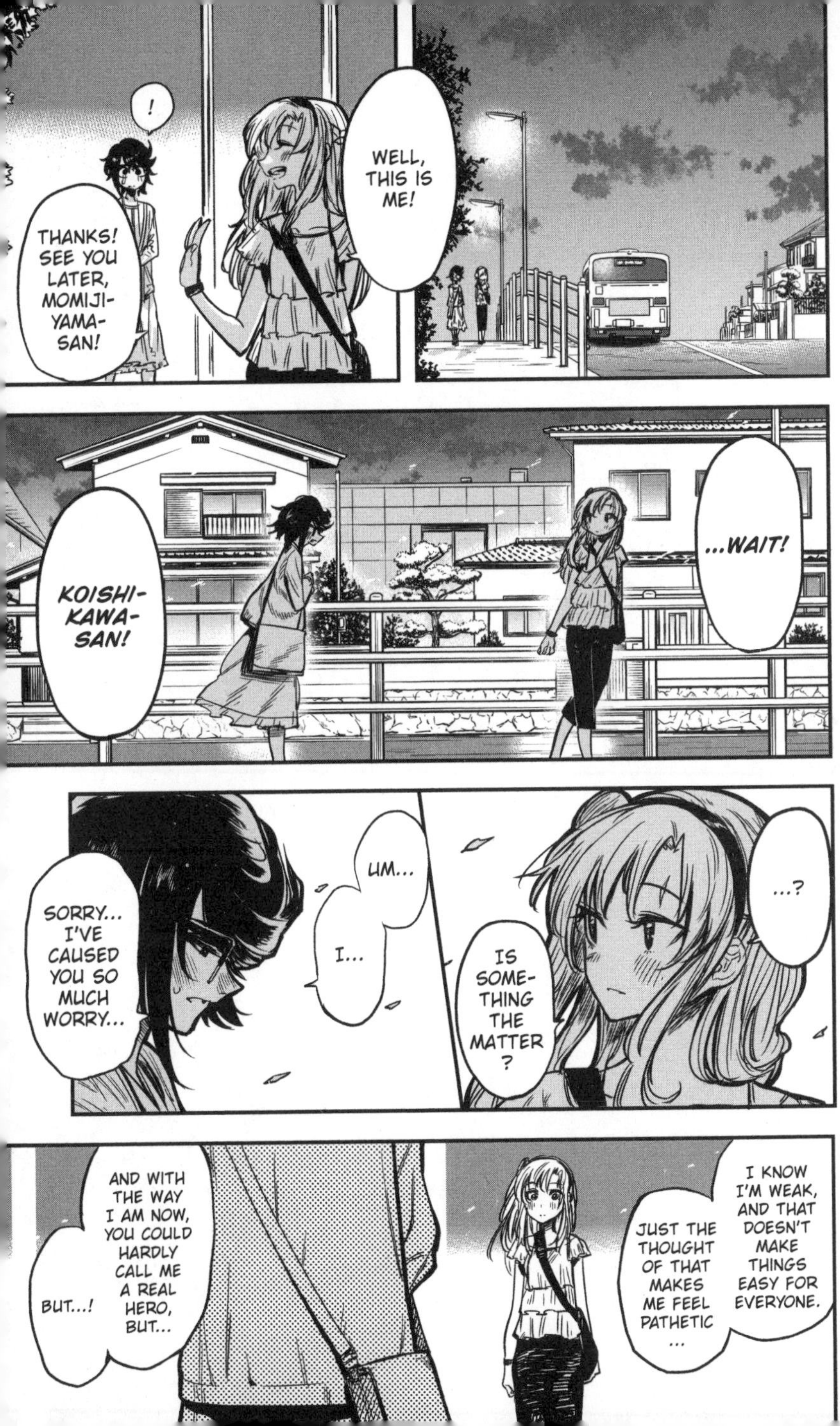
WELL, THIS IS ME!
!
THANKS! SEE YOU LATER, MOMIJI-YAMA-SAN!
...WAIT!
KOISHI-KAWA-SAN!
...?
IS SOME-THING THE MATTER?
UM...
I...
SORRY... I'VE CAUSED YOU SO MUCH WORRY...
I KNOW I'M WEAK, AND THAT DOESN'T MAKE THINGS EASY FOR EVERYONE.
JUST THE THOUGHT OF THAT MAKES ME FEEL PATHETIC...
AND WITH THE WAY I AM NOW, YOU COULD HARDLY CALL ME A REAL HERO, BUT...
BUT...!

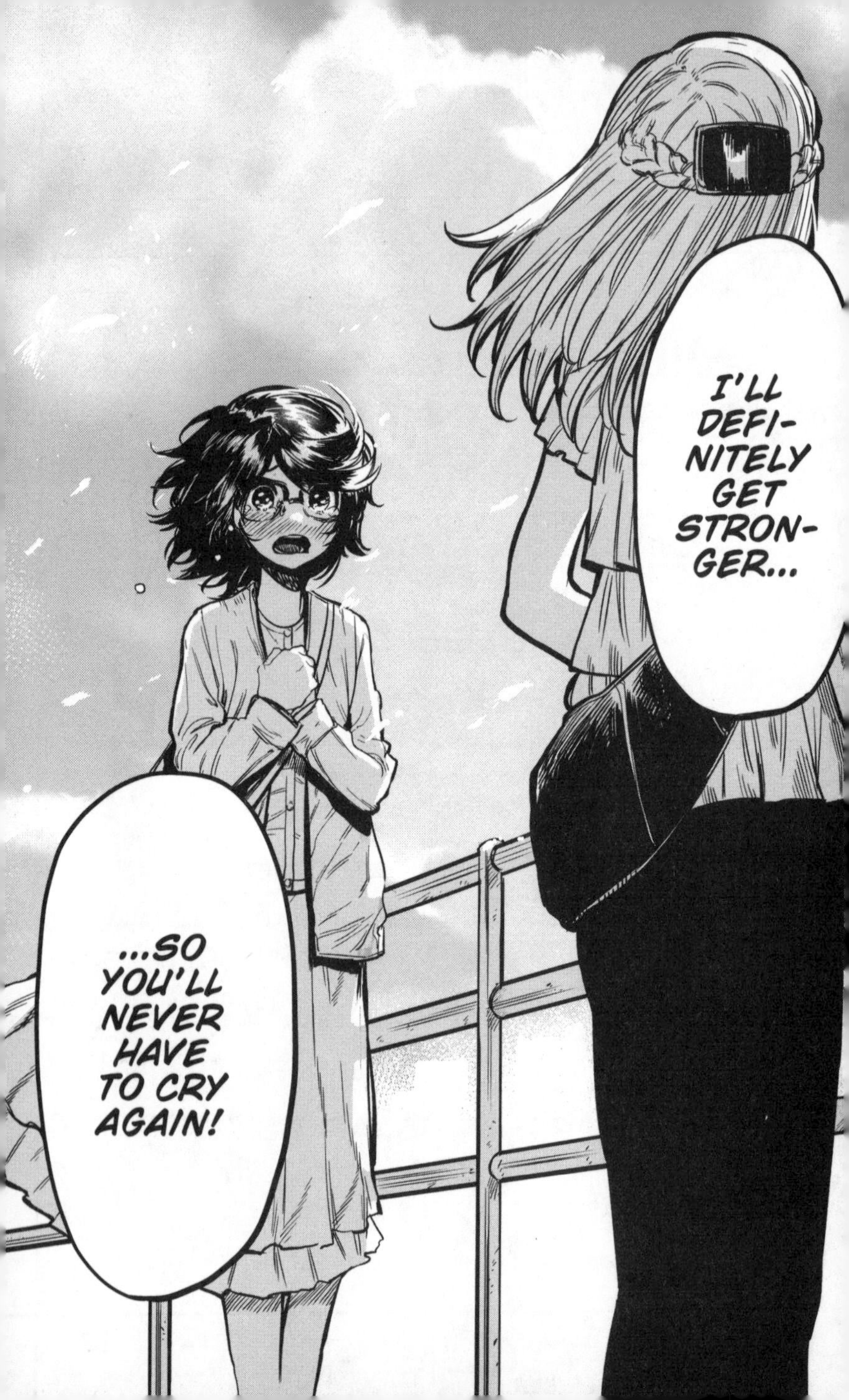
I'LL DEFINITELY GET STRONGER...
...SO YOU'LL NEVER HAVE TO CRY AGAIN!

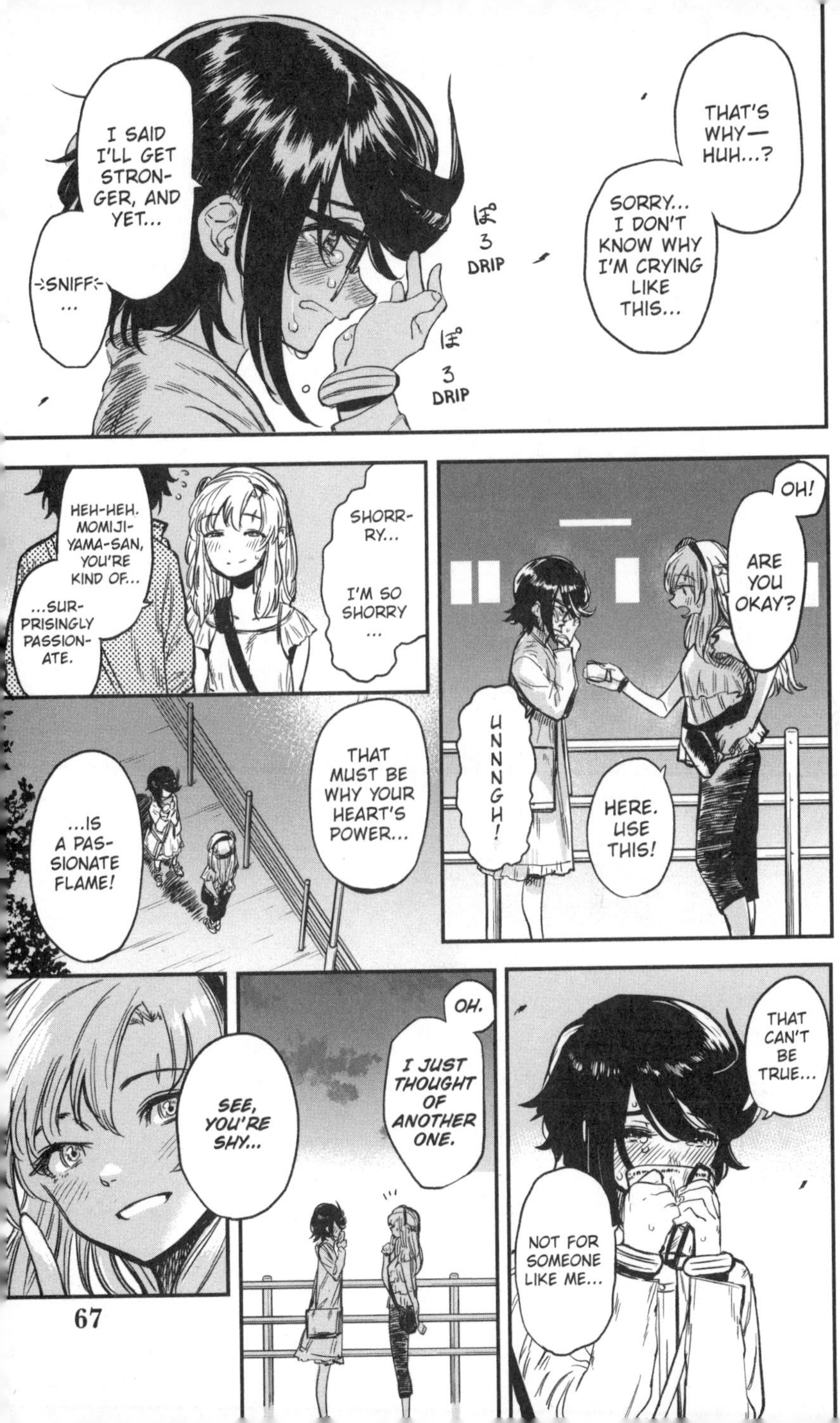
THAT'S WHY— HUH...?
SORRY... I DON'T KNOW WHY I'M CRYING LIKE THIS...
ぽろ DRIP
ぽろ DRIP
I SAID I'LL GET STRONGER, AND YET...
-SNIFF- ...
OH!
ARE YOU OKAY?
HERE. USE THIS!
UNNNGH!
SHORRRY...
I'M SO SHORRY...
HEH-HEH. MOMIJIYAMA-SAN, YOU'RE KIND OF...
...SURPRISINGLY PASSIONATE.
THAT MUST BE WHY YOUR HEART'S POWER...
...IS A PASSIONATE FLAME!
THAT CAN'T BE TRUE...
NOT FOR SOMEONE LIKE ME...
OH.
I JUST THOUGHT OF ANOTHER ONE.
SEE, YOU'RE SHY...

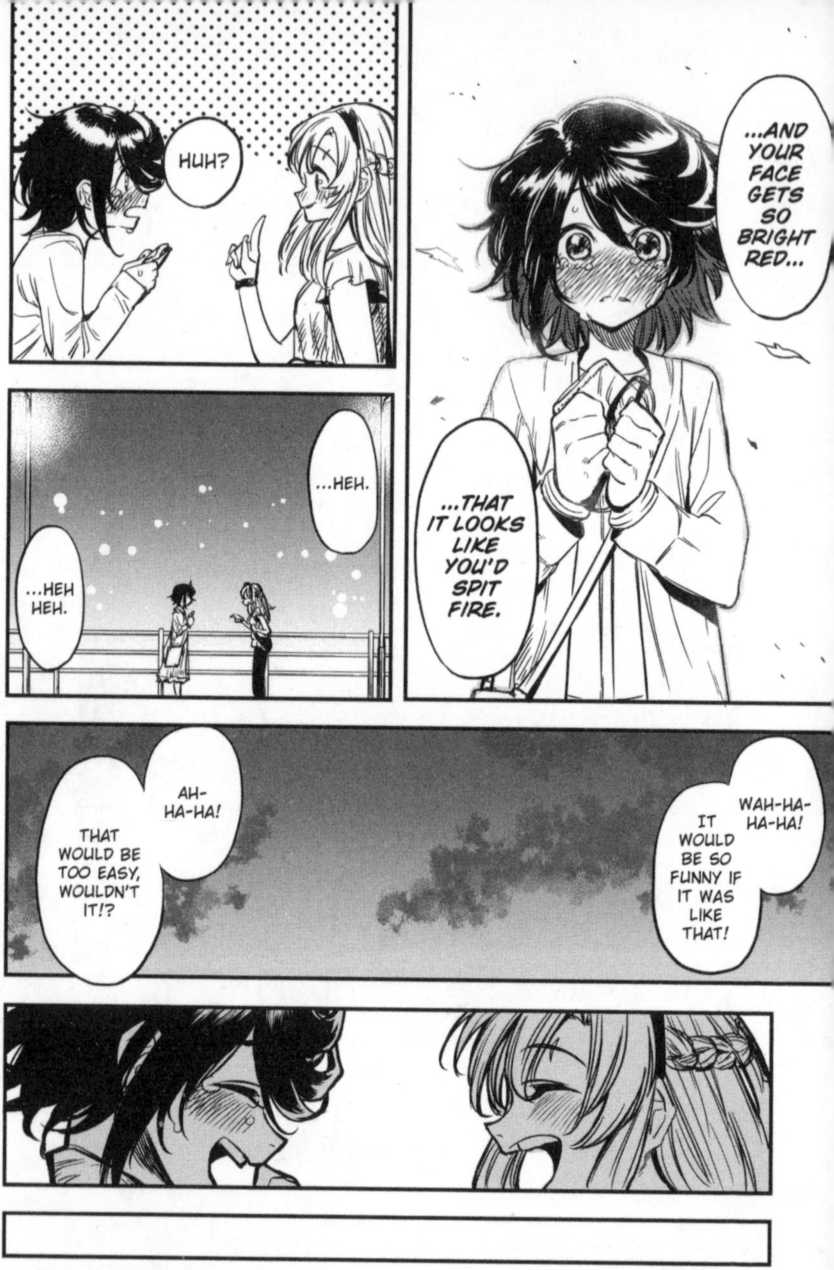
...AND YOUR FACE GETS SO BRIGHT RED...
...THAT IT LOOKS LIKE YOU'D SPIT FIRE.
HUH?
...HEH.
...HEH HEH.
WAH-HA-HA-HA!
IT WOULD BE SO FUNNY IF IT WAS LIKE THAT!
AH-HA-HA!
THAT WOULD BE TOO EASY, WOULDN'T IT!?

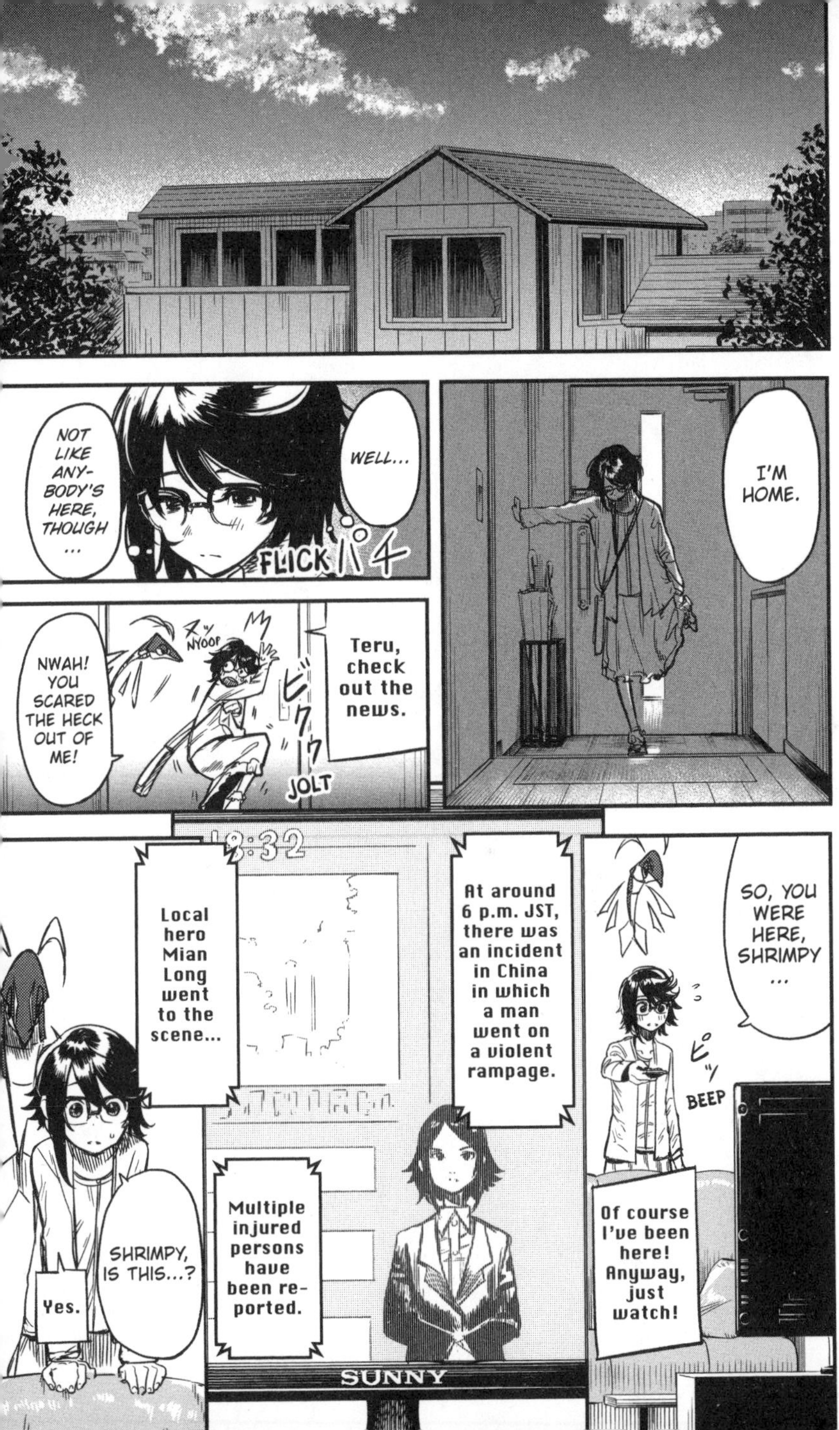
I'M HOME.
WELL...
NOT LIKE ANY-BODY'S HERE, THOUGH...
FLICK
Teru, check out the news.
NYOOP
JOLT
NWAH! YOU SCARED THE HECK OUT OF ME!
SO, YOU WERE HERE, SHRIMPY...
BEEP
Of course I've been here! Anyway, just watch!
18:32
At around 6 p.m. JST, there was an incident in China in which a man went on a violent rampage.
Multiple injured persons have been reported.
SUNNY
Local hero Mian Long went to the scene...
SHRIMPY, IS THIS...?
Yes.

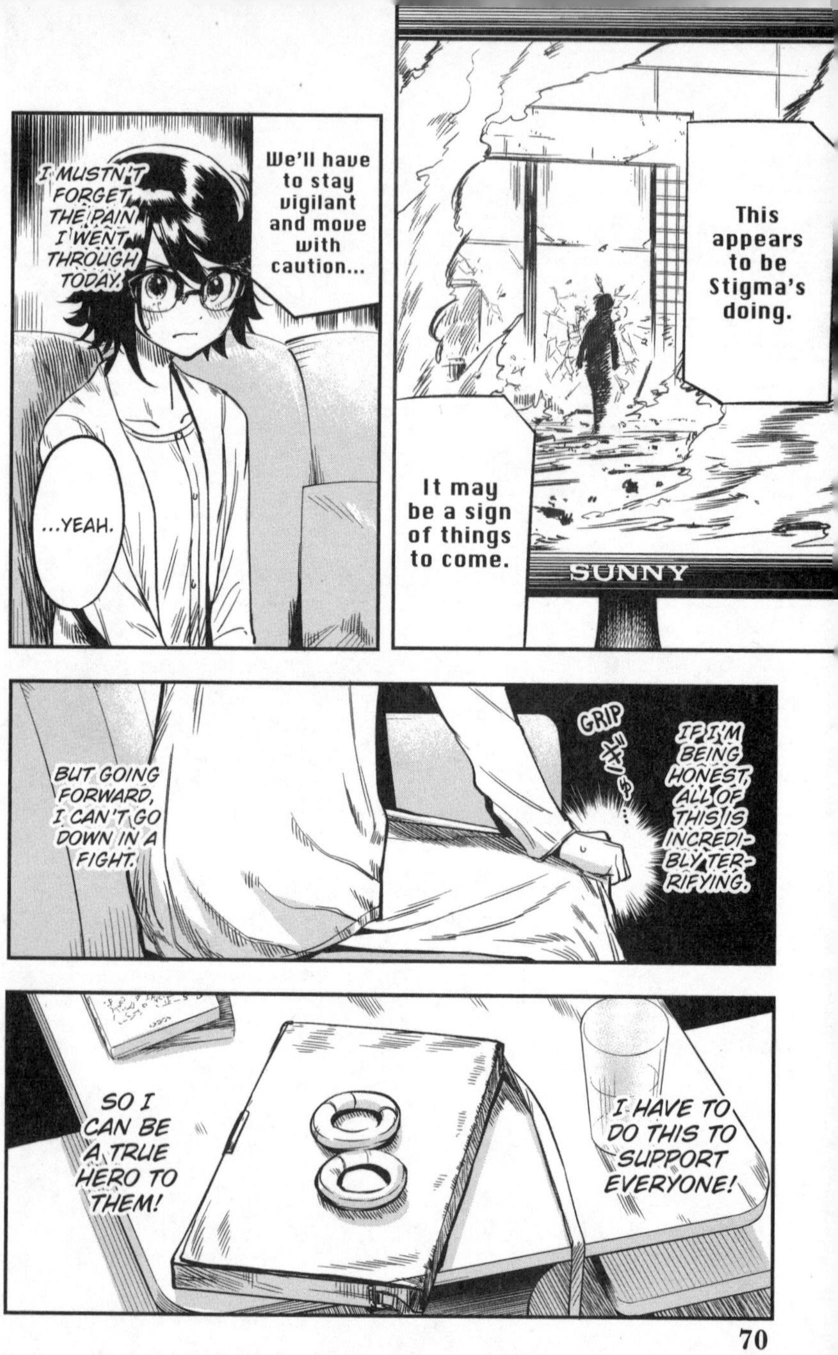
This appears to be Stigma's doing.
It may be a sign of things to come.
SUNNY
We'll have to stay vigilant and move with caution...
I MUSTN'T FORGET THE PAIN I WENT THROUGH TODAY.
...YEAH.
IF I'M BEING HONEST, ALL OF THIS IS INCREDIBLY TERRIFYING.
GRIP
BUT GOING FORWARD, I CAN'T GO DOWN IN A FIGHT.
I HAVE TO DO THIS TO SUPPORT EVERYONE!
SO I CAN BE A TRUE HERO TO THEM!

Chapter 10

I Hate Them

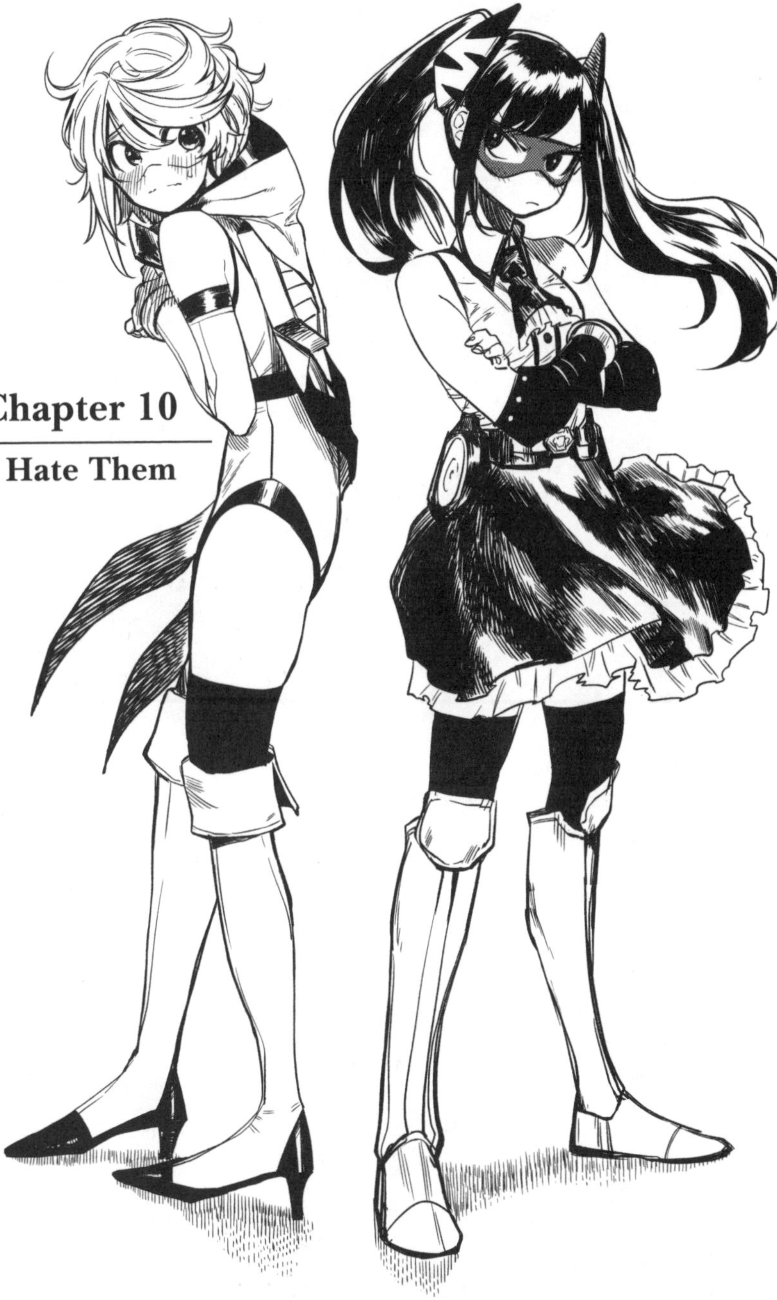

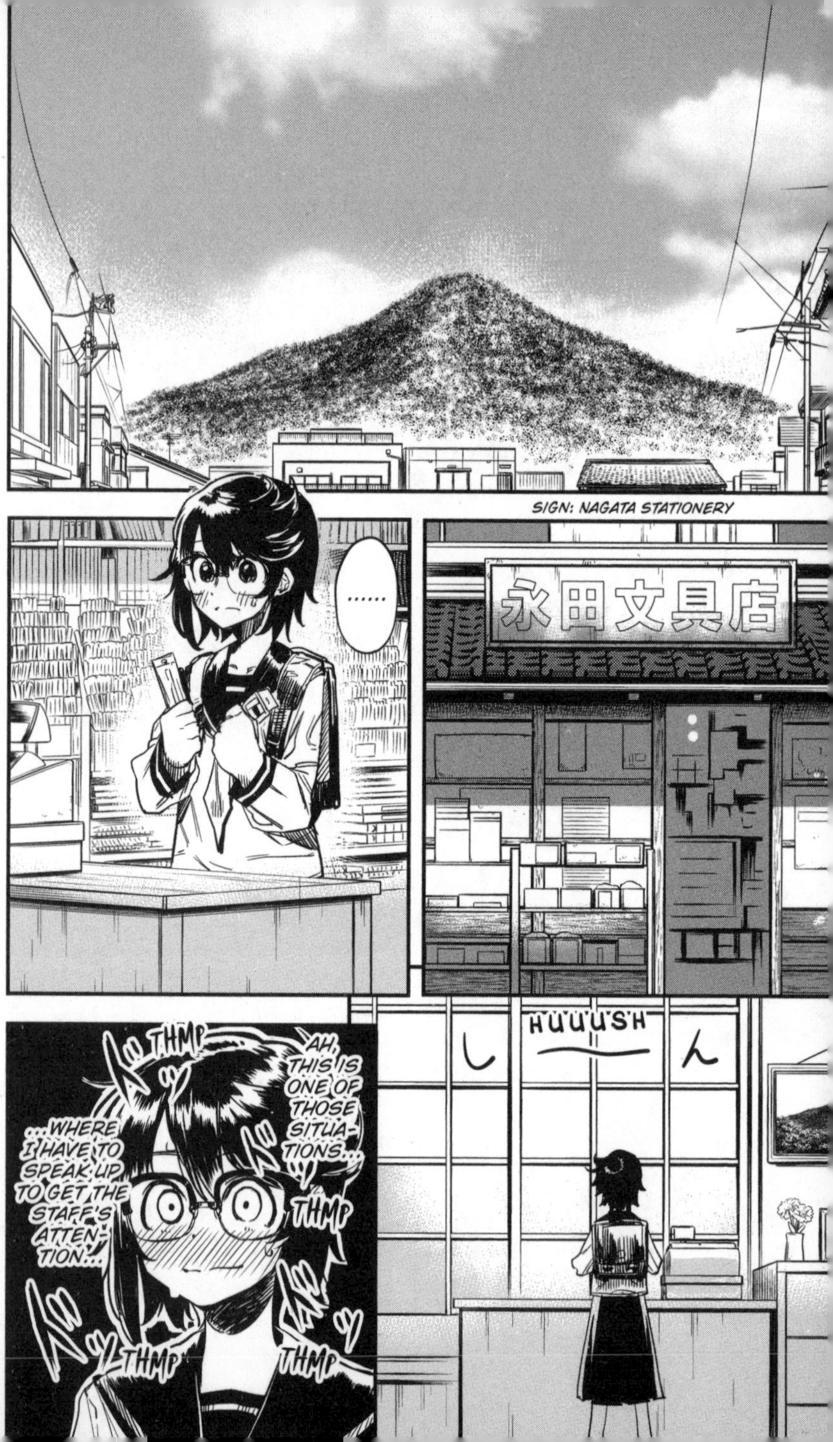
SIGN: NAGATA STATIONERY
永田文具店
......
HUUUSH
し——ん
THMP
AH, THIS IS ONE OF THOSE SITUA-TIONS...
...WHERE I HAVE TO SPEAK UP TO GET THE STAFF'S ATTEN-TION...
THMP
THMP
THMP

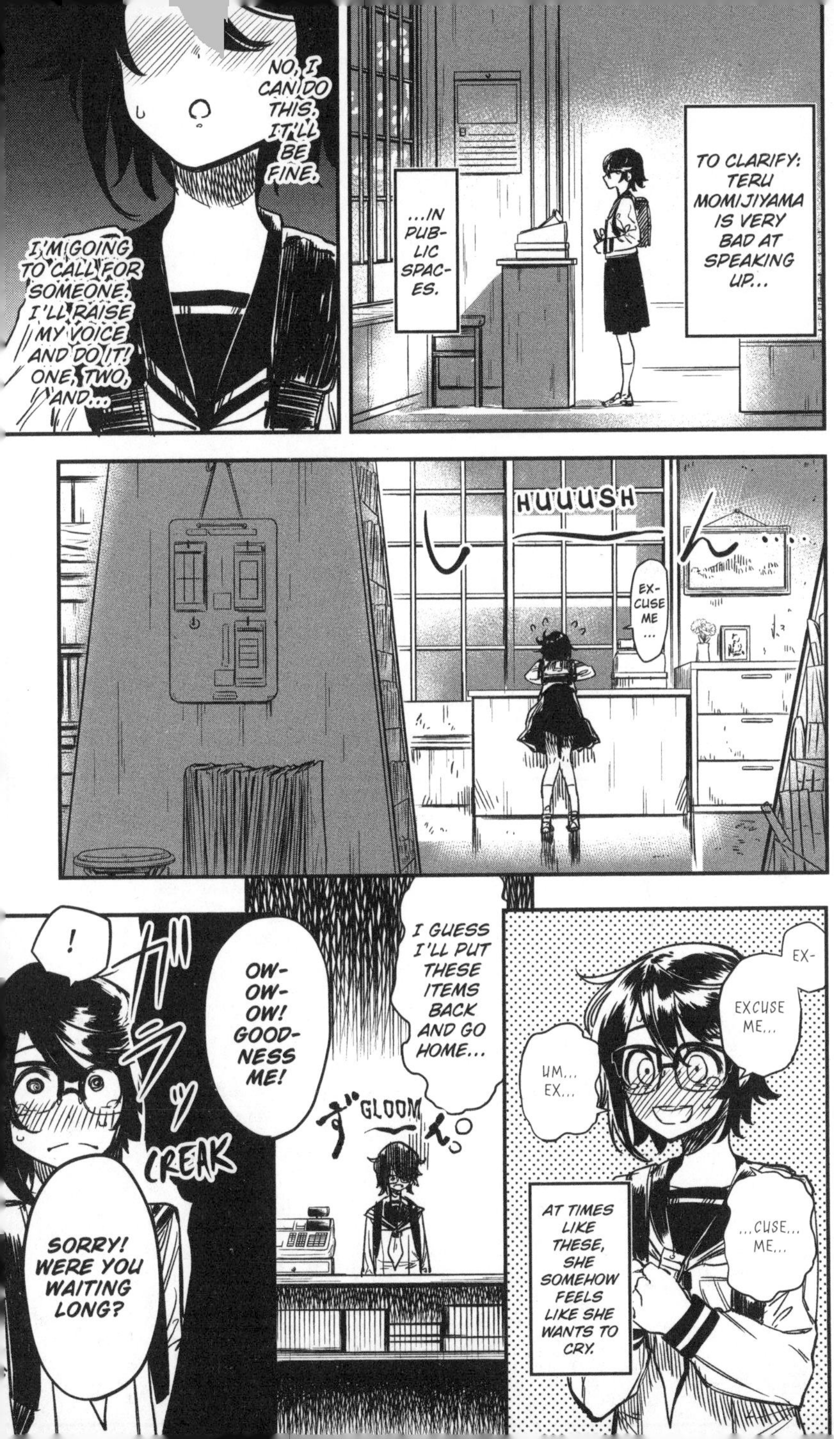

TO CLARIFY: TERU MOMIJIYAMA IS VERY BAD AT SPEAKING UP...
...IN PUBLIC SPACES.
NO, I CAN DO THIS. IT'LL BE FINE.
I'M GOING TO CALL FOR SOMEONE. I'LL RAISE MY VOICE AND DO IT! ONE, TWO, AND...
HUUUSH
EXCUSE ME...
EX-
EXCUSE ME...
UM... EX...
...CUSE... ME...
AT TIMES LIKE THESE, SHE SOMEHOW FEELS LIKE SHE WANTS TO CRY.
I GUESS I'LL PUT THESE ITEMS BACK AND GO HOME...
GLOOM
!
CREAK
OW-OW-OW! GOODNESS ME!
SORRY! WERE YOU WAITING LONG?

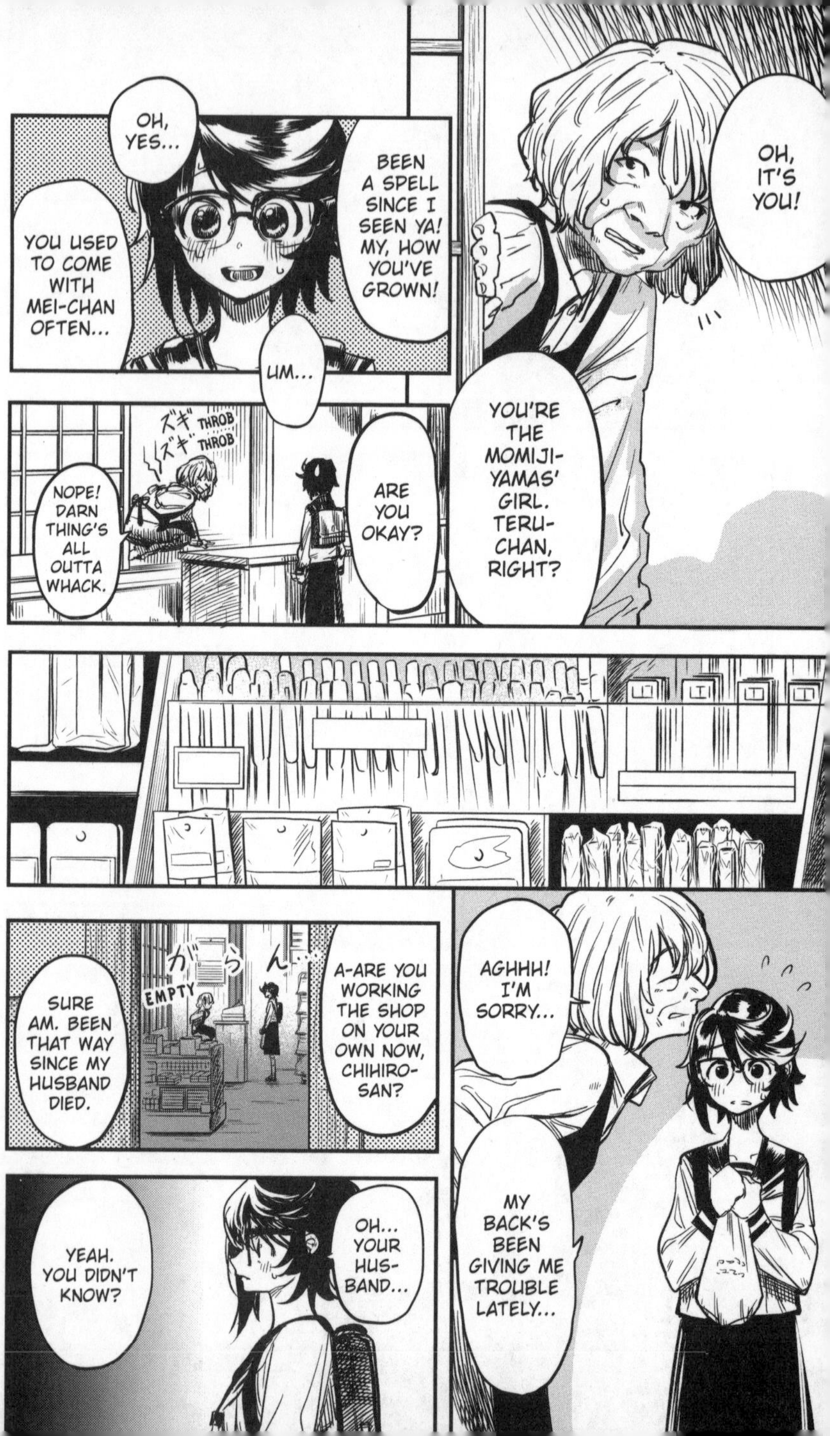
OH, IT'S YOU!
YOU'RE THE MOMIJI-YAMAS' GIRL. TERU-CHAN, RIGHT?
OH, YES...
BEEN A SPELL SINCE I SEEN YA! MY, HOW YOU'VE GROWN!
YOU USED TO COME WITH MEI-CHAN OFTEN...
UM...
ARE YOU OKAY?
ズキ THROB
ズキ THROB
NOPE! DARN THING'S ALL OUTTA WHACK.
AGHHH! I'M SORRY...
MY BACK'S BEEN GIVING ME TROUBLE LATELY...
A-ARE YOU WORKING THE SHOP ON YOUR OWN NOW, CHIHIRO-SAN?
がらん… EMPTY
SURE AM. BEEN THAT WAY SINCE MY HUSBAND DIED.
OH... YOUR HUS-BAND...
YEAH. YOU DIDN'T KNOW?

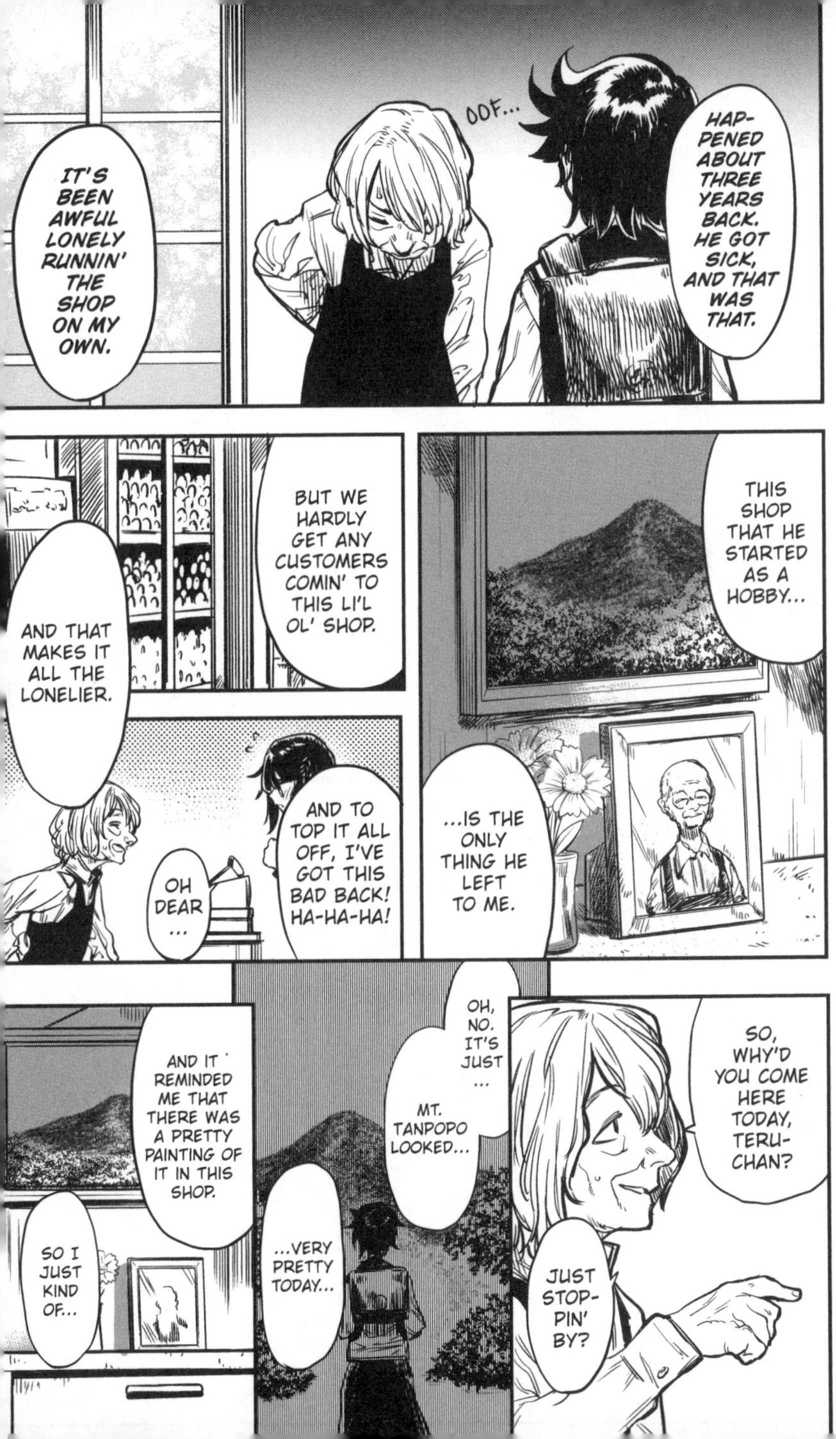
HAP-PENED ABOUT THREE YEARS BACK. HE GOT SICK, AND THAT WAS THAT.
OOF...
IT'S BEEN AWFUL LONELY RUNNIN' THE SHOP ON MY OWN.
THIS SHOP THAT HE STARTED AS A HOBBY...
...IS THE ONLY THING HE LEFT TO ME.
BUT WE HARDLY GET ANY CUSTOMERS COMIN' TO THIS LI'L OL' SHOP.
AND THAT MAKES IT ALL THE LONELIER.
AND TO TOP IT ALL OFF, I'VE GOT THIS BAD BACK! HA-HA-HA!
OH DEAR...
SO, WHY'D YOU COME HERE TODAY, TERU-CHAN?
JUST STOP-PIN' BY?
OH, NO. IT'S JUST...
MT. TANPOPO LOOKED...
...VERY PRETTY TODAY...
AND IT REMINDED ME THAT THERE WAS A PRETTY PAINTING OF IT IN THIS SHOP.
SO I JUST KIND OF...

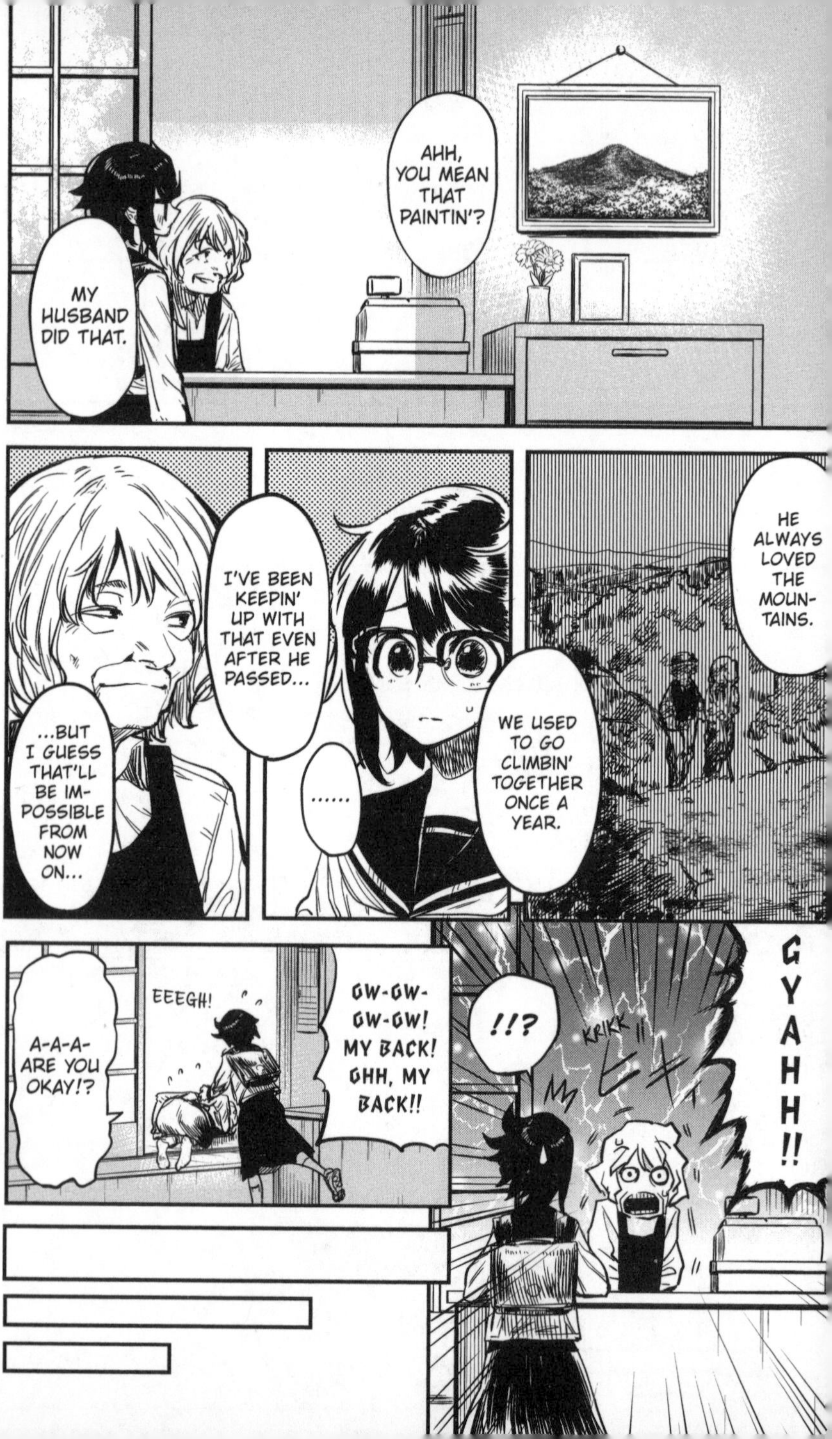
AHH, YOU MEAN THAT PAINTIN'?
MY HUSBAND DID THAT.
HE ALWAYS LOVED THE MOUN-TAINS.
WE USED TO GO CLIMBIN' TOGETHER ONCE A YEAR.
......
I'VE BEEN KEEPIN' UP WITH THAT EVEN AFTER HE PASSED...
...BUT I GUESS THAT'LL BE IM-POSSIBLE FROM NOW ON...
GYAHH!!
!!?
KRIKK
GW-GW-GW-GW! MY BACK! GHH, MY BACK!!
EEEGH!
A-A-A-ARE YOU OKAY!?

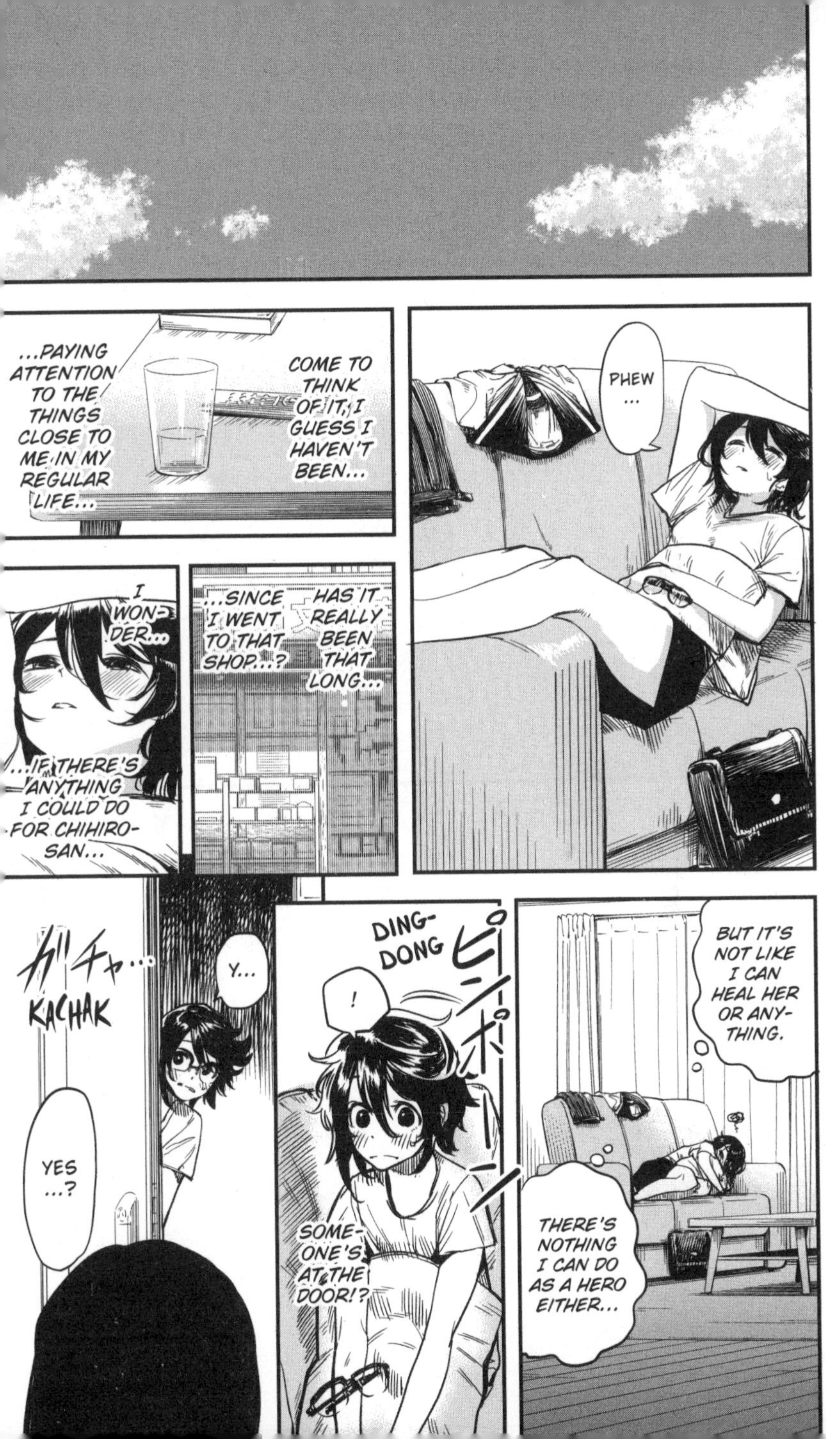
PHEW...
COME TO THINK OF IT, I GUESS I HAVEN'T BEEN...
...PAYING ATTENTION TO THE THINGS CLOSE TO ME IN MY REGULAR LIFE...
HAS IT REALLY BEEN THAT LONG...
...SINCE I WENT TO THAT SHOP...?
I WONDER...
...IF THERE'S ANYTHING I COULD DO FOR CHIHIRO-SAN...
BUT IT'S NOT LIKE I CAN HEAL HER OR ANYTHING.
THERE'S NOTHING I CAN DO AS A HERO EITHER...
ピンポーン
DING-DONG
!
SOME-ONE'S AT THE DOOR!?
ガチャ…
KACHAK
Y...
YES ...?

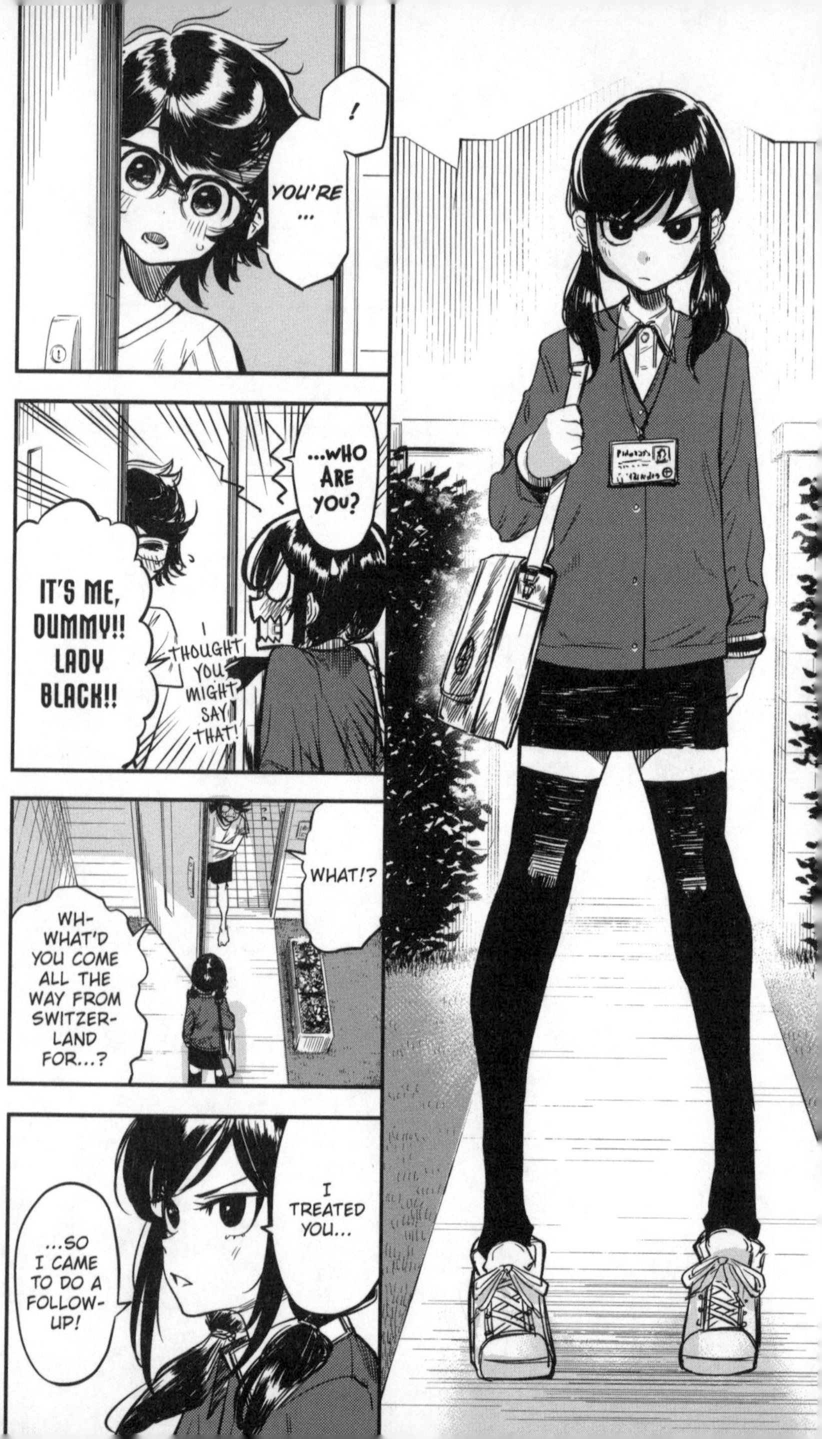
!
YOU'RE ...
...WHO ARE YOU?
IT'S ME, DUMMY!! LADY BLACK!!
I THOUGHT YOU MIGHT SAY THAT!
WHAT!?
WH-WHAT'D YOU COME ALL THE WAY FROM SWITZER-LAND FOR...?
I TREATED YOU...
...SO I CAME TO DO A FOLLOW-UP!

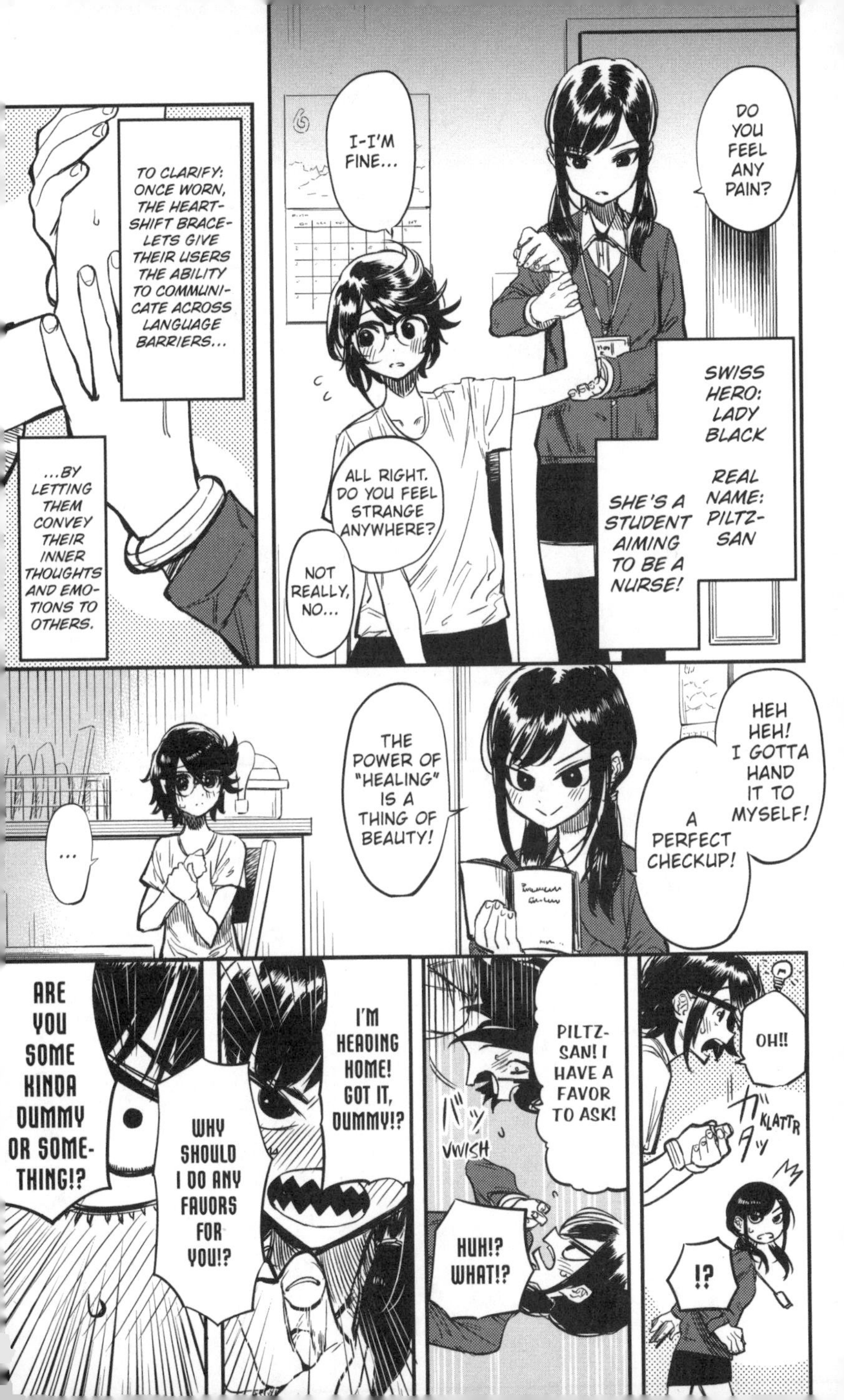
DO YOU FEEL ANY PAIN?
I-I'M FINE...
SWISS HERO: LADY BLACK
REAL NAME: PILTZ-SAN
SHE'S A STUDENT AIMING TO BE A NURSE!
ALL RIGHT. DO YOU FEEL STRANGE ANYWHERE?
NOT REALLY, NO...
TO CLARIFY: ONCE WORN, THE HEART-SHIFT BRACELETS GIVE THEIR USERS THE ABILITY TO COMMUNICATE ACROSS LANGUAGE BARRIERS...
...BY LETTING THEM CONVEY THEIR INNER THOUGHTS AND EMOTIONS TO OTHERS.
HEH HEH! I GOTTA HAND IT TO MYSELF!
A PERFECT CHECKUP!
THE POWER OF "HEALING" IS A THING OF BEAUTY!
...
OH!!
KLATTR
!?
PILTZ-SAN! I HAVE A FAVOR TO ASK!
VWISH
HUH!? WHAT!?
I'M HEADING HOME! GOT IT, DUMMY!?
ARE YOU SOME KINDA DUMMY OR SOMETHING!?
WHY SHOULD I DO ANY FAVORS FOR YOU!?

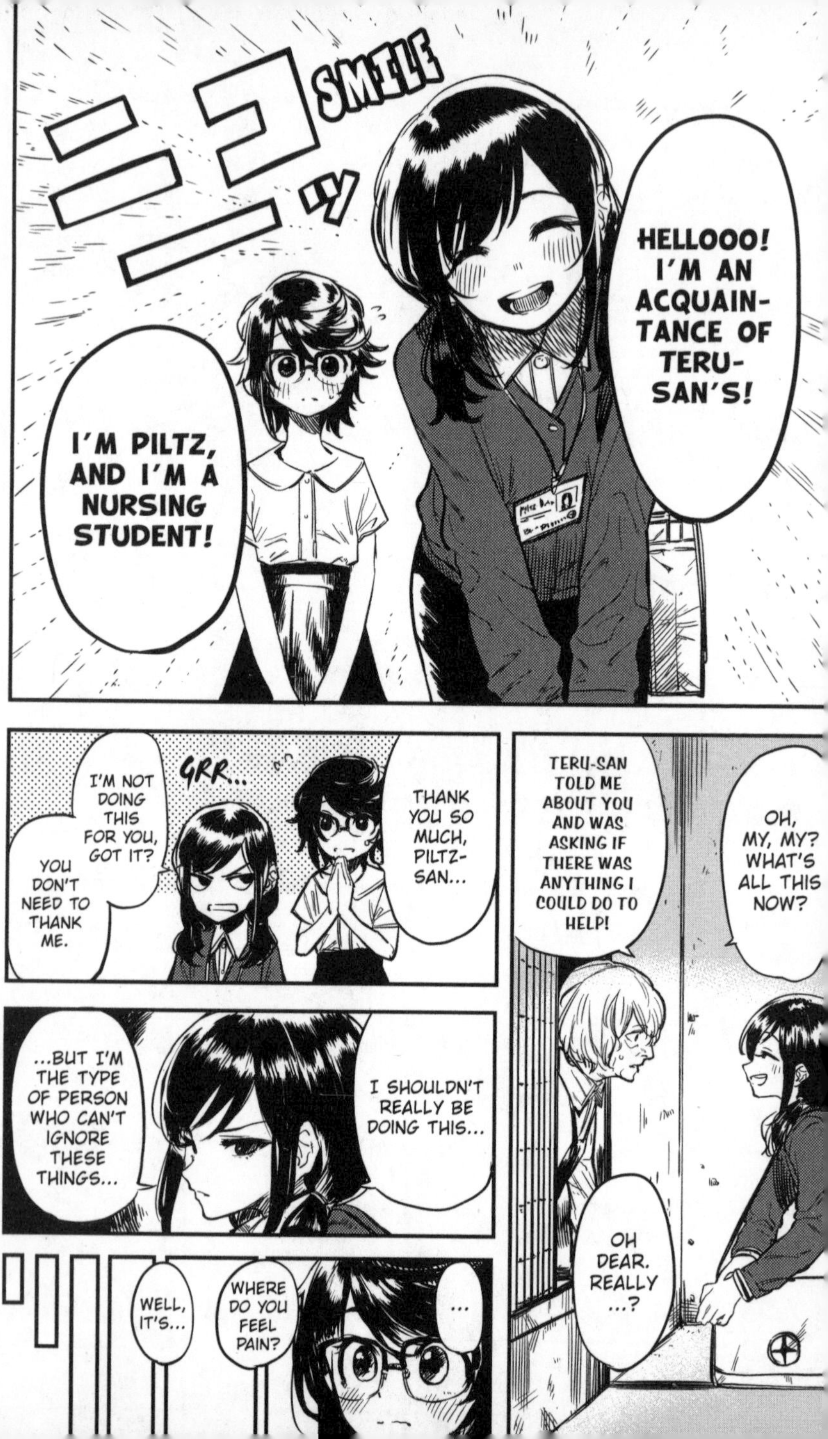
SMILE
HELLOOO! I'M AN ACQUAINTANCE OF TERU-SAN'S!
I'M PILTZ, AND I'M A NURSING STUDENT!
OH, MY, MY? WHAT'S ALL THIS NOW?
TERU-SAN TOLD ME ABOUT YOU AND WAS ASKING IF THERE WAS ANYTHING I COULD DO TO HELP!
OH DEAR. REALLY...?
THANK YOU SO MUCH, PILTZ-SAN...
GRR...
I'M NOT DOING THIS FOR YOU, GOT IT?
YOU DON'T NEED TO THANK ME.
I SHOULDN'T REALLY BE DOING THIS...
...BUT I'M THE TYPE OF PERSON WHO CAN'T IGNORE THESE THINGS...
...
WHERE DO YOU FEEL PAIN?
WELL, IT'S...

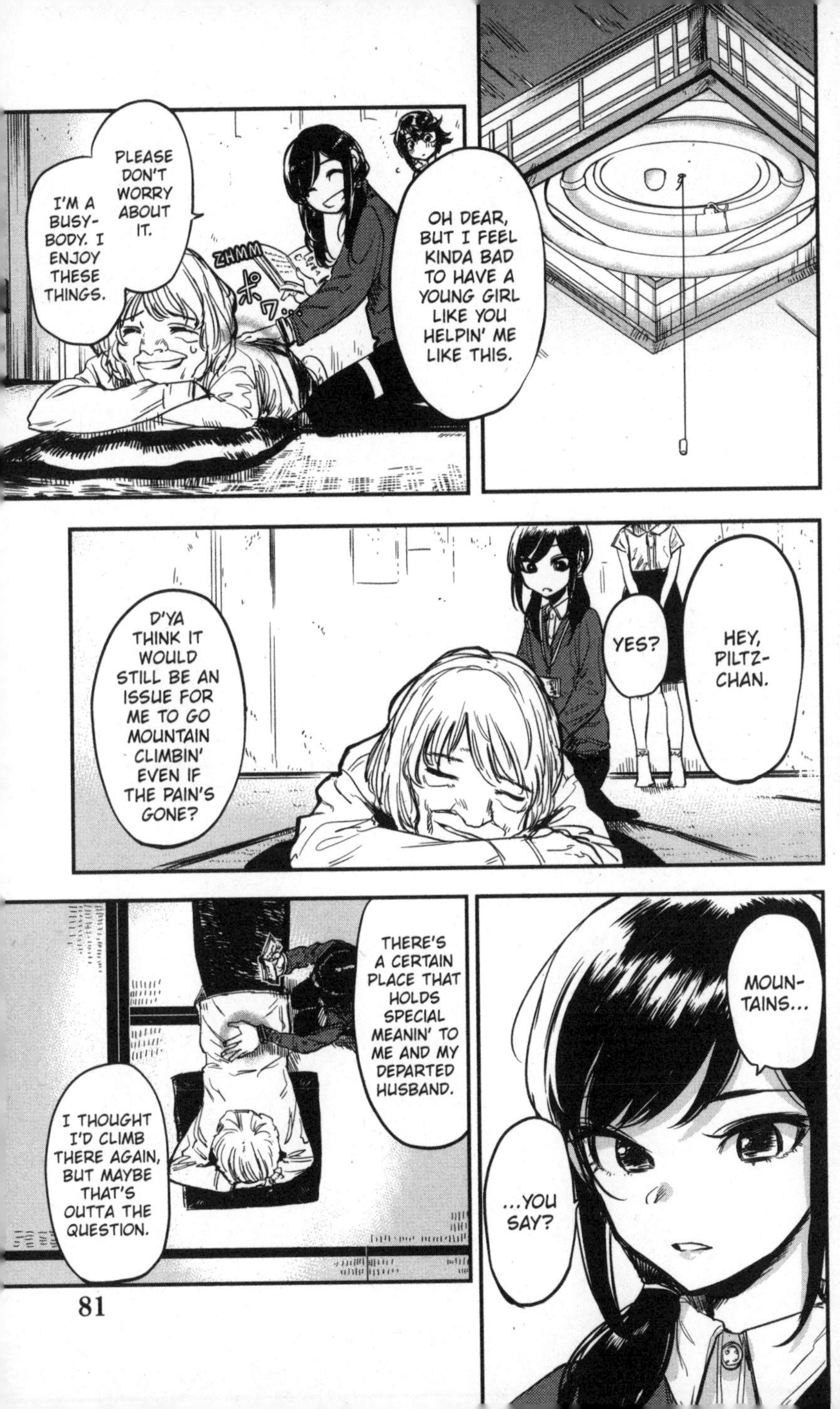
OH DEAR, BUT I FEEL KINDA BAD TO HAVE A YOUNG GIRL LIKE YOU HELPIN' ME LIKE THIS.
PLEASE DON'T WORRY ABOUT IT.
I'M A BUSY-BODY. I ENJOY THESE THINGS.
ZHMM
HEY, PILTZ-CHAN.
YES?
D'YA THINK IT WOULD STILL BE AN ISSUE FOR ME TO GO MOUNTAIN CLIMBIN' EVEN IF THE PAIN'S GONE?
MOUN-TAINS...
...YOU SAY?
THERE'S A CERTAIN PLACE THAT HOLDS SPECIAL MEANIN' TO ME AND MY DEPARTED HUSBAND.
I THOUGHT I'D CLIMB THERE AGAIN, BUT MAYBE THAT'S OUTTA THE QUESTION.

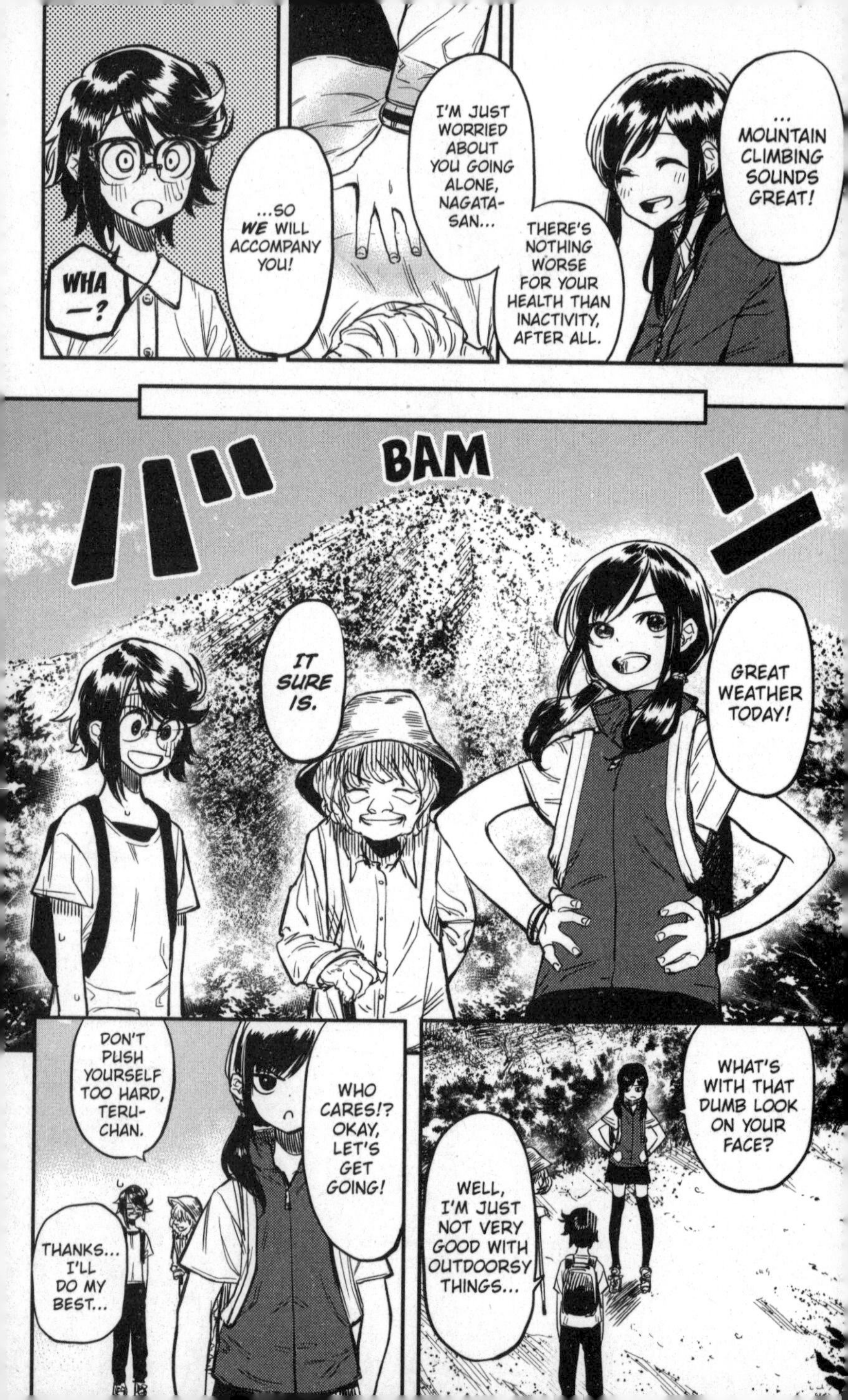
...MOUNTAIN CLIMBING SOUNDS GREAT!
THERE'S NOTHING WORSE FOR YOUR HEALTH THAN INACTIVITY, AFTER ALL.
I'M JUST WORRIED ABOUT YOU GOING ALONE, NAGATA-SAN...
...SO WE WILL ACCOMPANY YOU!
WHA—?
BAM
GREAT WEATHER TODAY!
IT SURE IS.
WHAT'S WITH THAT DUMB LOOK ON YOUR FACE?
WELL, I'M JUST NOT VERY GOOD WITH OUTDOORSY THINGS...
WHO CARES!? OKAY, LET'S GET GOING!
DON'T PUSH YOURSELF TOO HARD, TERU-CHAN.
THANKS... I'LL DO MY BEST...

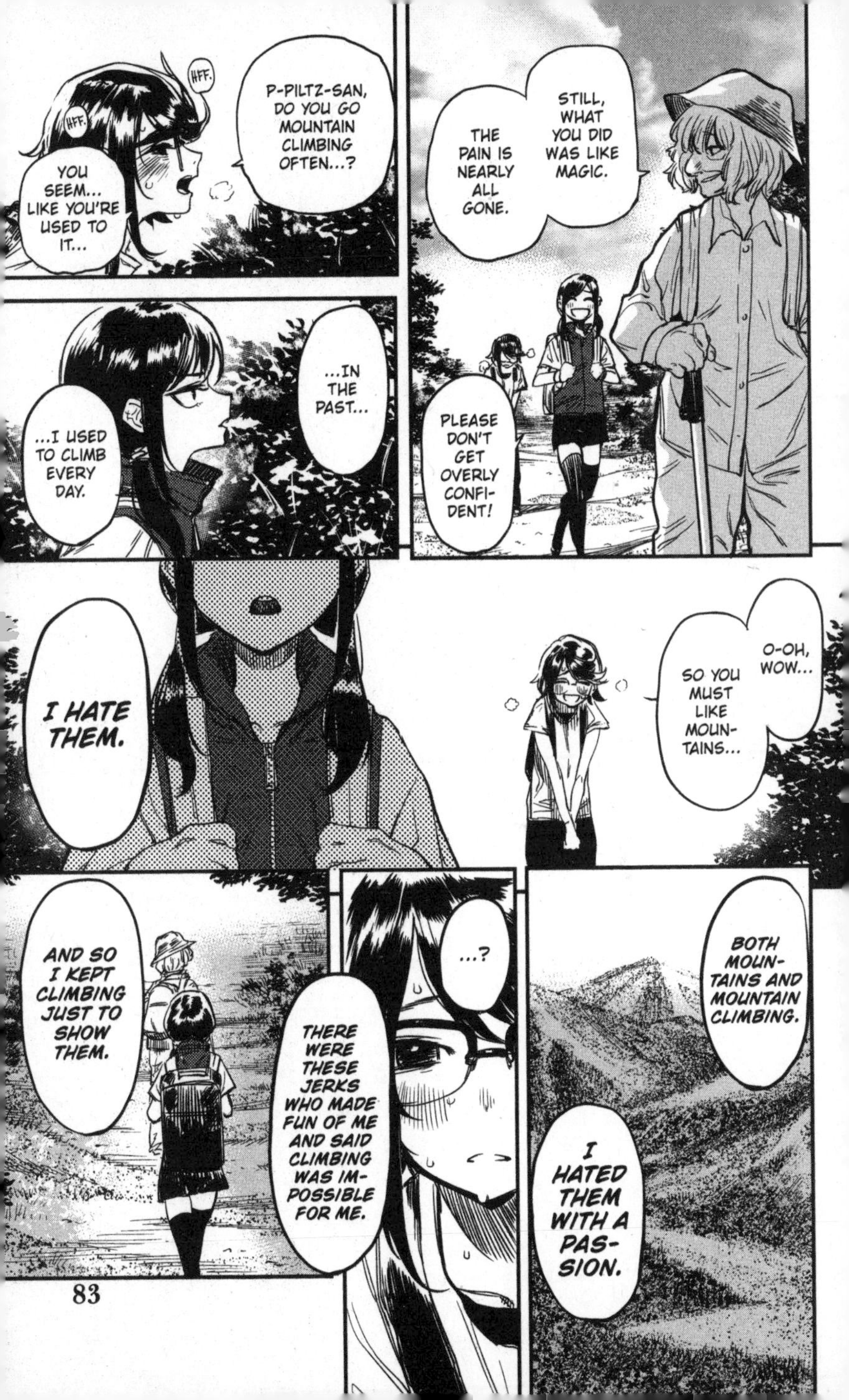
STILL, WHAT YOU DID WAS LIKE MAGIC.
THE PAIN IS NEARLY ALL GONE.
PLEASE DON'T GET OVERLY CONFIDENT!
HFF.
HFF.
P-PILTZ-SAN, DO YOU GO MOUNTAIN CLIMBING OFTEN...?
YOU SEEM... LIKE YOU'RE USED TO IT...
...IN THE PAST...
...I USED TO CLIMB EVERY DAY.
O-OH, WOW...
SO YOU MUST LIKE MOUNTAINS...
I HATE THEM.
BOTH MOUNTAINS AND MOUNTAIN CLIMBING.
I HATED THEM WITH A PASSION.
...?
THERE WERE THESE JERKS WHO MADE FUN OF ME AND SAID CLIMBING WAS IMPOSSIBLE FOR ME.
AND SO I KEPT CLIMBING JUST TO SHOW THEM.

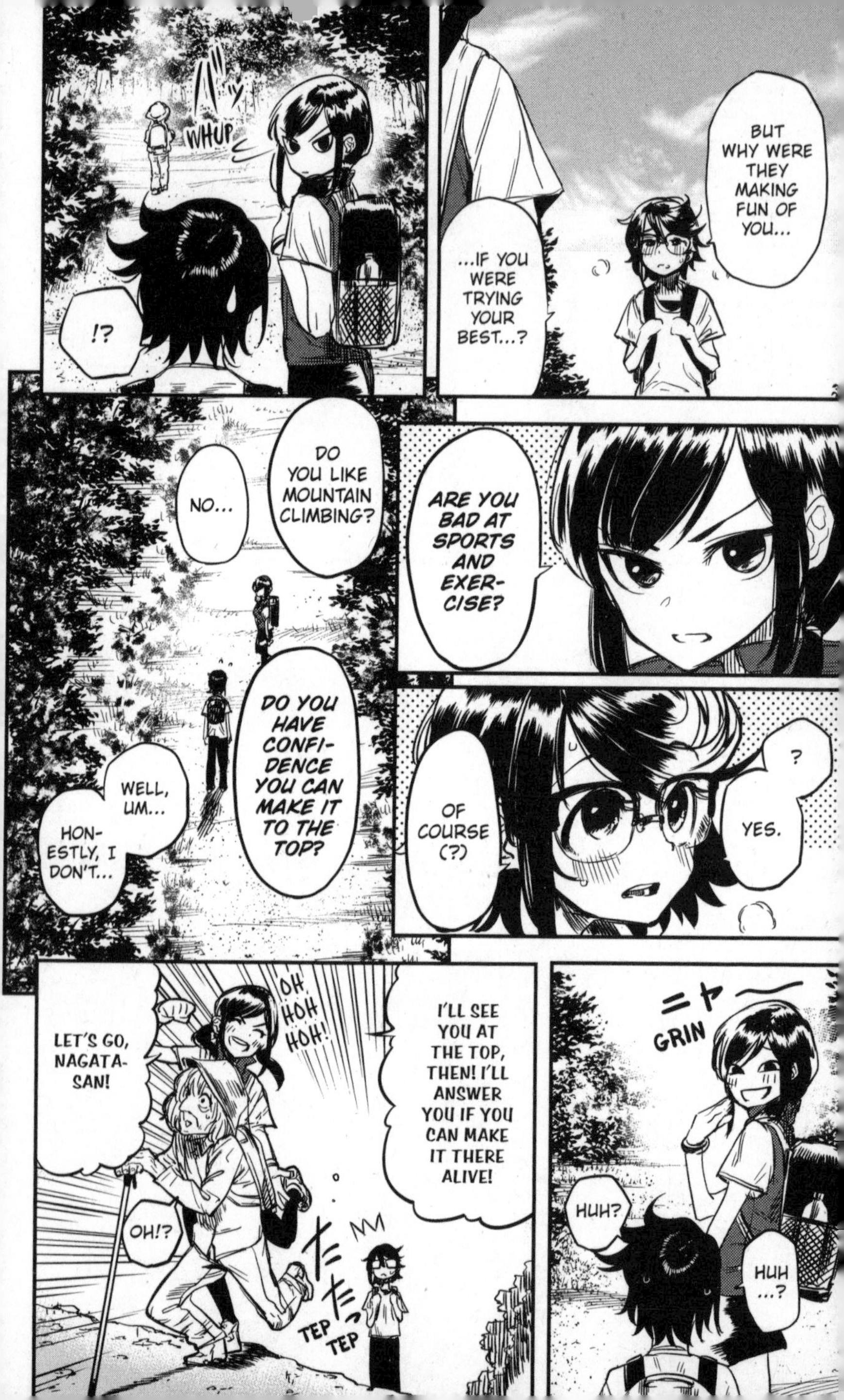
BUT WHY WERE THEY MAKING FUN OF YOU...
...IF YOU WERE TRYING YOUR BEST...?
WHUP
!?
ARE YOU BAD AT SPORTS AND EXER-CISE?
?
YES.
OF COURSE (?)
DO YOU LIKE MOUNTAIN CLIMBING?
NO...
DO YOU HAVE CONFI-DENCE YOU CAN MAKE IT TO THE TOP?
WELL, UM...
HON-ESTLY, I DON'T...
GRIN
HUH?
HUH ...?
I'LL SEE YOU AT THE TOP, THEN! I'LL ANSWER YOU IF YOU CAN MAKE IT THERE ALIVE!
OH HOH HOH!
LET'S GO, NAGATA-SAN!
OH!?
TEP TEP

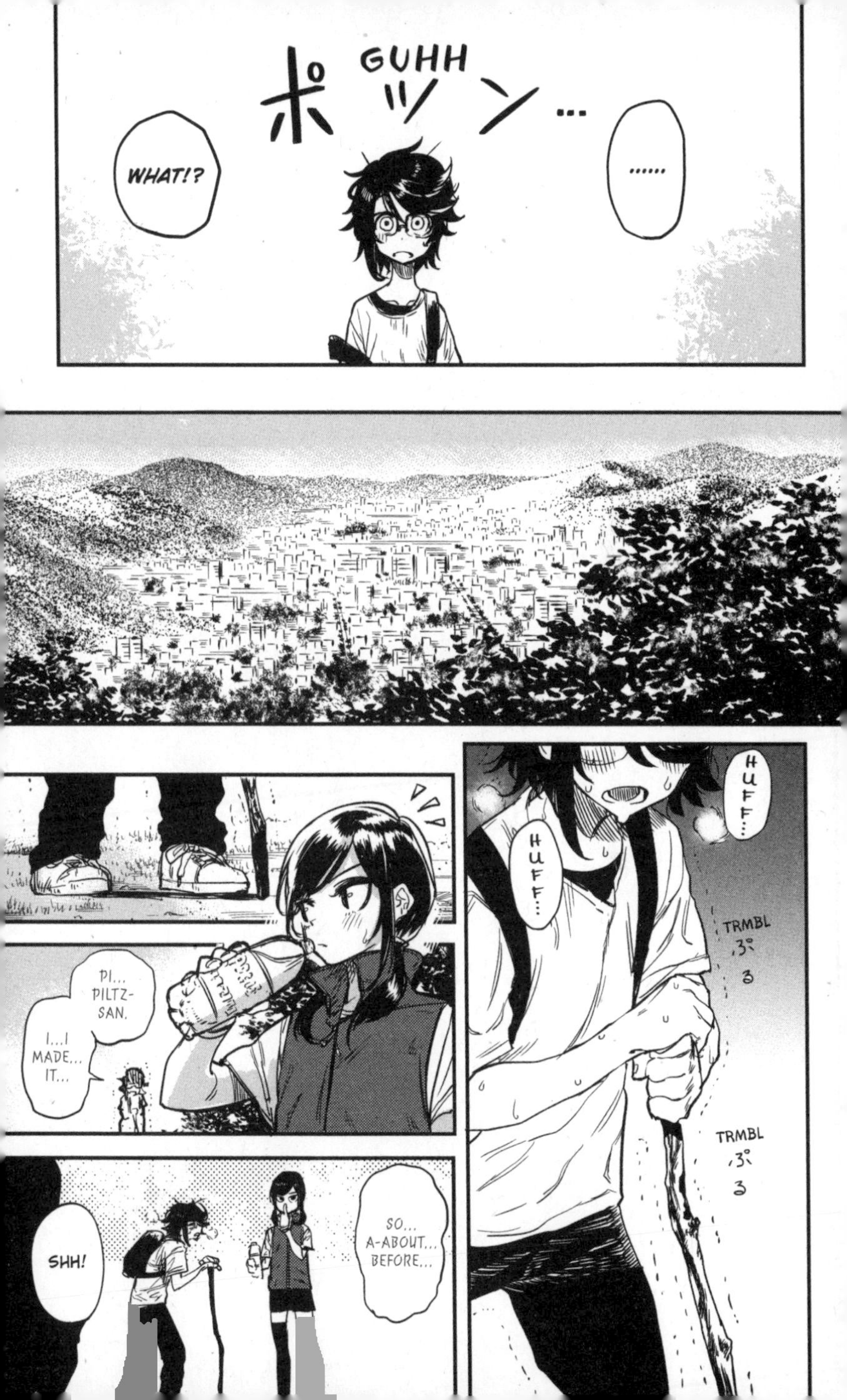
GUHH
ポツン…
......
WHAT!?
HUFF...
HUFF...
TRMBL ぷる
TRMBL ぷる
PI... PILTZ-SAN.
I...I MADE... IT...
SO... A-ABOUT... BEFORE...
SHH!

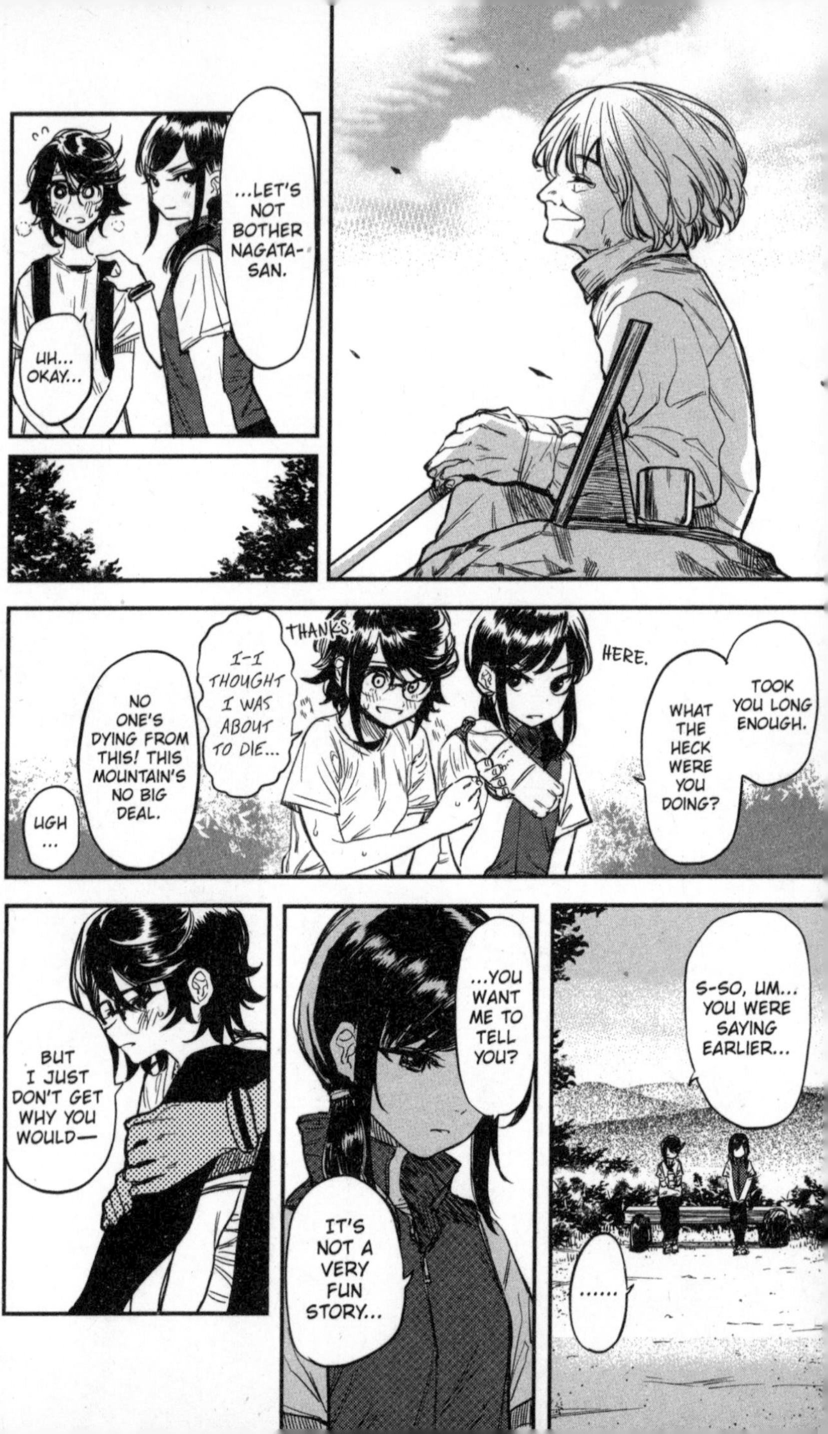
...LET'S NOT BOTHER NAGATA-SAN.
UH... OKAY...
TOOK YOU LONG ENOUGH.
WHAT THE HECK WERE YOU DOING?
HERE.
THANKS.
I-I THOUGHT I WAS ABOUT TO DIE...
NO ONE'S DYING FROM THIS! THIS MOUNTAIN'S NO BIG DEAL.
UGH...
S-SO, UM... YOU WERE SAYING EARLIER...
......
...YOU WANT ME TO TELL YOU?
IT'S NOT A VERY FUN STORY...
BUT I JUST DON'T GET WHY YOU WOULD—

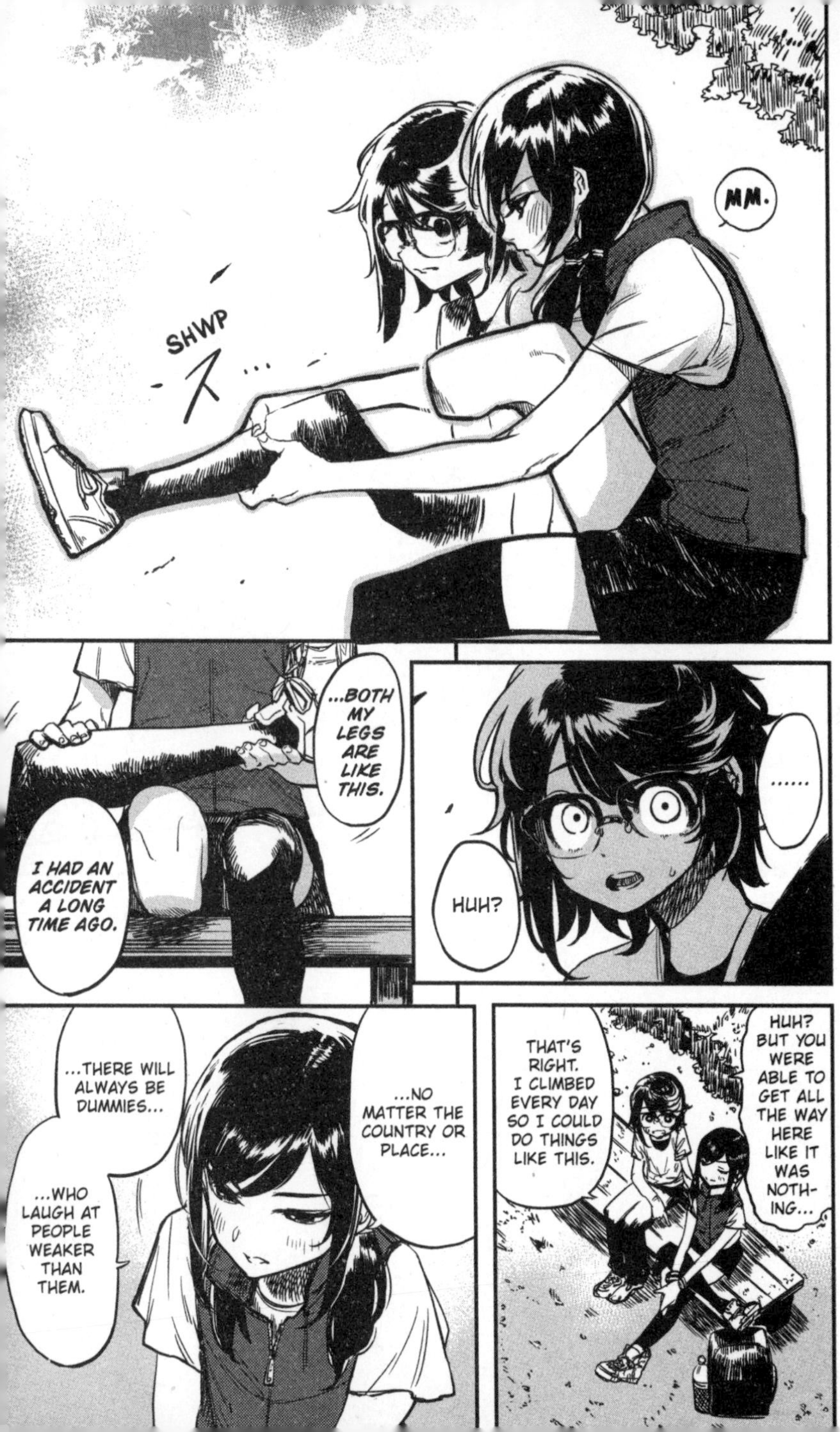
MM.
SHWP
......
HUH?
...BOTH MY LEGS ARE LIKE THIS.
I HAD AN ACCIDENT A LONG TIME AGO.
HUH? BUT YOU WERE ABLE TO GET ALL THE WAY HERE LIKE IT WAS NOTH-ING...
THAT'S RIGHT. I CLIMBED EVERY DAY SO I COULD DO THINGS LIKE THIS.
...NO MATTER THE COUNTRY OR PLACE...
...THERE WILL ALWAYS BE DUMMIES...
...WHO LAUGH AT PEOPLE WEAKER THAN THEM.

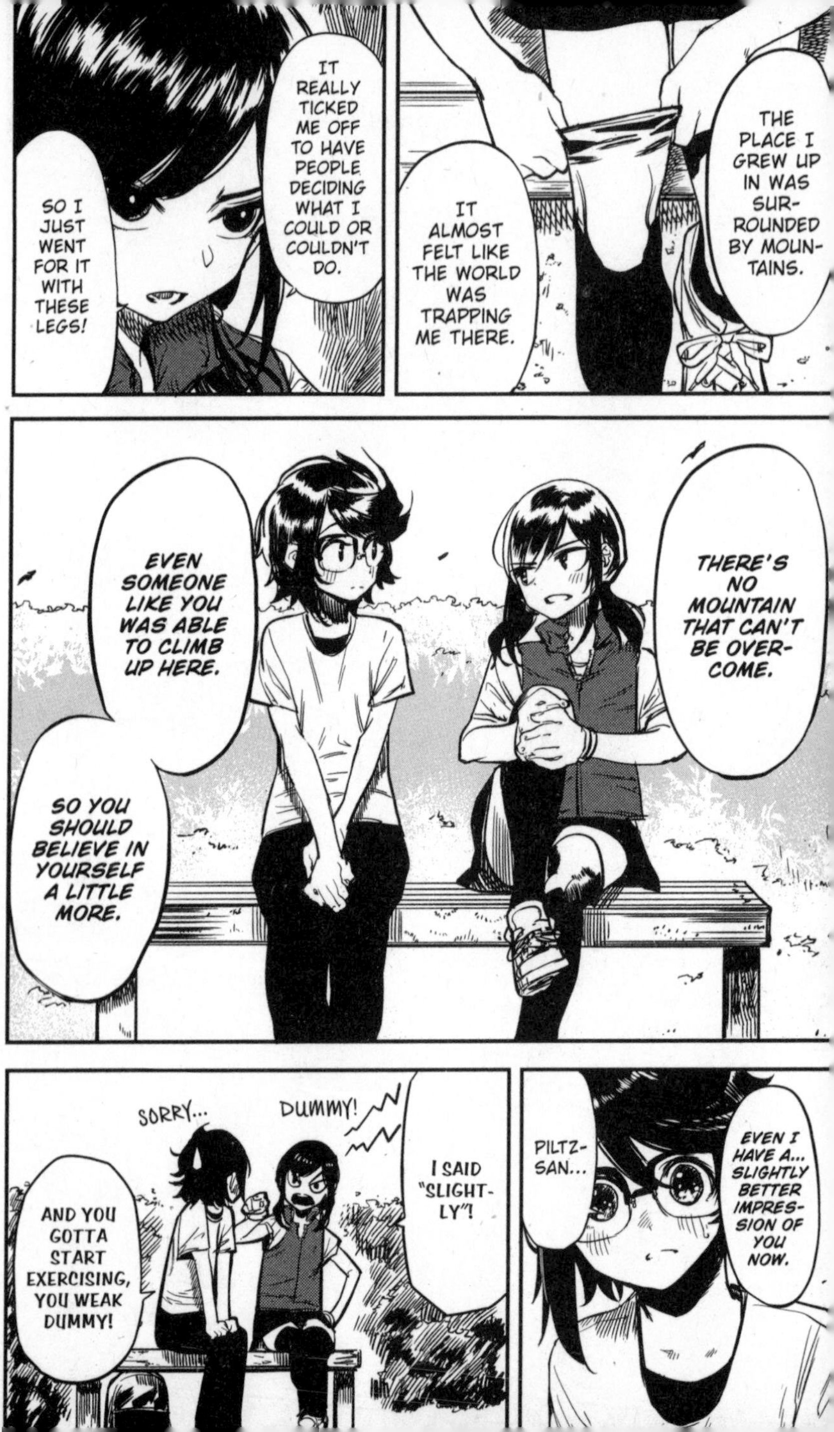
THE PLACE I GREW UP IN WAS SURROUNDED BY MOUNTAINS.
IT ALMOST FELT LIKE THE WORLD WAS TRAPPING ME THERE.
IT REALLY TICKED ME OFF TO HAVE PEOPLE DECIDING WHAT I COULD OR COULDN'T DO.
SO I JUST WENT FOR IT WITH THESE LEGS!
THERE'S NO MOUNTAIN THAT CAN'T BE OVERCOME.
EVEN SOMEONE LIKE YOU WAS ABLE TO CLIMB UP HERE.
SO YOU SHOULD BELIEVE IN YOURSELF A LITTLE MORE.
EVEN I HAVE A... SLIGHTLY BETTER IMPRESSION OF YOU NOW.
PILTZ-SAN...
I SAID "SLIGHTLY"!
DUMMY!
SORRY...
AND YOU GOTTA START EXERCISING, YOU WEAK DUMMY!

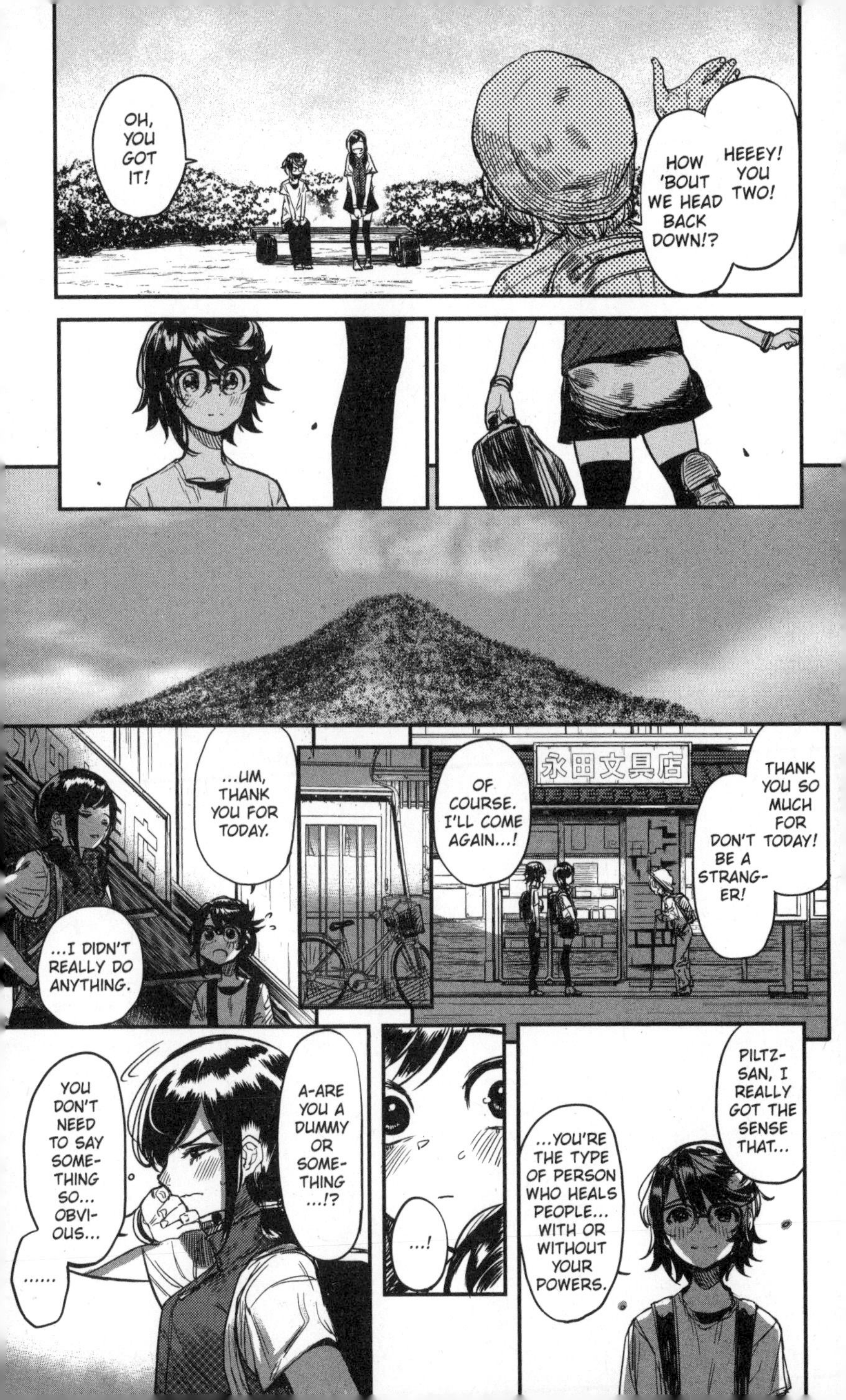
HEEEY! YOU TWO!
HOW 'BOUT WE HEAD BACK DOWN!?
OH, YOU GOT IT!
THANK YOU SO MUCH FOR TODAY!
永田文具店
DON'T BE A STRANGER!
OF COURSE. I'LL COME AGAIN...!
...UM, THANK YOU FOR TODAY.
...I DIDN'T REALLY DO ANYTHING.
PILTZ-SAN, I REALLY GOT THE SENSE THAT...
...YOU'RE THE TYPE OF PERSON WHO HEALS PEOPLE... WITH OR WITHOUT YOUR POWERS.
...!
A-ARE YOU A DUMMY OR SOMETHING...!?
YOU DON'T NEED TO SAY SOMETHING SO... OBVIOUS...
......

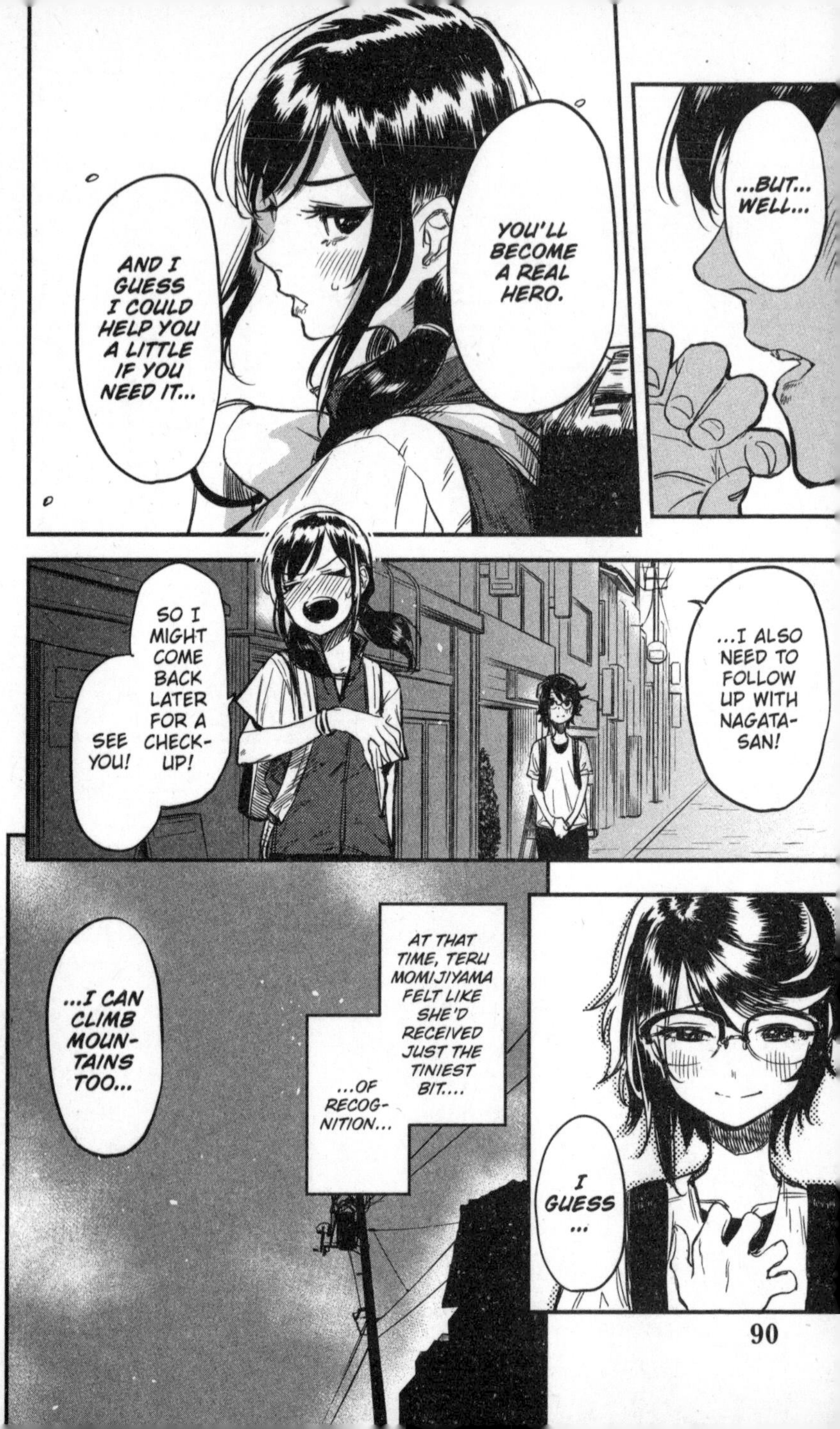
...BUT... WELL...
YOU'LL BECOME A REAL HERO.
AND I GUESS I COULD HELP YOU A LITTLE IF YOU NEED IT...
...I ALSO NEED TO FOLLOW UP WITH NAGATA-SAN!
SO I MIGHT COME BACK LATER FOR A CHECK-UP!
SEE YOU!
I GUESS...
AT THAT TIME, TERU MOMIJIYAMA FELT LIKE SHE'D RECEIVED JUST THE TINIEST BIT....
...OF RECOGNITION...
...I CAN CLIMB MOUNTAINS TOO...

SHY

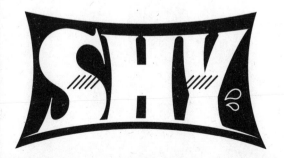

CHARACTERS FILE

PILTZ DUNANT

Hero name: Lady Black

NATIONALITY: SWISS
AGE: 16
BIRTH DATE: SEPTEMBER 6
BLOOD TYPE: B
HEIGHT: 155 CM
WEIGHT: 45 KG
LIKES: VOLUNTEER WORK, BLACK THINGS

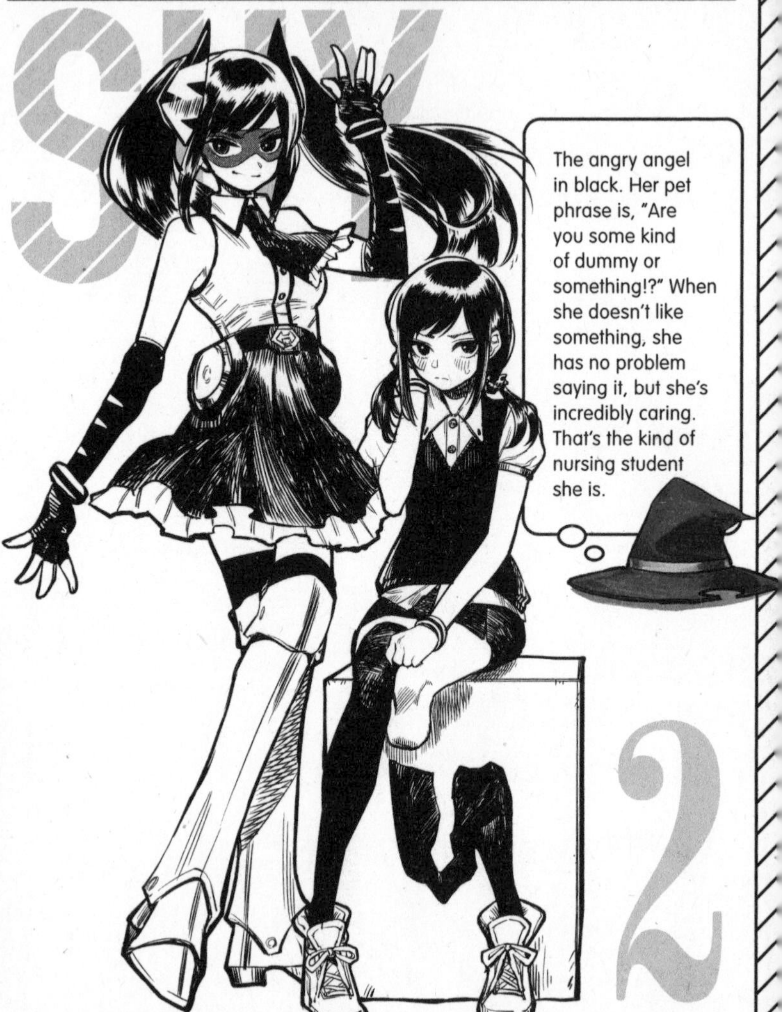
SHY
The angry angel in black. Her pet phrase is, "Are you some kind of dummy or something!?" When she doesn't like something, she has no problem saying it, but she's incredibly caring. That's the kind of nursing student she is.
2

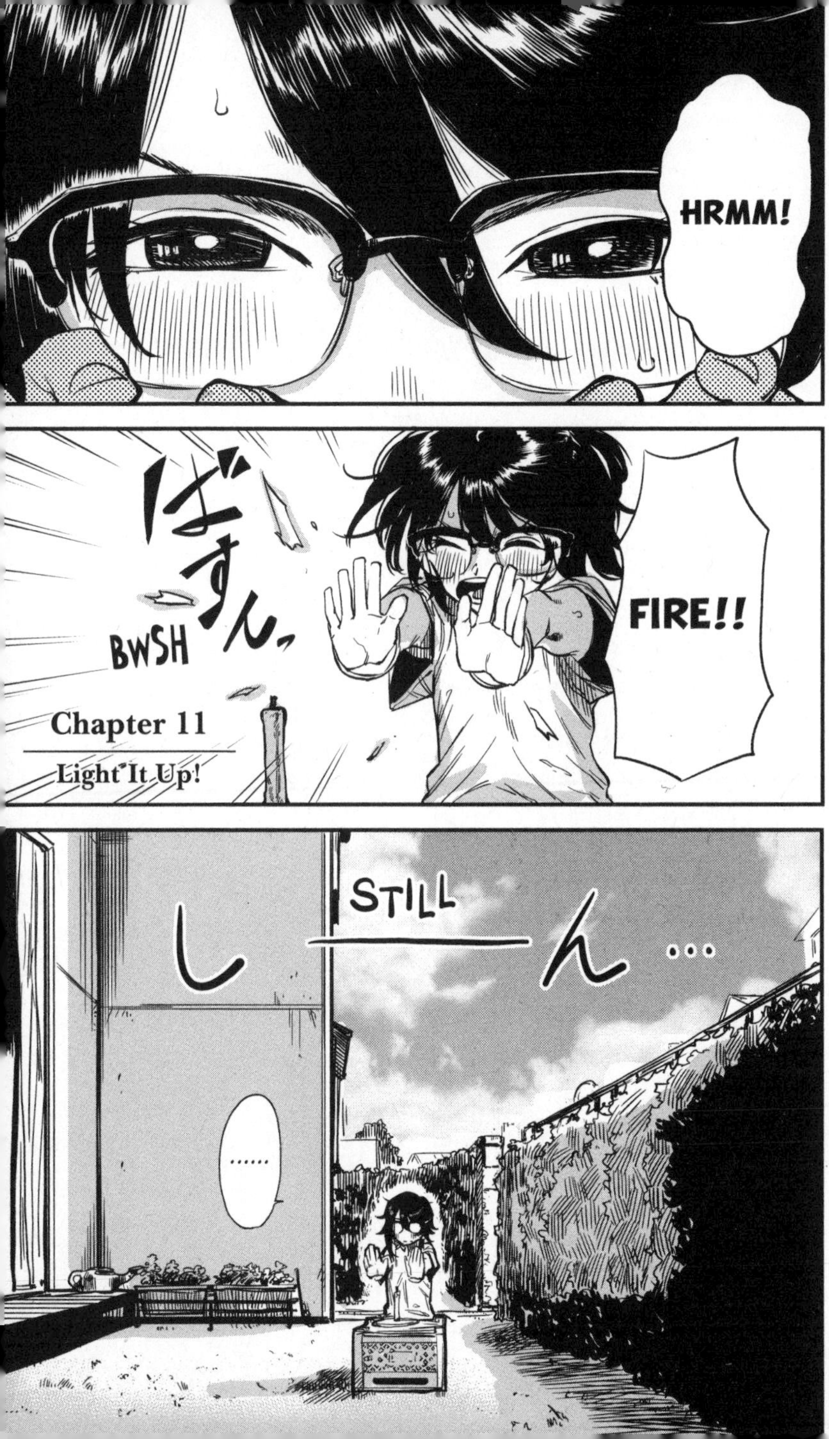
HRMM!
FIRE!!
ばすん
BWSH
Chapter 11
Light It Up!
STILL
し——ん…
......

Chapter 11

Light It Up!

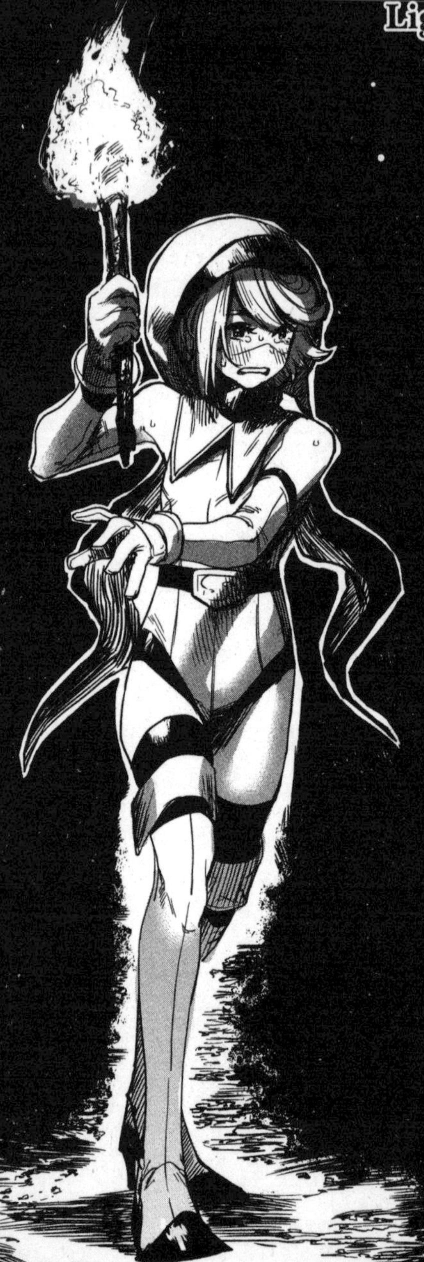

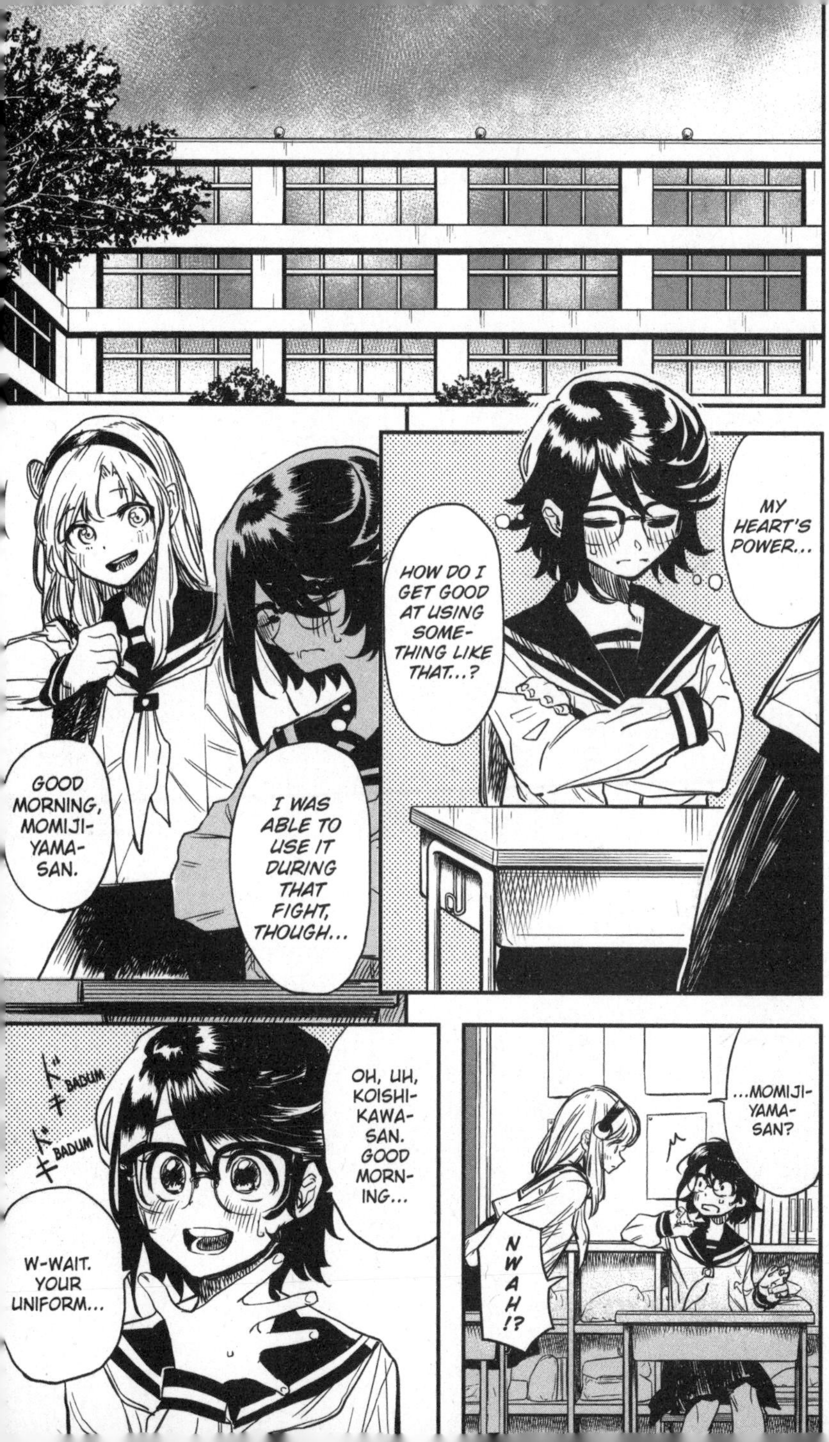
MY HEART'S POWER...
HOW DO I GET GOOD AT USING SOMETHING LIKE THAT...?
I WAS ABLE TO USE IT DURING THAT FIGHT, THOUGH...
GOOD MORNING, MOMIJIYAMA-SAN.
...MOMIJIYAMA-SAN?
NWAH!?
OH, UH, KOISHIKAWA-SAN. GOOD MORNING...
BADUM
BADUM
W-WAIT. YOUR UNIFORM...

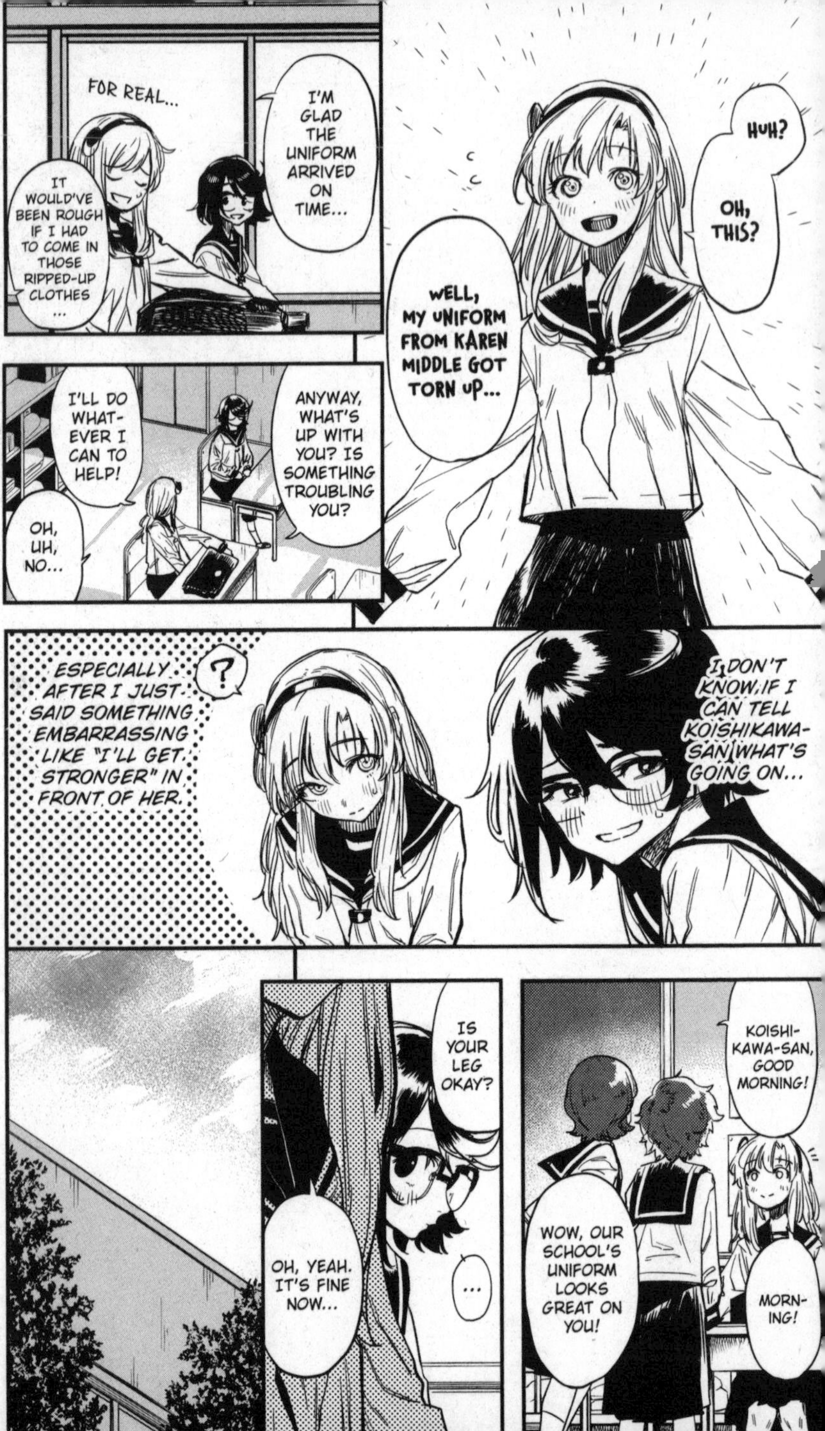
HUH?
OH, THIS?
WELL, MY UNIFORM FROM KAREN MIDDLE GOT TORN UP...
I'M GLAD THE UNIFORM ARRIVED ON TIME...
FOR REAL...
IT WOULD'VE BEEN ROUGH IF I HAD TO COME IN THOSE RIPPED-UP CLOTHES...
ANYWAY, WHAT'S UP WITH YOU? IS SOMETHING TROUBLING YOU?
I'LL DO WHATEVER I CAN TO HELP!
OH, UH, NO...
I DON'T KNOW IF I CAN TELL KOISHIKAWA-SAN WHAT'S GOING ON...
?
ESPECIALLY AFTER I JUST SAID SOMETHING EMBARRASSING LIKE "I'LL GET STRONGER" IN FRONT OF HER.
KOISHIKAWA-SAN, GOOD MORNING!
MORNING!
WOW, OUR SCHOOL'S UNIFORM LOOKS GREAT ON YOU!
IS YOUR LEG OKAY?
OH, YEAH. IT'S FINE NOW...
...

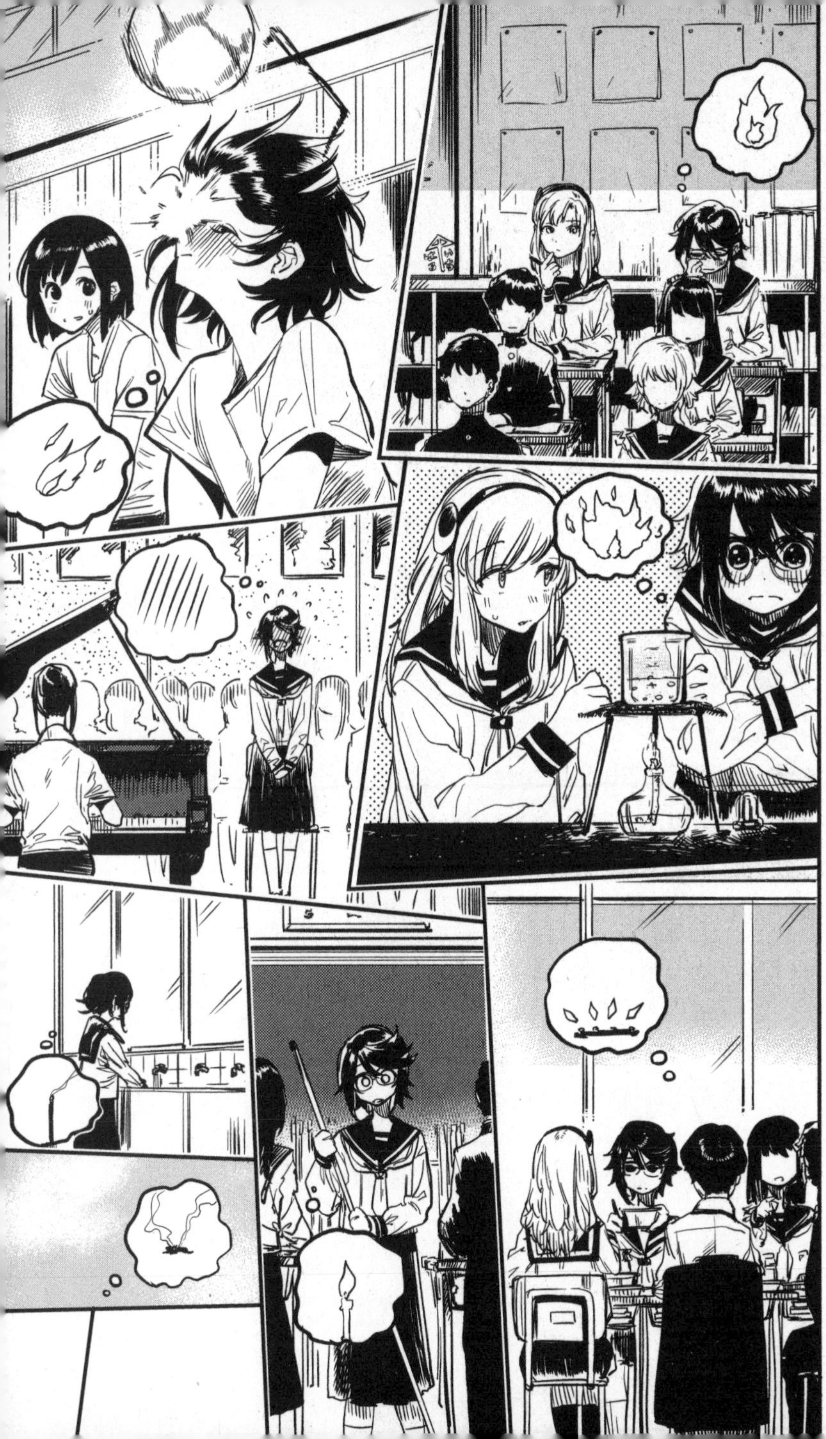

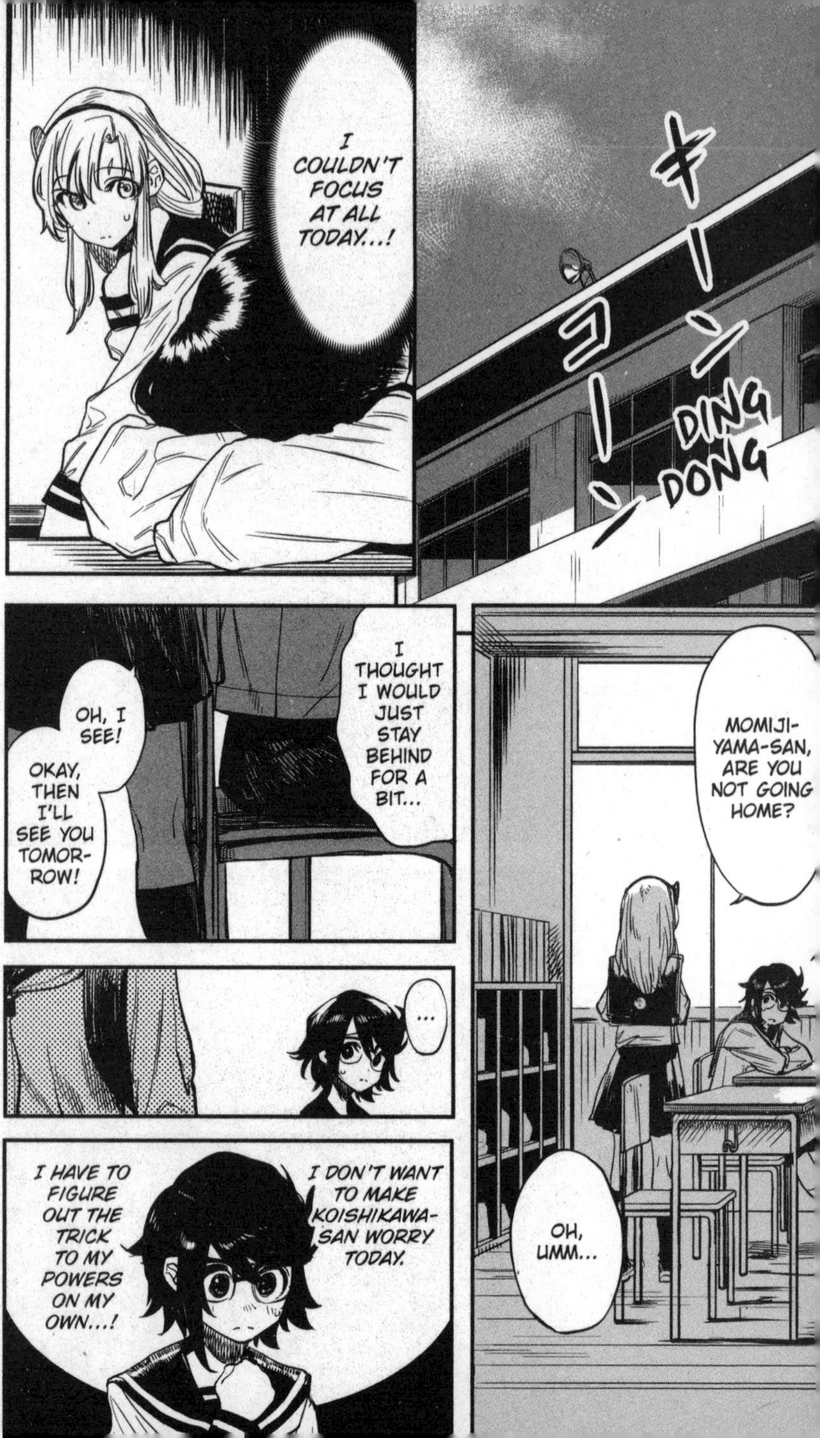
キーンコーン
DING DONG
I COULDN'T FOCUS AT ALL TODAY...!
MOMIJI-YAMA-SAN, ARE YOU NOT GOING HOME?
OH, UMM...
I THOUGHT I WOULD JUST STAY BEHIND FOR A BIT...
OH, I SEE!
OKAY, THEN I'LL SEE YOU TOMOR-ROW!
...
I DON'T WANT TO MAKE KOISHIKAWA-SAN WORRY TODAY.
I HAVE TO FIGURE OUT THE TRICK TO MY POWERS ON MY OWN...!

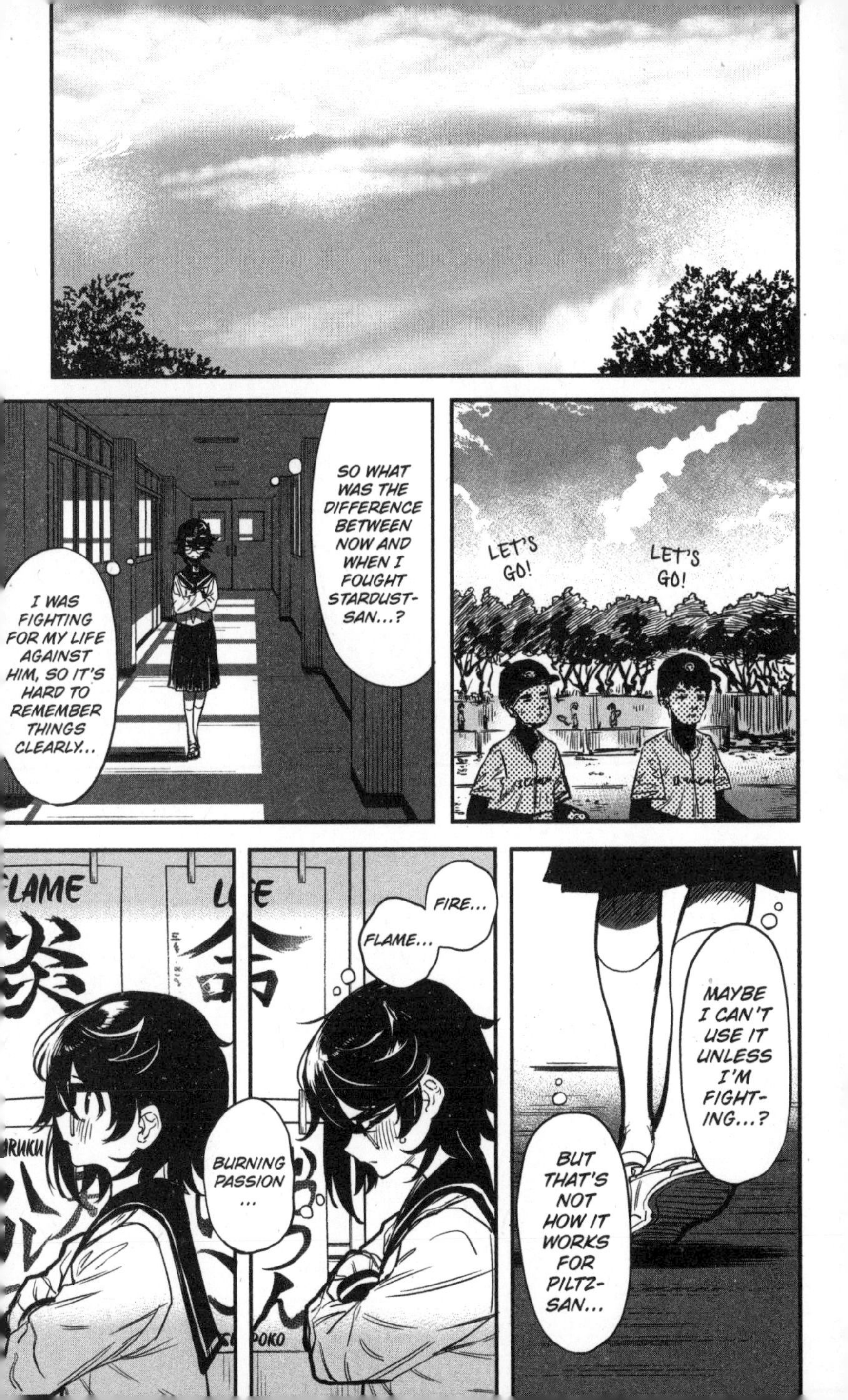
LET'S GO!
LET'S GO!
SO WHAT WAS THE DIFFERENCE BETWEEN NOW AND WHEN I FOUGHT STARDUST-SAN...?
I WAS FIGHTING FOR MY LIFE AGAINST HIM, SO IT'S HARD TO REMEMBER THINGS CLEARLY...
MAYBE I CAN'T USE IT UNLESS I'M FIGHTING...?
BUT THAT'S NOT HOW IT WORKS FOR PILTZ-SAN...
FIRE...
FLAME...
BURNING PASSION...
FLAME

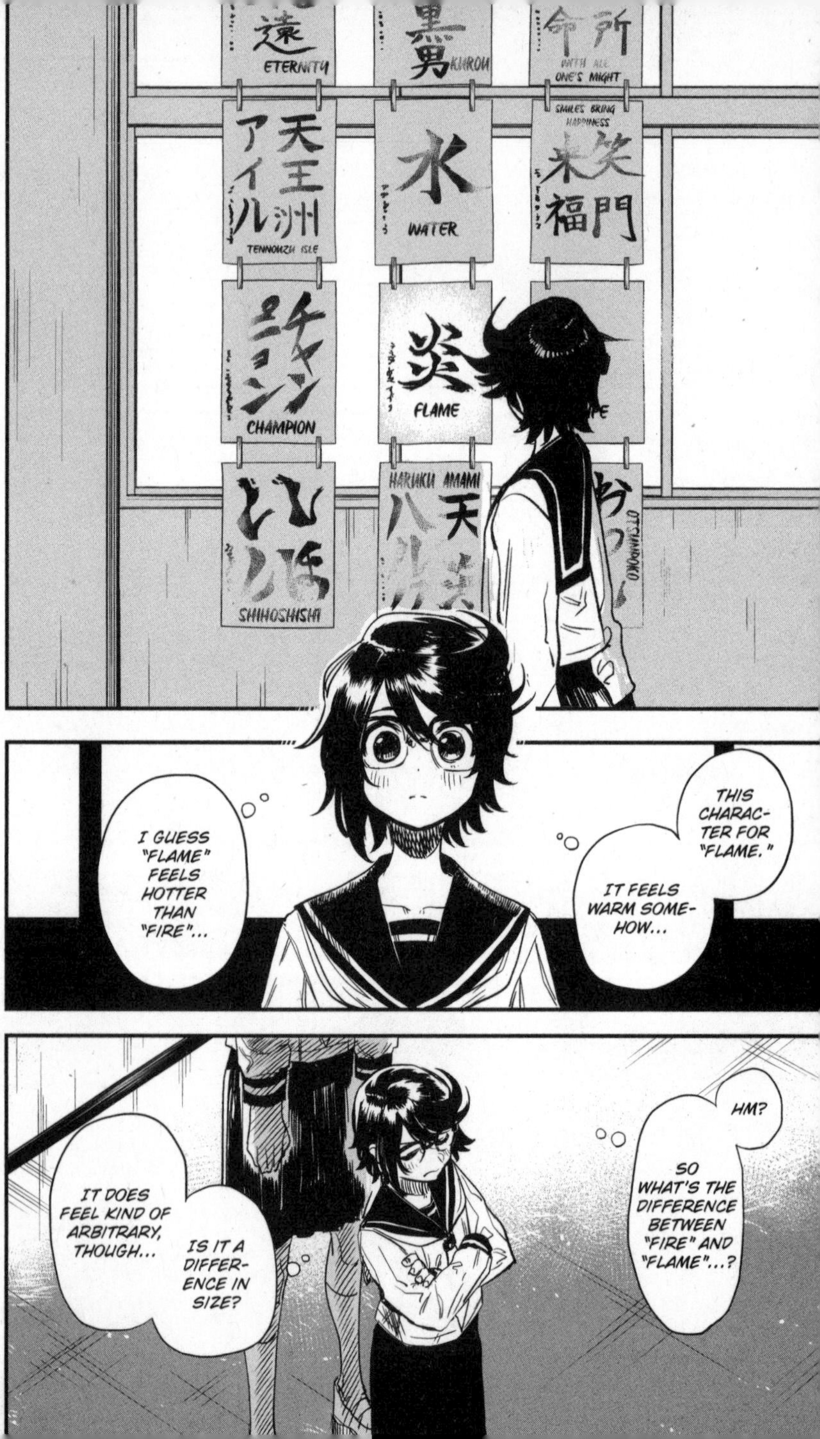
WITH ALL ONE'S MIGHT
KUROU
ETERNITY
SMILES BRING HAPPINESS
WATER
TENNOUZU ISLE
FLAME
CHAMPION
HARUKU AMAMI
SHIHOSHISHI
THIS CHARACTER FOR "FLAME."
IT FEELS WARM SOME-HOW...
I GUESS "FLAME" FEELS HOTTER THAN "FIRE"...
HM?
SO WHAT'S THE DIFFERENCE BETWEEN "FIRE" AND "FLAME"...?
IS IT A DIFFER-ENCE IN SIZE?
IT DOES FEEL KIND OF ARBITRARY, THOUGH...

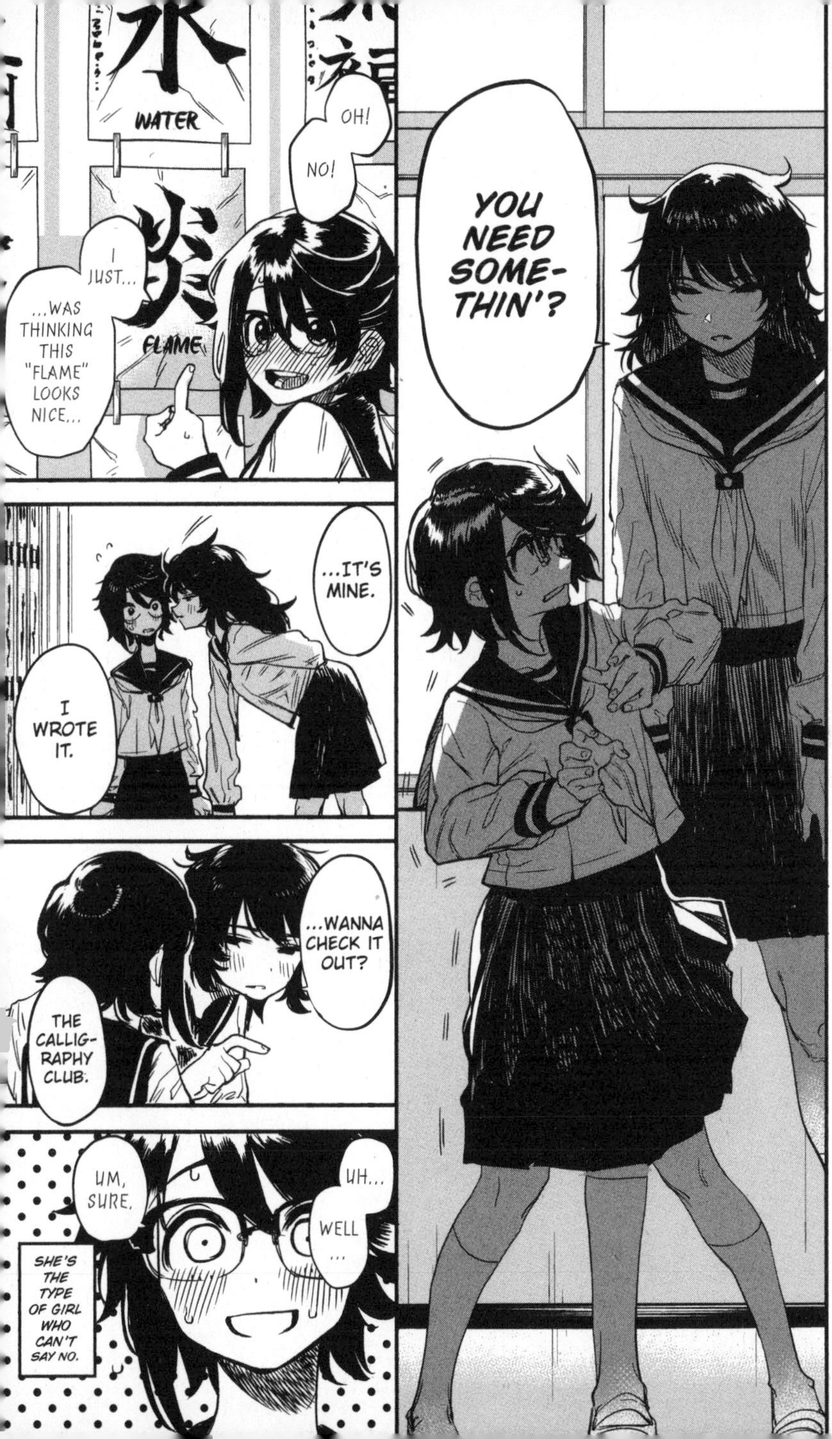
YOU NEED SOME-THIN'?
WATER
FLAME
OH! NO!
I JUST...
...WAS THINKING THIS "FLAME" LOOKS NICE...
...IT'S MINE.
I WROTE IT.
...WANNA CHECK IT OUT?
THE CALLIG-RAPHY CLUB.
UH... WELL...
UM, SURE.
SHE'S THE TYPE OF GIRL WHO CAN'T SAY NO.

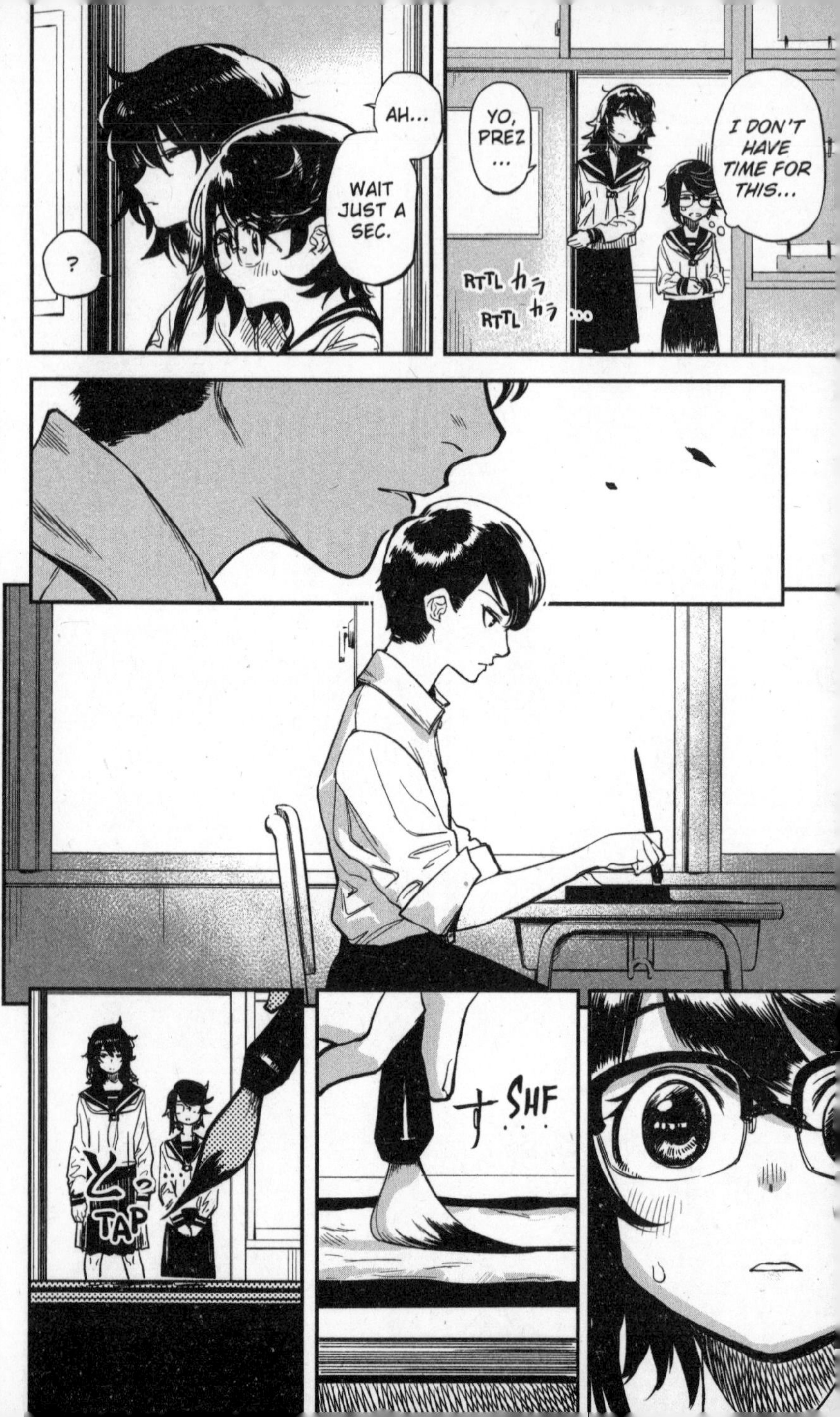
I DON'T HAVE TIME FOR THIS...
YO, PREZ...
RTTL カラ
RTTL カラ...
AH...
WAIT JUST A SEC.
?
す SHF...
と TAP

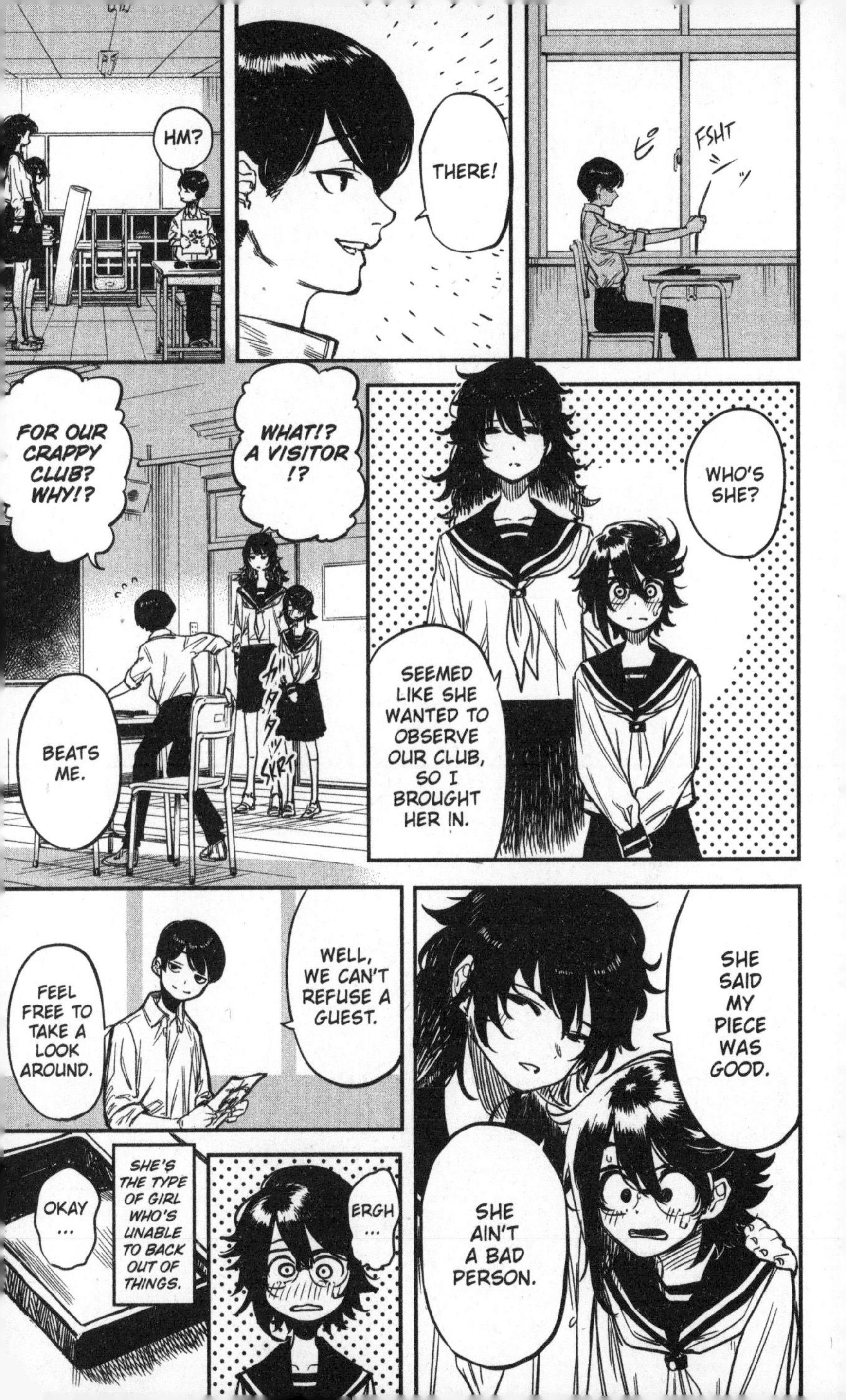
FSHT
THERE!
HM?
WHO'S SHE?
SEEMED LIKE SHE WANTED TO OBSERVE OUR CLUB, SO I BROUGHT HER IN.
WHAT!? A VISITOR !?
FOR OUR CRAPPY CLUB? WHY!?
SKRT
BEATS ME.
SHE SAID MY PIECE WAS GOOD.
SHE AIN'T A BAD PERSON.
WELL, WE CAN'T REFUSE A GUEST.
FEEL FREE TO TAKE A LOOK AROUND.
ERGH ...
SHE'S THE TYPE OF GIRL WHO'S UNABLE TO BACK OUT OF THINGS.
OKAY ...

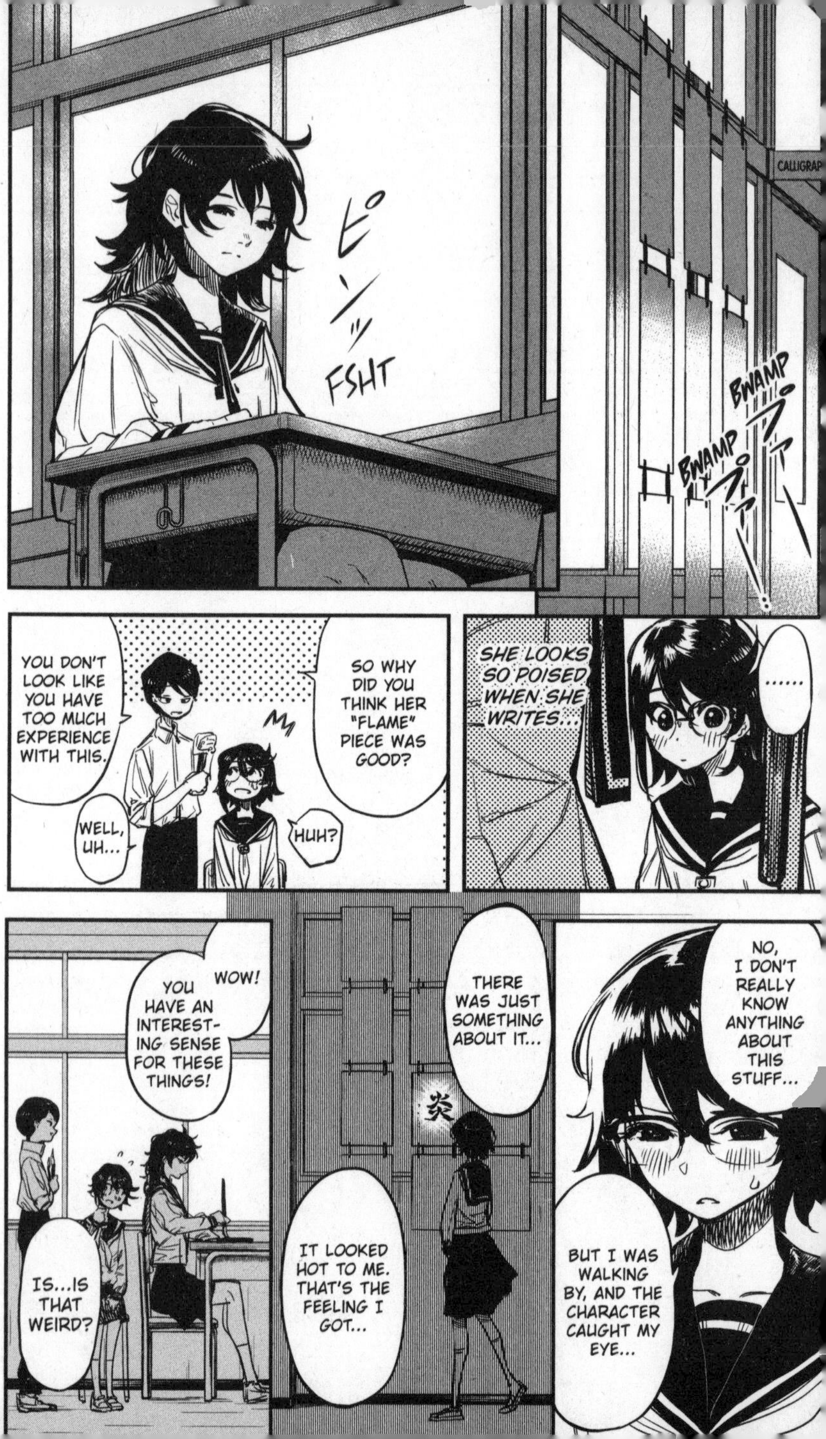
CALLIGRAP
BWAMP
BWAMP
FSHT
......
SHE LOOKS SO POISED WHEN SHE WRITES...
SO WHY DID YOU THINK HER "FLAME" PIECE WAS GOOD?
YOU DON'T LOOK LIKE YOU HAVE TOO MUCH EXPERIENCE WITH THIS.
HUH?
WELL, UH...
NO, I DON'T REALLY KNOW ANYTHING ABOUT THIS STUFF...
BUT I WAS WALKING BY, AND THE CHARACTER CAUGHT MY EYE...
THERE WAS JUST SOMETHING ABOUT IT...
炎
IT LOOKED HOT TO ME. THAT'S THE FEELING I GOT...
WOW!
YOU HAVE AN INTEREST-ING SENSE FOR THESE THINGS!
IS...IS THAT WEIRD?

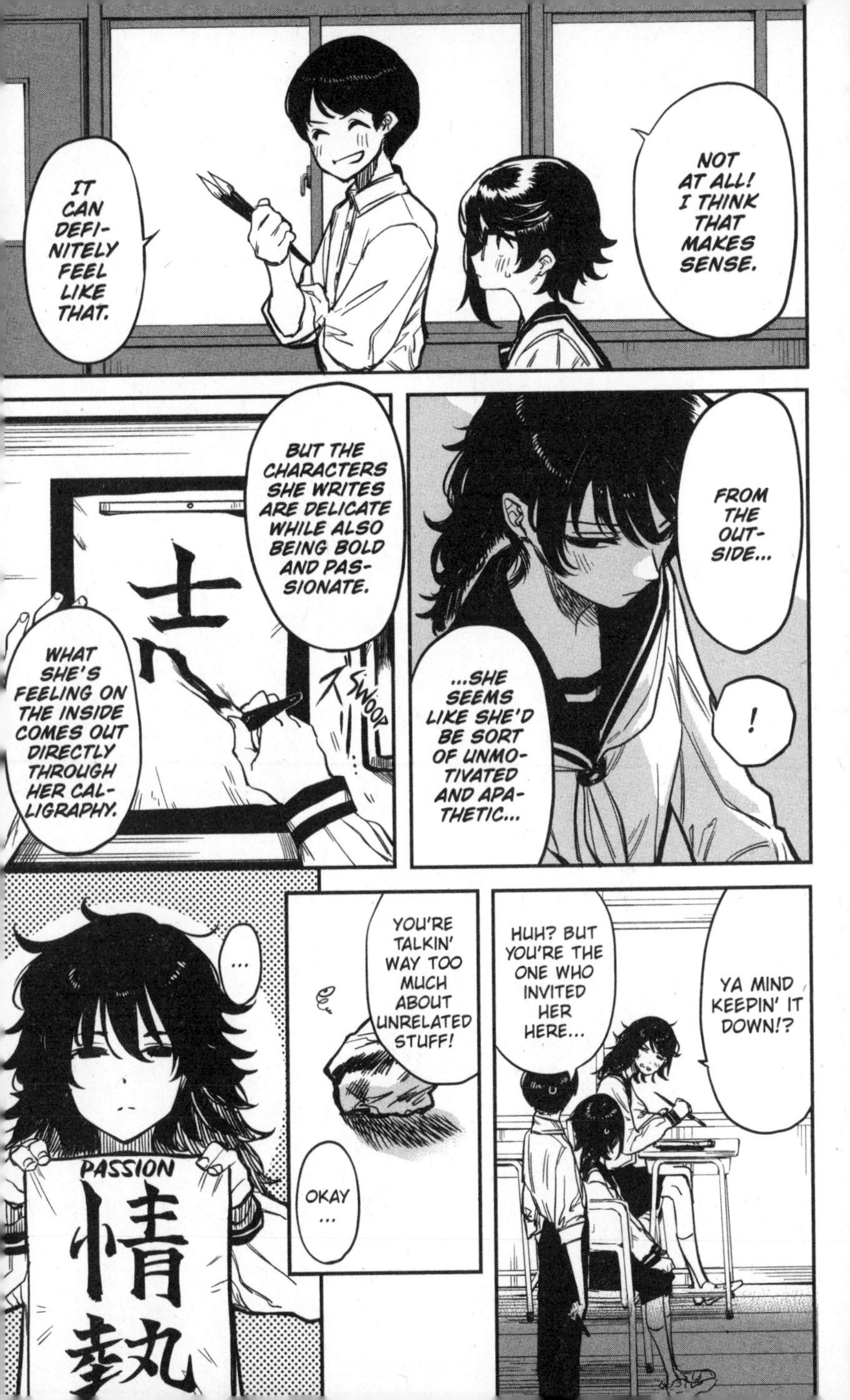
NOT AT ALL! I THINK THAT MAKES SENSE.
IT CAN DEFI-NITELY FEEL LIKE THAT.
FROM THE OUT-SIDE...
...SHE SEEMS LIKE SHE'D BE SORT OF UNMO-TIVATED AND APA-THETIC...
!
BUT THE CHARACTERS SHE WRITES ARE DELICATE WHILE ALSO BEING BOLD AND PAS-SIONATE.
WHAT SHE'S FEELING ON THE INSIDE COMES OUT DIRECTLY THROUGH HER CAL-LIGRAPHY.
SWOOP
YA MIND KEEPIN' IT DOWN!?
HUH? BUT YOU'RE THE ONE WHO INVITED HER HERE...
YOU'RE TALKIN' WAY TOO MUCH ABOUT UNRELATED STUFF!
OKAY...
...
PASSION
情熱

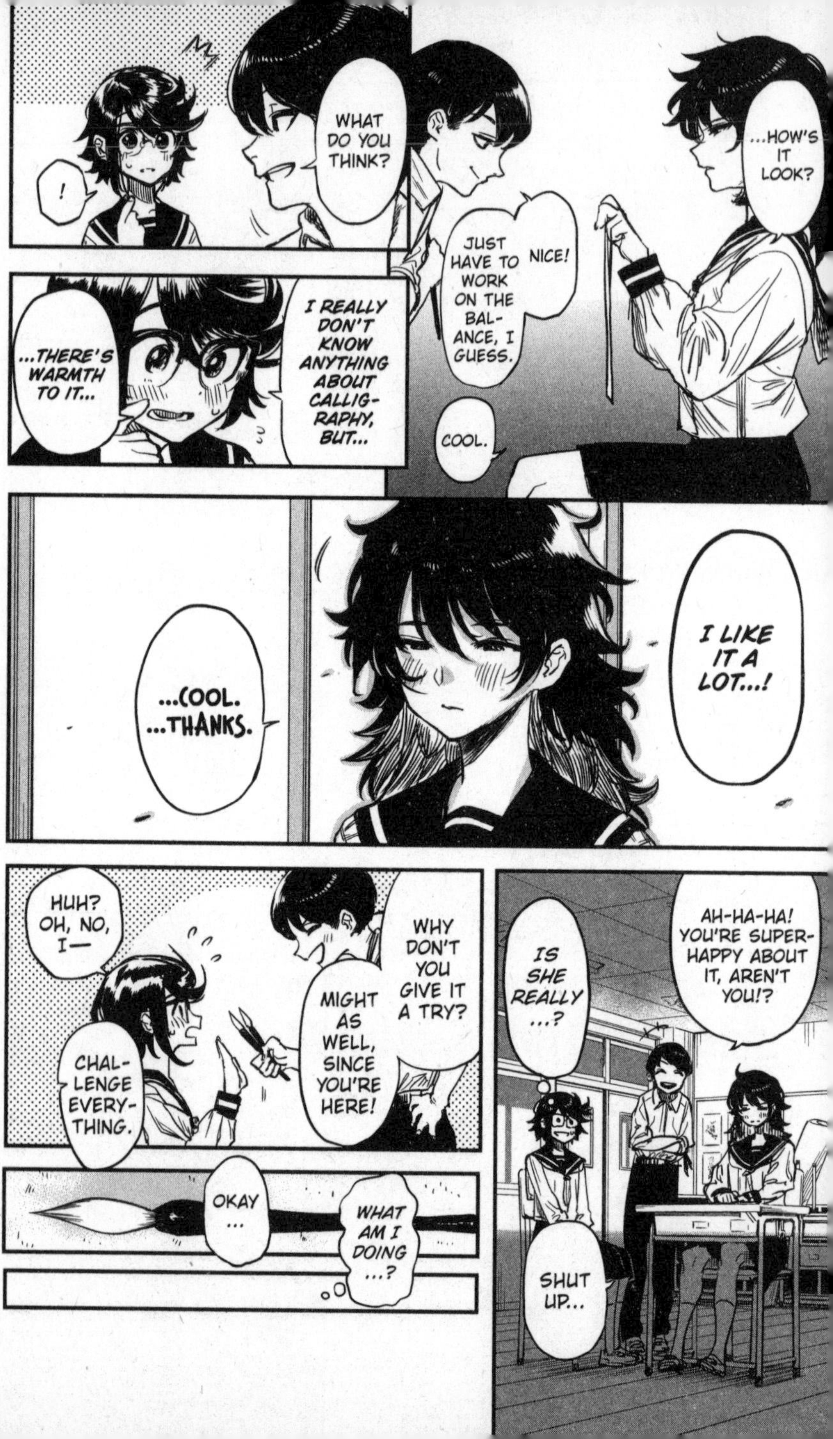
...HOW'S IT LOOK?
NICE!
JUST HAVE TO WORK ON THE BAL-ANCE, I GUESS.
COOL.
WHAT DO YOU THINK?
!
I REALLY DON'T KNOW ANYTHING ABOUT CALLIG-RAPHY, BUT...
...THERE'S WARMTH TO IT...
I LIKE IT A LOT...!
...COOL. ...THANKS.
AH-HA-HA! YOU'RE SUPER-HAPPY ABOUT IT, AREN'T YOU!?
IS SHE REALLY ...?
SHUT UP...
WHY DON'T YOU GIVE IT A TRY?
MIGHT AS WELL, SINCE YOU'RE HERE!
HUH? OH, NO, I—
CHAL-LENGE EVERY-THING.
WHAT AM I DOING ...?
OKAY ...

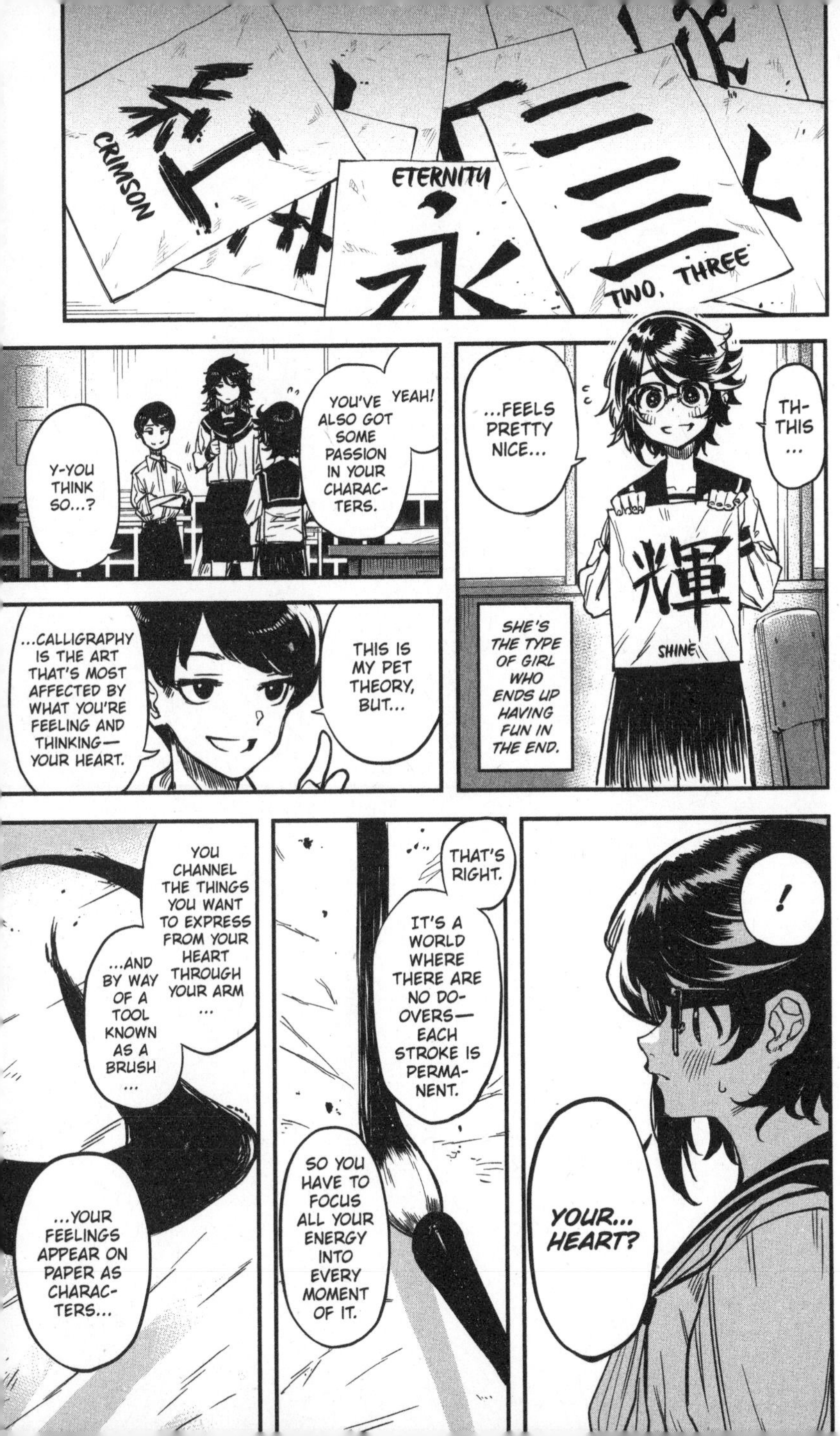
TWO, THREE
ETERNITY
CRIMSON
TH-THIS...
...FEELS PRETTY NICE...
SHINE
SHE'S THE TYPE OF GIRL WHO ENDS UP HAVING FUN IN THE END.
YEAH!
YOU'VE ALSO GOT SOME PASSION IN YOUR CHARACTERS.
Y-YOU THINK SO...?
THIS IS MY PET THEORY, BUT...
...CALLIGRAPHY IS THE ART THAT'S MOST AFFECTED BY WHAT YOU'RE FEELING AND THINKING—YOUR HEART.
!
YOUR... HEART?
THAT'S RIGHT.
IT'S A WORLD WHERE THERE ARE NO DO-OVERS—EACH STROKE IS PERMANENT.
SO YOU HAVE TO FOCUS ALL YOUR ENERGY INTO EVERY MOMENT OF IT.
YOU CHANNEL THE THINGS YOU WANT TO EXPRESS FROM YOUR HEART THROUGH YOUR ARM...
...AND BY WAY OF A TOOL KNOWN AS A BRUSH...
...YOUR FEELINGS APPEAR ON PAPER AS CHARACTERS...

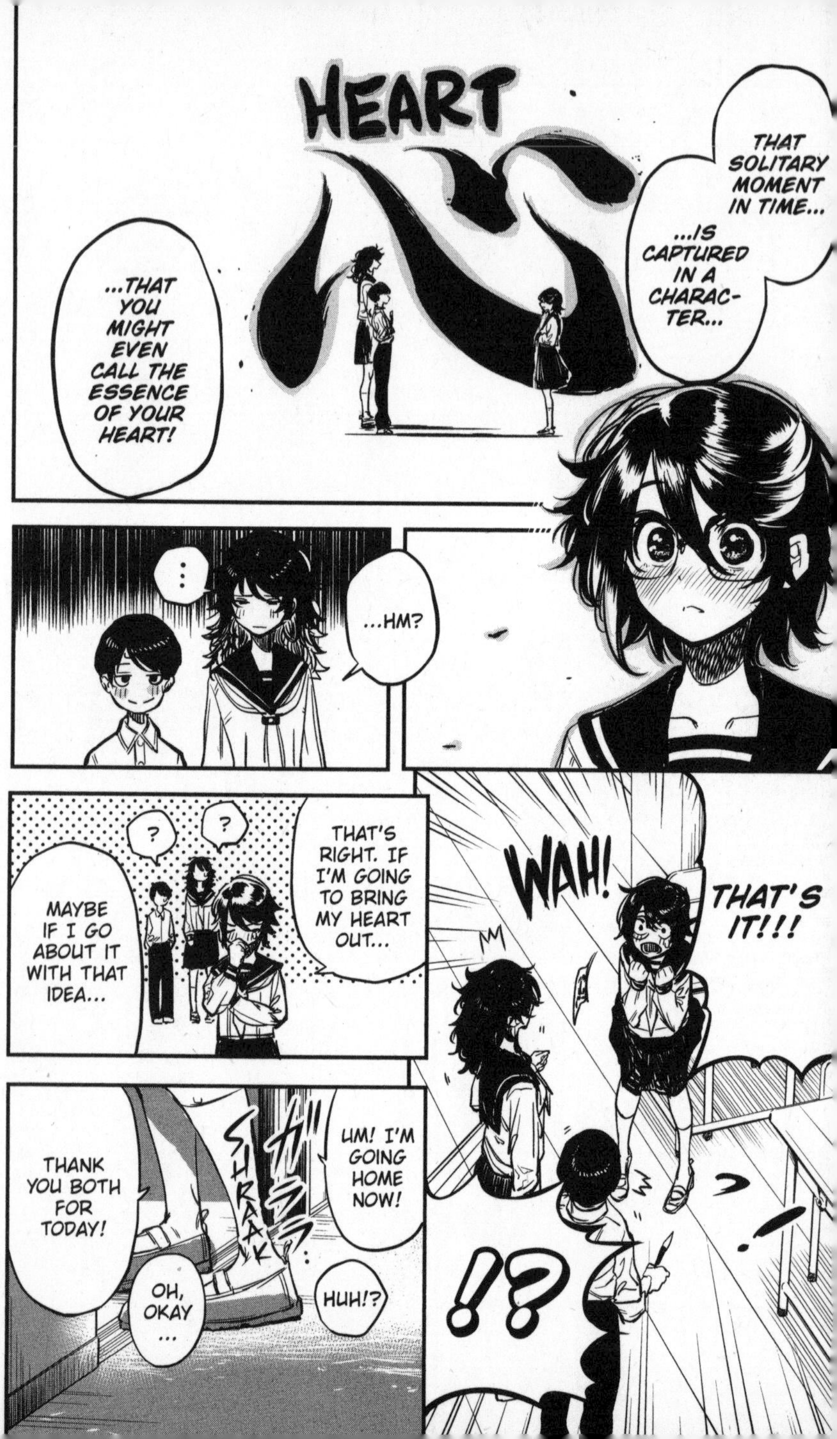
THAT SOLITARY MOMENT IN TIME...
...IS CAPTURED IN A CHARAC-TER...
HEART
...THAT YOU MIGHT EVEN CALL THE ESSENCE OF YOUR HEART!
...HM?
...
THAT'S IT!!!
WAH!
!?
?
!
THAT'S RIGHT. IF I'M GOING TO BRING MY HEART OUT...
?
?
MAYBE IF I GO ABOUT IT WITH THAT IDEA...
UM! I'M GOING HOME NOW!
SHRAAK
HUH!?
THANK YOU BOTH FOR TODAY!
OH, OKAY ...

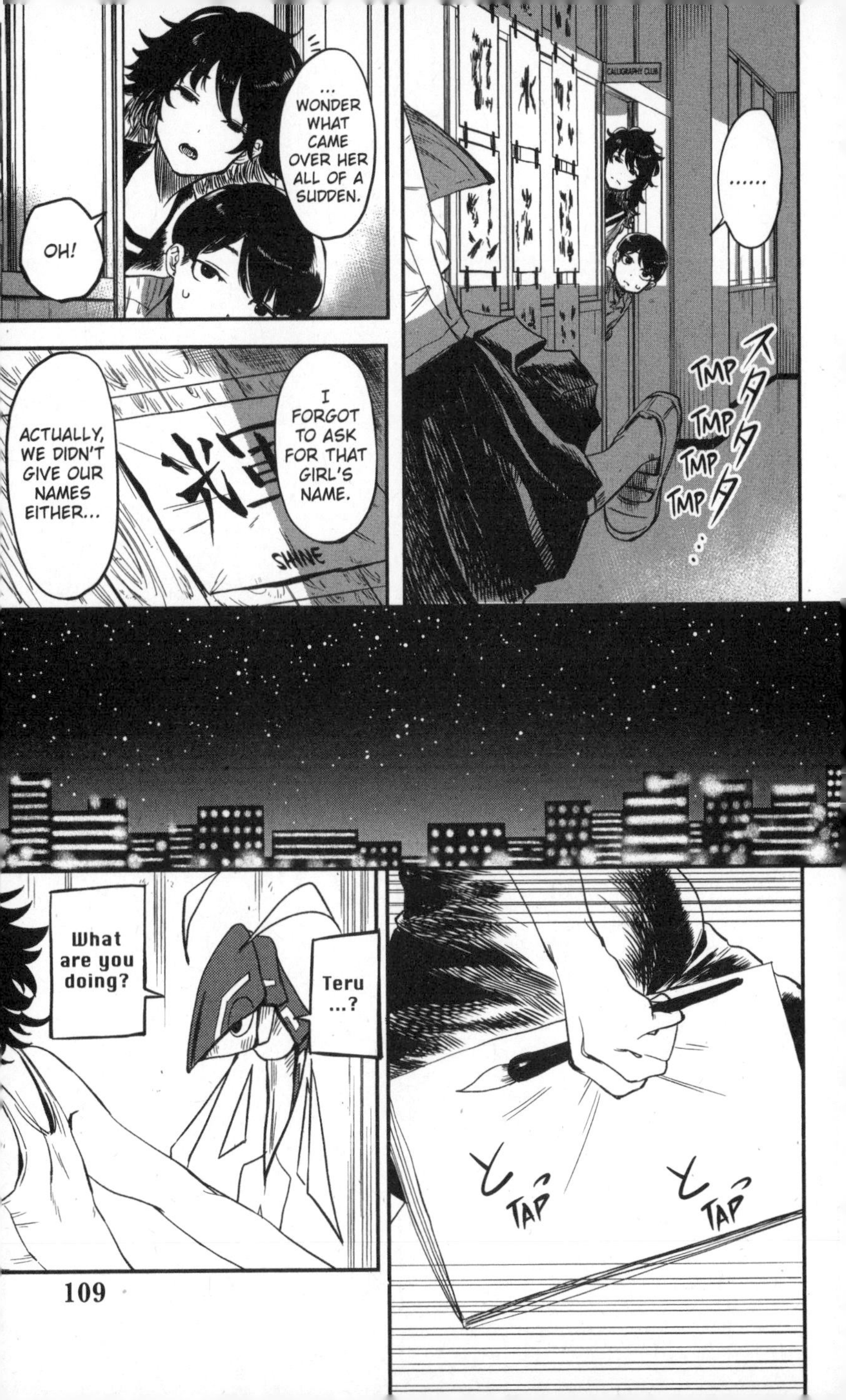
CALLIGRAPHY CLUB
......
スタタタ
TMP TMP TMP TMP
... WONDER WHAT CAME OVER HER ALL OF A SUDDEN.
OH!
I FORGOT TO ASK FOR THAT GIRL'S NAME.
ACTUALLY, WE DIDN'T GIVE OUR NAMES EITHER...
SHINE
と TAP
と TAP
Teru ...?
What are you doing?

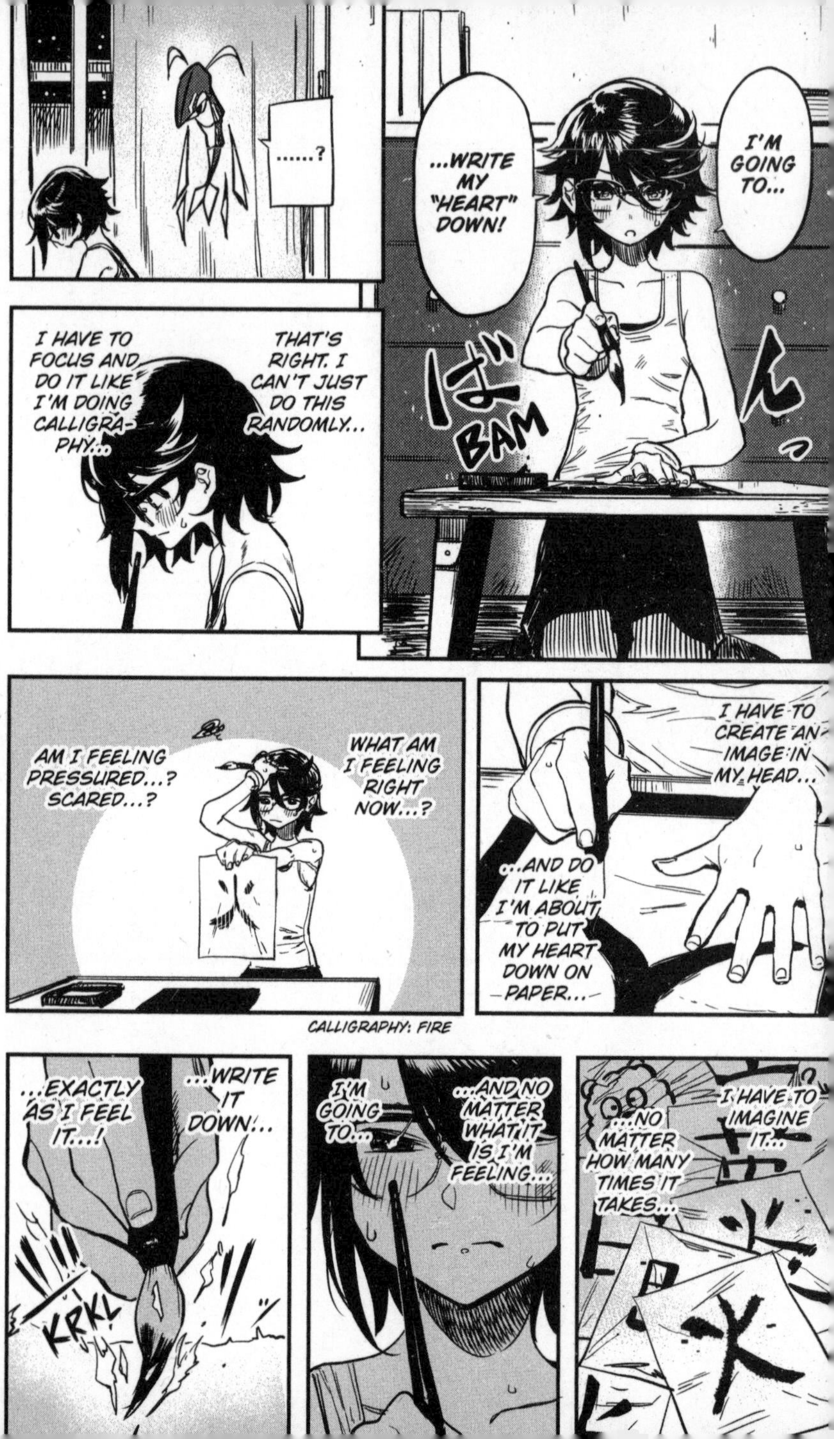
I'M GOING TO...
...WRITE MY "HEART" DOWN!
BAM
......?
THAT'S RIGHT. I CAN'T JUST DO THIS RANDOMLY...
I HAVE TO FOCUS AND DO IT LIKE I'M DOING CALLIGRAPHY...
I HAVE TO CREATE AN IMAGE IN MY HEAD...
...AND DO IT LIKE I'M ABOUT TO PUT MY HEART DOWN ON PAPER...
WHAT AM I FEELING RIGHT NOW...?
AM I FEELING PRESSURED...? SCARED...?
CALLIGRAPHY: FIRE
I HAVE TO IMAGINE IT...
...NO MATTER HOW MANY TIMES IT TAKES...
...AND NO MATTER WHAT IT IS I'M FEELING...
I'M GOING TO...
...WRITE IT DOWN...
...EXACTLY AS I FEEL IT...!
KRKL

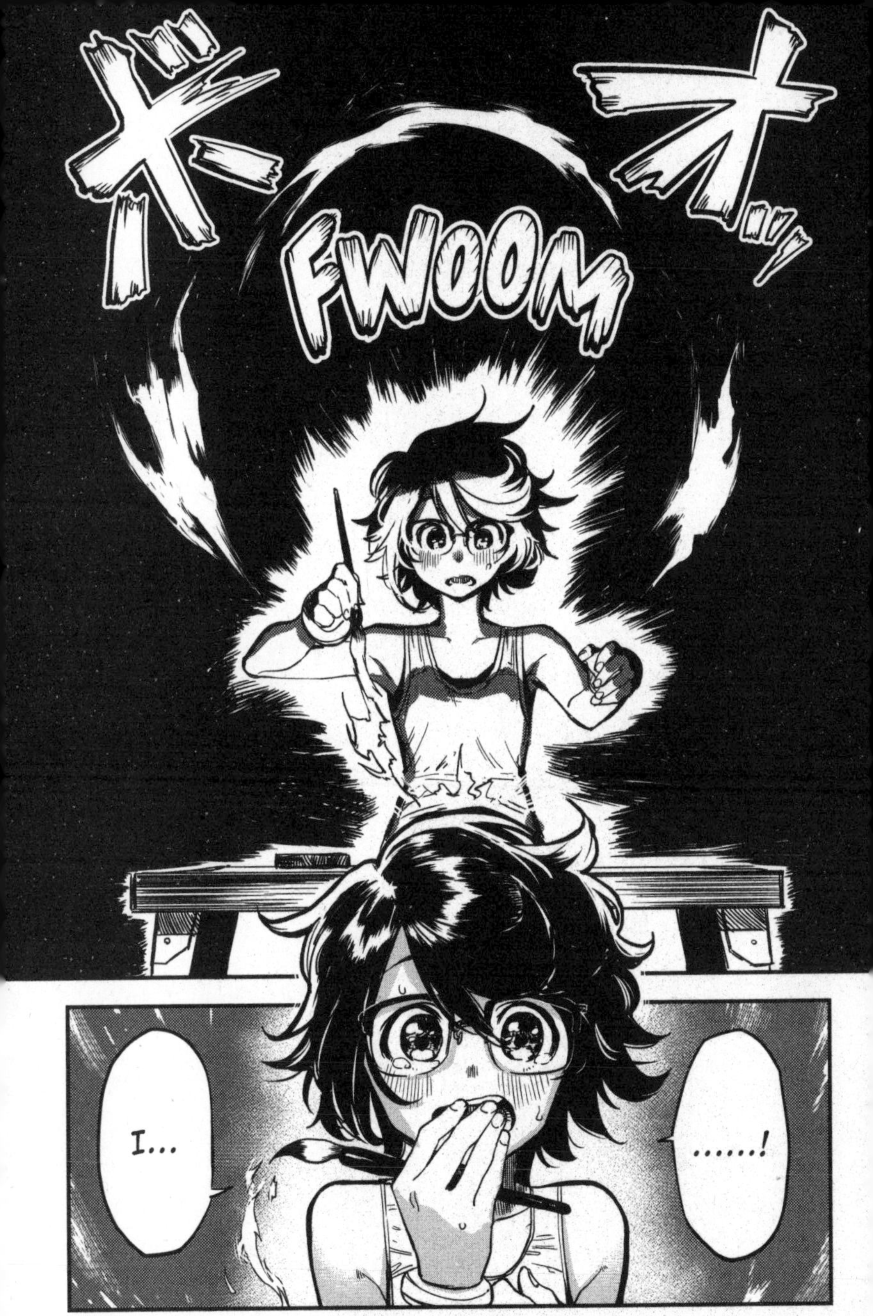
FWOOM
......!
I...

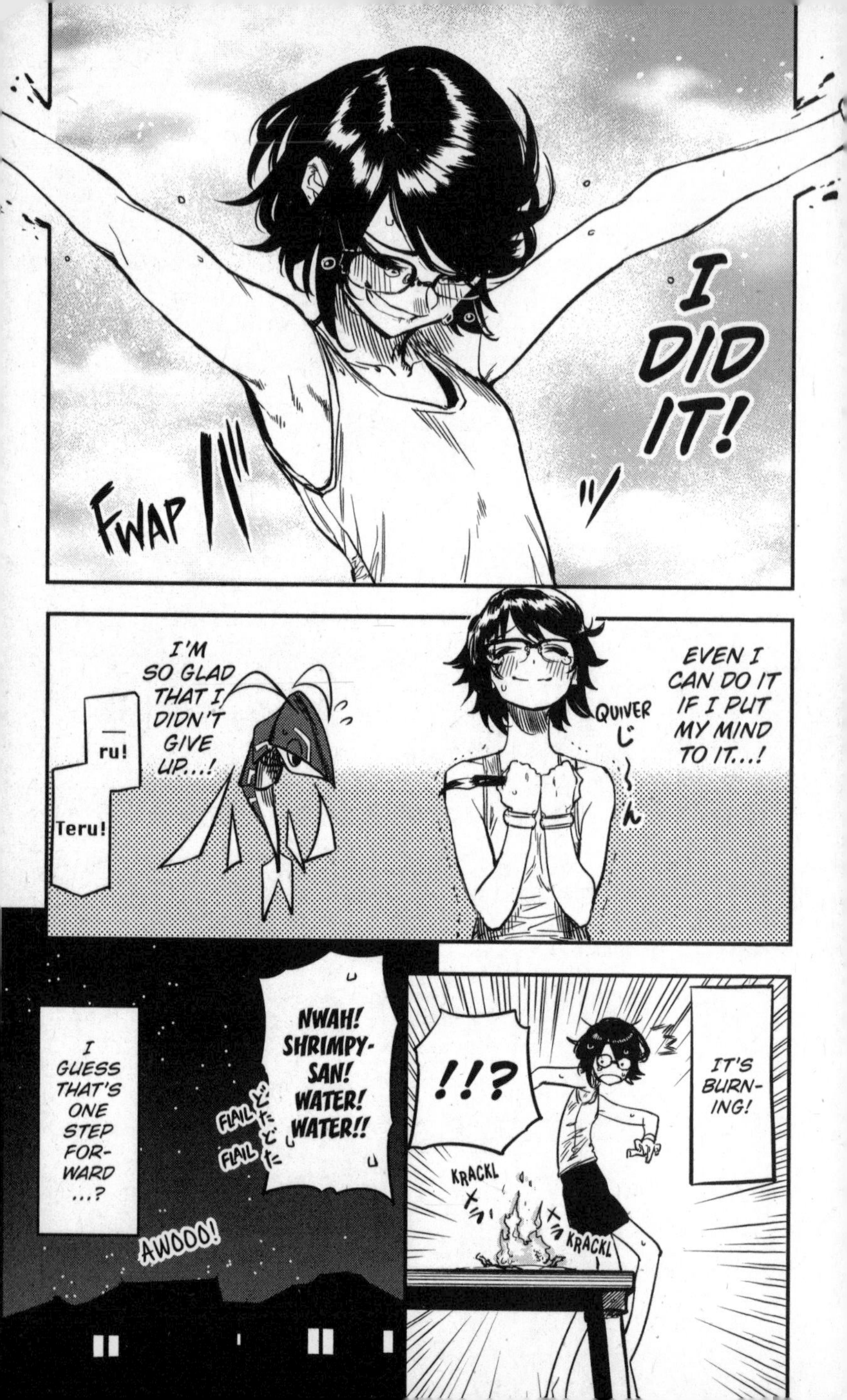
I DID IT!
FWAP
EVEN I CAN DO IT IF I PUT MY MIND TO IT...!
QUIVER じ~ん
I'M SO GLAD THAT I DIDN'T GIVE UP...!
—ru!
Teru!
IT'S BURN-ING!
!!?
KRACKL
KRACKL
NWAH! SHRIMPY-SAN! WATER! WATER!!
FLAIL どたどた FLAIL
I GUESS THAT'S ONE STEP FOR-WARD...?
AWOOO!

Chapter 12

A Revolution in the Department Store

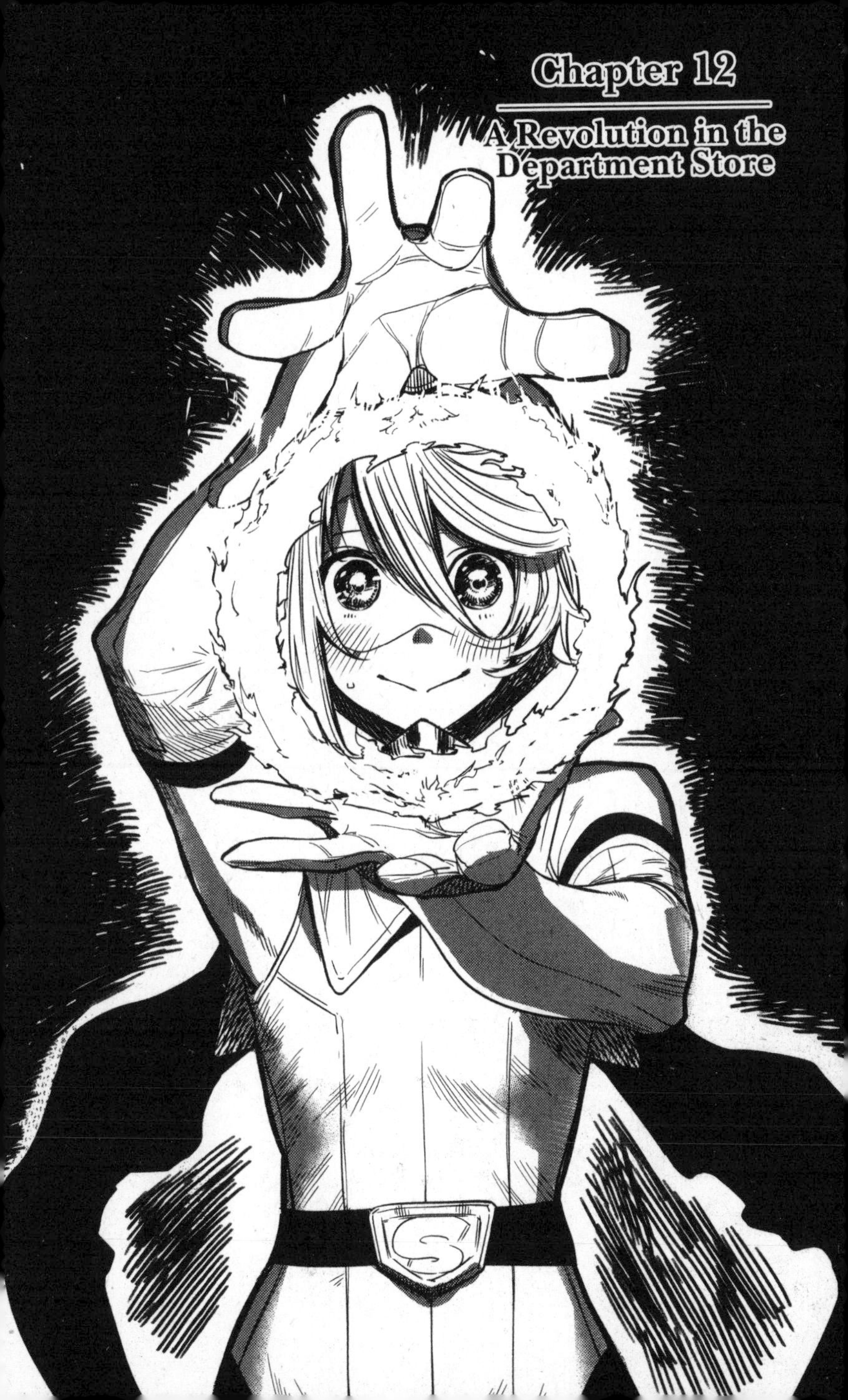

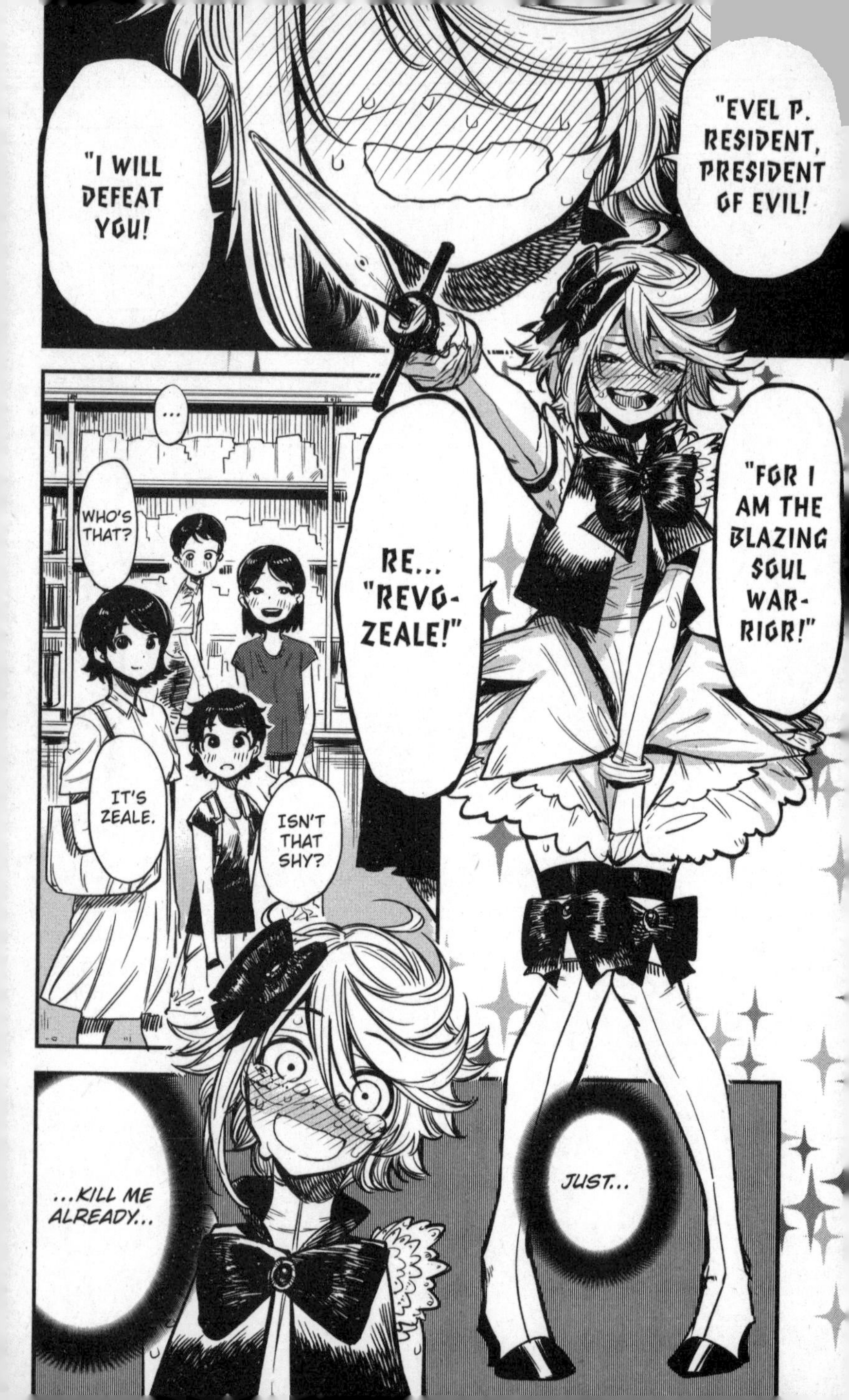
"EVEL P. RESIDENT, PRESIDENT OF EVIL!
"I WILL DEFEAT YOU!
"FOR I AM THE BLAZING SOUL WARRIOR!"
RE... "REVO-ZEALE!"
...
WHO'S THAT?
IT'S ZEALE.
ISN'T THAT SHY?
JUST...
...KILL ME ALREADY...

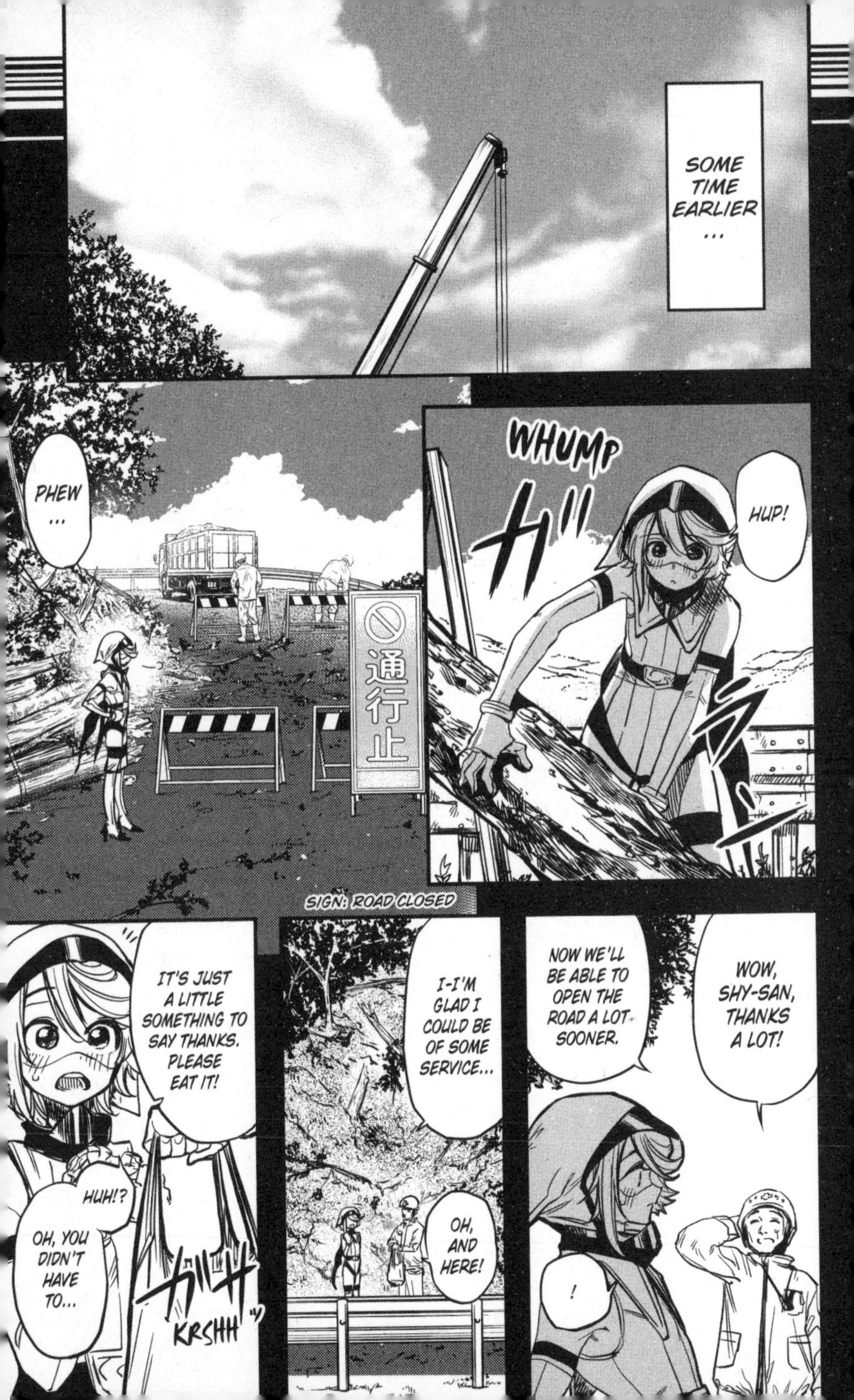
SOME TIME EARLIER...
WHUMP
HUP!
PHEW...
通行止
SIGN: ROAD CLOSED
WOW, SHY-SAN, THANKS A LOT!
NOW WE'LL BE ABLE TO OPEN THE ROAD A LOT SOONER.
!
I-I'M GLAD I COULD BE OF SOME SERVICE...
OH, AND HERE!
IT'S JUST A LITTLE SOMETHING TO SAY THANKS. PLEASE EAT IT!
HUH!?
OH, YOU DIDN'T HAVE TO...
KRSHH

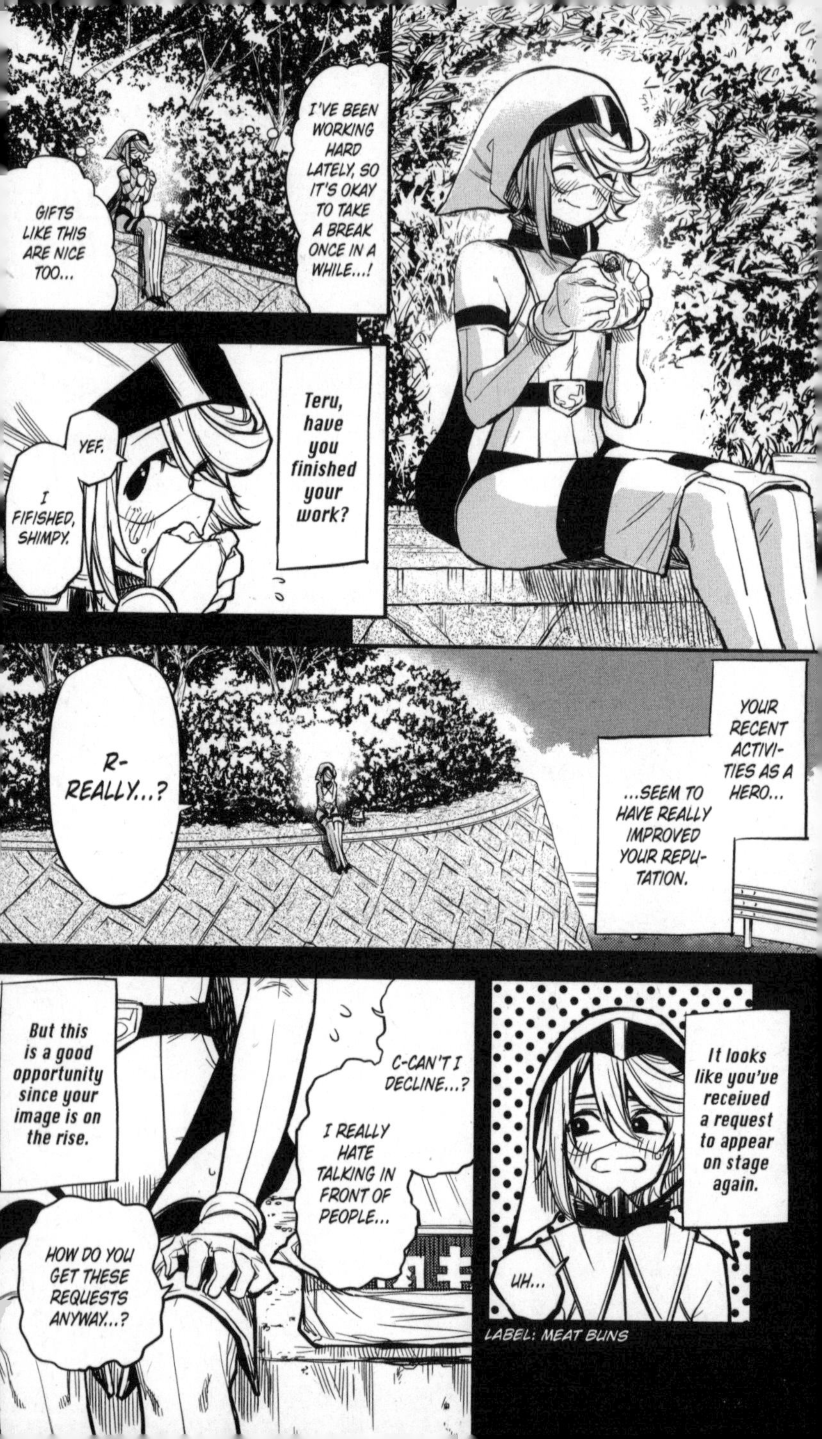
I'VE BEEN WORKING HARD LATELY, SO IT'S OKAY TO TAKE A BREAK ONCE IN A WHILE...!
GIFTS LIKE THIS ARE NICE TOO...
Teru, have you finished your work?
YEF.
I FIFISHED, SHIMPY.
YOUR RECENT ACTIVITIES AS A HERO...
...SEEM TO HAVE REALLY IMPROVED YOUR REPUTATION.
R-REALLY...?
It looks like you've received a request to appear on stage again.
UH...
LABEL: MEAT BUNS
C-CAN'T I DECLINE...?
I REALLY HATE TALKING IN FRONT OF PEOPLE...
But this is a good opportunity since your image is on the rise.
HOW DO YOU GET THESE REQUESTS ANYWAY...?

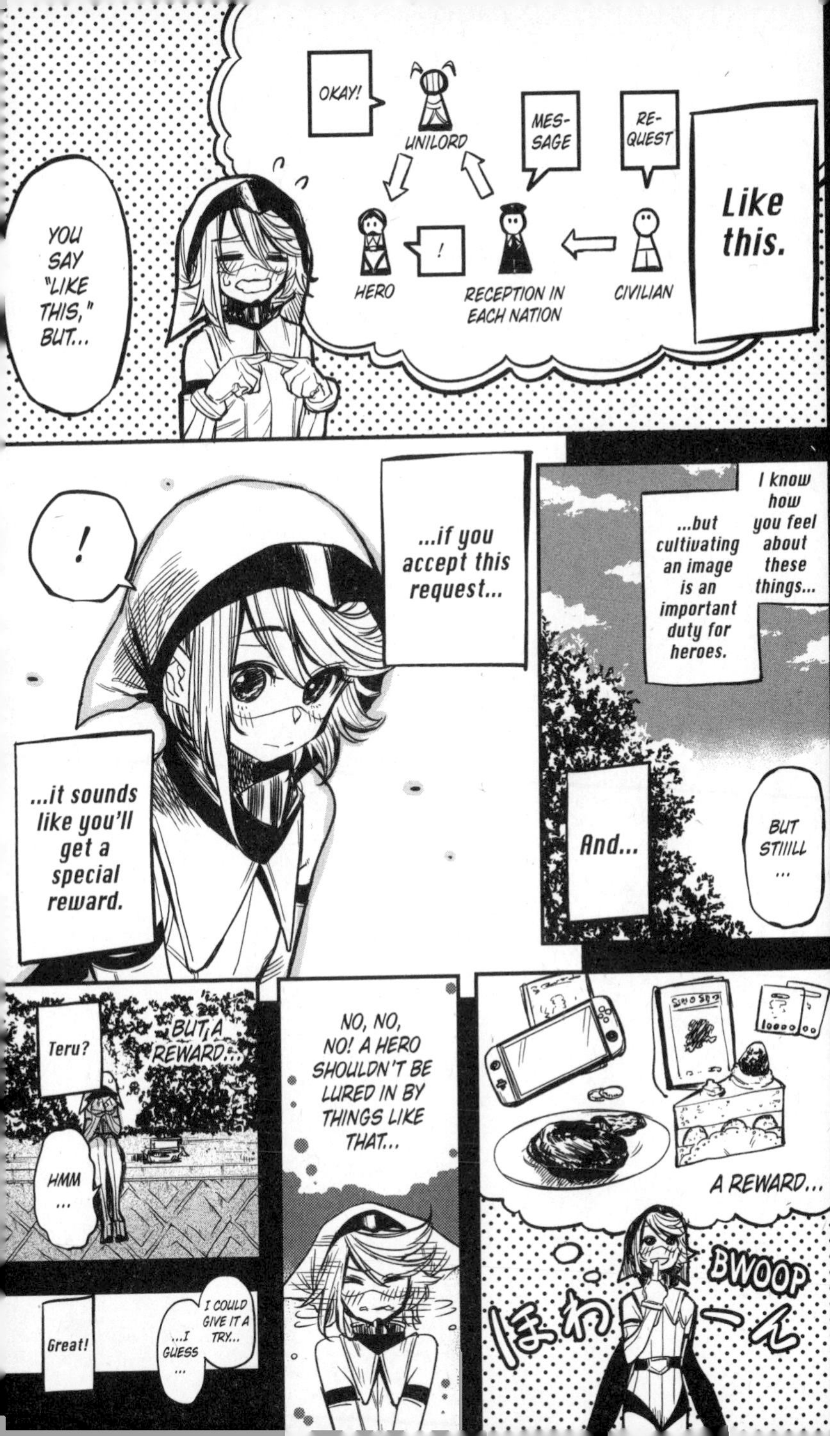
Like this.
RE-
QUEST
MES-
SAGE
OKAY!
UNILORD
!
CIVILIAN
RECEPTION IN EACH NATION
HERO
YOU SAY "LIKE THIS," BUT...
I know how you feel about these things...
...but cultivating an image is an important duty for heroes.
BUT STIIILL...
And...
...if you accept this request...
!
...it sounds like you'll get a special reward.
A REWARD...
BWOOP
ほわーん
NO, NO, NO! A HERO SHOULDN'T BE LURED IN BY THINGS LIKE THAT...
BUT, A REWARD...
Teru?
HMM...
I COULD GIVE IT A TRY...
...I GUESS...
Great!

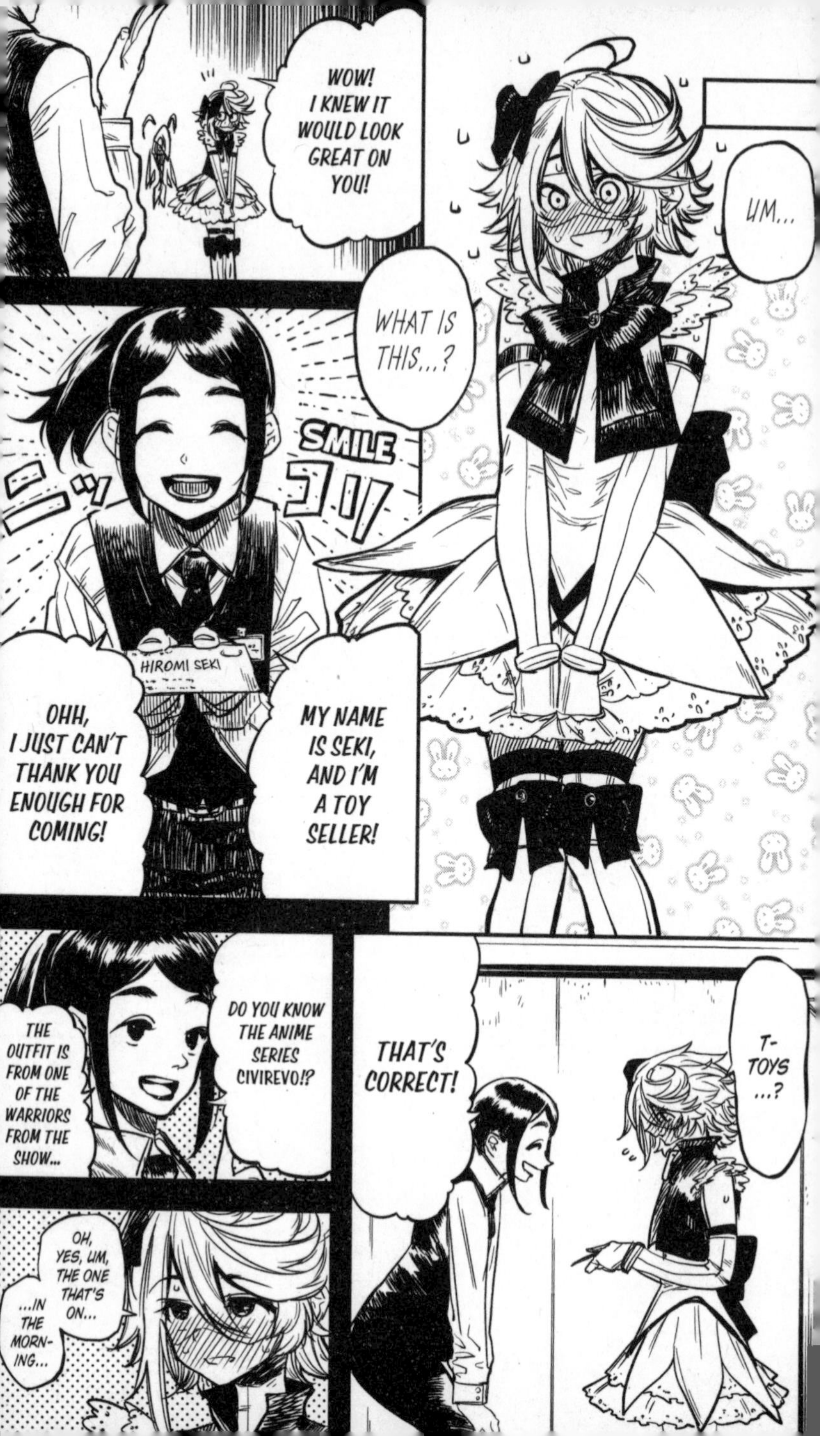
UM...
WHAT IS THIS...?
WOW! I KNEW IT WOULD LOOK GREAT ON YOU!
SMILE
HIROMI SEKI
MY NAME IS SEKI, AND I'M A TOY SELLER!
OHH, I JUST CAN'T THANK YOU ENOUGH FOR COMING!
T-TOYS ...?
THAT'S CORRECT!
DO YOU KNOW THE ANIME SERIES CIVIREVO!?
THE OUTFIT IS FROM ONE OF THE WARRIORS FROM THE SHOW...
OH, YES, UM, THE ONE THAT'S ON...
...IN THE MORNING...

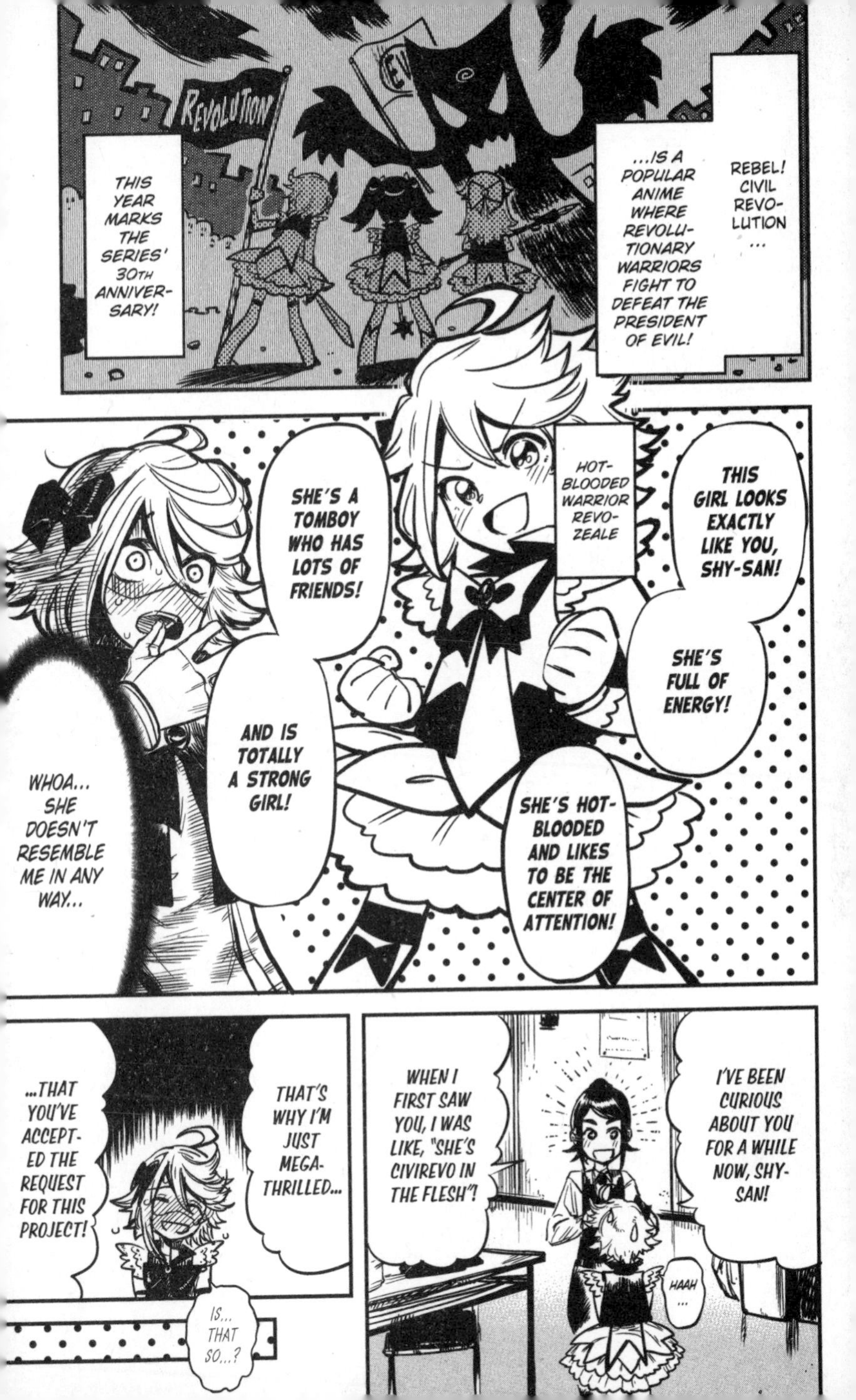
REBEL! CIVIL REVOLUTION ...
...IS A POPULAR ANIME WHERE REVOLUTIONARY WARRIORS FIGHT TO DEFEAT THE PRESIDENT OF EVIL!
REVOLUTION
THIS YEAR MARKS THE SERIES' 30TH ANNIVERSARY!
THIS GIRL LOOKS EXACTLY LIKE YOU, SHY-SAN!
HOT-BLOODED WARRIOR REVO-ZEALE
SHE'S FULL OF ENERGY!
SHE'S A TOMBOY WHO HAS LOTS OF FRIENDS!
SHE'S HOT-BLOODED AND LIKES TO BE THE CENTER OF ATTENTION!
AND IS TOTALLY A STRONG GIRL!
WHOA... SHE DOESN'T RESEMBLE ME IN ANY WAY...
I'VE BEEN CURIOUS ABOUT YOU FOR A WHILE NOW, SHY-SAN!
WHEN I FIRST SAW YOU, I WAS LIKE, "SHE'S CIVIREVO IN THE FLESH"!
HAAH ...
THAT'S WHY I'M JUST MEGA-THRILLED...
...THAT YOU'VE ACCEPTED THE REQUEST FOR THIS PROJECT!
IS... THAT SO...?

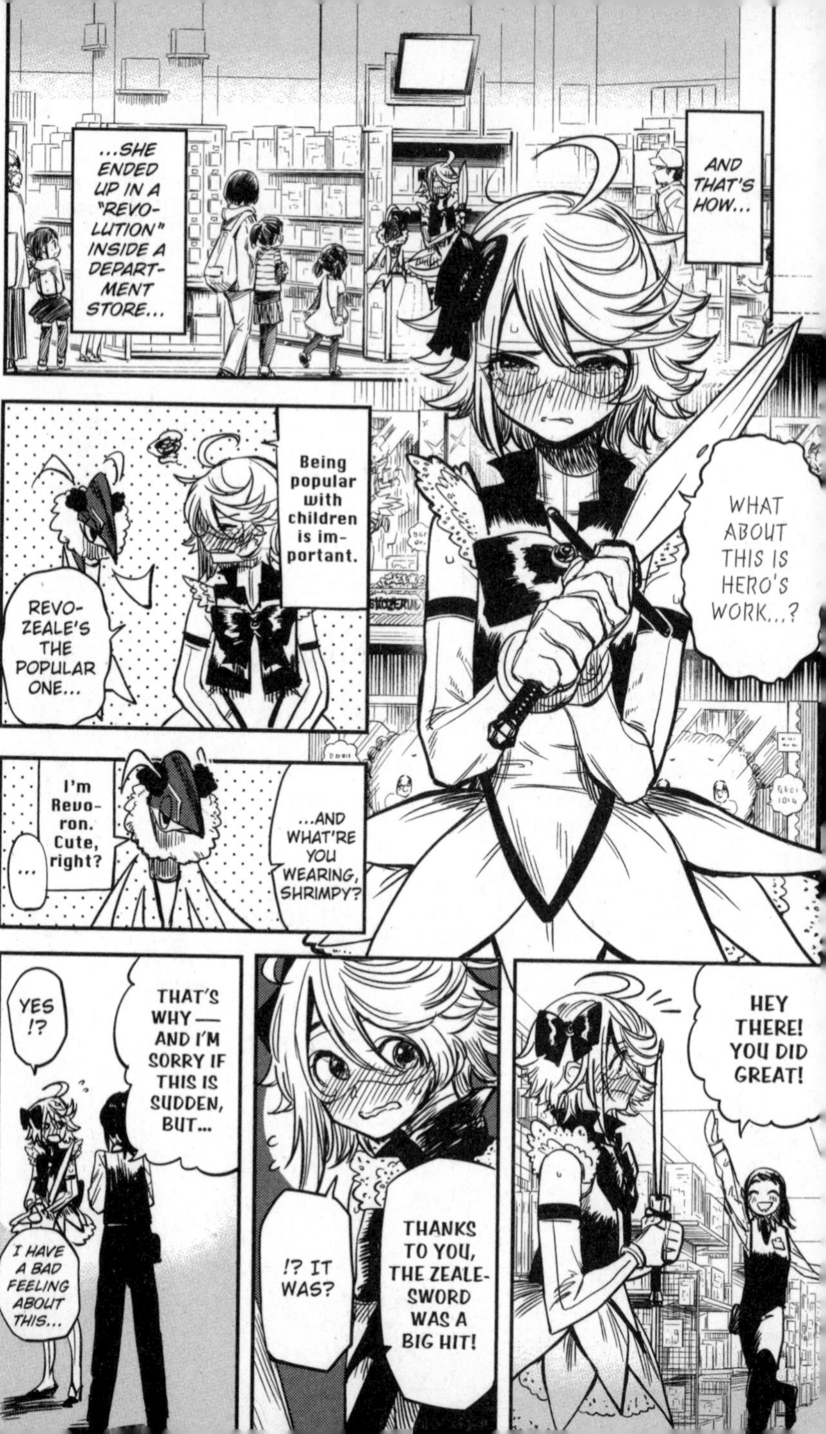
AND THAT'S HOW...
...SHE ENDED UP IN A "REVOLUTION" INSIDE A DEPARTMENT STORE...
WHAT ABOUT THIS IS HERO'S WORK...?
Being popular with children is important.
REVO-ZEALE'S THE POPULAR ONE...
...AND WHAT'RE YOU WEARING, SHRIMPY?
I'm Revoron. Cute, right?
...
HEY THERE! YOU DID GREAT!
THANKS TO YOU, THE ZEALE-SWORD WAS A BIG HIT!
!? IT WAS?
THAT'S WHY— AND I'M SORRY IF THIS IS SUDDEN, BUT...
YES !?
I HAVE A BAD FEELING ABOUT THIS...

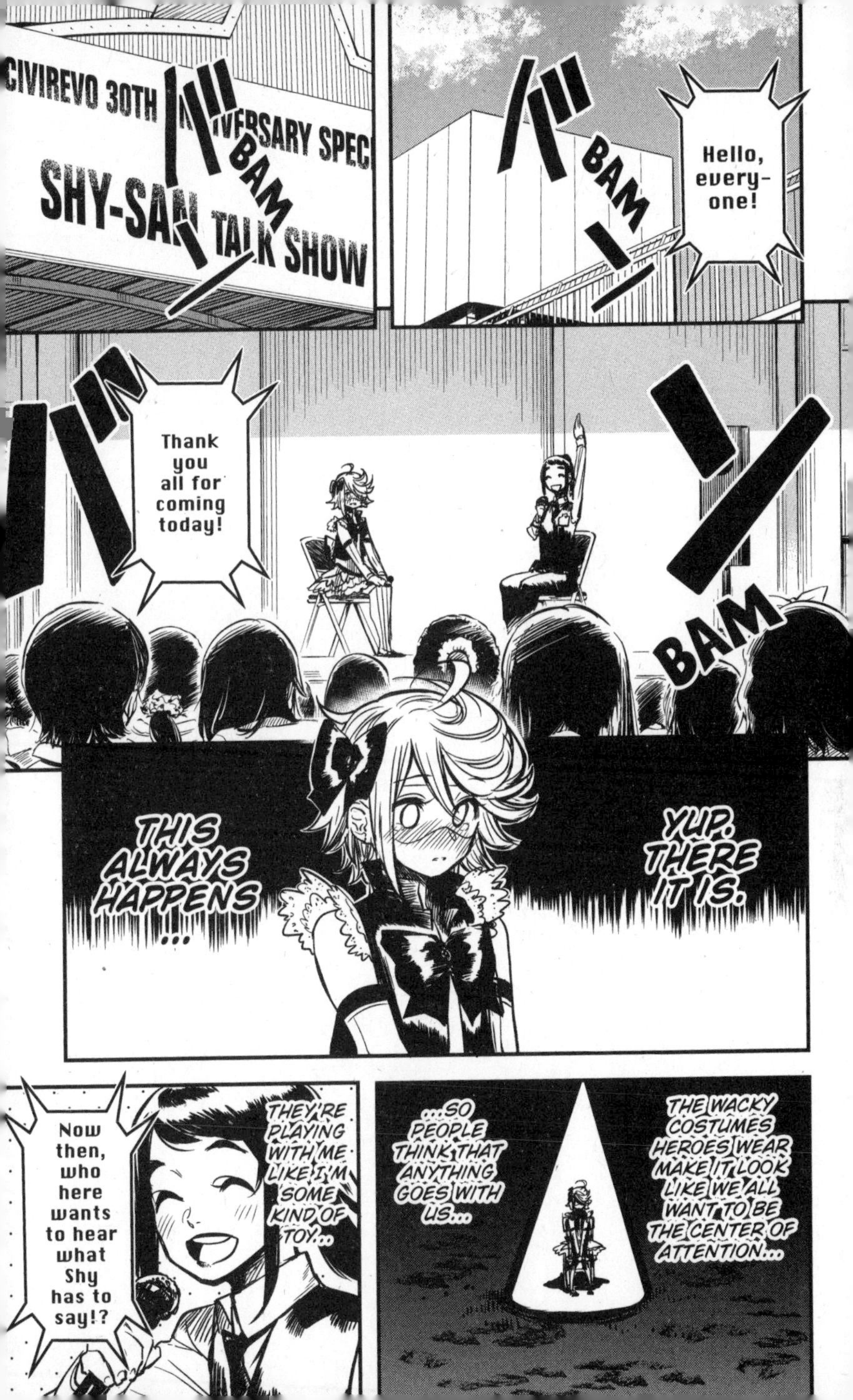
BAM
Hello, everyone!
CIVIREVO 30TH
VERSARY SPEC
SHY-SAN
TA K SHOW
BAM
Thank you all for coming today!
BAM
YUP. THERE IT IS.
THIS ALWAYS HAPPENS...
THE WACKY COSTUMES HEROES WEAR MAKE IT LOOK LIKE WE ALL WANT TO BE THE CENTER OF ATTENTION...
...SO PEOPLE THINK THAT ANYTHING GOES WITH US...
THEY'RE PLAYING WITH ME LIKE I'M SOME KIND OF TOY...
Now then, who here wants to hear what Shy has to say!?

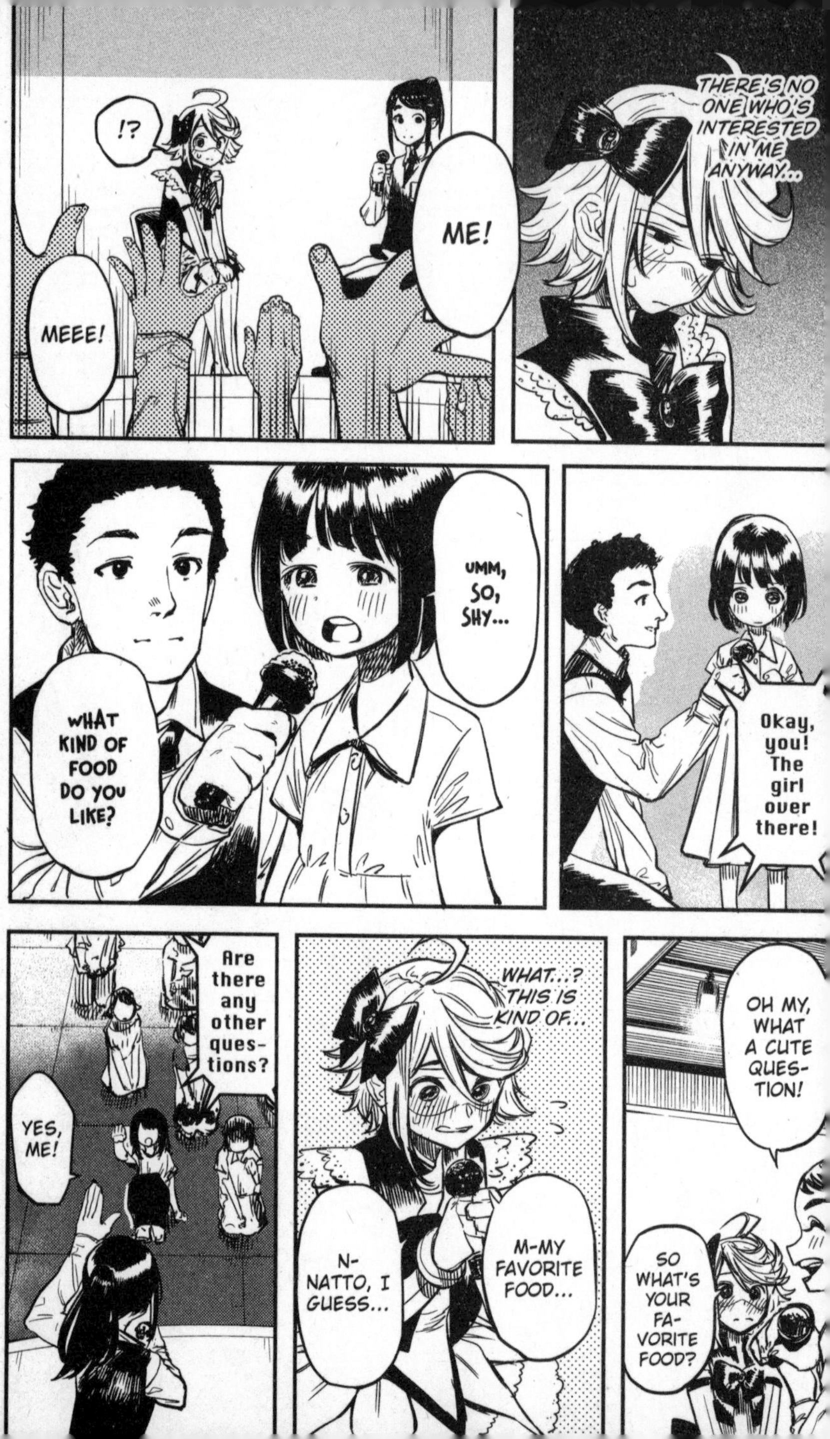
THERE'S NO ONE WHO'S INTERESTED IN ME ANYWAY...
ME!
!?
MEEE!
Okay, you! The girl over there!
UMM, SO, SHY...
WHAT KIND OF FOOD DO YOU LIKE?
OH MY, WHAT A CUTE QUES-TION!
SO WHAT'S YOUR FA-VORITE FOOD?
WHAT...? THIS IS KIND OF...
M-MY FAVORITE FOOD...
N-NATTO, I GUESS...
Are there any other ques-tions?
YES, ME!

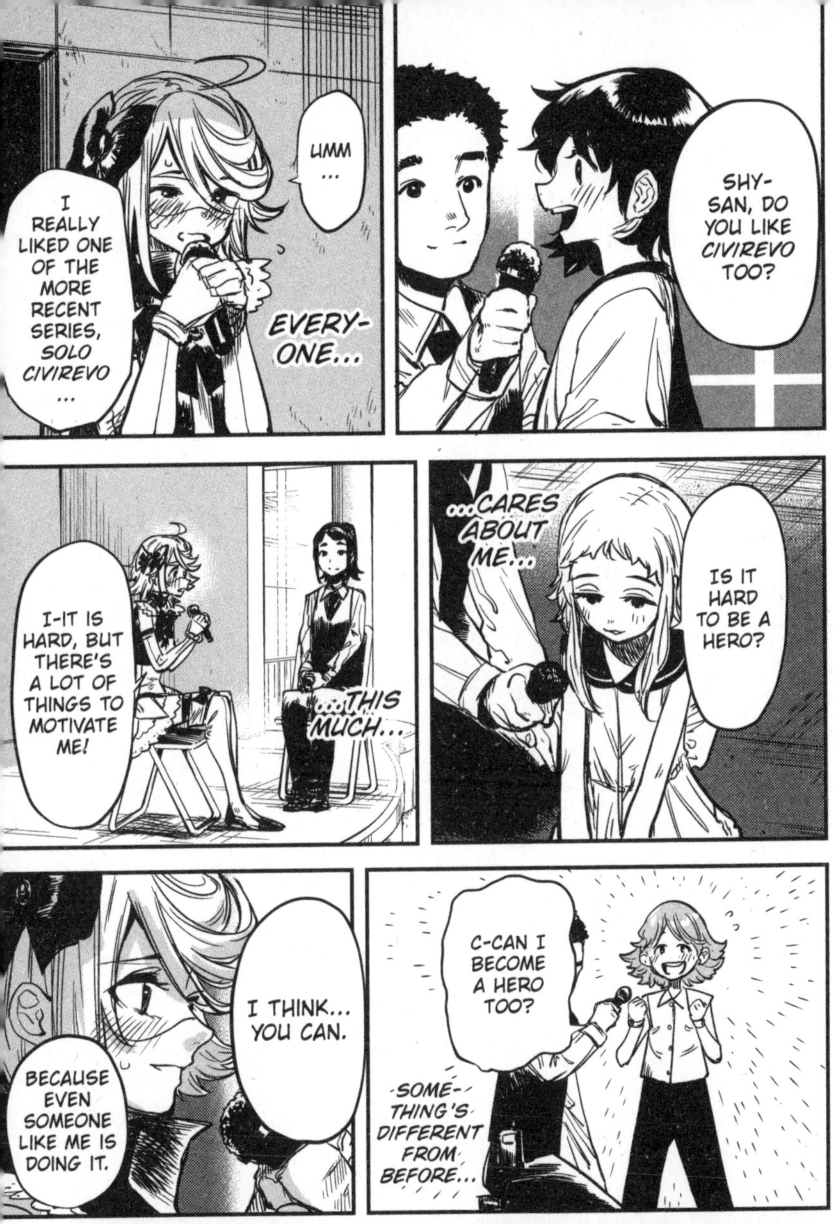
SHY-SAN, DO YOU LIKE CIVIREVO TOO?
UMM ...
I REALLY LIKED ONE OF THE MORE RECENT SERIES, SOLO CIVIREVO ...
EVERY-ONE...
...CARES ABOUT ME...
IS IT HARD TO BE A HERO?
I-IT IS HARD, BUT THERE'S A LOT OF THINGS TO MOTIVATE ME!
...THIS MUCH...
C-CAN I BECOME A HERO TOO?
SOME-THING'S DIFFERENT FROM BEFORE...
I THINK... YOU CAN.
BECAUSE EVEN SOMEONE LIKE ME IS DOING IT.

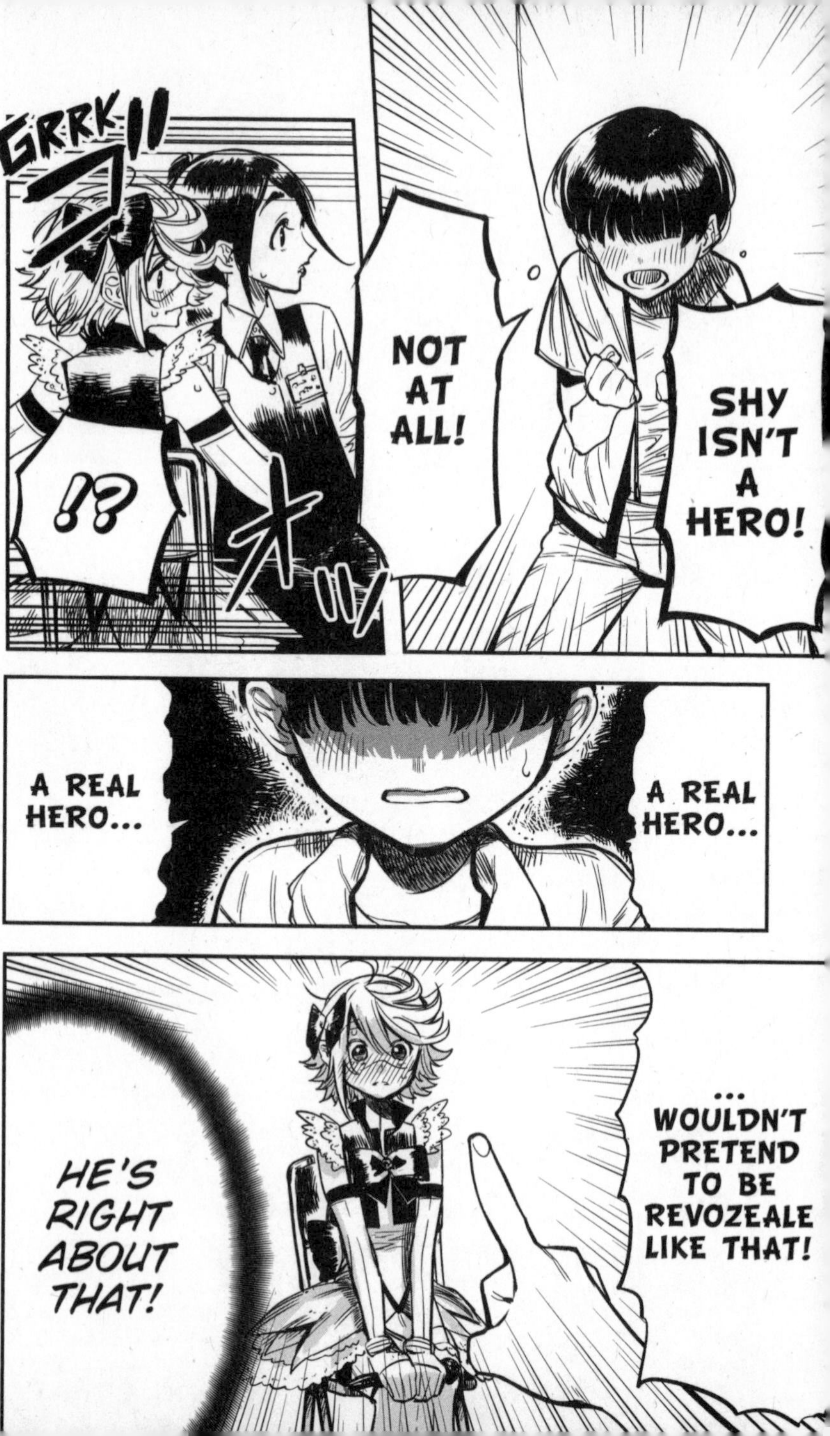
SHY ISN'T A HERO!
NOT AT ALL!
GRRK!!
!?
A REAL HERO...
A REAL HERO...
...WOULDN'T PRETEND TO BE REVOZEALE LIKE THAT!
HE'S RIGHT ABOUT THAT!

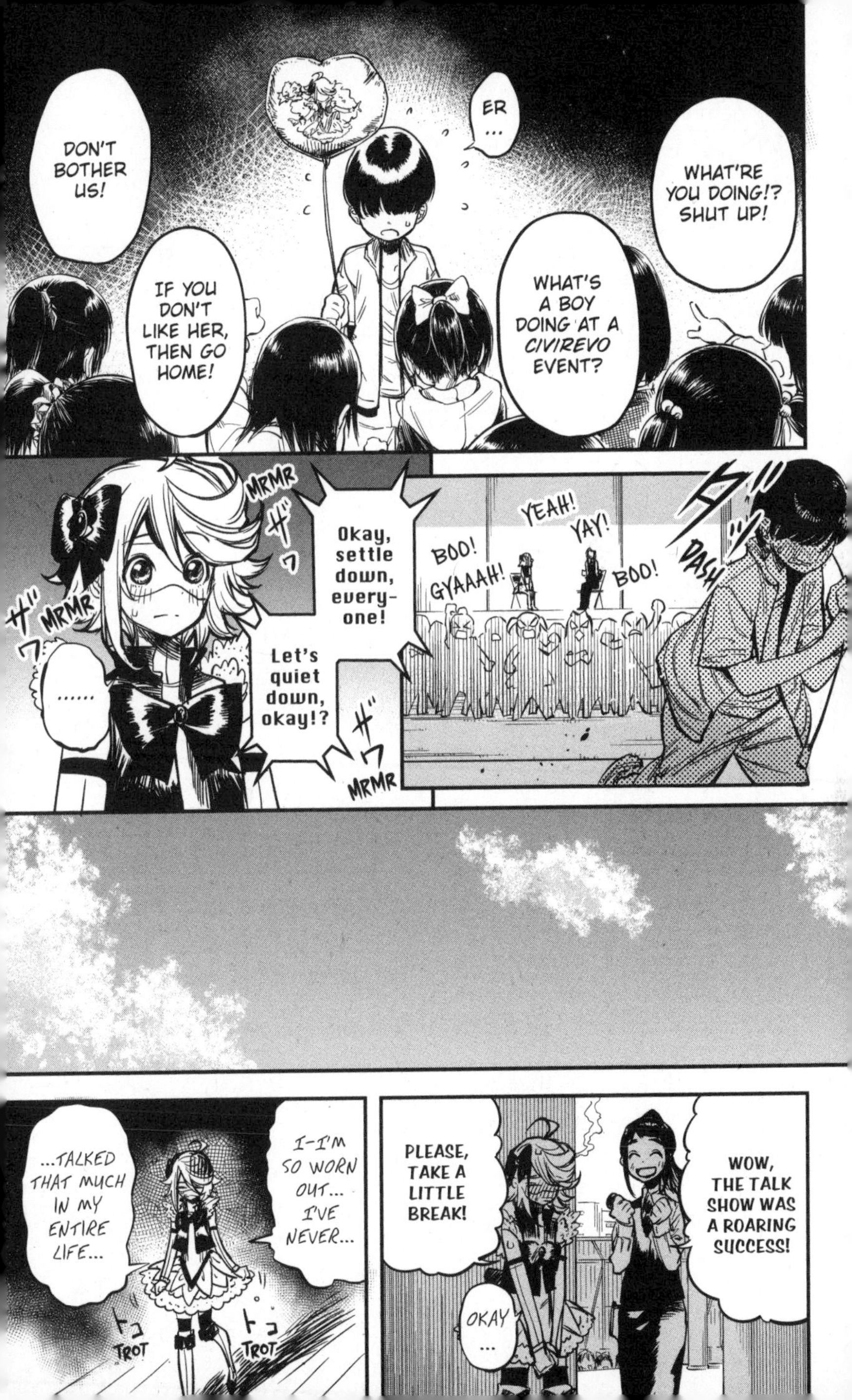
WHAT'RE YOU DOING!? SHUT UP!
ER ...
DON'T BOTHER US!
WHAT'S A BOY DOING AT A CIVIREVO EVENT?
IF YOU DON'T LIKE HER, THEN GO HOME!
DASH
YEAH!
YAY!
BOO!
BOO!
GYAAAH!
MRMR
Okay, settle down, every-one!
Let's quiet down, okay!?
MRMR
......
MRMR
WOW, THE TALK SHOW WAS A ROARING SUCCESS!
PLEASE, TAKE A LITTLE BREAK!
OKAY ...
I-I'M SO WORN OUT... I'VE NEVER...
...TALKED THAT MUCH IN MY ENTIRE LIFE...
TROT
TROT

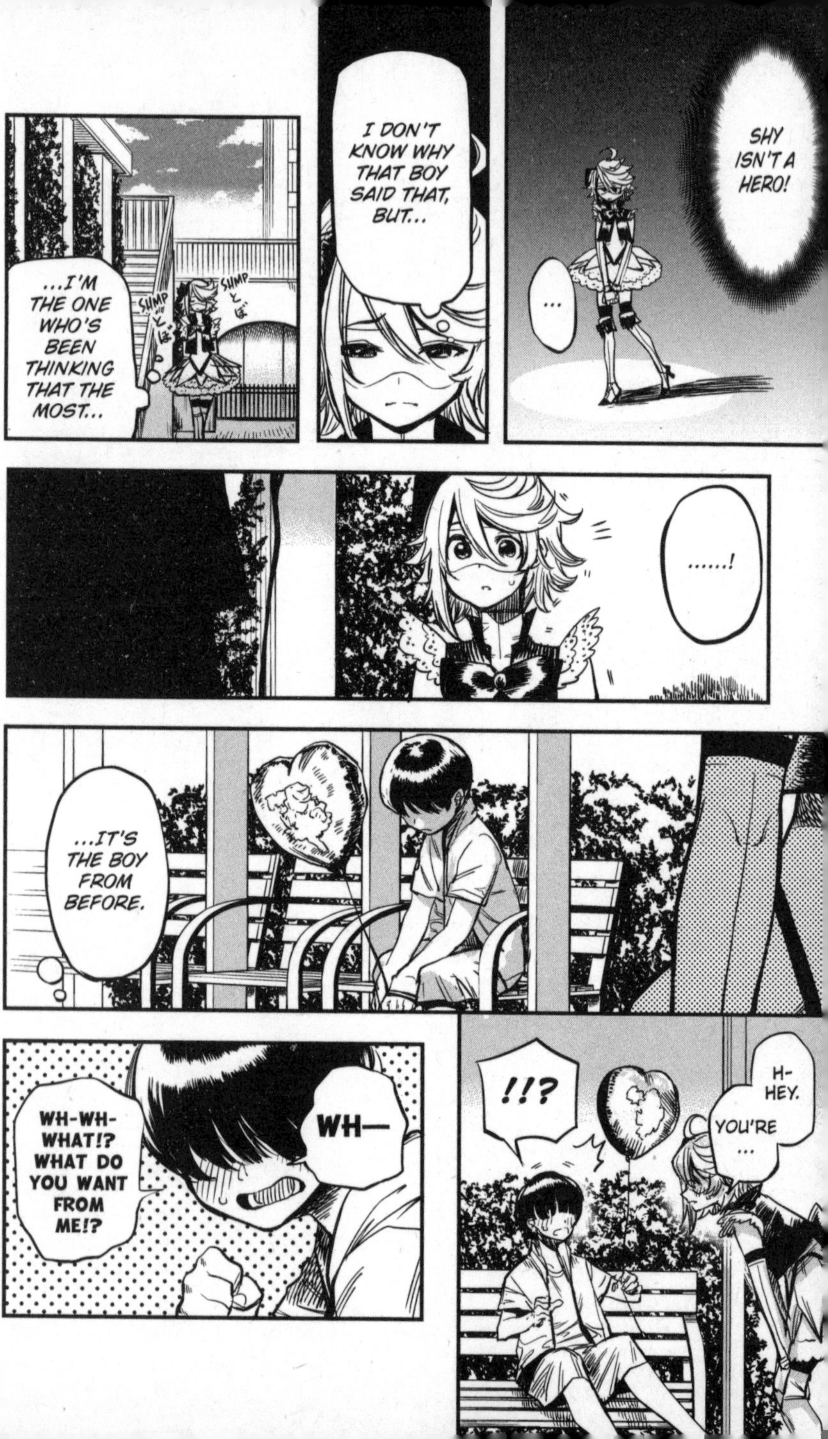
SHY ISN'T A HERO!
...
I DON'T KNOW WHY THAT BOY SAID THAT, BUT...
SHMP とぼ
SHMP とぼ
...I'M THE ONE WHO'S BEEN THINKING THAT THE MOST...
......!
...IT'S THE BOY FROM BEFORE.
H- HEY.
YOU'RE ...
!!?
WH—
WH-WH-WHAT!? WHAT DO YOU WANT FROM ME!?

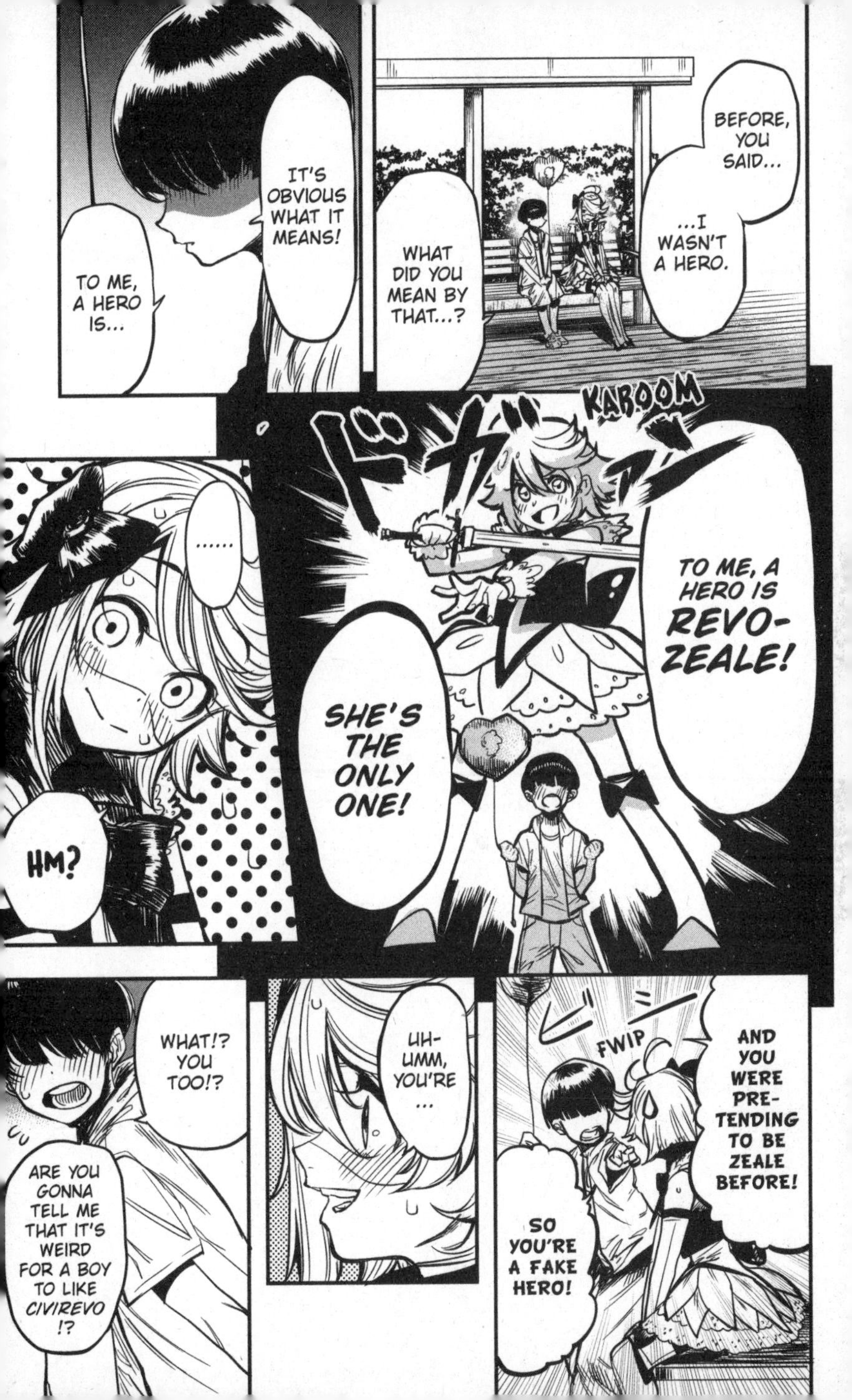
BEFORE, YOU SAID...
...I WASN'T A HERO.
WHAT DID YOU MEAN BY THAT...?
IT'S OBVIOUS WHAT IT MEANS!
TO ME, A HERO IS...
KABOOM
TO ME, A HERO IS REVO-ZEALE!
SHE'S THE ONLY ONE!
......
HM?
FWIP
AND YOU WERE PRE-TENDING TO BE ZEALE BEFORE!
SO YOU'RE A FAKE HERO!
UH-UMM, YOU'RE ...
WHAT!? YOU TOO!?
ARE YOU GONNA TELL ME THAT IT'S WEIRD FOR A BOY TO LIKE CIVIREVO!?

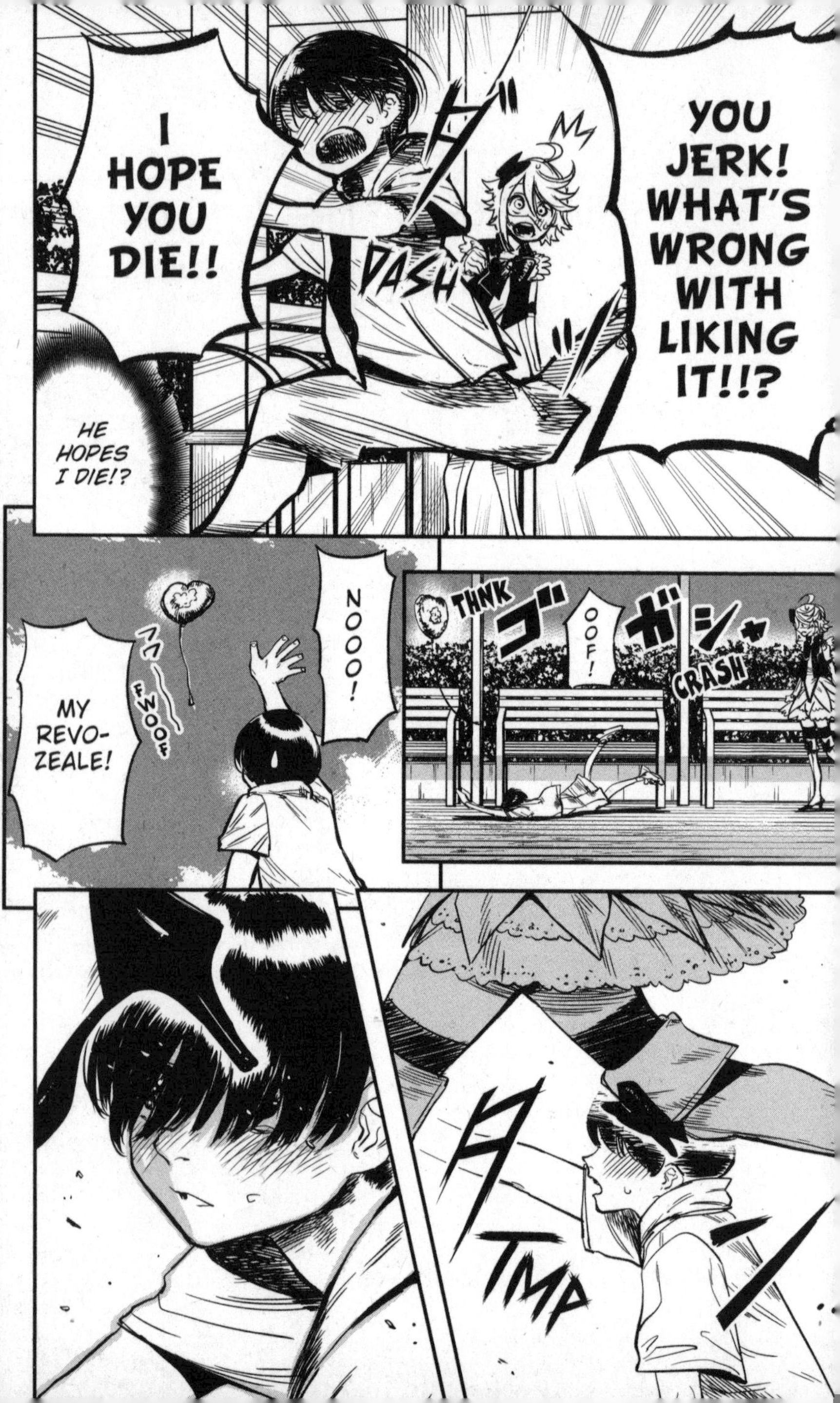
YOU JERK! WHAT'S WRONG WITH LIKING IT!!?
DASH
I HOPE YOU DIE!!
HE HOPES I DIE!?
THNK
OOF!
CRASH
NOOOO!
FWOOF
MY REVO-ZEALE!
TMP

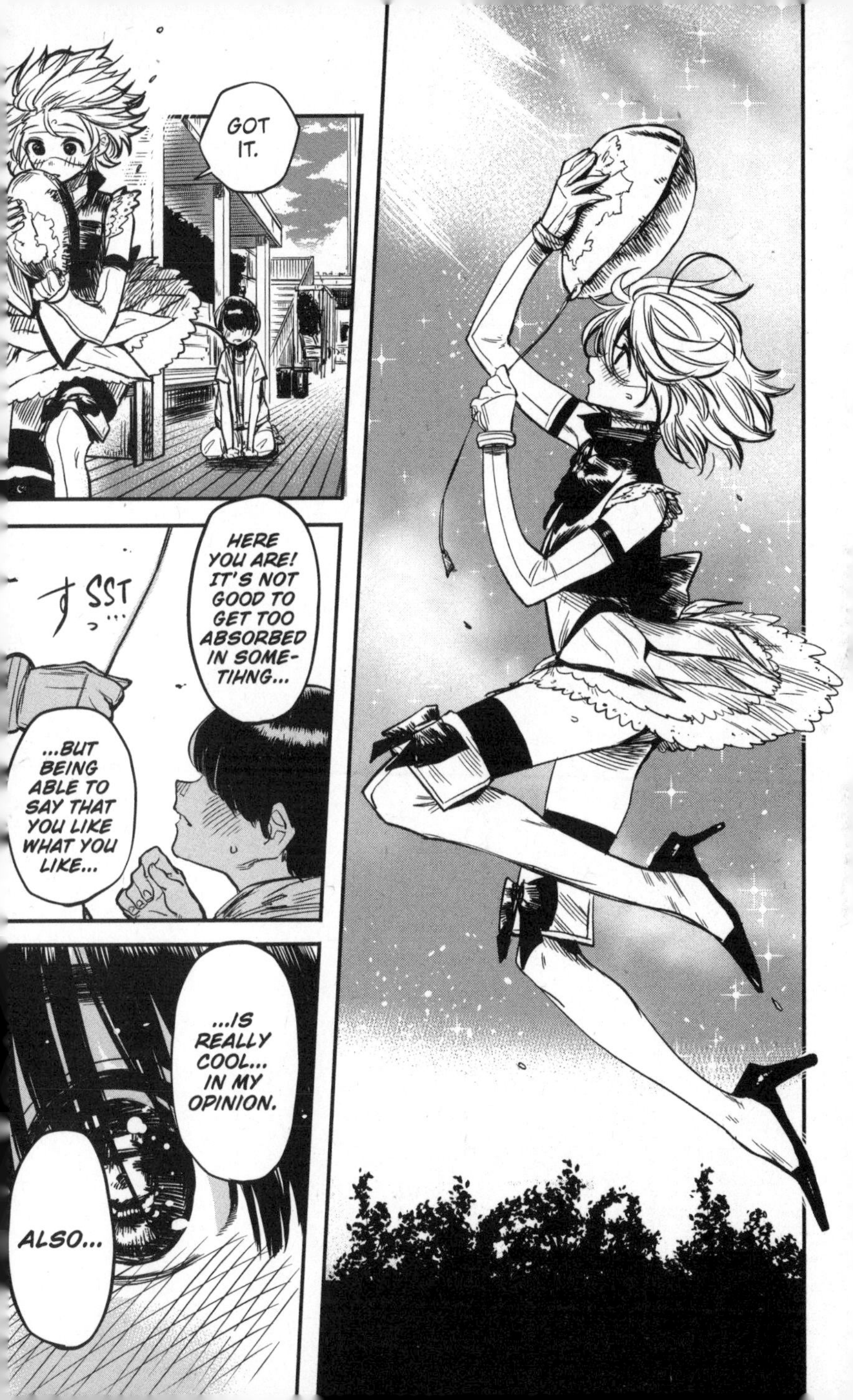
GOT IT.
すっ… SST
HERE YOU ARE! IT'S NOT GOOD TO GET TOO ABSORBED IN SOMETIHNG...
...BUT BEING ABLE TO SAY THAT YOU LIKE WHAT YOU LIKE...
...IS REALLY COOL... IN MY OPINION.
ALSO...

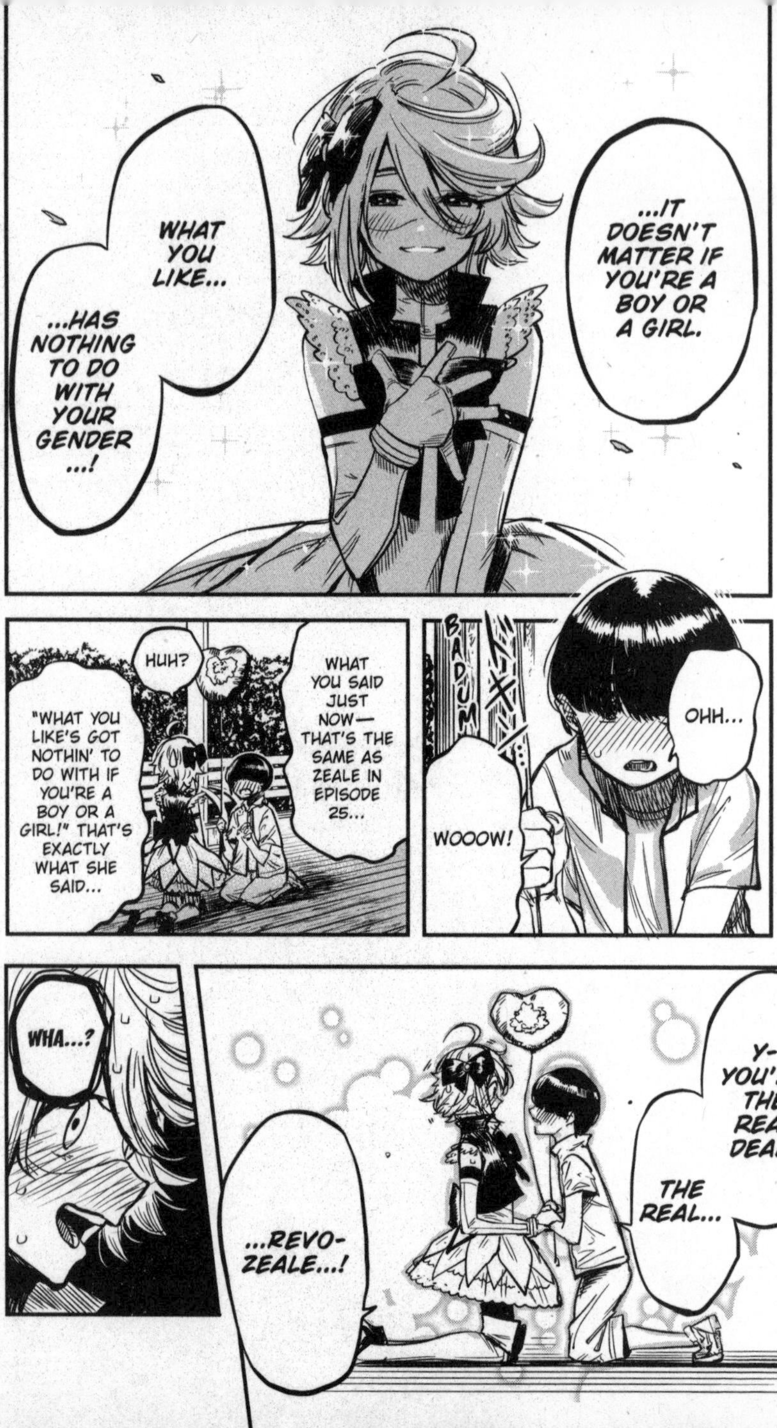
...IT DOESN'T MATTER IF YOU'RE A BOY OR A GIRL.
WHAT YOU LIKE...
...HAS NOTHING TO DO WITH YOUR GENDER ...!
BADUM
OHH...
WOOOW!
WHAT YOU SAID JUST NOW—THAT'S THE SAME AS ZEALE IN EPISODE 25...
HUH?
"WHAT YOU LIKE'S GOT NOTHIN' TO DO WITH IF YOU'RE A BOY OR A GIRL!" THAT'S EXACTLY WHAT SHE SAID...
Y-YOU'RE THE REAL DEAL!
THE REAL...
...REVO-ZEALE...!
WHA...?

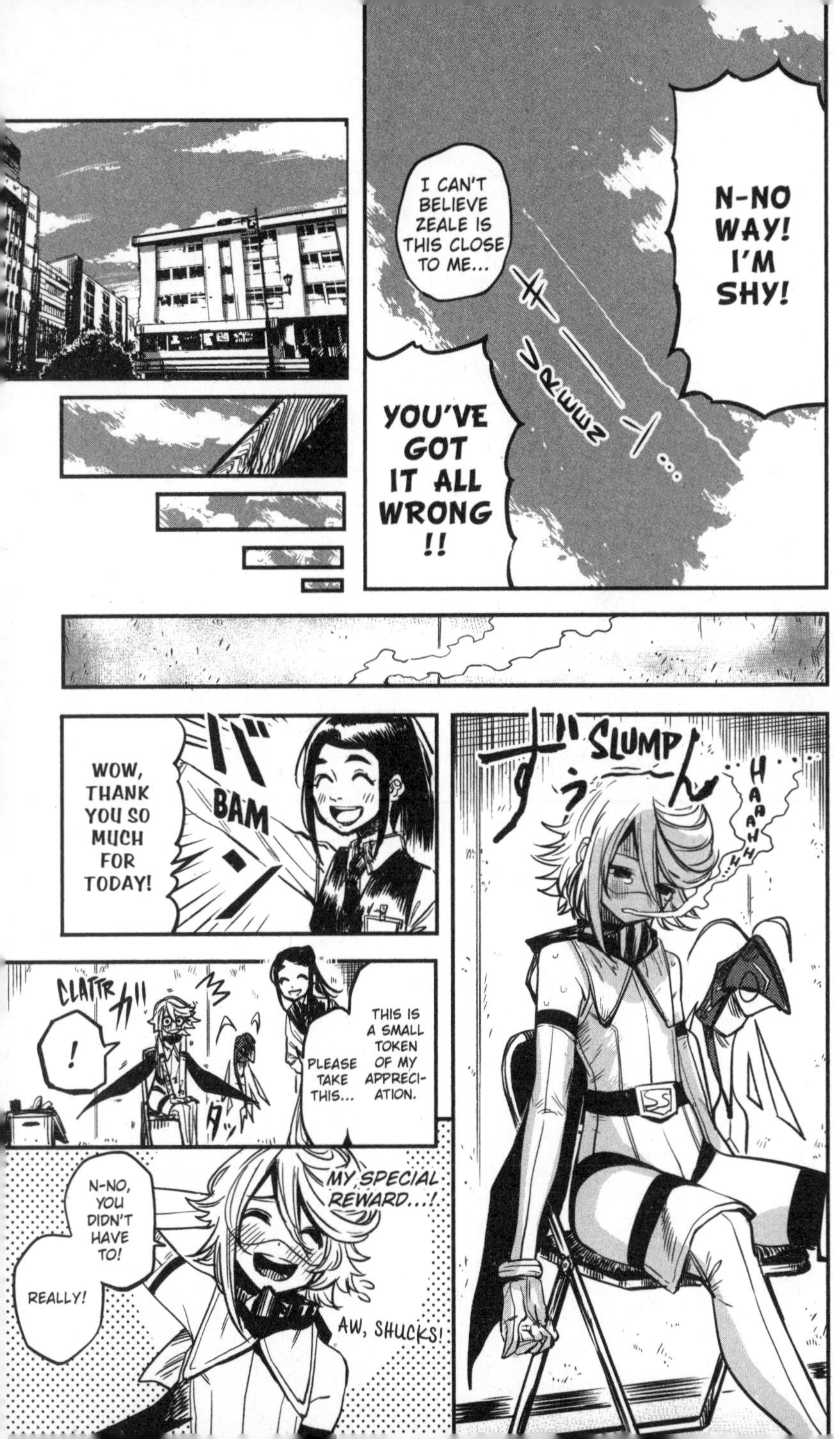
N-NO WAY! I'M SHY!
I CAN'T BELIEVE ZEALE IS THIS CLOSE TO ME...
YOU'VE GOT IT ALL WRONG!!
SLUMP
HAAAHH...
WOW, THANK YOU SO MUCH FOR TODAY!
BAM
THIS IS A SMALL TOKEN OF MY APPRECIATION.
PLEASE TAKE THIS...
CLATTR
!
MY SPECIAL REWARD...!
N-NO, YOU DIDN'T HAVE TO!
REALLY!
AW, SHUCKS!

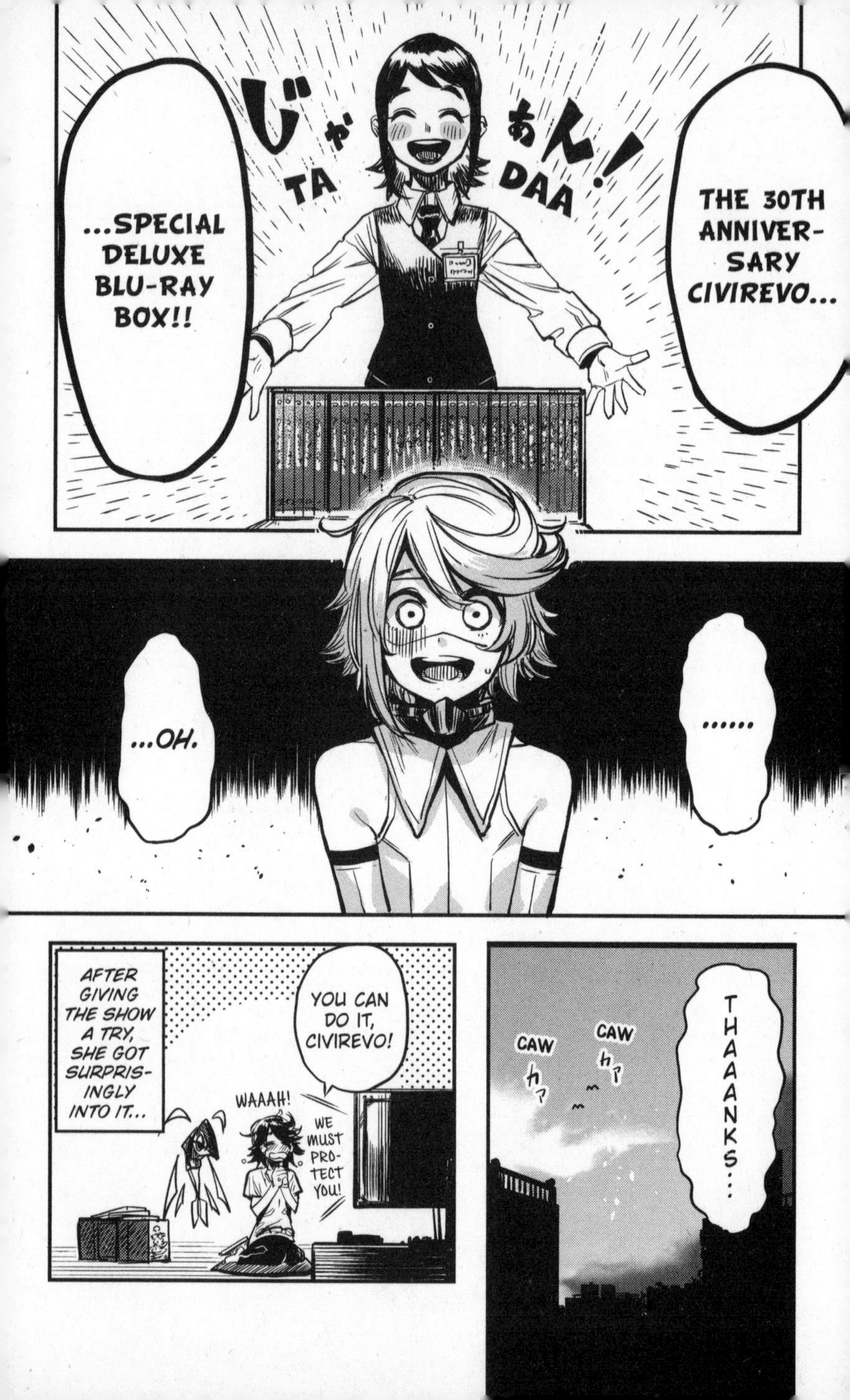
THE 30TH ANNIVER-SARY CIVIREVO...
じゃあん!
TA DAA
...SPECIAL DELUXE BLU-RAY BOX!!
......
...OH.
THAAAANKS...
CAW カァ
CAW カァ
YOU CAN DO IT, CIVIREVO!
AFTER GIVING THE SHOW A TRY, SHE GOT SURPRIS-INGLY INTO IT...
WE MUST PRO-TECT YOU!
WAAAH!

SHY

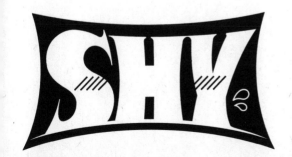

PEPESHA ANDREANOVA

Hero name: Spirit

NATIONALITY: RUSSIAN
AGE: 27
BIRTH DATE: NOVEMBER 30
BLOOD TYPE: O
HEIGHT: 174 CM
WEIGHT: 58 KG
LIKES: ALCOHOL, BREAD

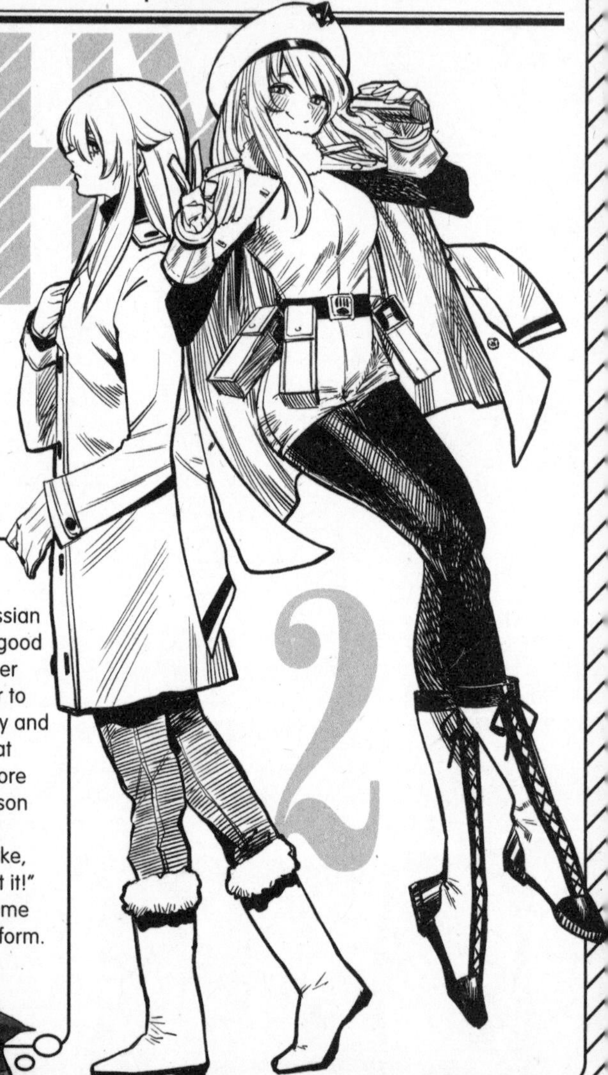

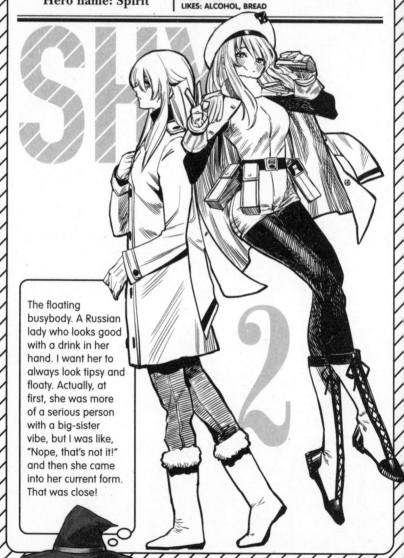

The floating busybody. A Russian lady who looks good with a drink in her hand. I want her to always look tipsy and floaty. Actually, at first, she was more of a serious person with a big-sister vibe, but I was like, "Nope, that's not it!" and then she came into her current form. That was close!

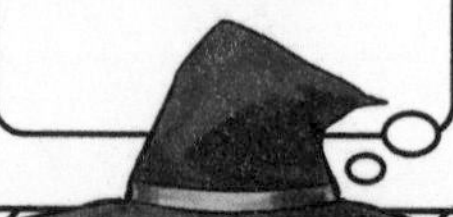

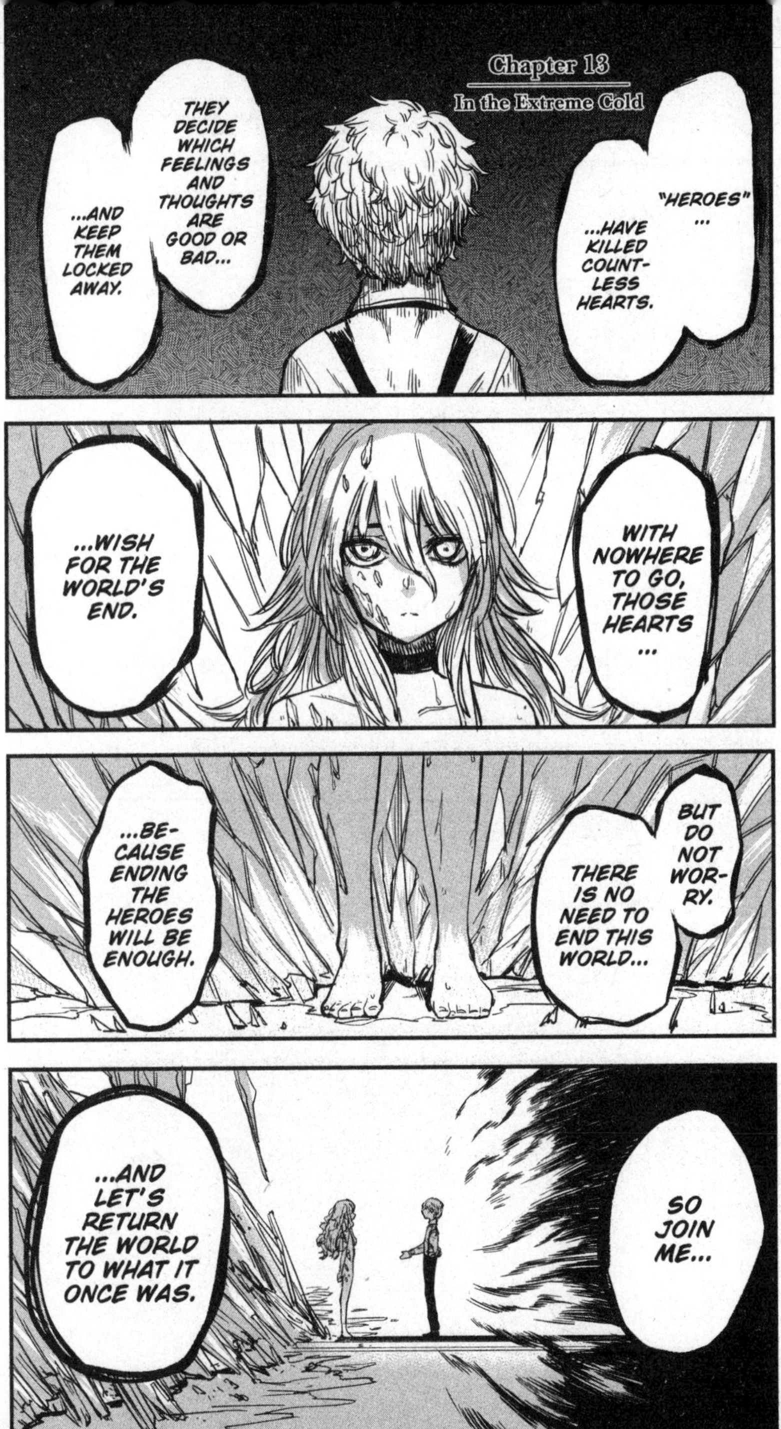
Chapter 13
In the Extreme Cold
"HEROES"...
...HAVE KILLED COUNT-LESS HEARTS.
THEY DECIDE WHICH FEELINGS AND THOUGHTS ARE GOOD OR BAD...
...AND KEEP THEM LOCKED AWAY.
WITH NOWHERE TO GO, THOSE HEARTS...
...WISH FOR THE WORLD'S END.
BUT DO NOT WOR-RY.
THERE IS NO NEED TO END THIS WORLD...
...BE-CAUSE ENDING THE HEROES WILL BE ENOUGH.
SO JOIN ME...
...AND LET'S RETURN THE WORLD TO WHAT IT ONCE WAS.

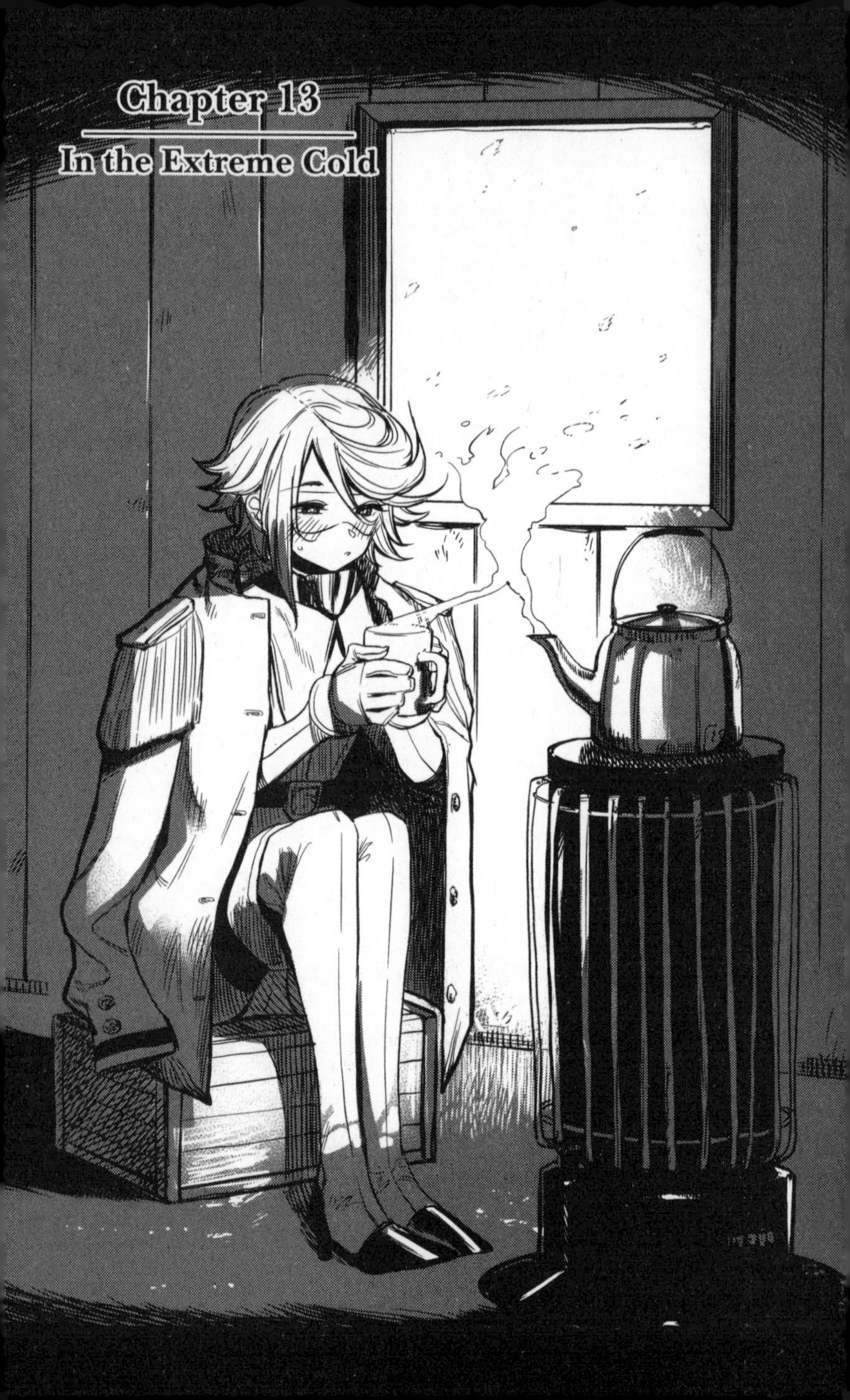
Chapter 13
In the Extreme Cold

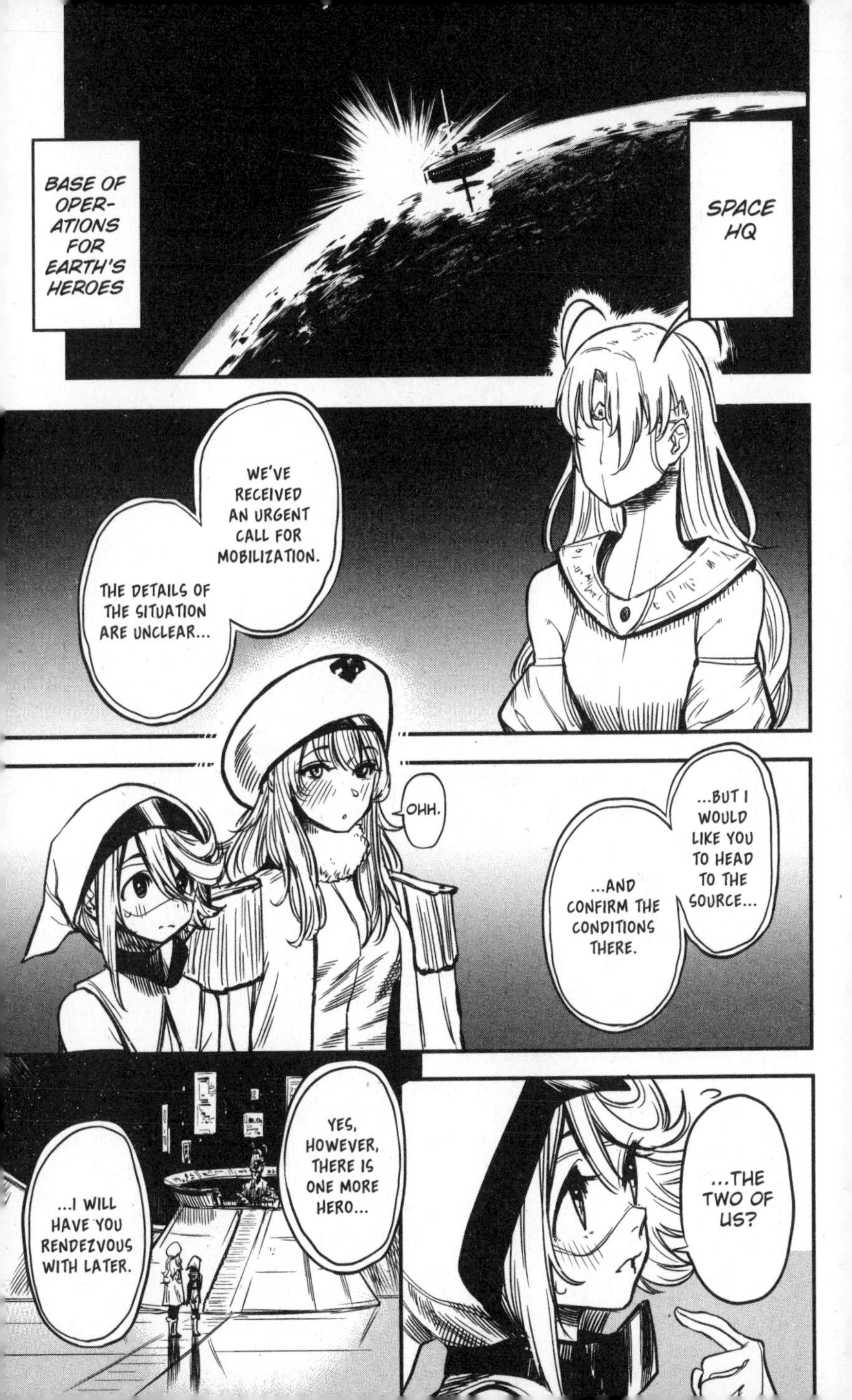
SPACE HQ
BASE OF OPER-ATIONS FOR EARTH'S HEROES
WE'VE RECEIVED AN URGENT CALL FOR MOBILIZATION.
THE DETAILS OF THE SITUATION ARE UNCLEAR...
...BUT I WOULD LIKE YOU TO HEAD TO THE SOURCE...
...AND CONFIRM THE CONDITIONS THERE.
OHH.
...THE TWO OF US?
YES, HOWEVER, THERE IS ONE MORE HERO...
...I WILL HAVE YOU RENDEZVOUS WITH LATER.

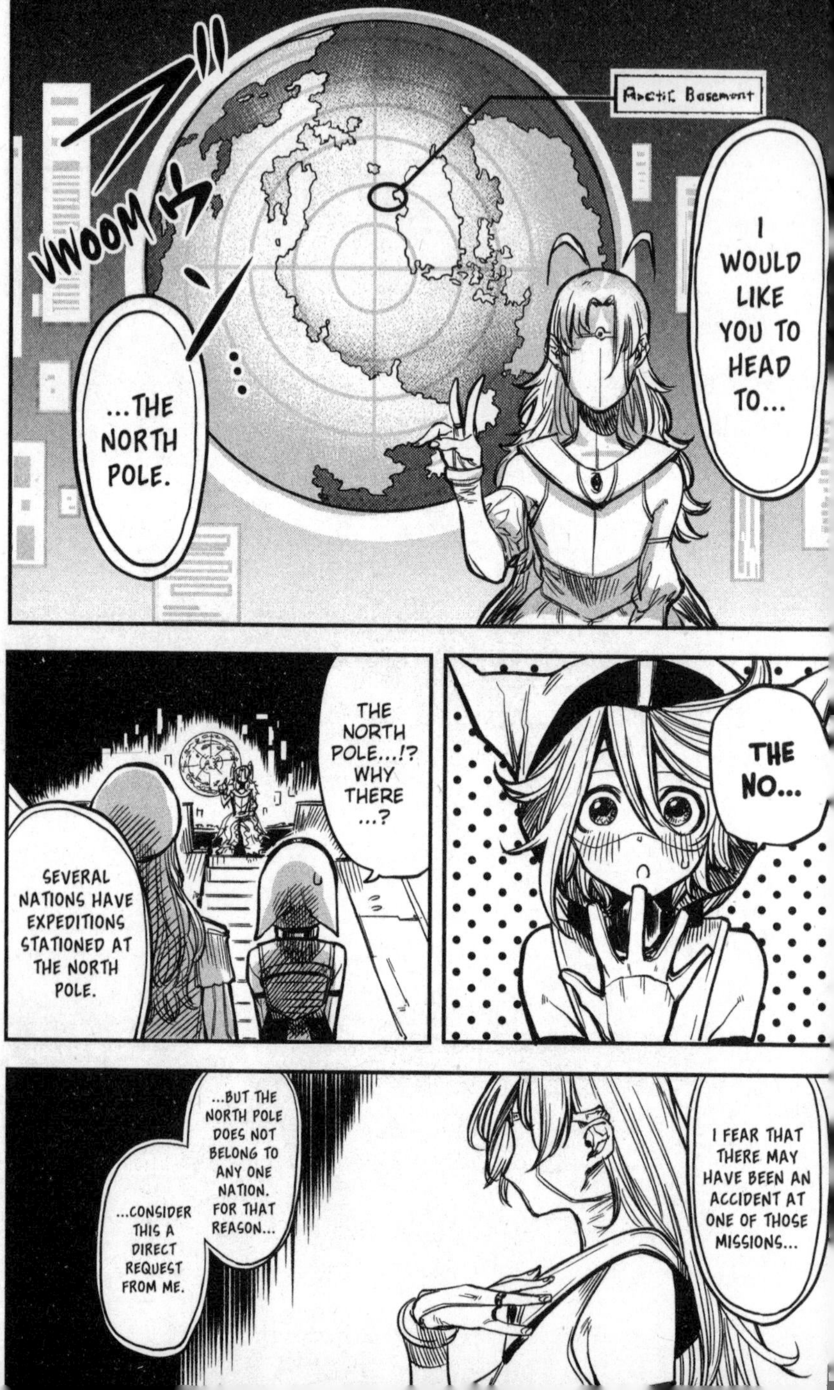
I WOULD LIKE YOU TO HEAD TO...
Arctic Basement
VWOOM
...THE NORTH POLE.
THE NO...
THE NORTH POLE...!? WHY THERE ...?
SEVERAL NATIONS HAVE EXPEDITIONS STATIONED AT THE NORTH POLE.
I FEAR THAT THERE MAY HAVE BEEN AN ACCIDENT AT ONE OF THOSE MISSIONS...
...BUT THE NORTH POLE DOES NOT BELONG TO ANY ONE NATION. FOR THAT REASON...
...CONSIDER THIS A DIRECT REQUEST FROM ME.

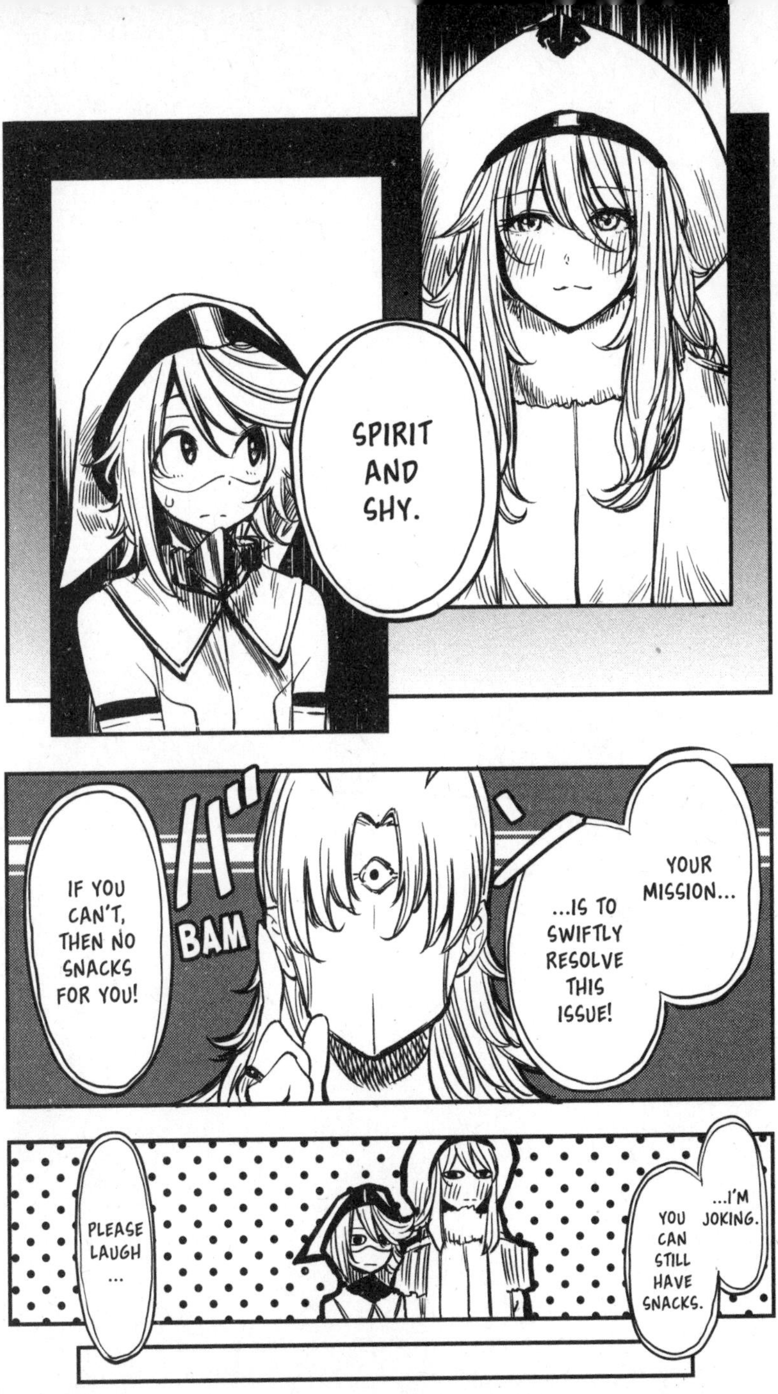
SPIRIT AND SHY.
YOUR MISSION...
...IS TO SWIFTLY RESOLVE THIS ISSUE!
BAM
IF YOU CAN'T, THEN NO SNACKS FOR YOU!
...I'M JOKING.
YOU CAN STILL HAVE SNACKS.
PLEASE LAUGH...

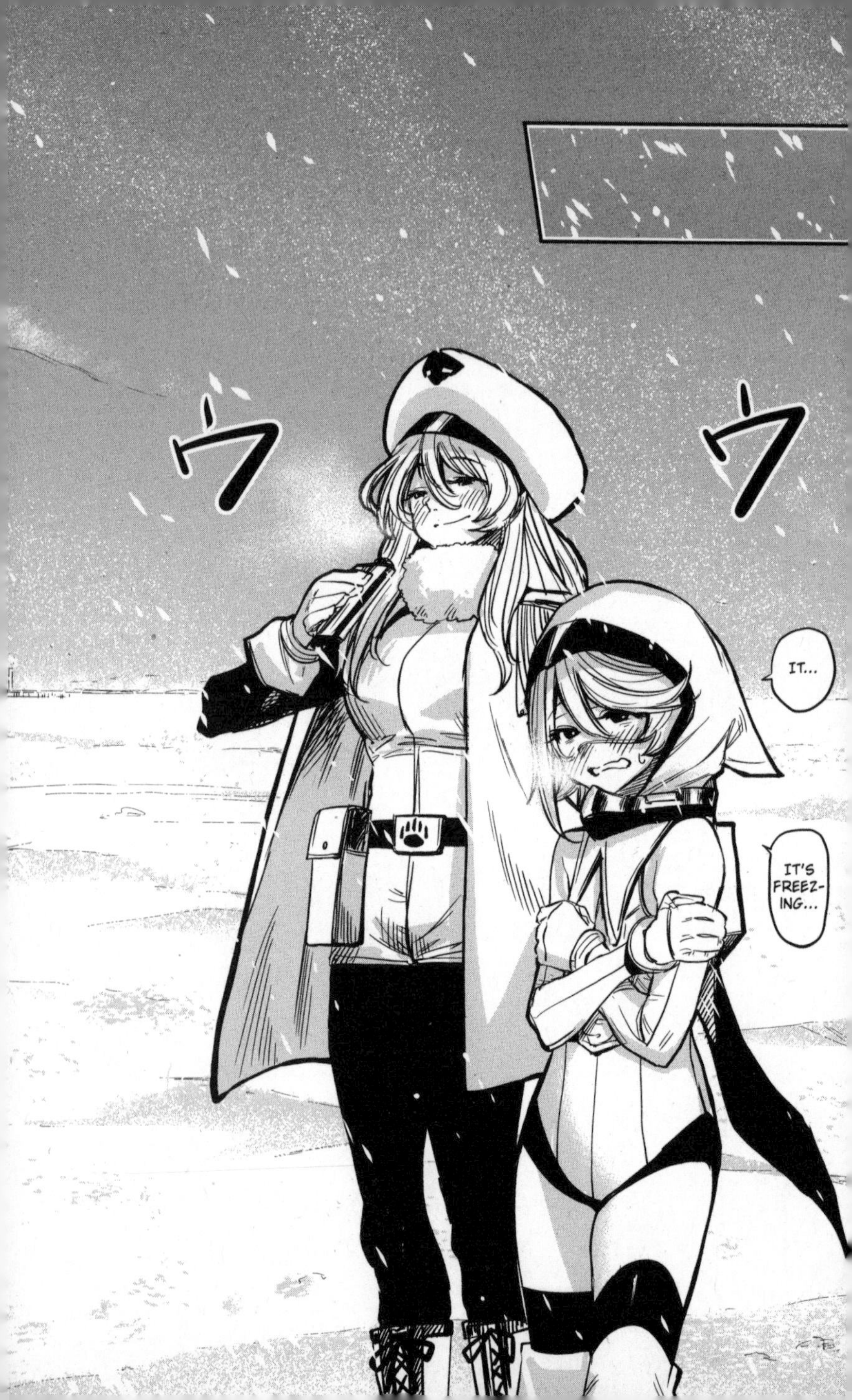
ウ
ウ
IT...
IT'S FREEZ-ING...

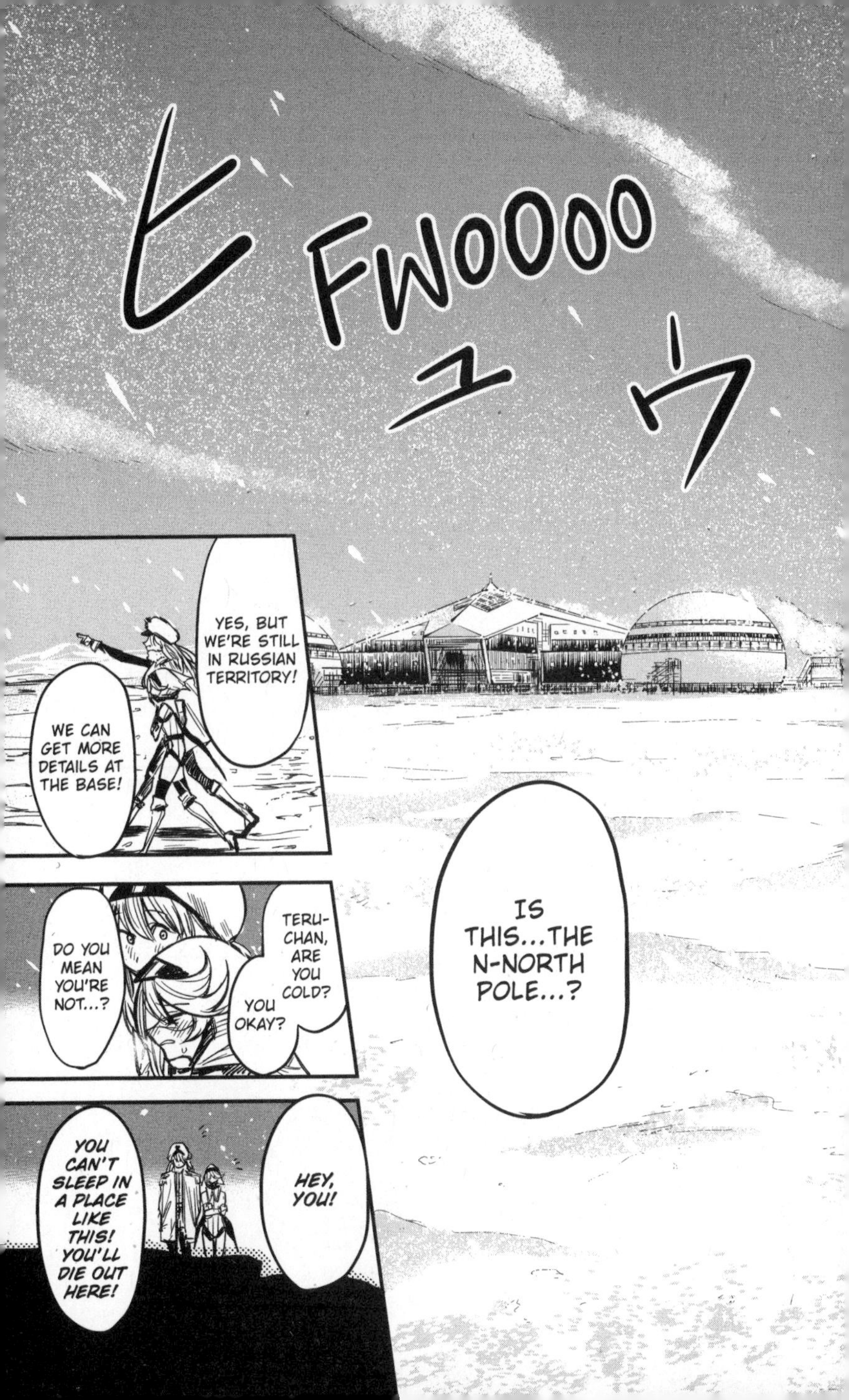
ヒュウ
FWOOOO
IS THIS...THE N-NORTH POLE...?
YES, BUT WE'RE STILL IN RUSSIAN TERRITORY!
WE CAN GET MORE DETAILS AT THE BASE!
TERU-CHAN, ARE YOU COLD?
YOU OKAY?
DO YOU MEAN YOU'RE NOT...?
HEY, YOU!
YOU CAN'T SLEEP IN A PLACE LIKE THIS! YOU'LL DIE OUT HERE!

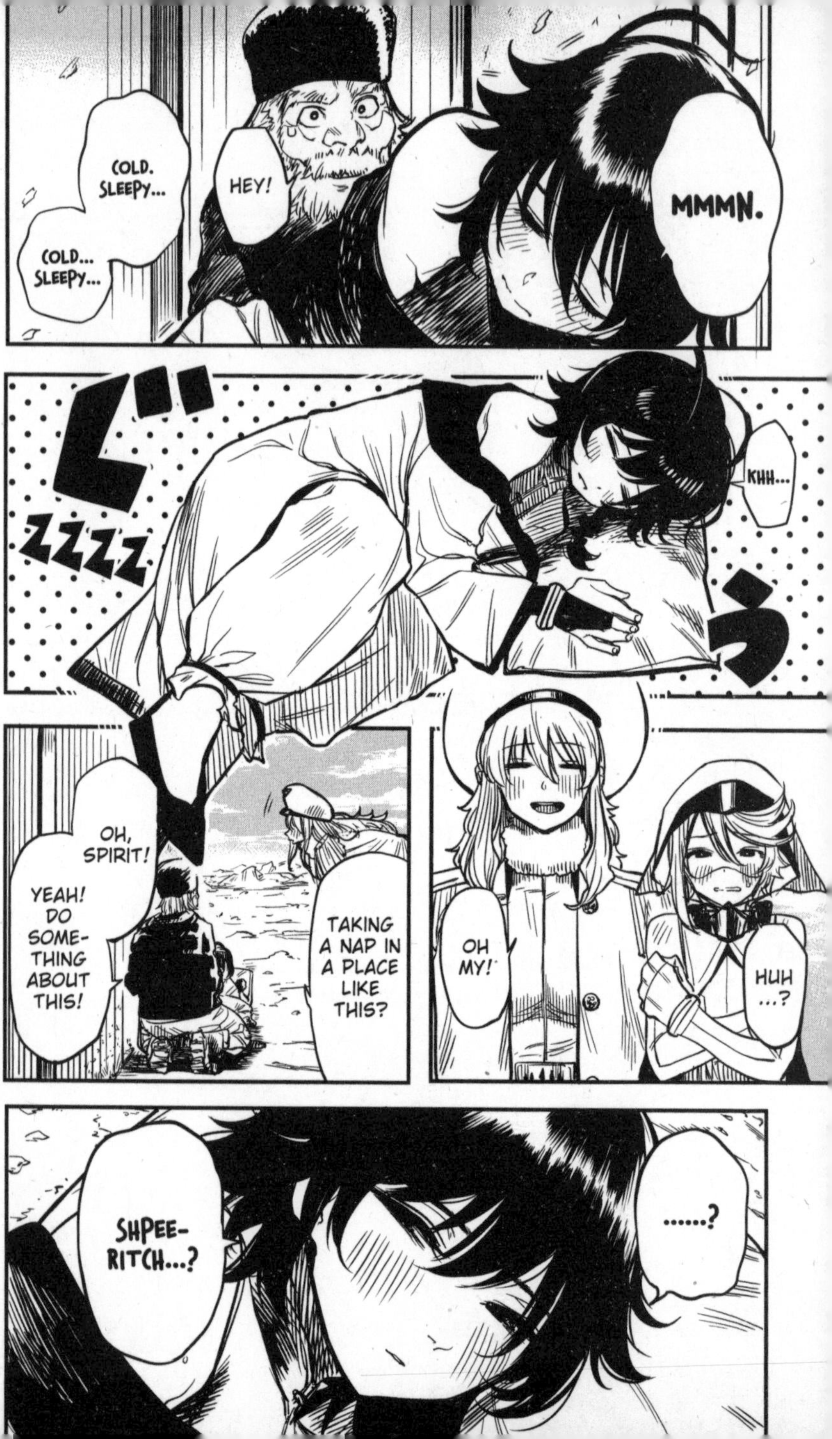
MMMN.
HEY!
COLD. SLEEPY...
COLD... SLEEPY...
KHH...
う
ぐ
ZZZZ
HUH ...?
OH MY!
TAKING A NAP IN A PLACE LIKE THIS?
OH, SPIRIT!
YEAH! DO SOME-THING ABOUT THIS!
......?
SHPEE-RITCH...?

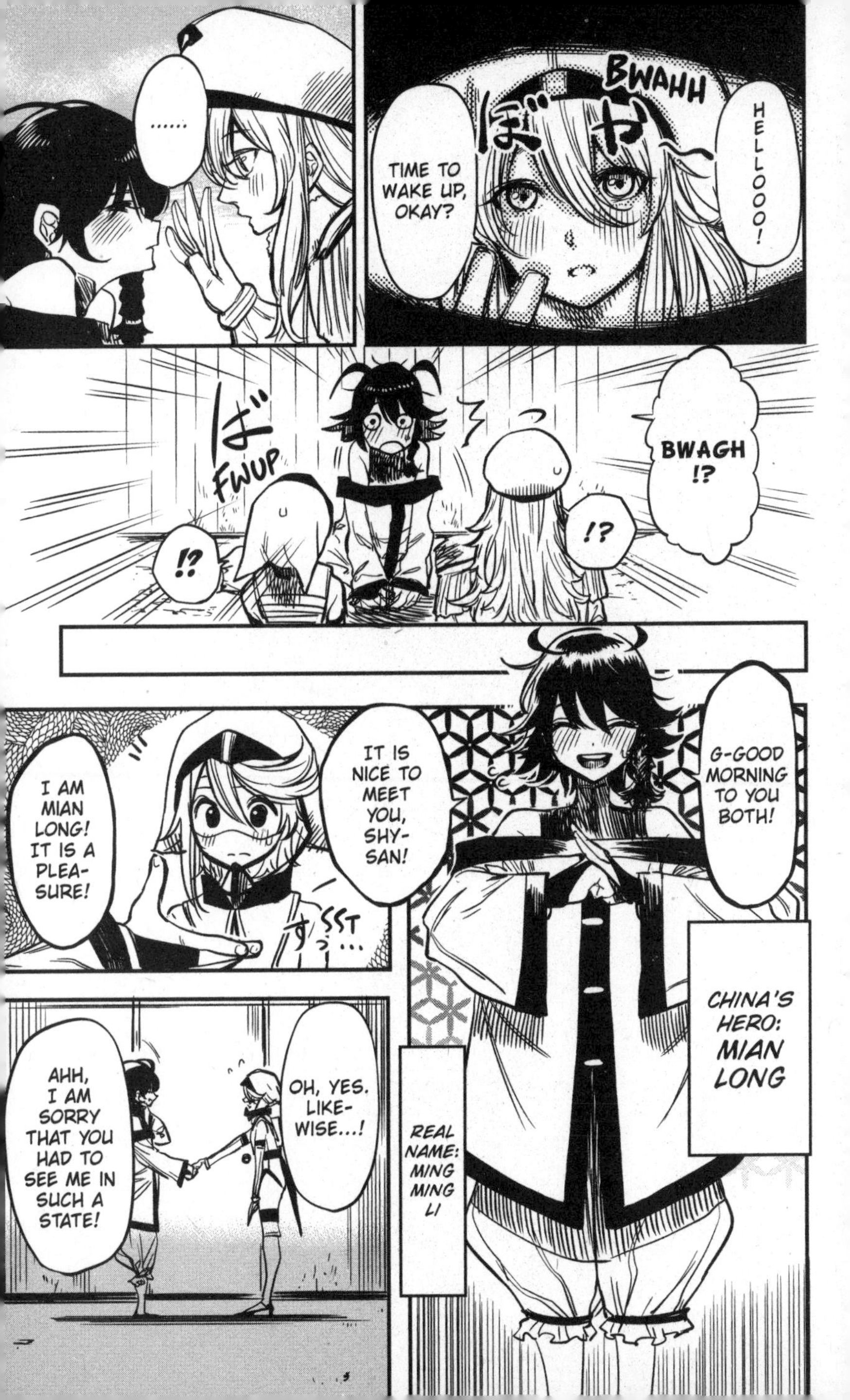
BWAHH
HELLOOOO!
TIME TO WAKE UP, OKAY?
......
BWAGH!?
!?
FWUP
!?
G-GOOD MORNING TO YOU BOTH!
CHINA'S HERO: MIAN LONG
REAL NAME: MING MING LI
IT IS NICE TO MEET YOU, SHY-SAN!
I AM MIAN LONG! IT IS A PLEA-SURE!
SSST...
OH, YES. LIKE-WISE...!
AHH, I AM SORRY THAT YOU HAD TO SEE ME IN SUCH A STATE!

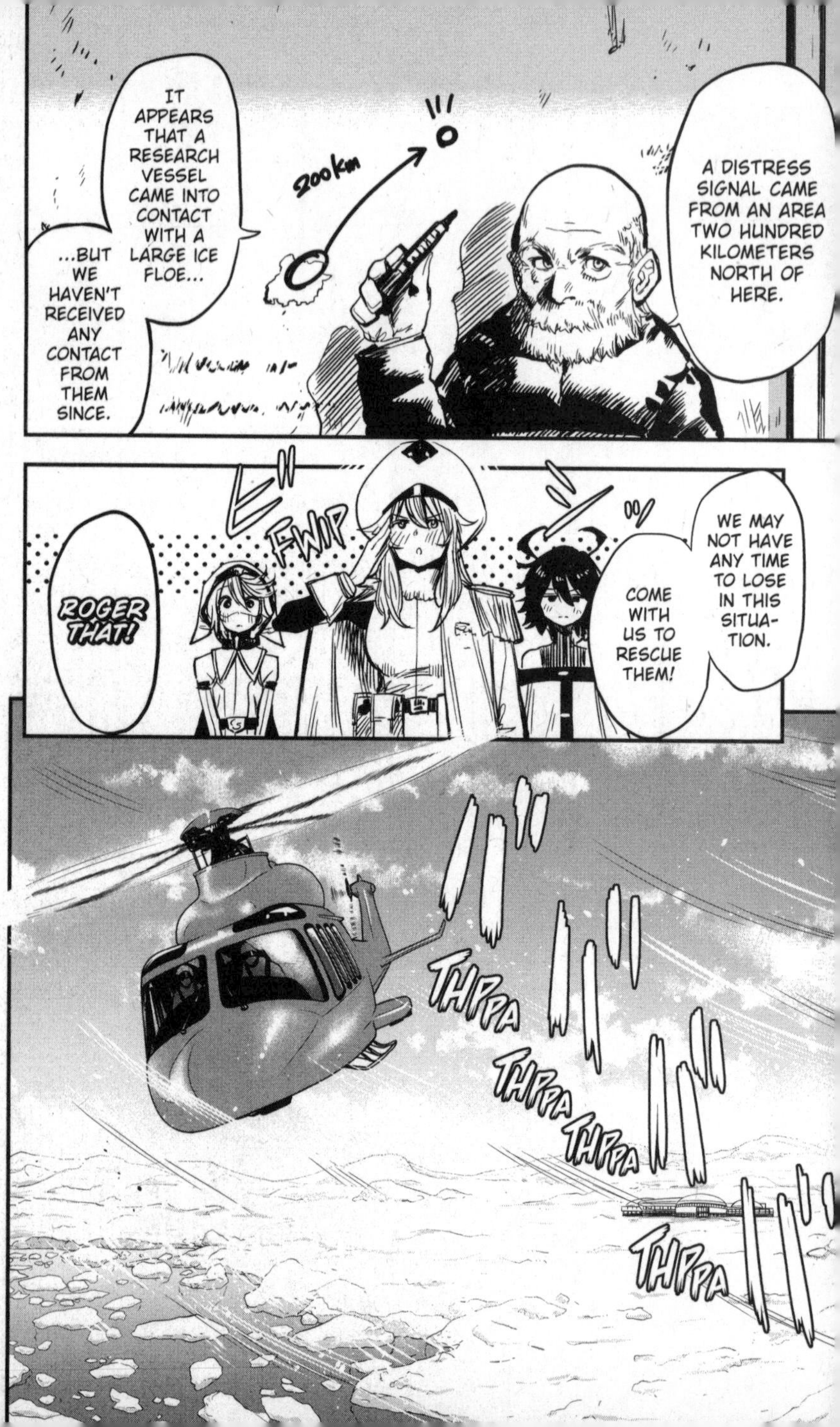
A DISTRESS SIGNAL CAME FROM AN AREA TWO HUNDRED KILOMETERS NORTH OF HERE.
200km
IT APPEARS THAT A RESEARCH VESSEL CAME INTO CONTACT WITH A LARGE ICE FLOE...
...BUT WE HAVEN'T RECEIVED ANY CONTACT FROM THEM SINCE.
WE MAY NOT HAVE ANY TIME TO LOSE IN THIS SITUA-TION.
COME WITH US TO RESCUE THEM!
FWIP
ROGER THAT!
THPPA
THPPA
THPPA
THPPA

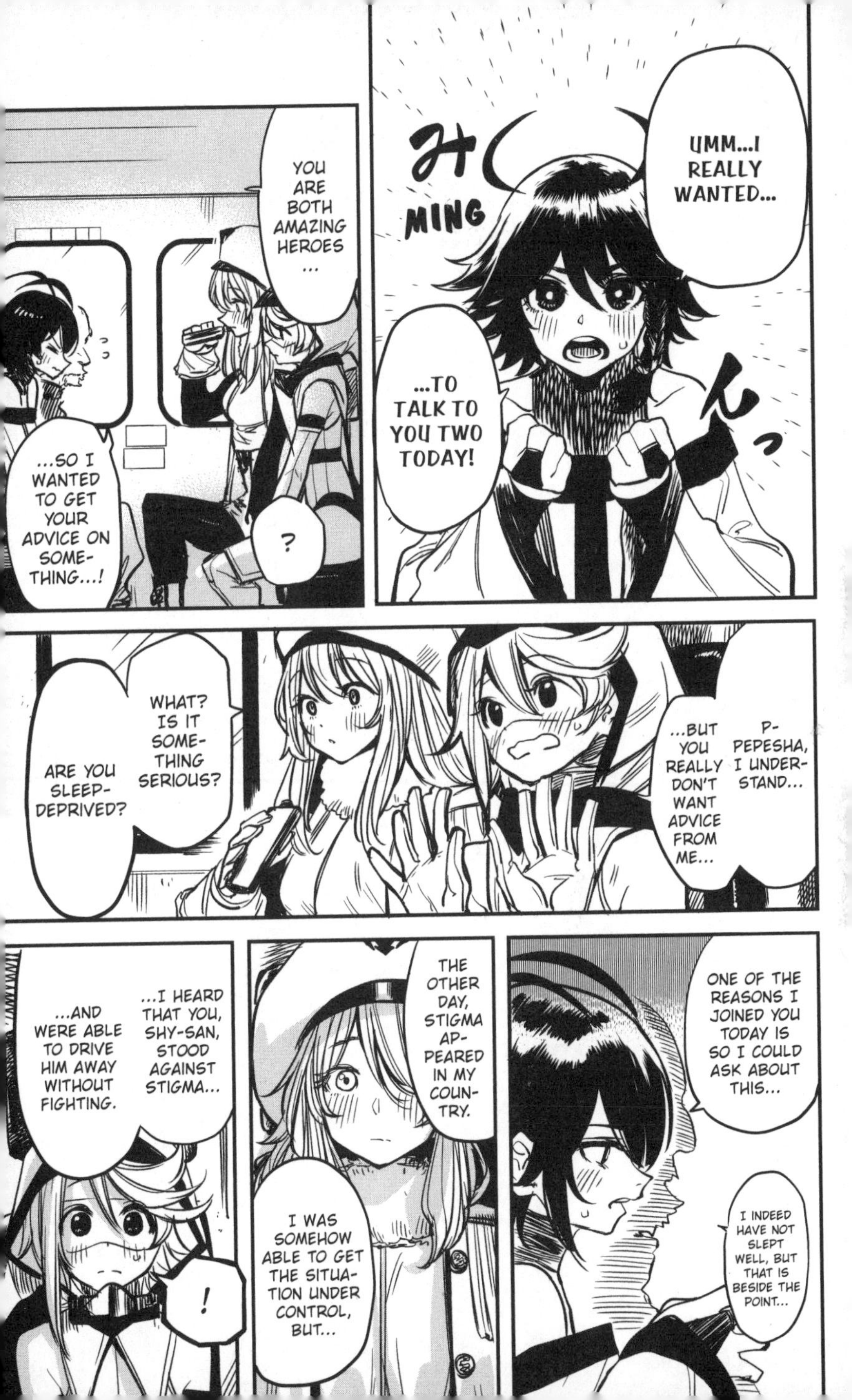

み
MING
UMM...I REALLY WANTED...
...TO TALK TO YOU TWO TODAY!
ん
YOU ARE BOTH AMAZING HEROES ...
...SO I WANTED TO GET YOUR ADVICE ON SOME-THING...!
?
P-PEPESHA, I UNDER-STAND...
...BUT YOU REALLY DON'T WANT ADVICE FROM ME...
WHAT? IS IT SOME-THING SERIOUS?
ARE YOU SLEEP-DEPRIVED?
ONE OF THE REASONS I JOINED YOU TODAY IS SO I COULD ASK ABOUT THIS...
I INDEED HAVE NOT SLEPT WELL, BUT THAT IS BESIDE THE POINT...
THE OTHER DAY, STIGMA AP-PEARED IN MY COUN-TRY.
I WAS SOMEHOW ABLE TO GET THE SITUA-TION UNDER CONTROL, BUT...
...I HEARD THAT YOU, SHY-SAN, STOOD AGAINST STIGMA...
...AND WERE ABLE TO DRIVE HIM AWAY WITHOUT FIGHTING.
!

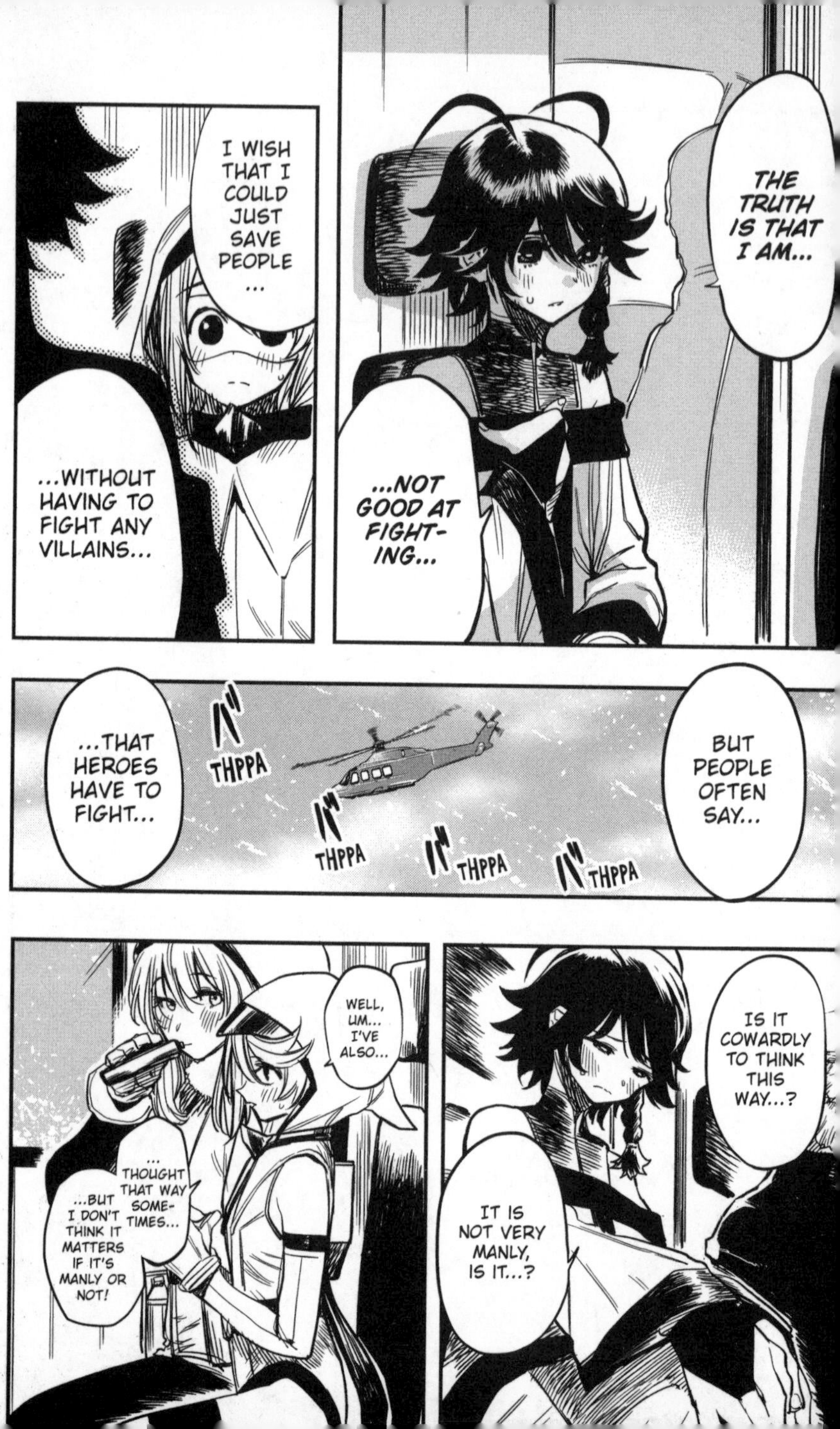
THE TRUTH IS THAT I AM...
...NOT GOOD AT FIGHTING...
I WISH THAT I COULD JUST SAVE PEOPLE...
...WITHOUT HAVING TO FIGHT ANY VILLAINS...
BUT PEOPLE OFTEN SAY...
THPPA
THPPA
THPPA
THPPA
...THAT HEROES HAVE TO FIGHT...
IS IT COWARDLY TO THINK THIS WAY...?
IT IS NOT VERY MANLY, IS IT...?
WELL, UM... I'VE ALSO...
...THOUGHT THAT WAY SOMETIMES...
...BUT I DON'T THINK IT MATTERS IF IT'S MANLY OR NOT!

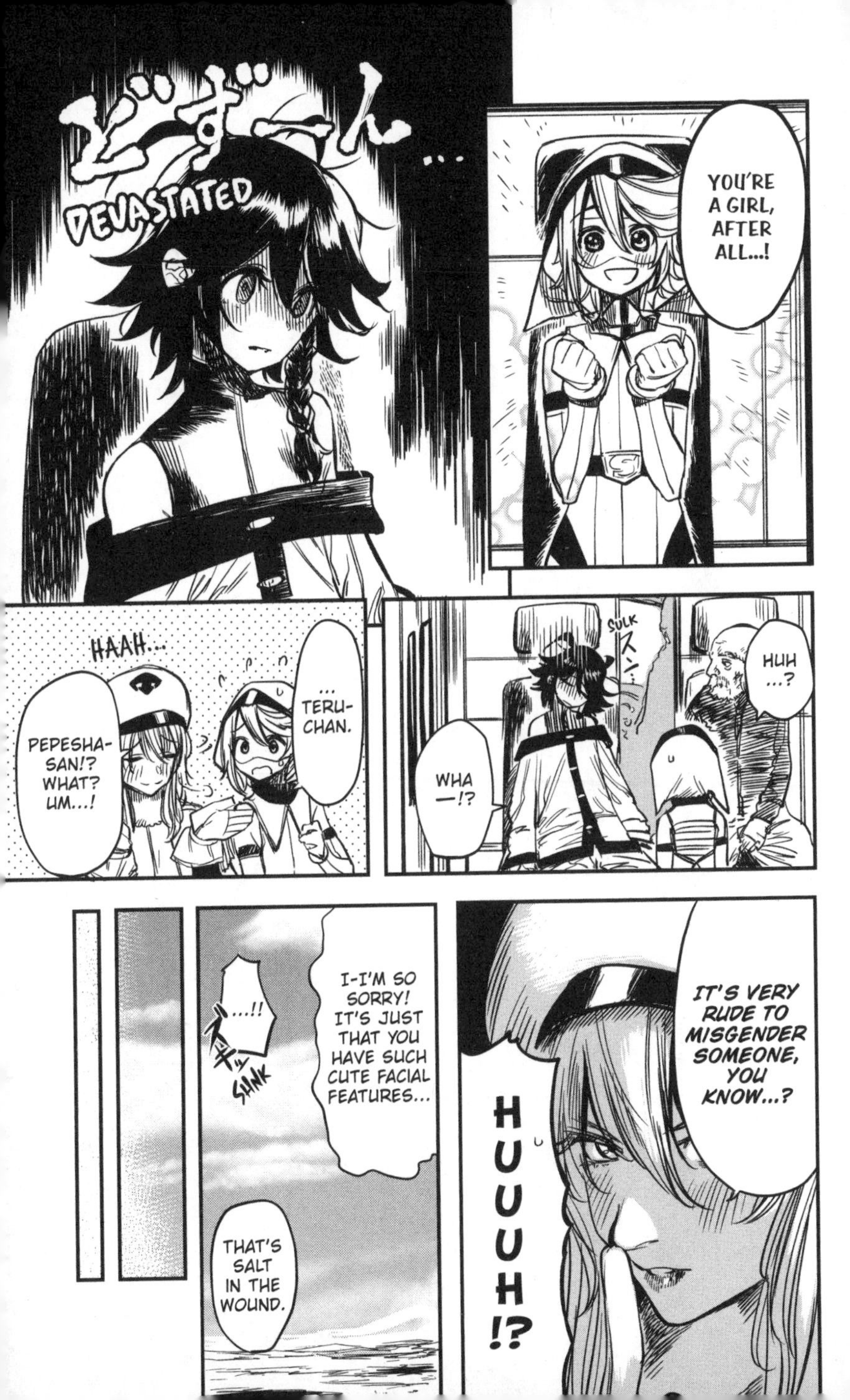
YOU'RE A GIRL, AFTER ALL...!
どずーん...
DEVASTATED
SULK
スン...
HUH ...?
WHA —!?
... TERU-CHAN.
HAAH...
PEPESHA-SAN!? WHAT? UM...!
IT'S VERY RUDE TO MISGENDER SOMEONE, YOU KNOW...?
HUUUH!?
I-I'M SO SORRY! IT'S JUST THAT YOU HAVE SUCH CUTE FACIAL FEATURES...
...!!
ズキッ
SHINK
THAT'S SALT IN THE WOUND.

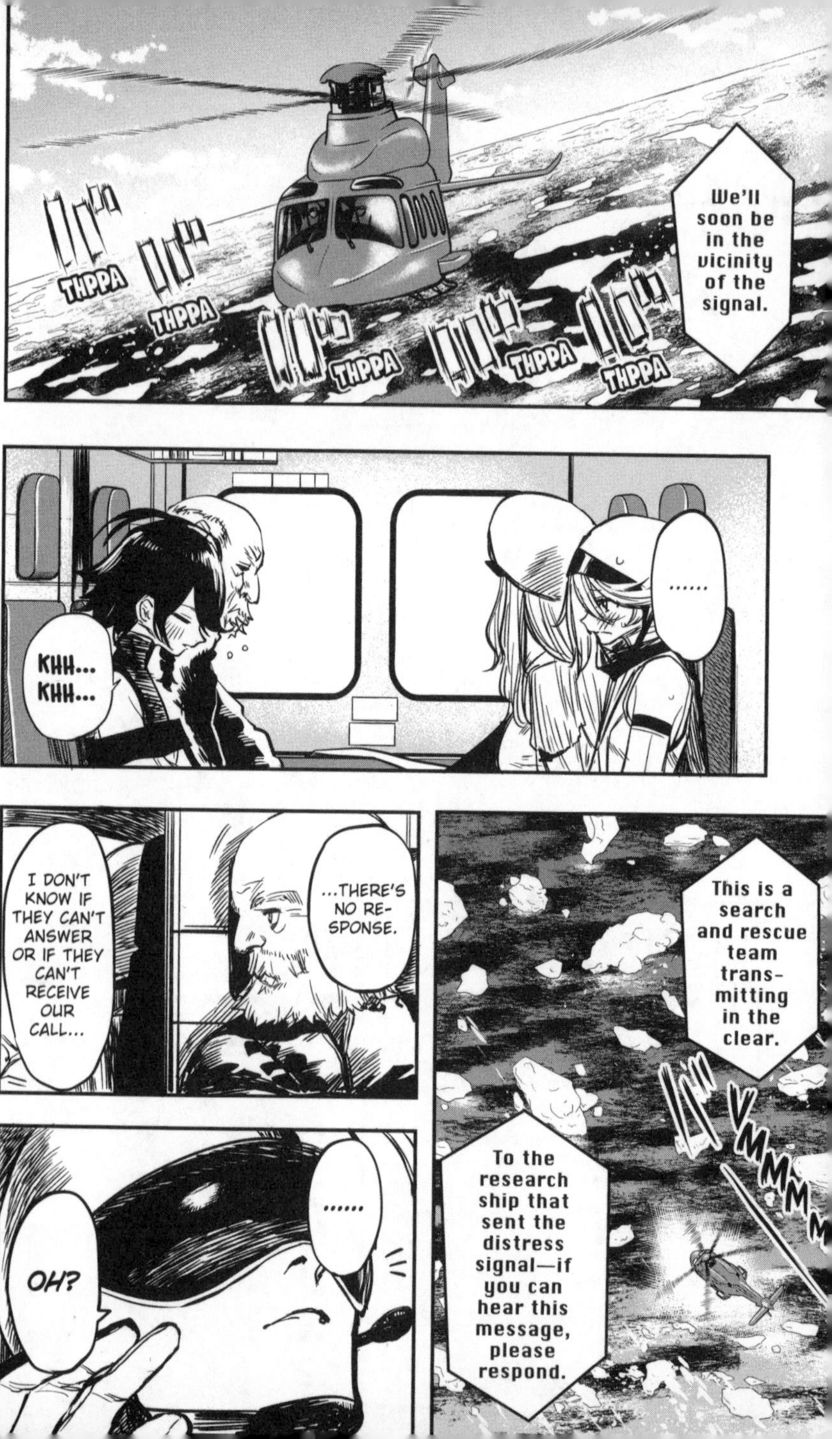
We'll soon be in the vicinity of the signal.
THPPA
THPPA
THPPA
THPPA
THPPA
......
KHH... KHH...
This is a search and rescue team trans-mitting in the clear.
VMMMM
To the research ship that sent the distress signal—if you can hear this message, please respond.
...THERE'S NO RE-SPONSE.
I DON'T KNOW IF THEY CAN'T ANSWER OR IF THEY CAN'T RECEIVE OUR CALL...
......
OH?

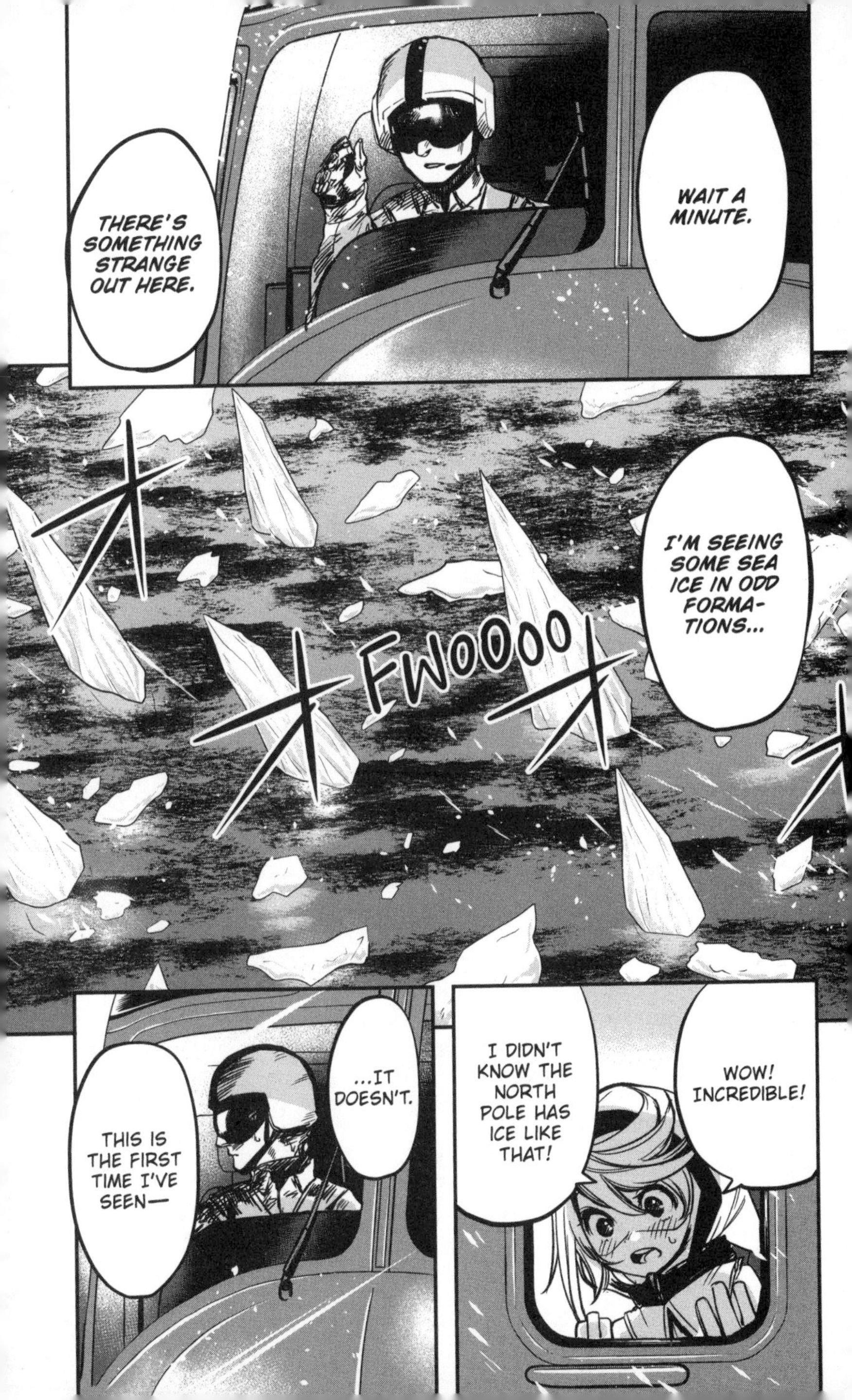
WAIT A MINUTE.
THERE'S SOMETHING STRANGE OUT HERE.
I'M SEEING SOME SEA ICE IN ODD FORMATIONS...
FWOOOO
WOW! INCREDIBLE!
I DIDN'T KNOW THE NORTH POLE HAS ICE LIKE THAT!
...IT DOESN'T.
THIS IS THE FIRST TIME I'VE SEEN—

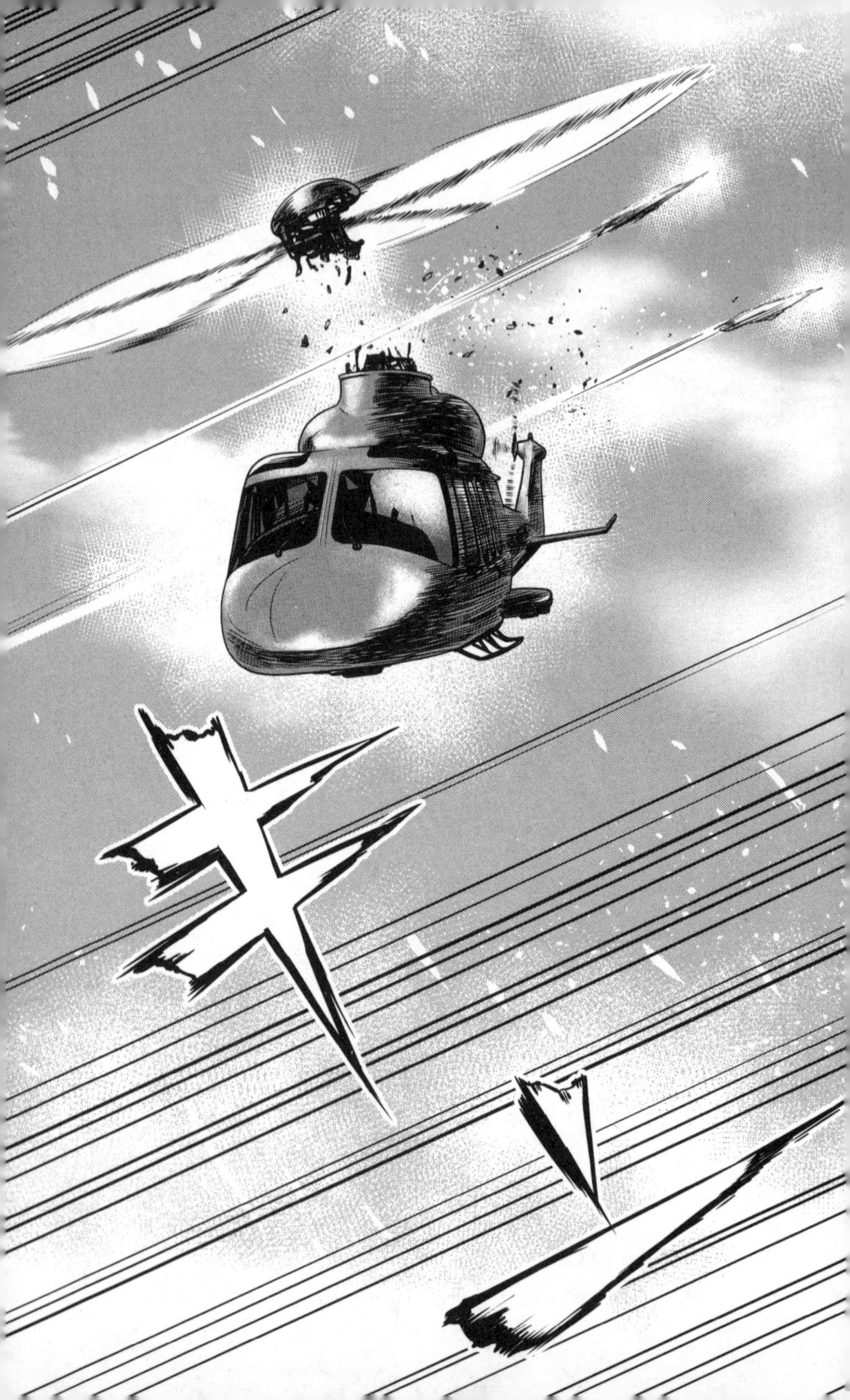
キン

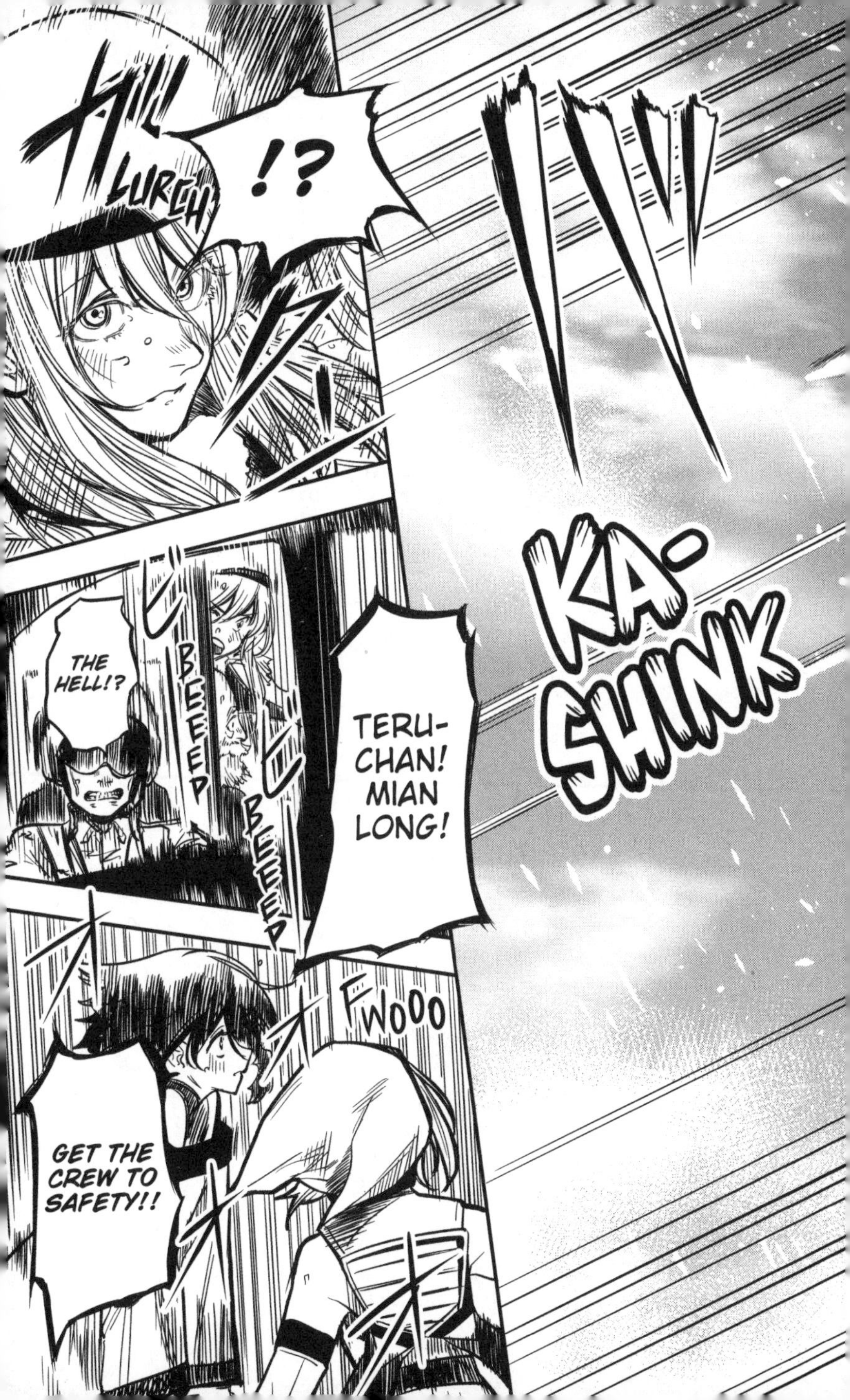
KA-SHINK
LURCH
!?
TERU-CHAN! MIAN LONG!
BEEEP BEEEP
THE HELL!?
FWOOO
GET THE CREW TO SAFETY!!

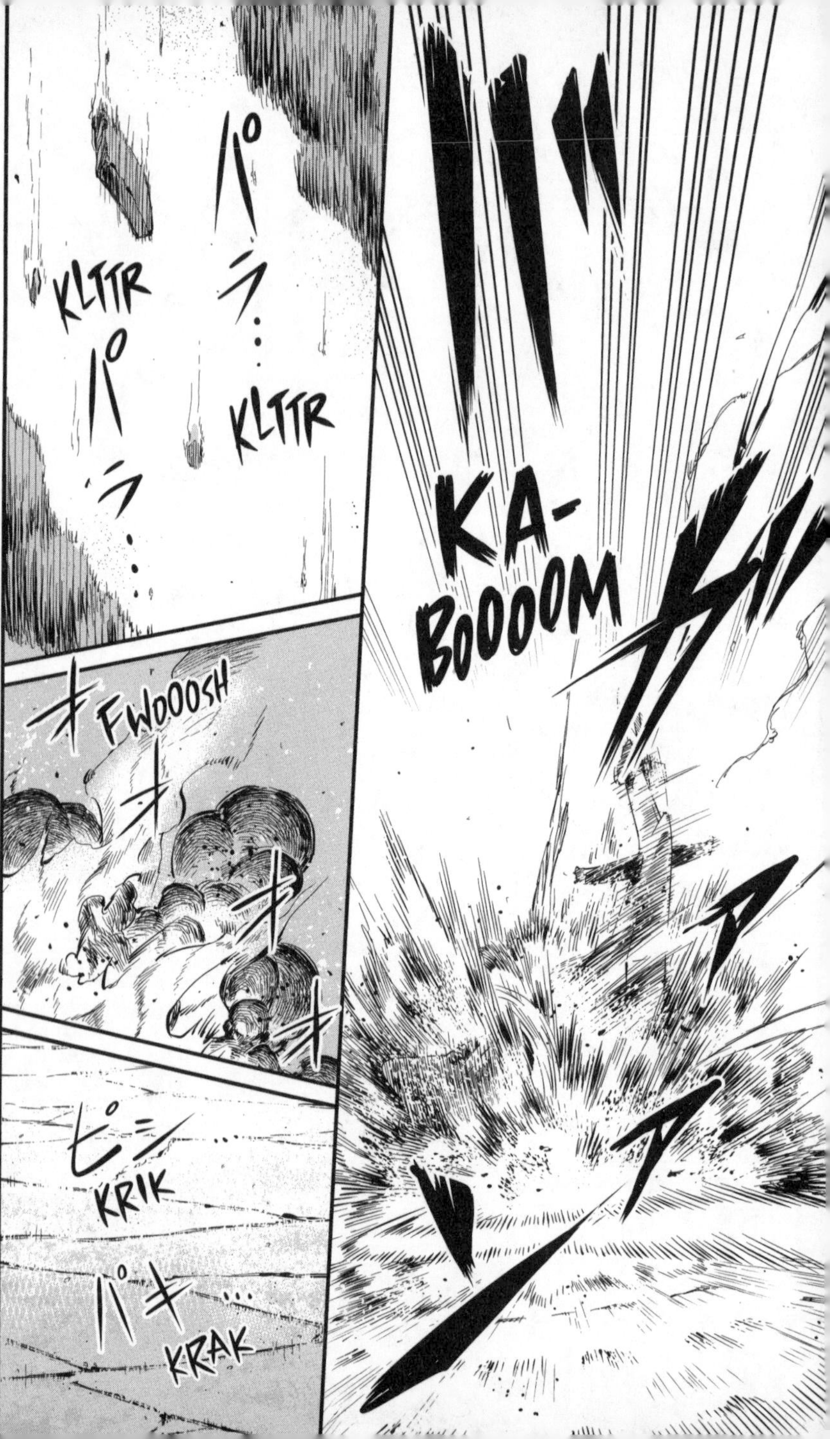

KA-BOOOOM
パラ…
KLTTR
パラ…
KLTTR
FWOOOSH
KRIK
パキ…
KRAK

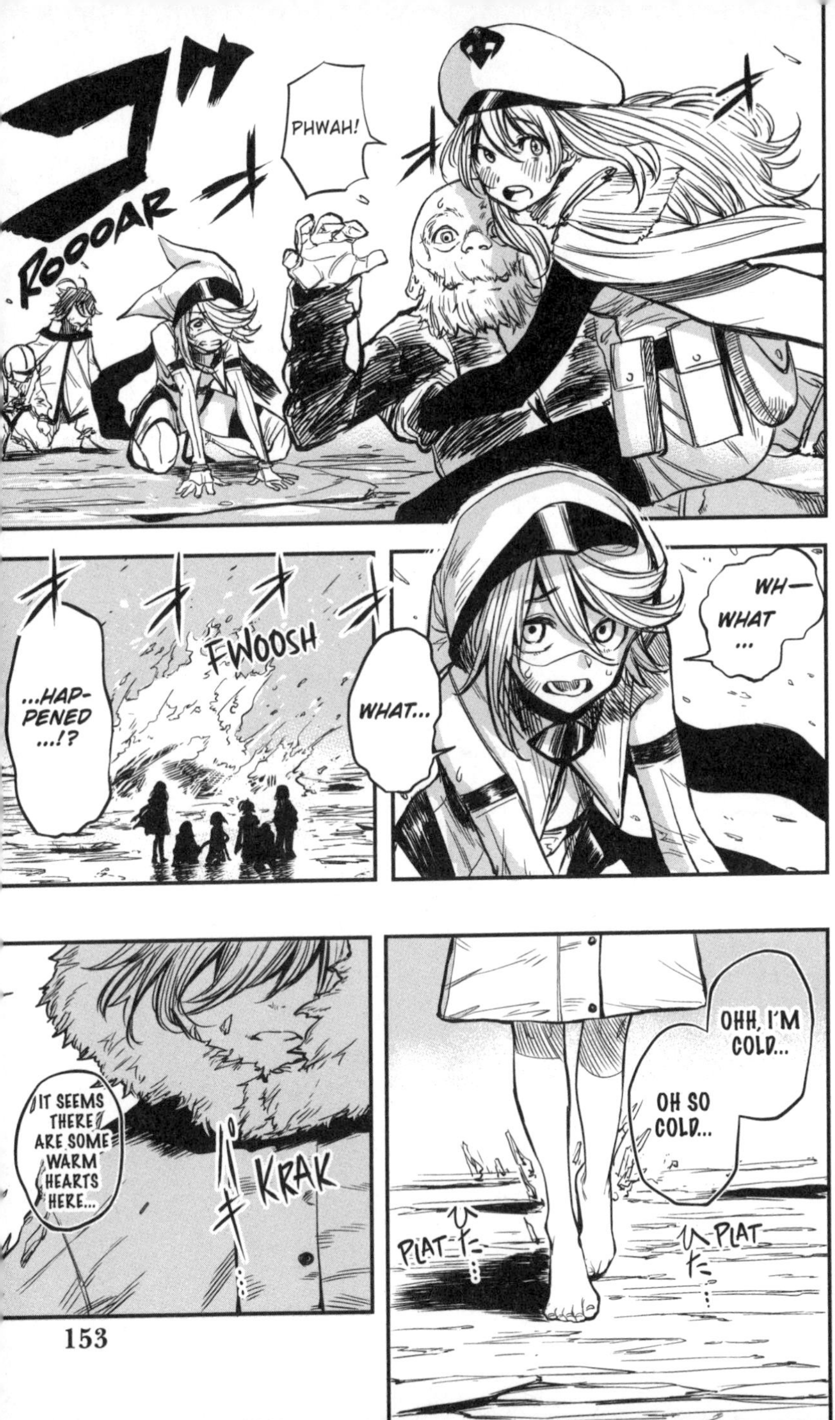
ROOOAR
PHWAH!
WH— WHAT ...
WHAT...
FWOOSH
...HAP-PENED ...!?
OHH, I'M COLD...
OH SO COLD...
PLAT
PLAT
KRAK
IT SEEMS THERE ARE SOME WARM HEARTS HERE...

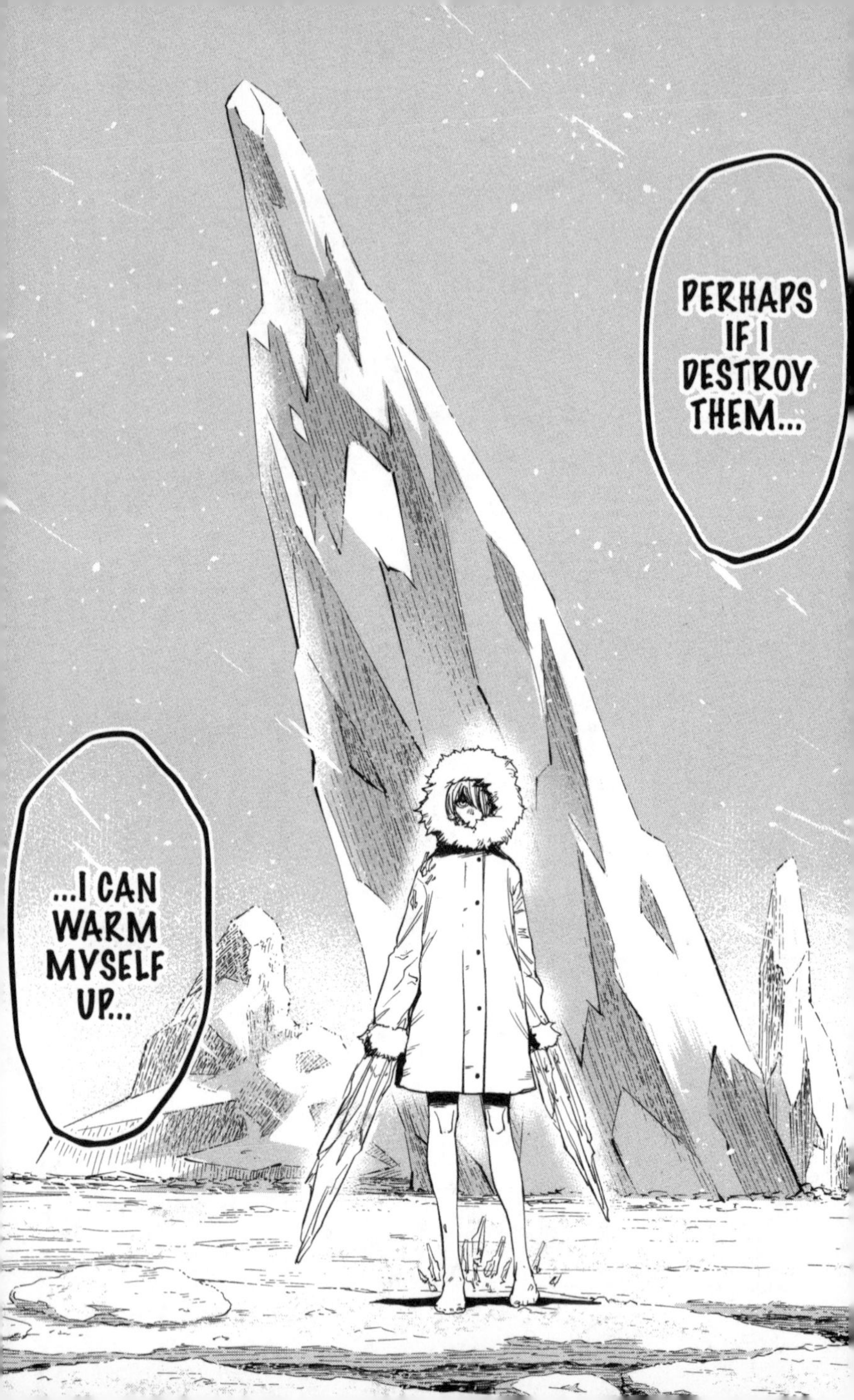
PERHAPS IF I DESTROY THEM...
...I CAN WARM MYSELF UP...

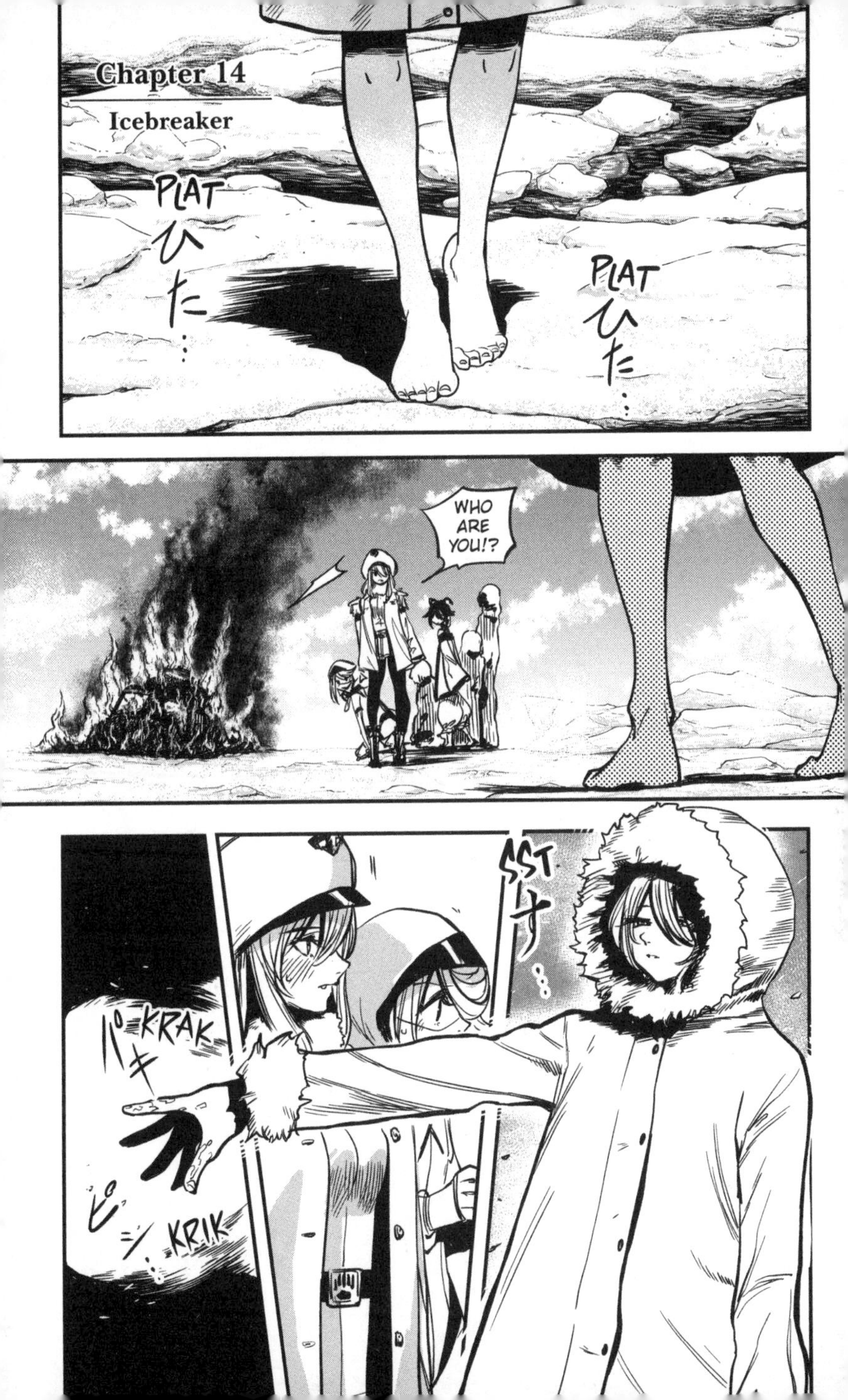
Chapter 14
Icebreaker
PLAT ひた…
PLAT ひた…
WHO ARE YOU!?
SST す…
KRAK パキ
KRIK ピシ

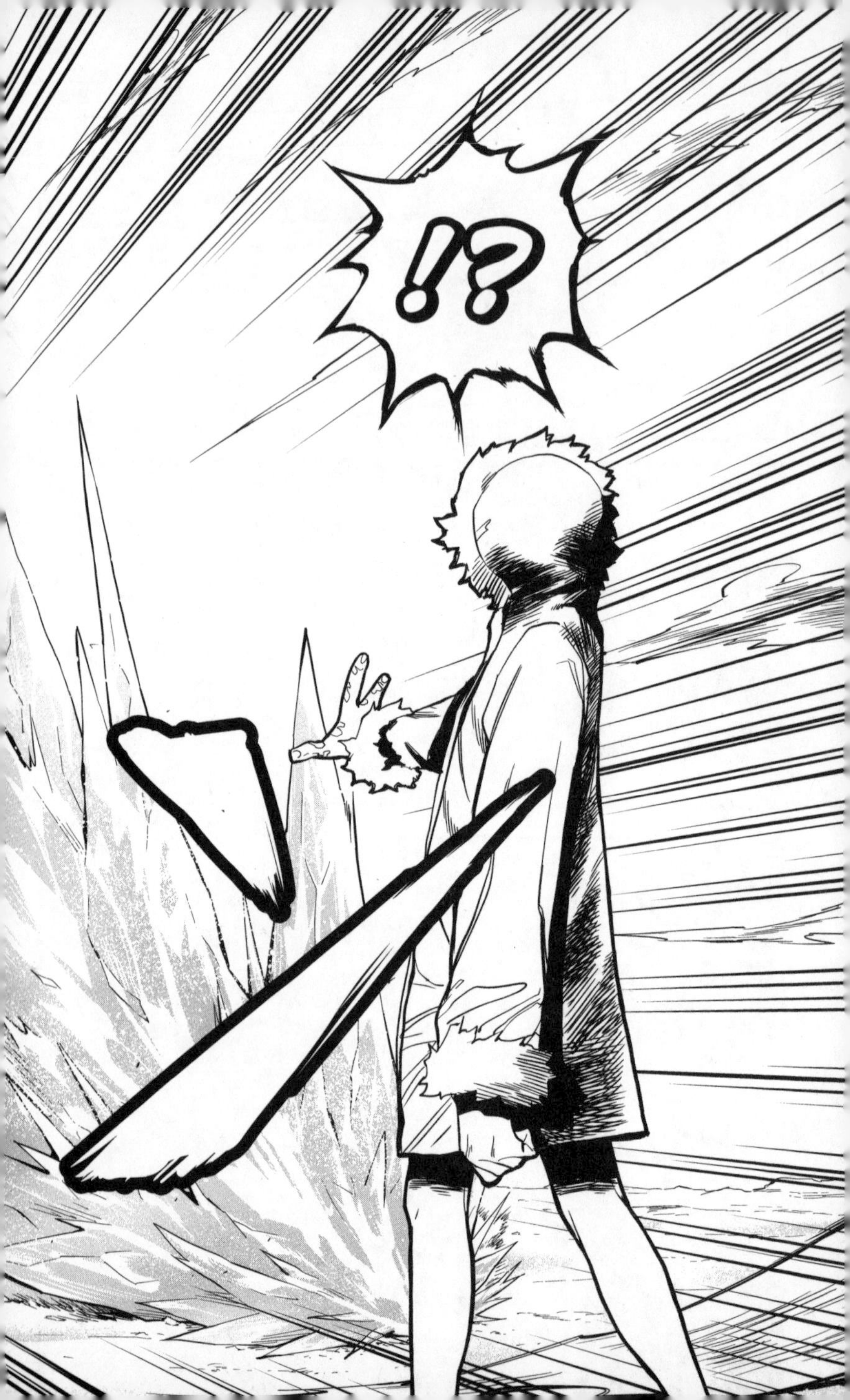
!?

Chapter 14

Ice Breaker

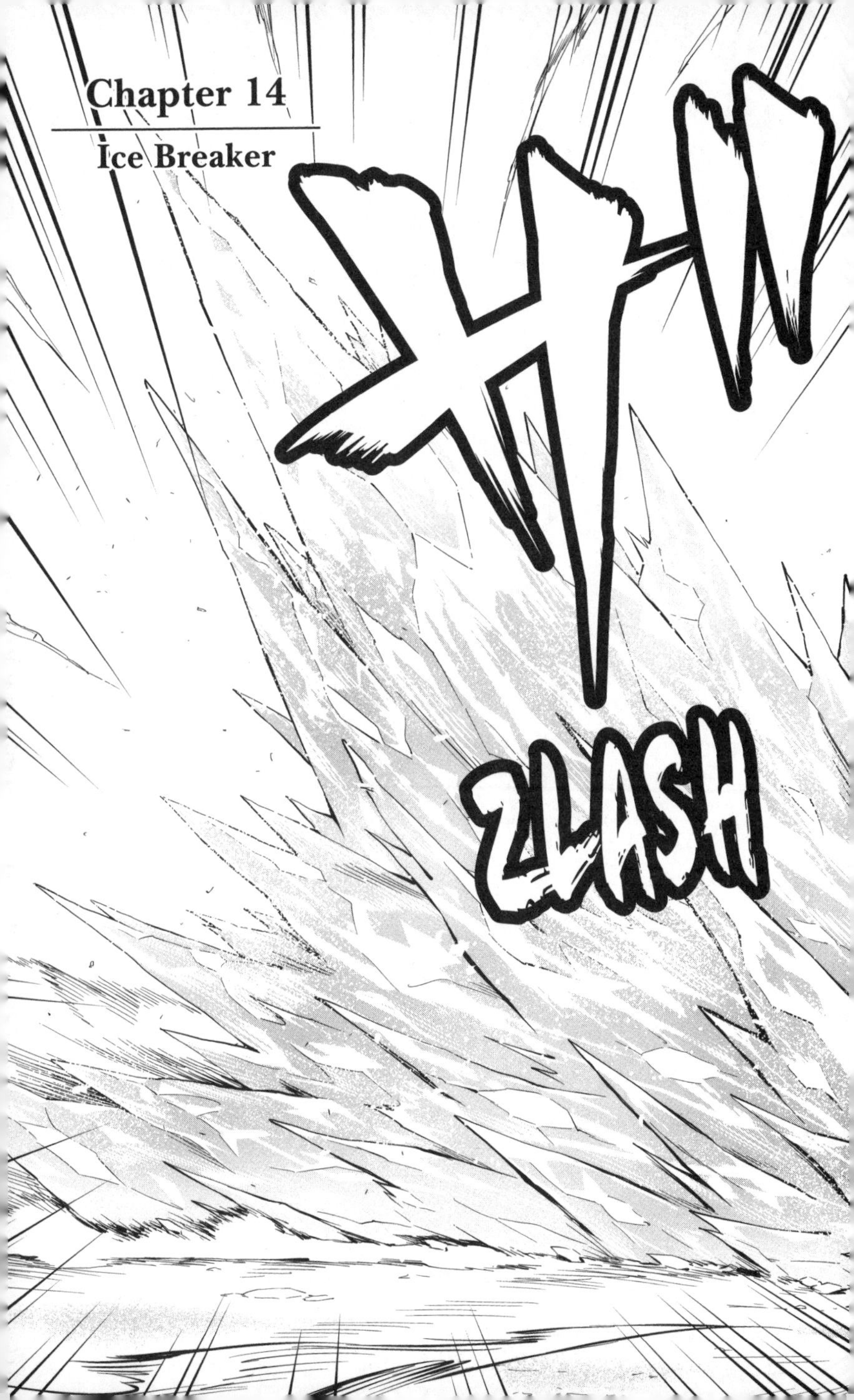
ZLASH

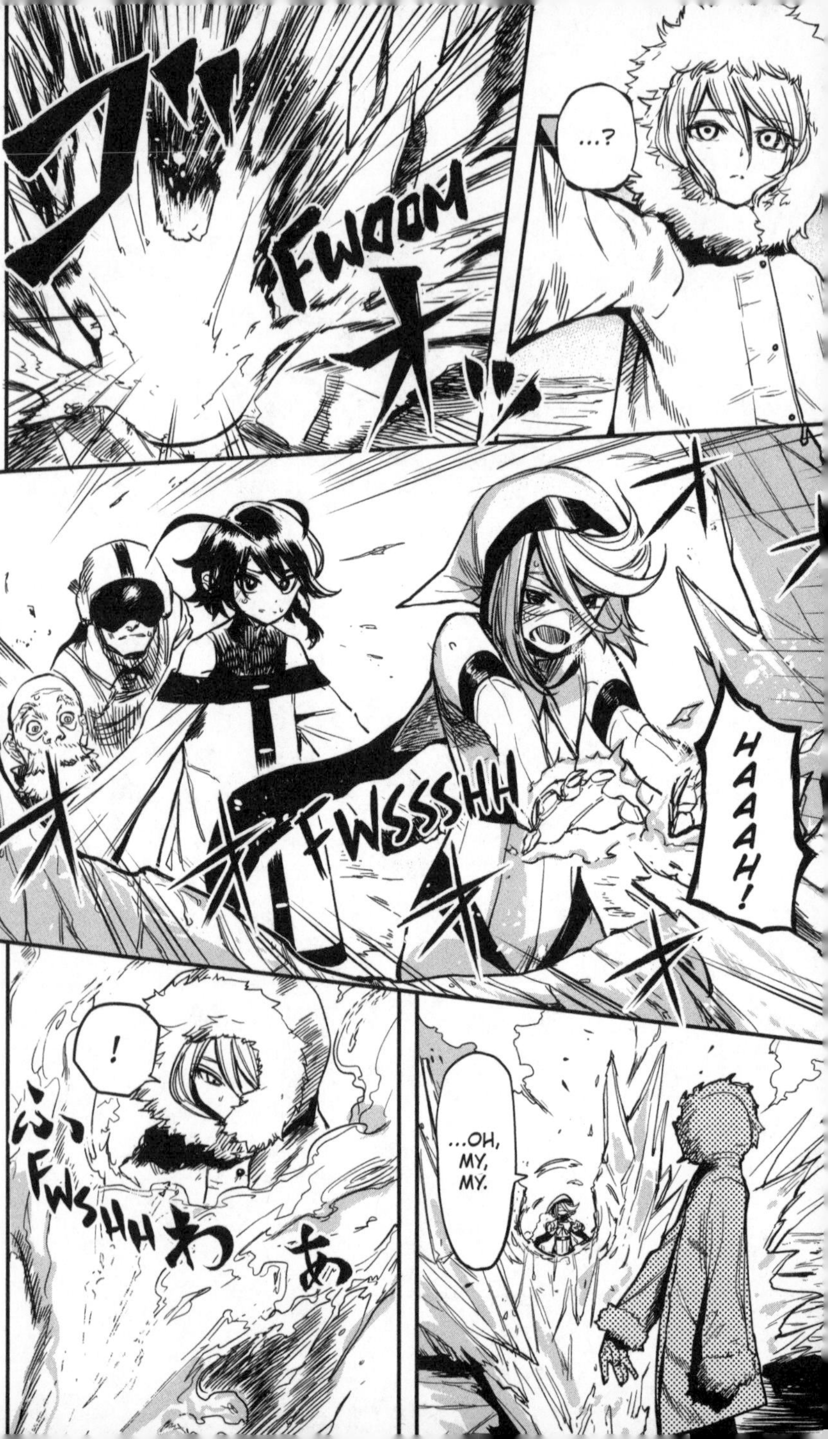
...?
FWOOM
HAAAH!
FWSSSHH
...OH, MY, MY.
!
ふわあ
FWSHH

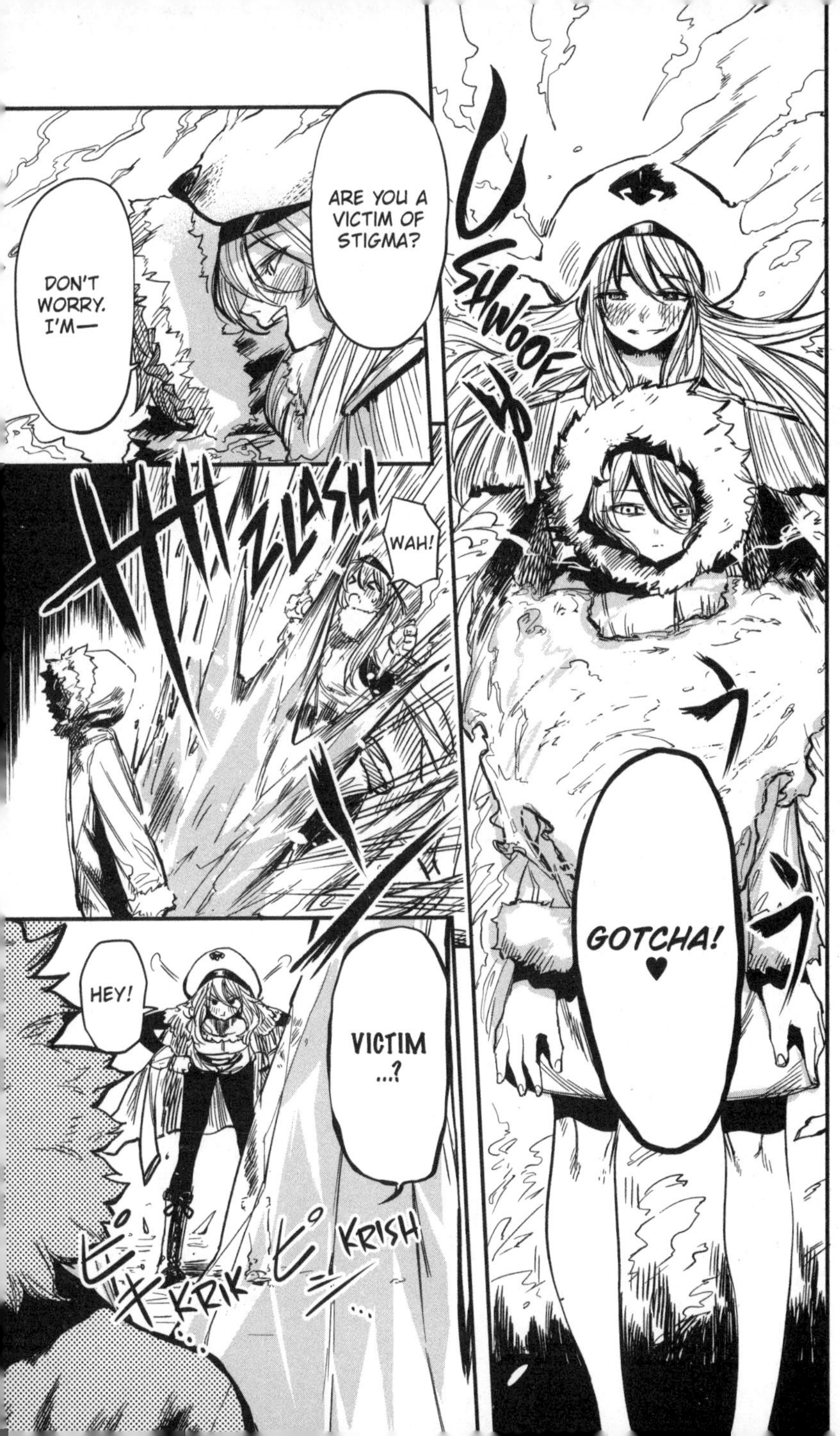
SHWOOF
GOTCHA! ♥
ARE YOU A VICTIM OF STIGMA?
DON'T WORRY. I'M—
ZLASH
WAH!
HEY!
VICTIM ...?
KRIK
KRISH
...
...

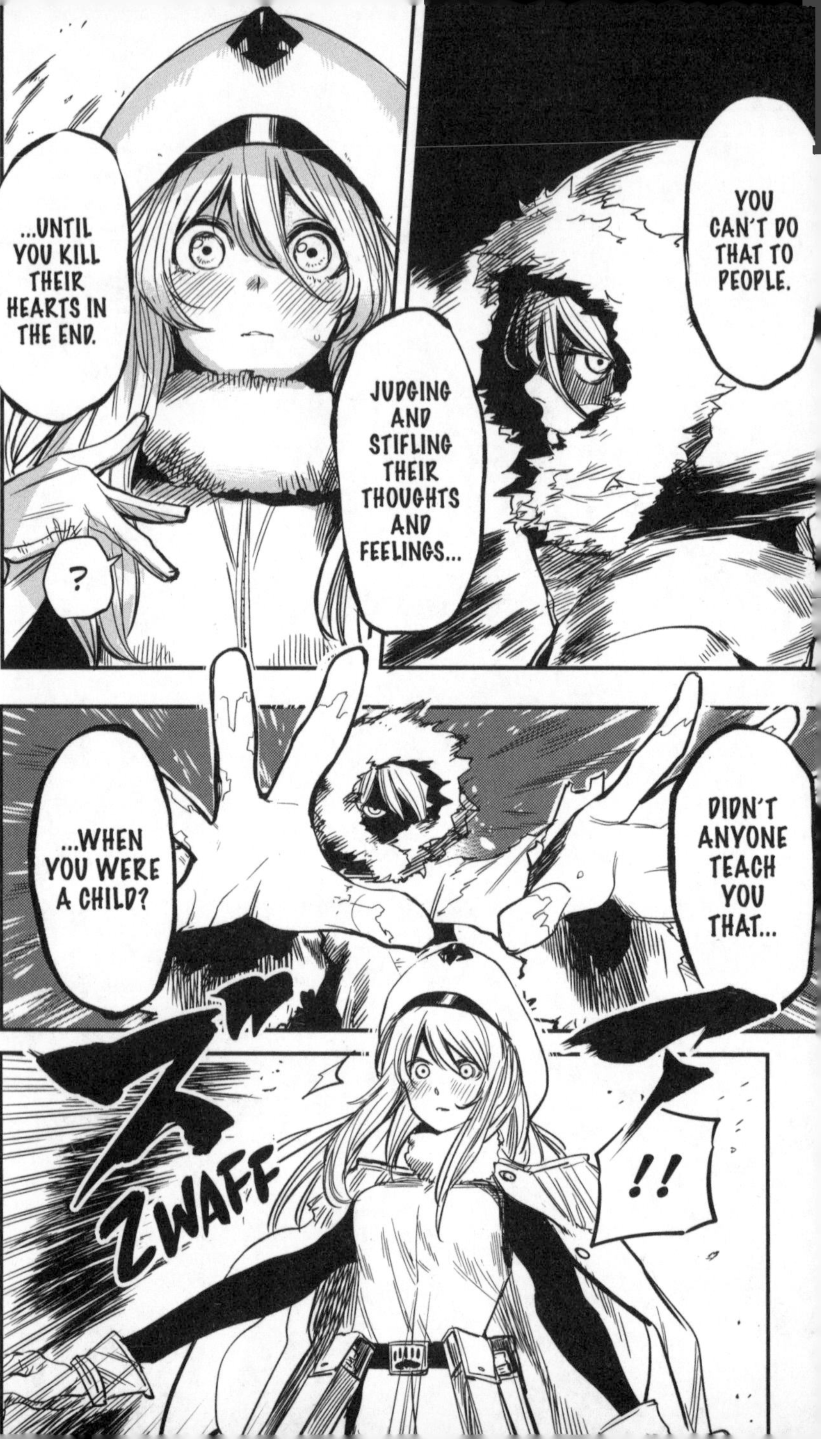

YOU CAN'T DO THAT TO PEOPLE.
JUDGING AND STIFLING THEIR THOUGHTS AND FEELINGS...
...UNTIL YOU KILL THEIR HEARTS IN THE END.
?
DIDN'T ANYONE TEACH YOU THAT...
...WHEN YOU WERE A CHILD?
!!
ZWAFF

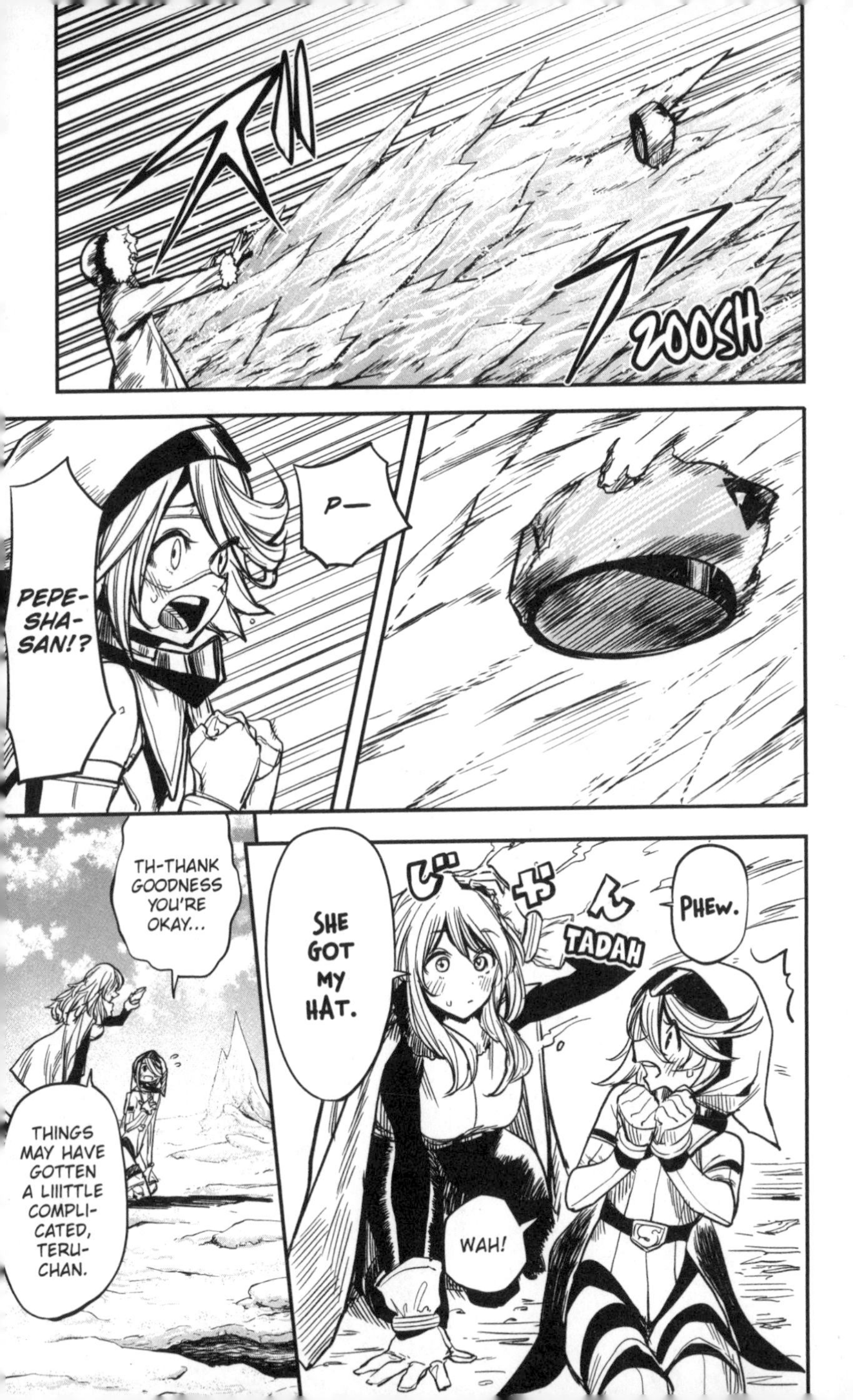
ZOOSH
P—
PEPESHA-SAN!?
PHEW.
TADAH
SHE GOT MY HAT.
WAH!
TH-THANK GOODNESS YOU'RE OKAY...
THINGS MAY HAVE GOTTEN A LIIITTLE COMPLICATED, TERU-CHAN.

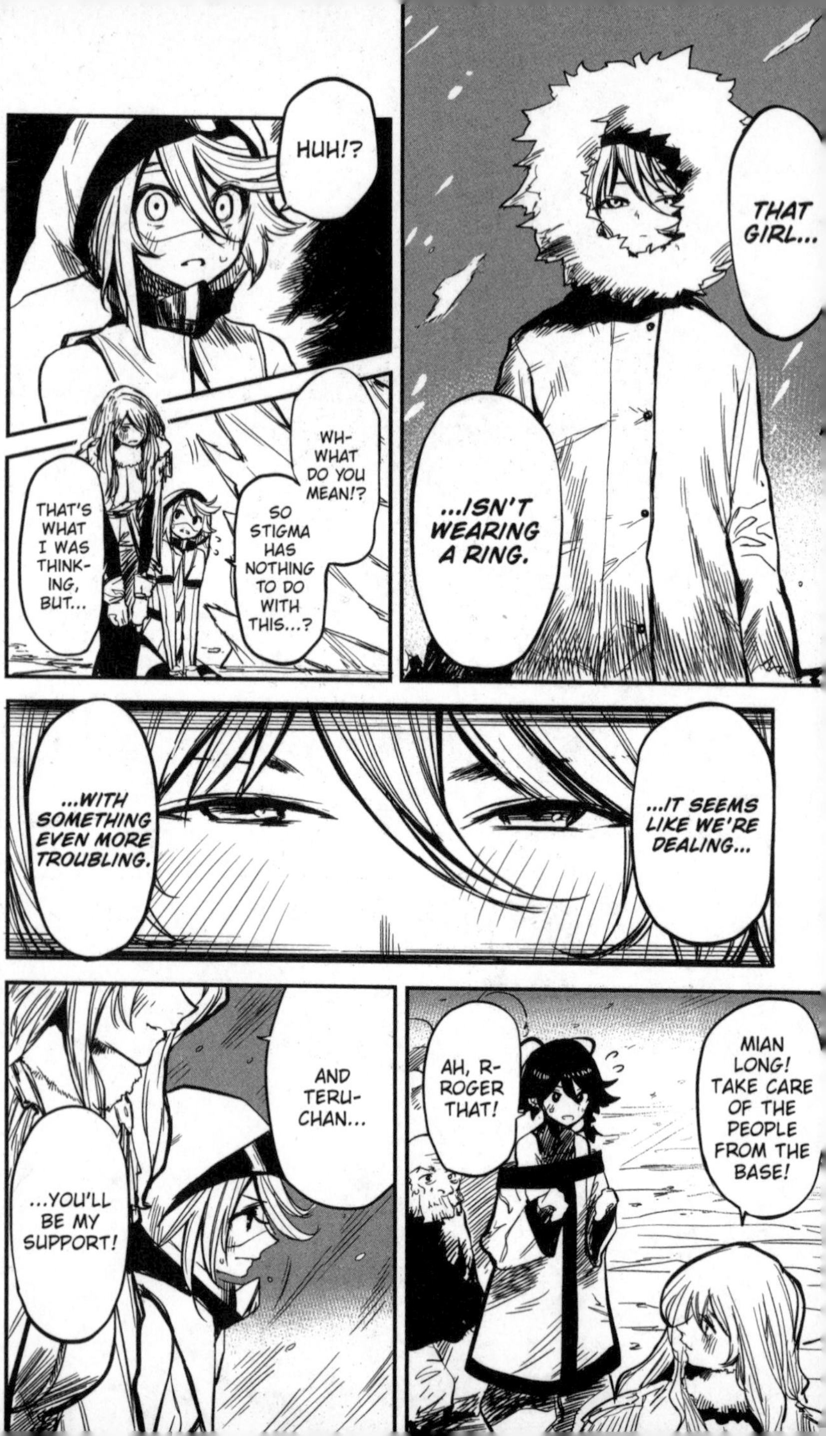
THAT GIRL...
...ISN'T WEARING A RING.
HUH!?
WH- WHAT DO YOU MEAN!?
SO STIGMA HAS NOTHING TO DO WITH THIS...?
THAT'S WHAT I WAS THINKING, BUT...
...IT SEEMS LIKE WE'RE DEALING...
...WITH SOMETHING EVEN MORE TROUBLING.
MIAN LONG! TAKE CARE OF THE PEOPLE FROM THE BASE!
AH, R-ROGER THAT!
AND TERU-CHAN...
...YOU'LL BE MY SUPPORT!

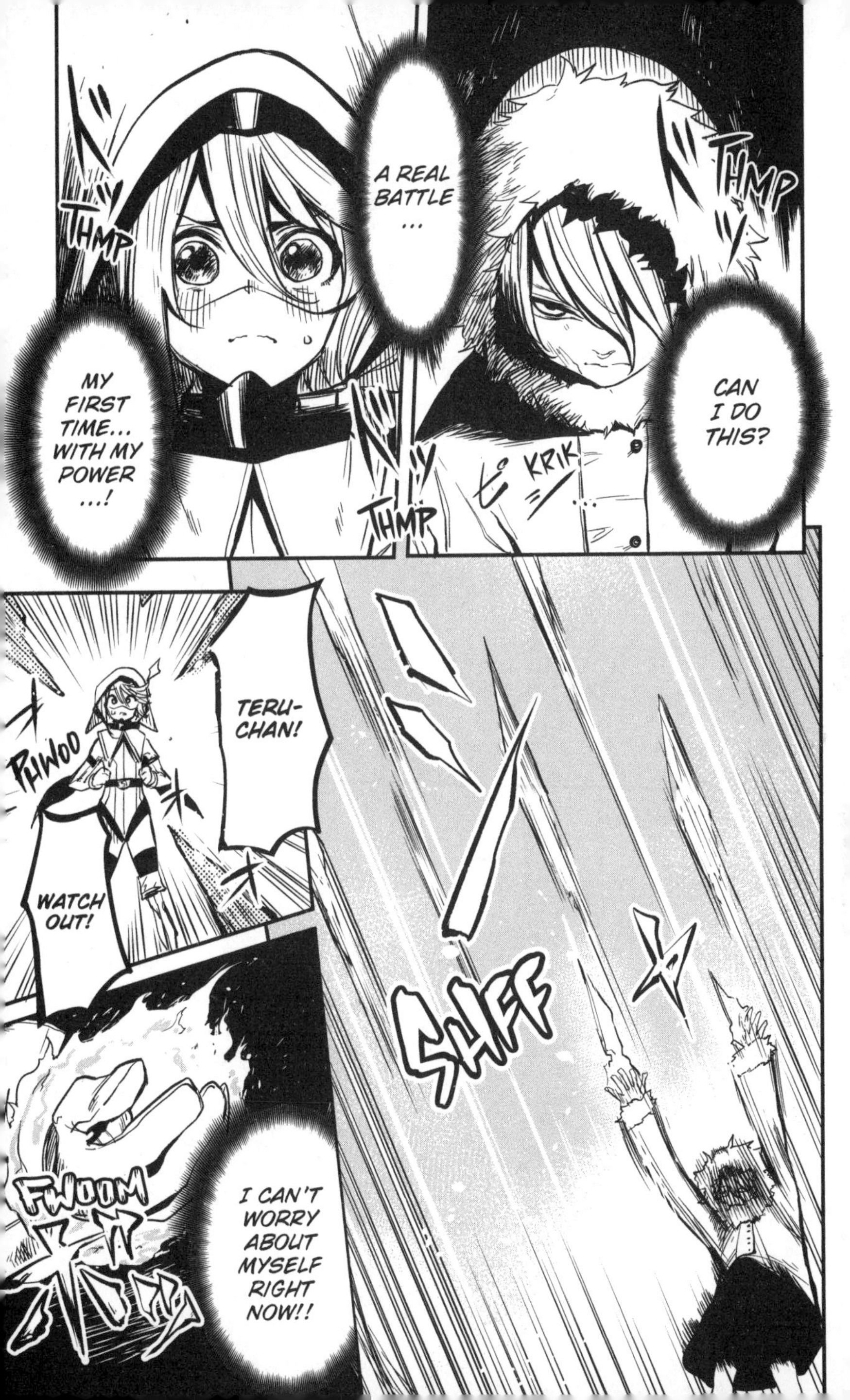
THMP
A REAL BATTLE …
CAN I DO THIS?
KRIK
THMP
THMP
MY FIRST TIME… WITH MY POWER …!
SHFF
TERU-CHAN!
WATCH OUT!
PHWOO
FWOOM
I CAN'T WORRY ABOUT MYSELF RIGHT NOW!!

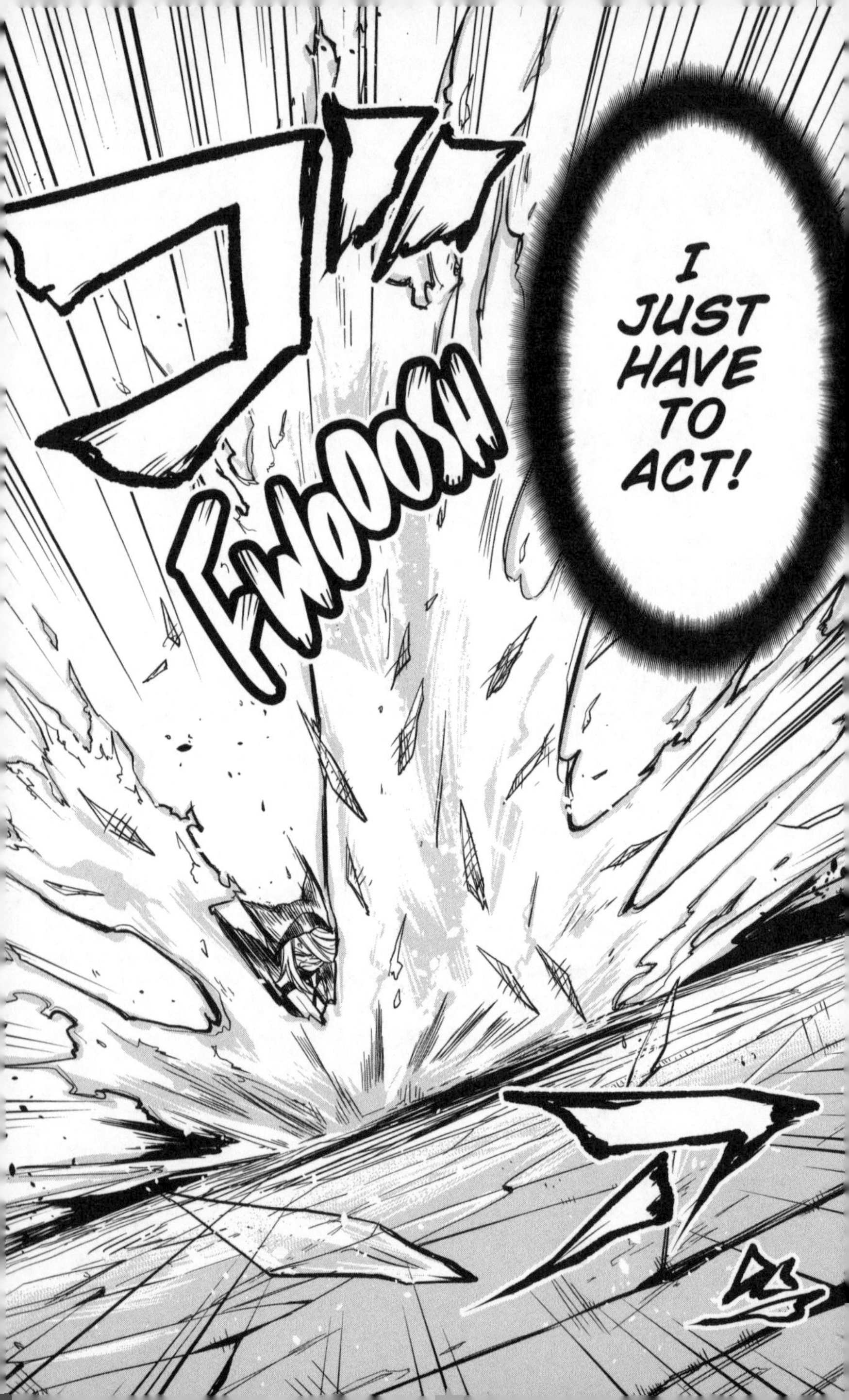
I JUST HAVE TO ACT!
FWOOOSH

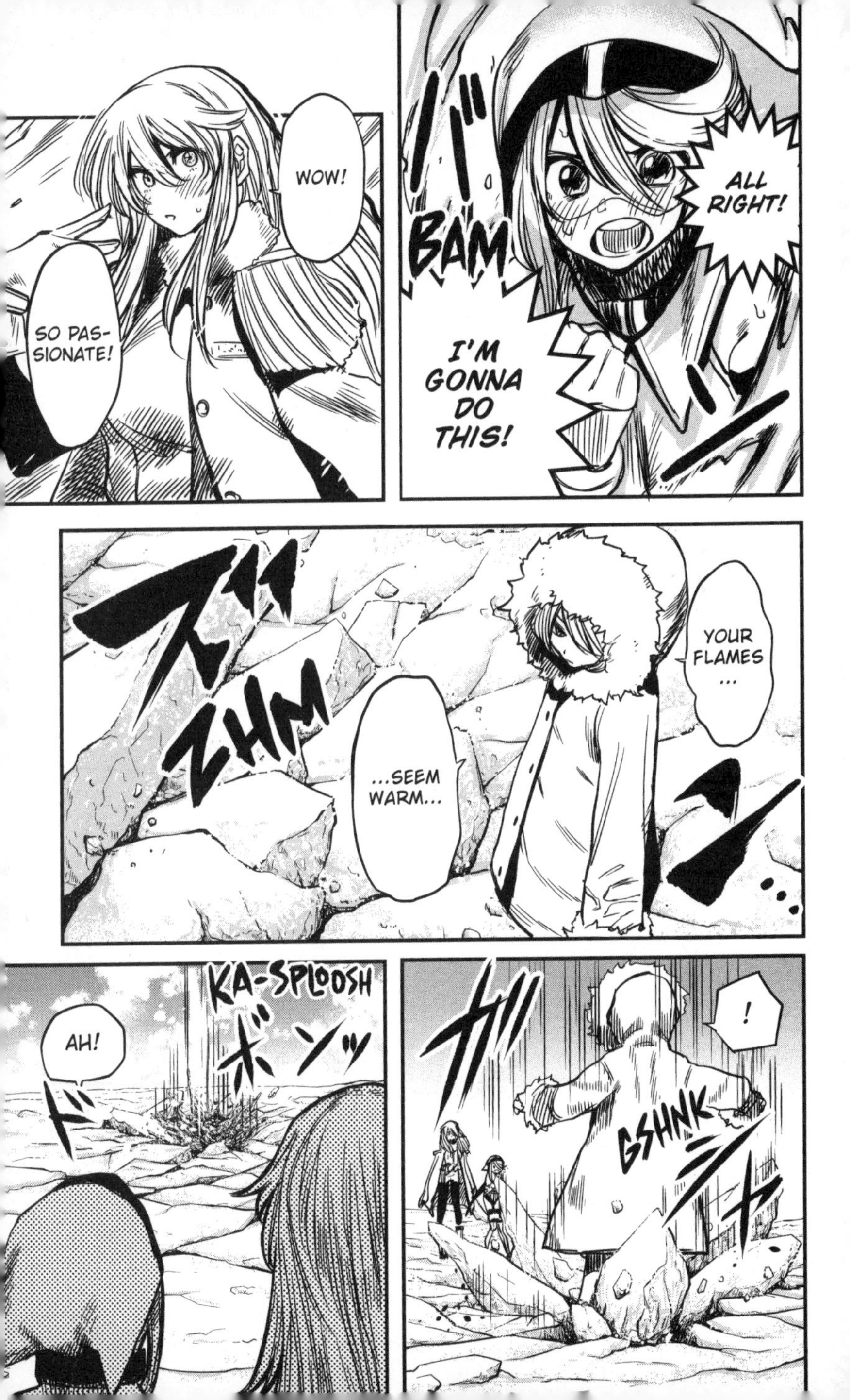
BAM
ALL RIGHT!
I'M GONNA DO THIS!
WOW!
SO PAS-SIONATE!
ZHM
YOUR FLAMES...
...SEEM WARM...
!
GSHNK
KA-SPLOOSH
AH!

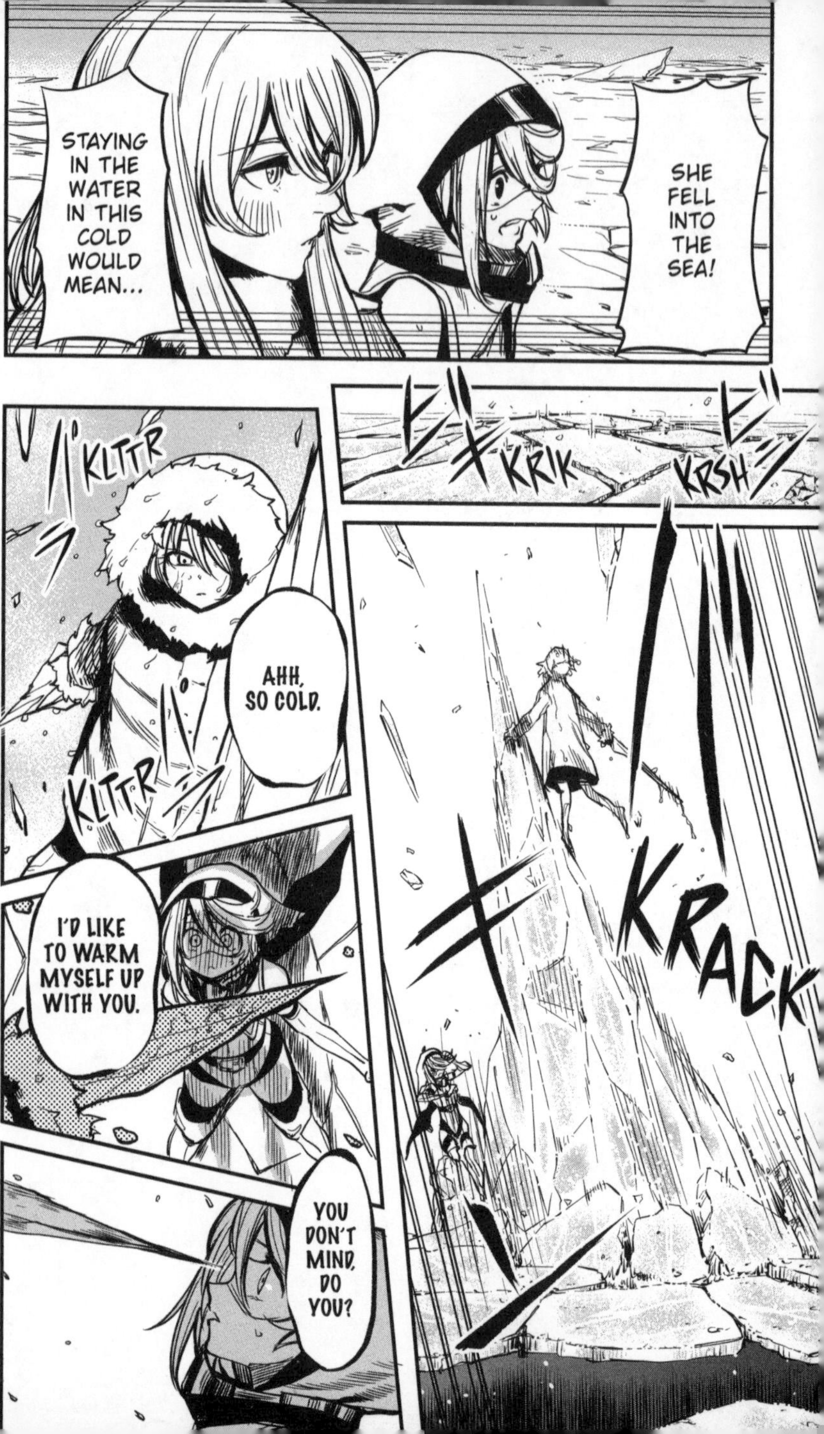
SHE FELL INTO THE SEA!
STAYING IN THE WATER IN THIS COLD WOULD MEAN...
KRIK
KRSH
KRACK
KLTTR
AHH, SO COLD.
KLTTR
I'D LIKE TO WARM MYSELF UP WITH YOU.
YOU DON'T MIND, DO YOU?

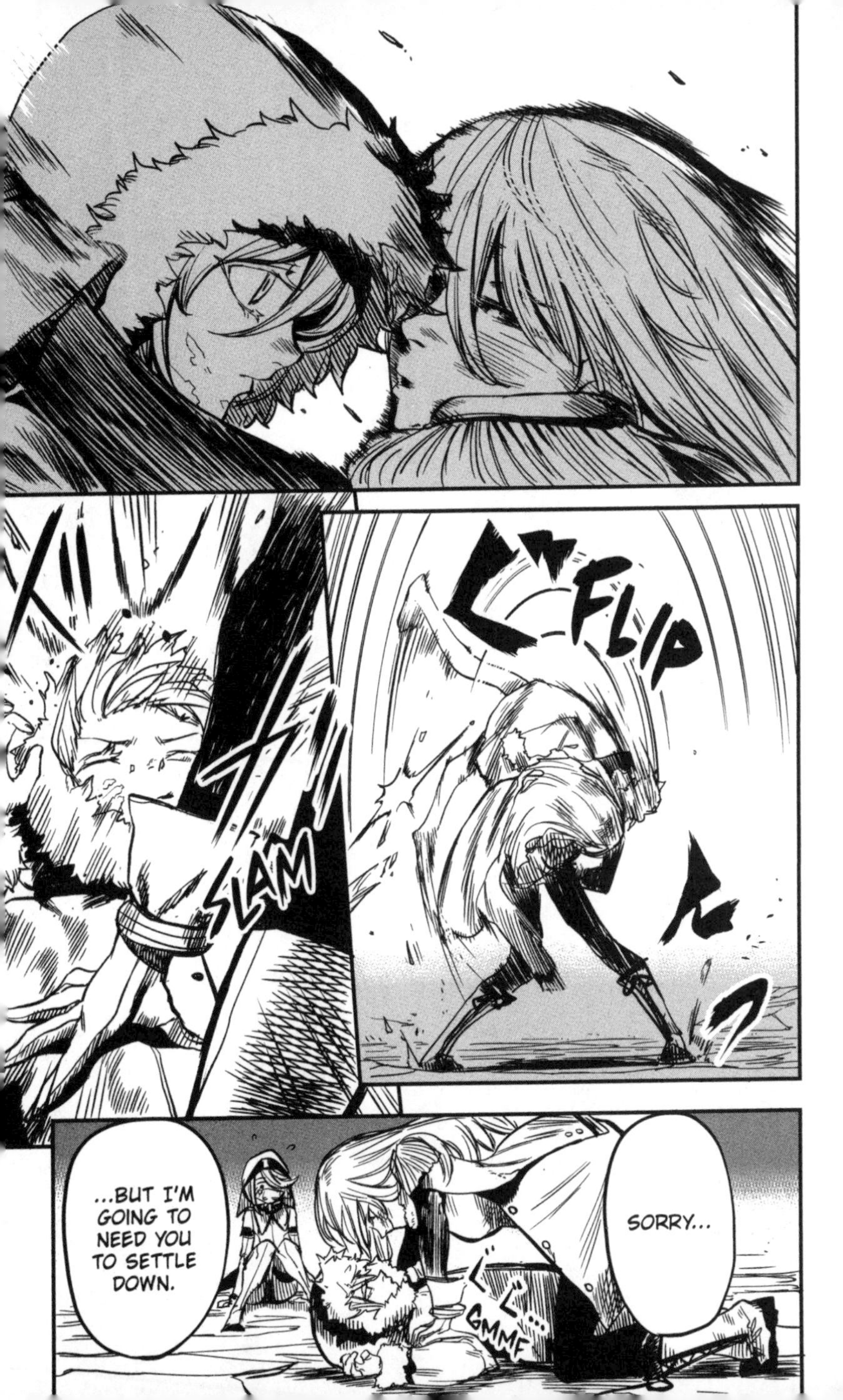
FLIP
SLAM
SORRY...
...BUT I'M GOING TO NEED YOU TO SETTLE DOWN.
GMMF

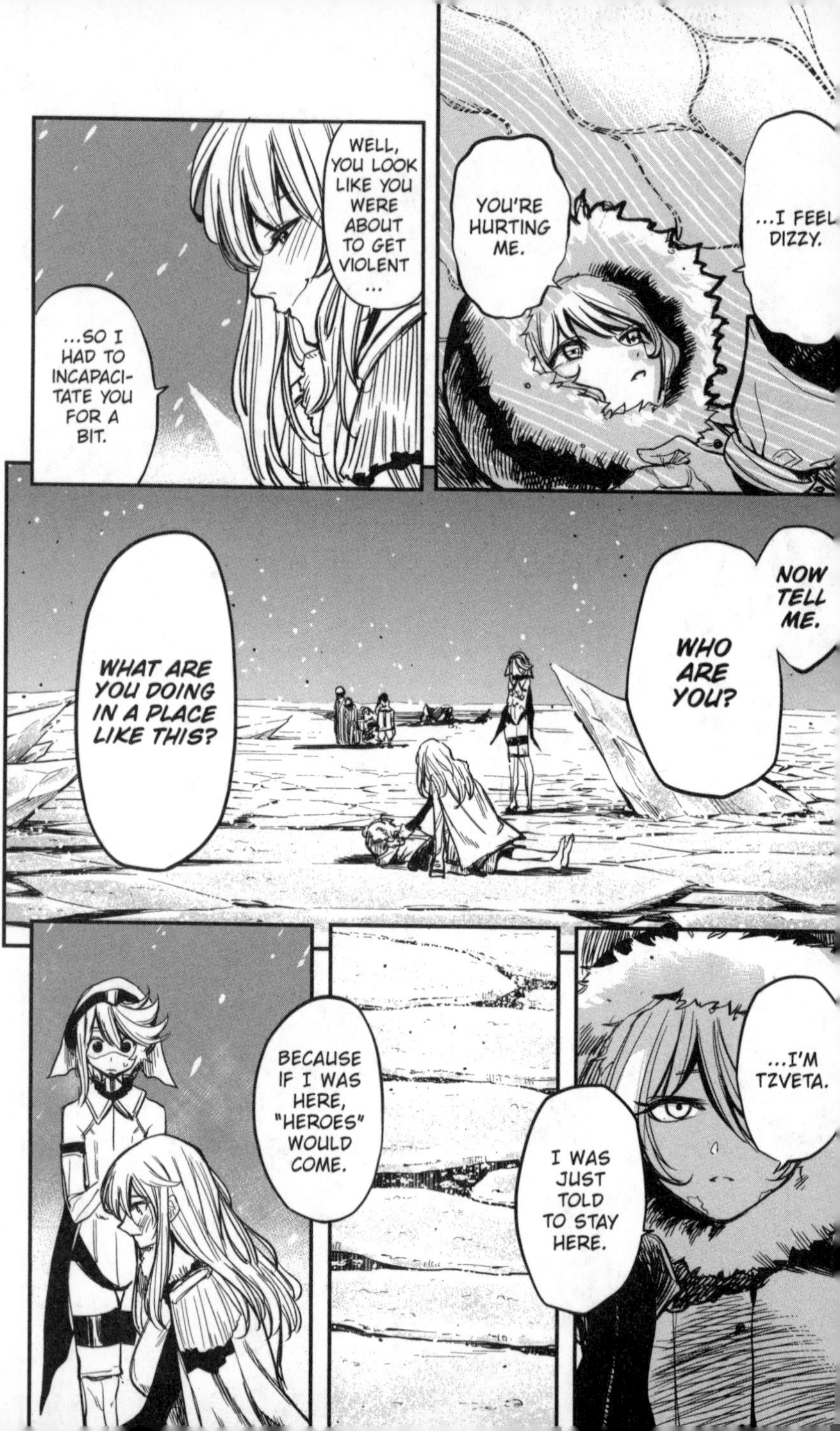
...I FEEL DIZZY.
YOU'RE HURTING ME.
WELL, YOU LOOK LIKE YOU WERE ABOUT TO GET VIOLENT ...
...SO I HAD TO INCAPACI-TATE YOU FOR A BIT.
NOW TELL ME.
WHO ARE YOU?
WHAT ARE YOU DOING IN A PLACE LIKE THIS?
...I'M TZVETA.
I WAS JUST TOLD TO STAY HERE.
BECAUSE IF I WAS HERE, "HEROES" WOULD COME.

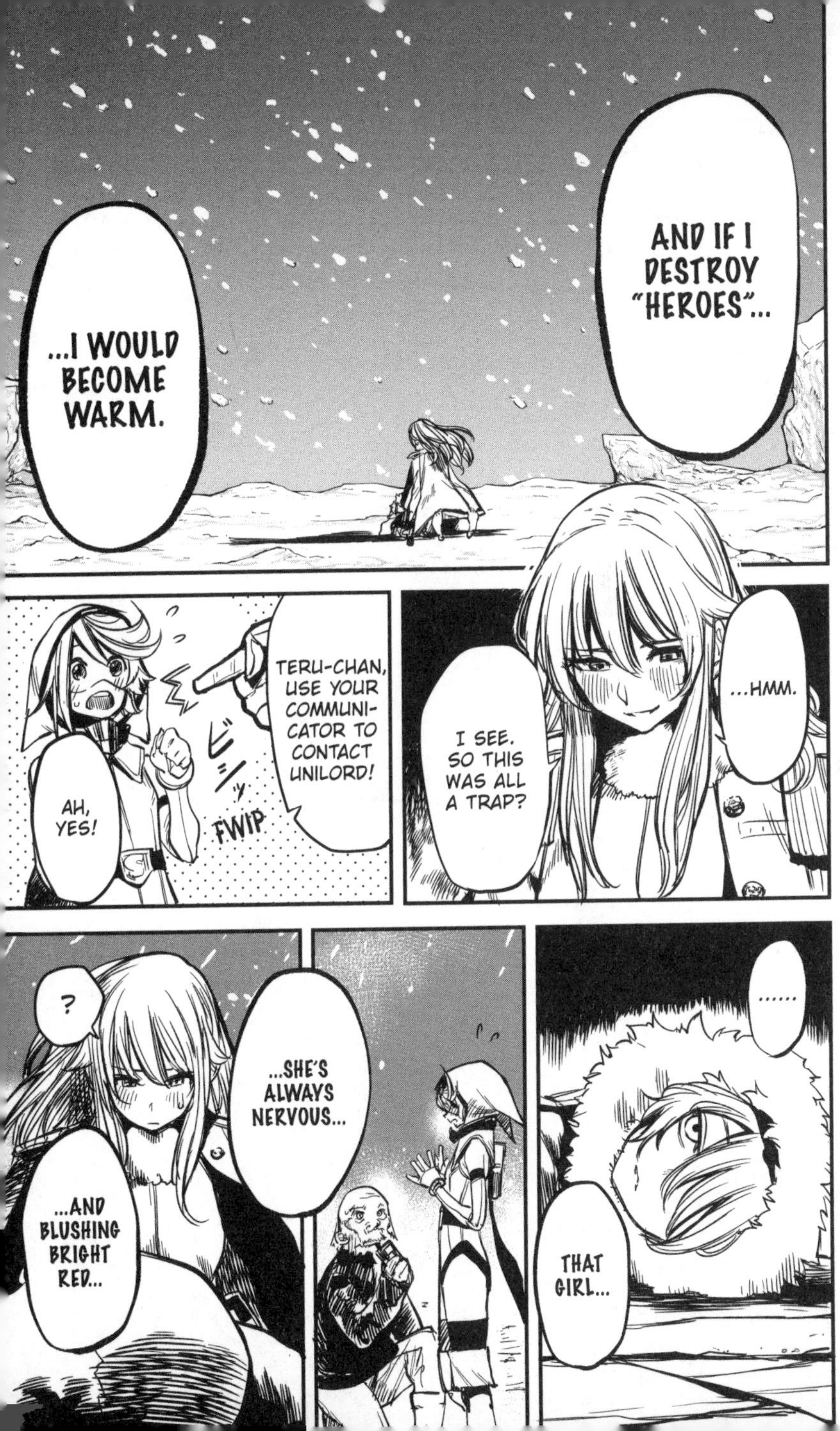
AND IF I DESTROY "HEROES"...
...I WOULD BECOME WARM.
...HMM.
I SEE. SO THIS WAS ALL A TRAP?
TERU-CHAN, USE YOUR COMMUNICATOR TO CONTACT UNILORD!
ビシッ
FWIP
AH, YES!
......
THAT GIRL...
...SHE'S ALWAYS NERVOUS...
?
...AND BLUSHING BRIGHT RED...

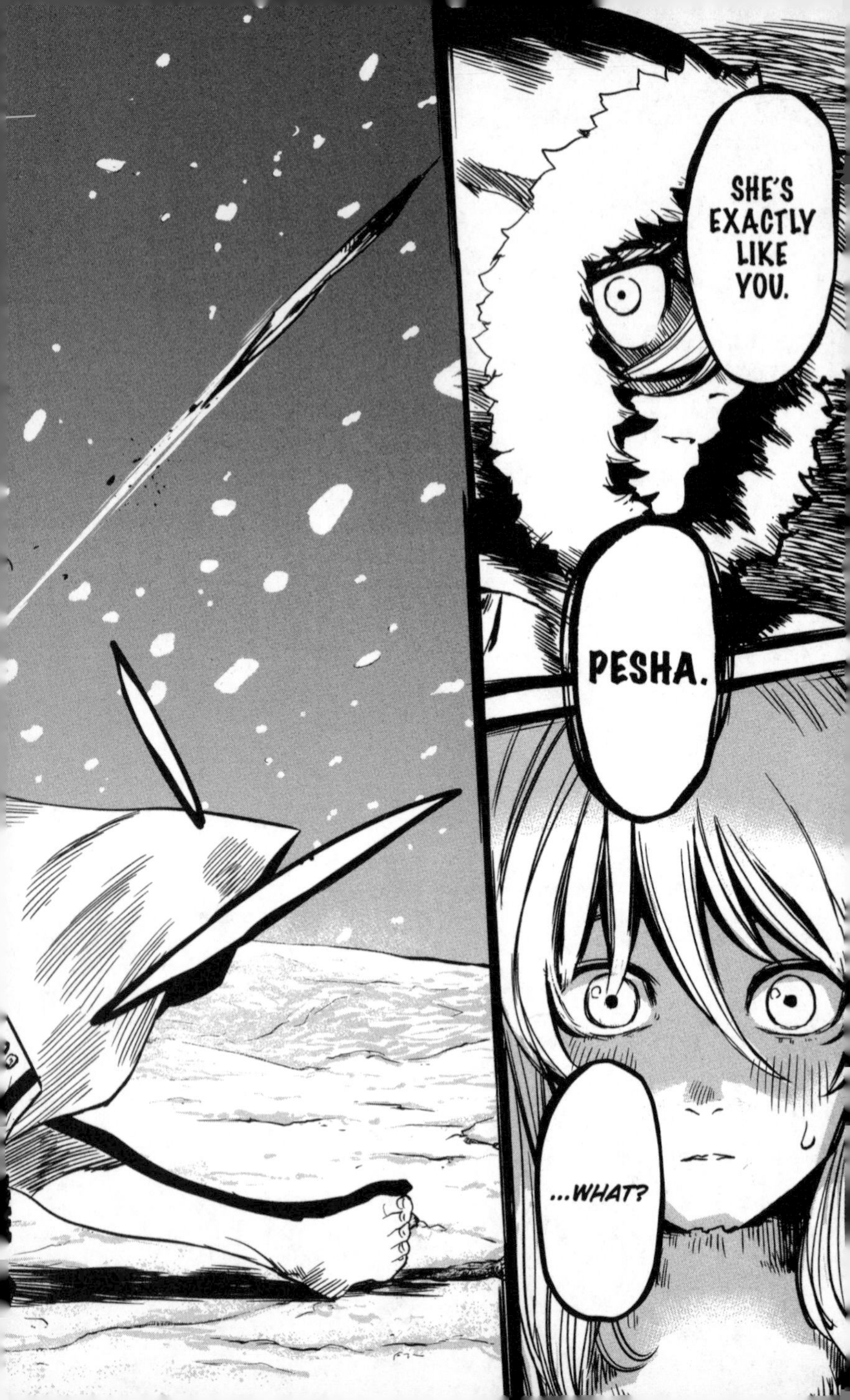
SHE'S EXACTLY LIKE YOU.
PESHA.
...WHAT?

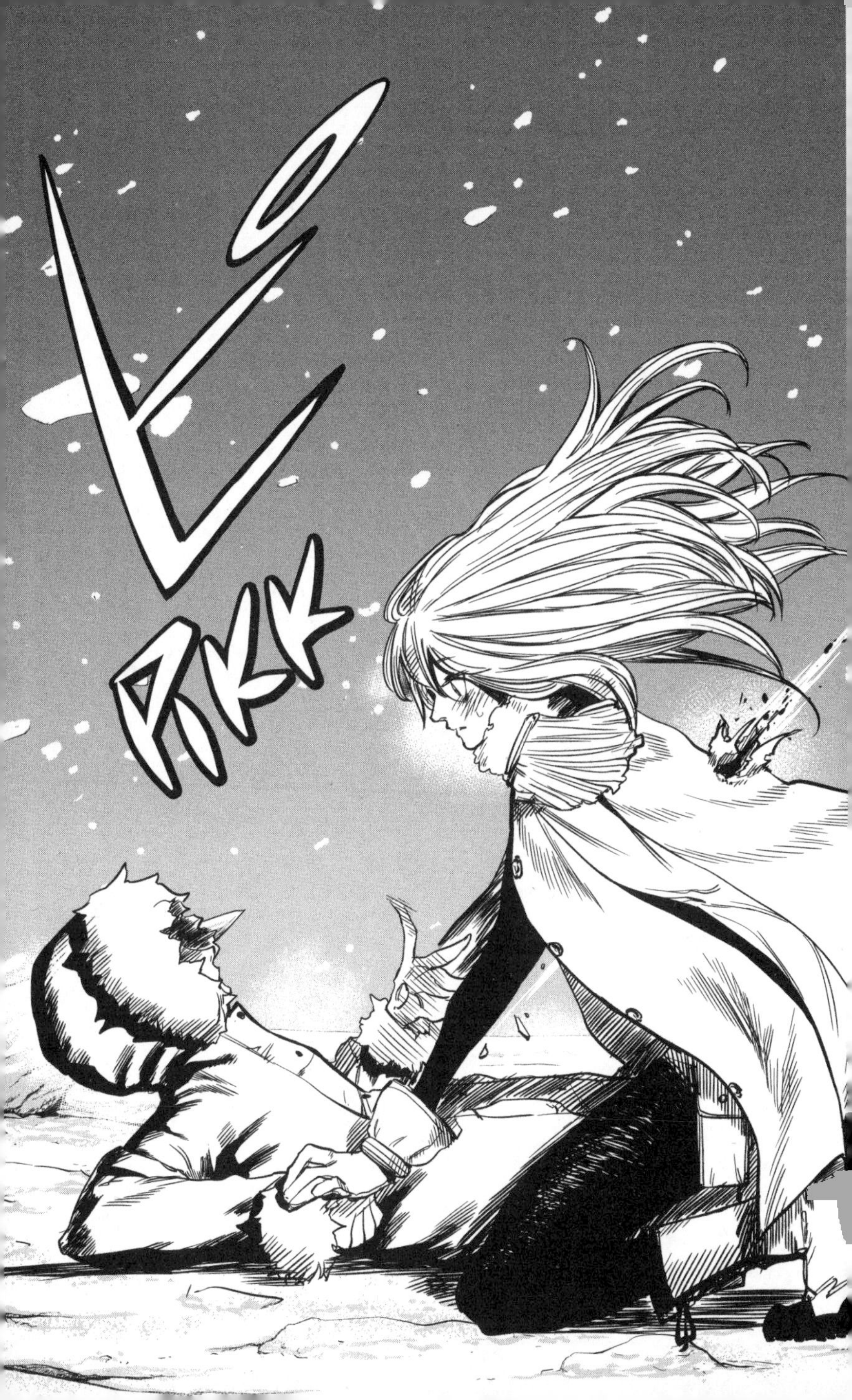
PIKK

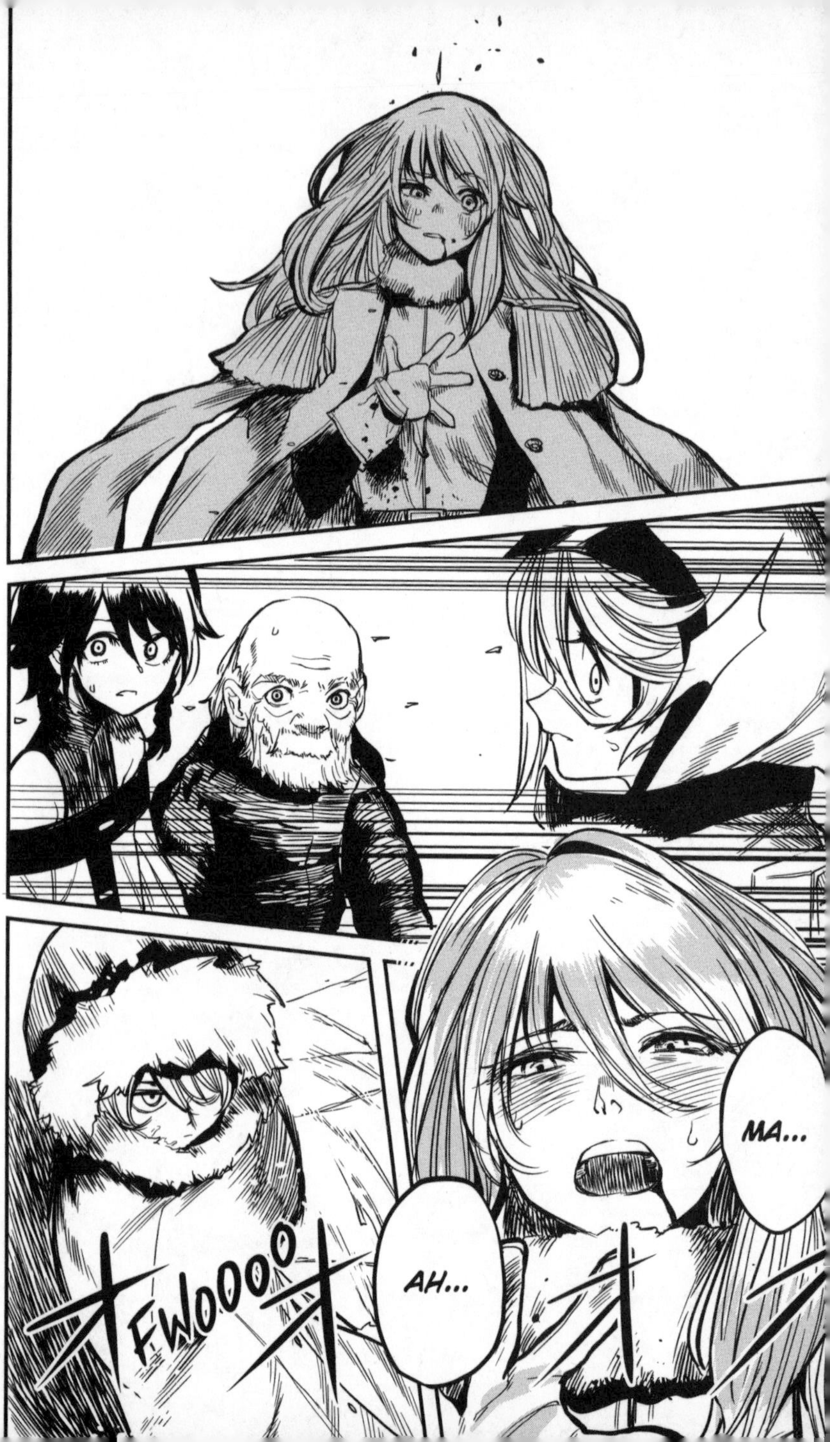
MA...
AH...
FWOOOO

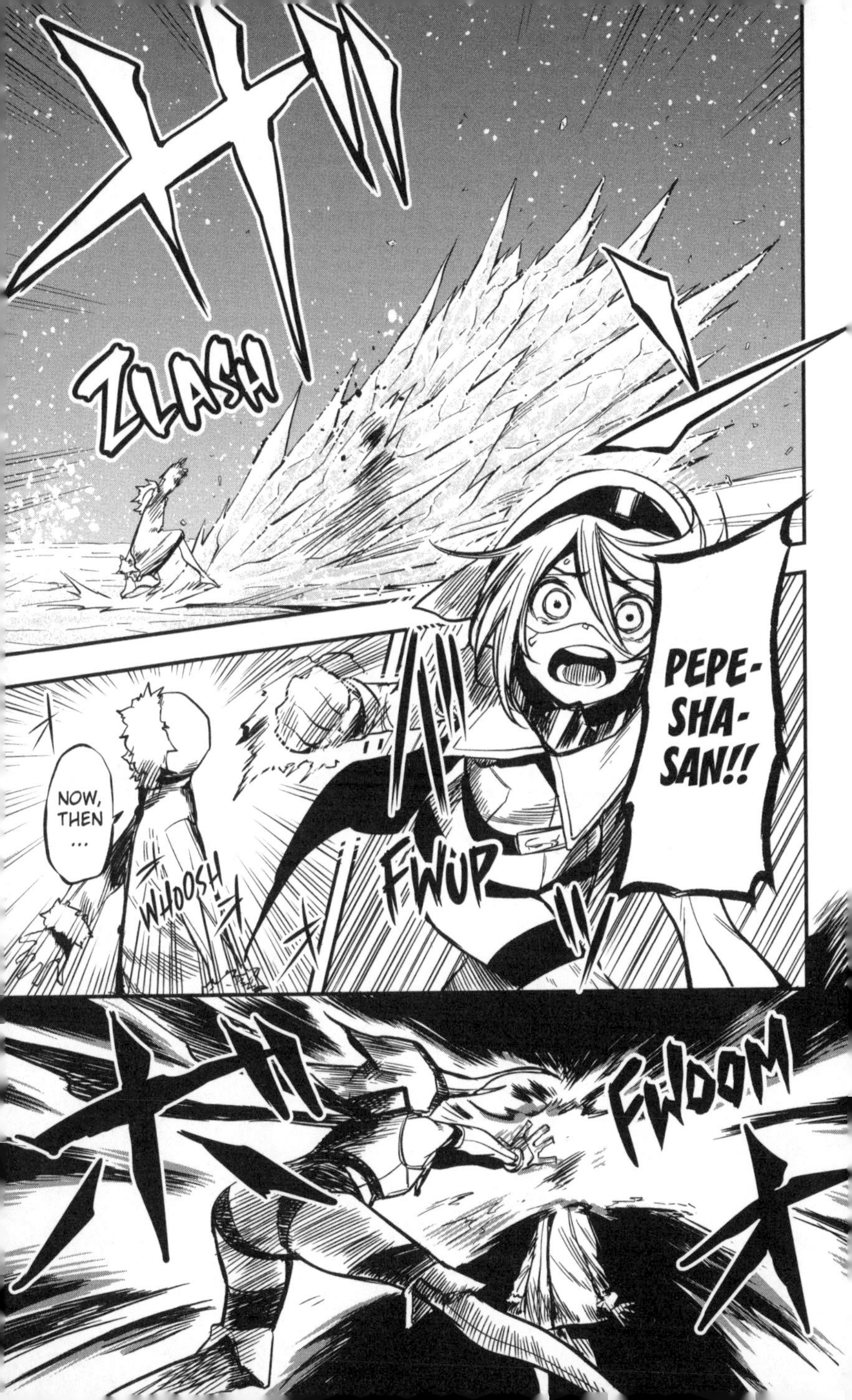
ZLASH
PEPE-SHA-SAN!!
FWUP
NOW, THEN ...
WHOOSH
FWOOM

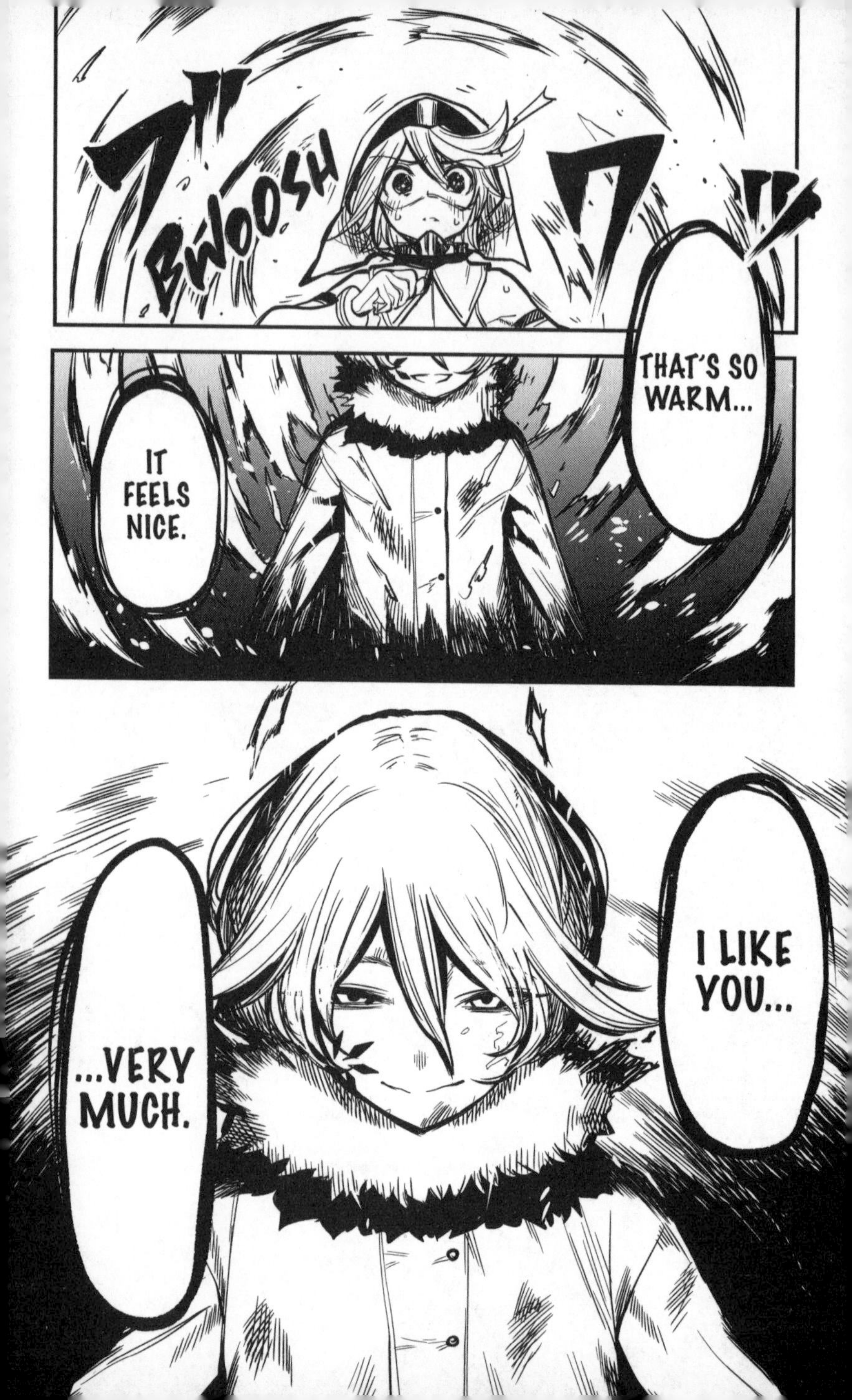
BWOOSH
THAT'S SO WARM...
IT FEELS NICE.
I LIKE YOU...
...VERY MUCH.

SHY

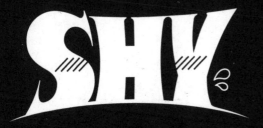

Chapter 15
Ice White

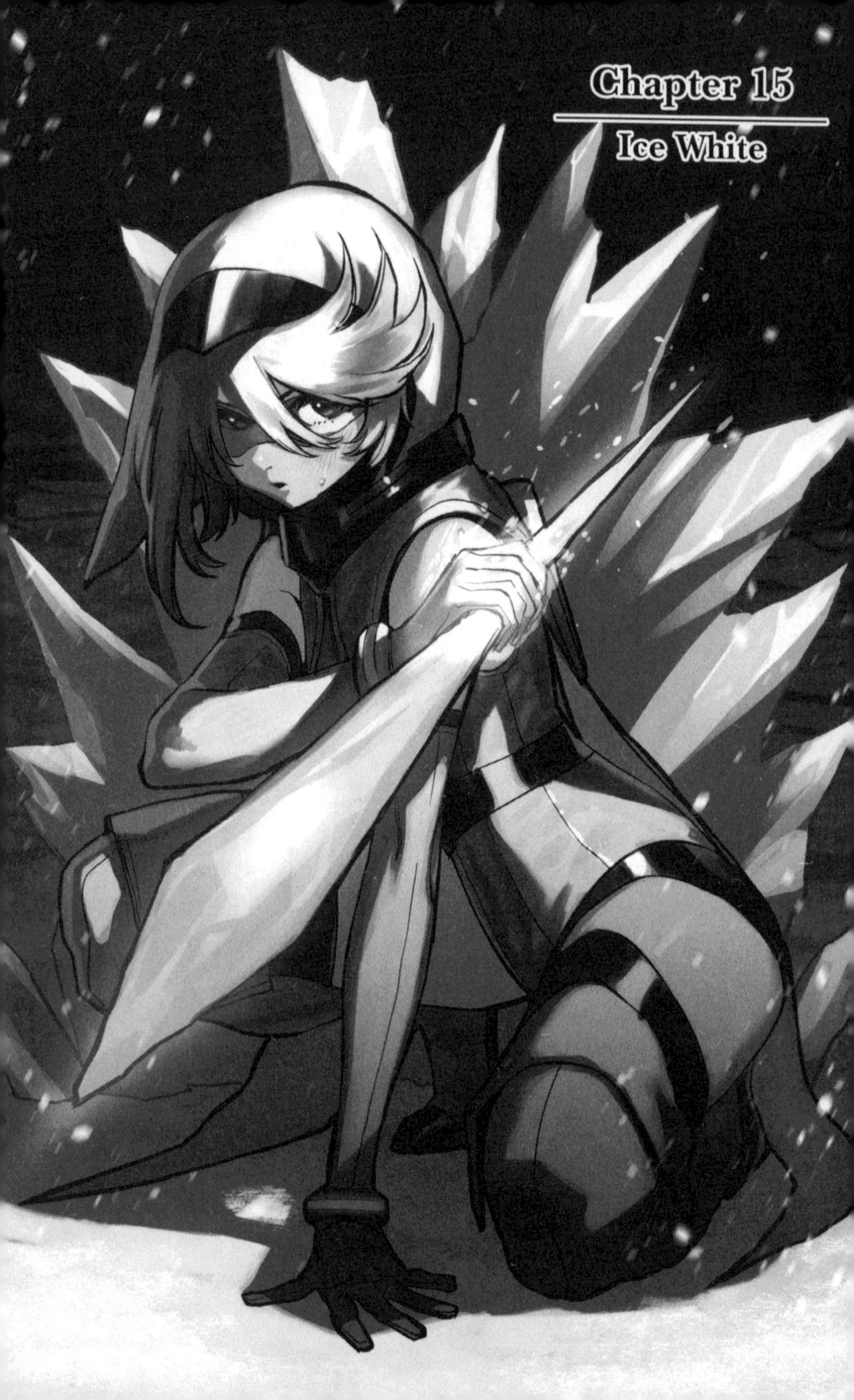

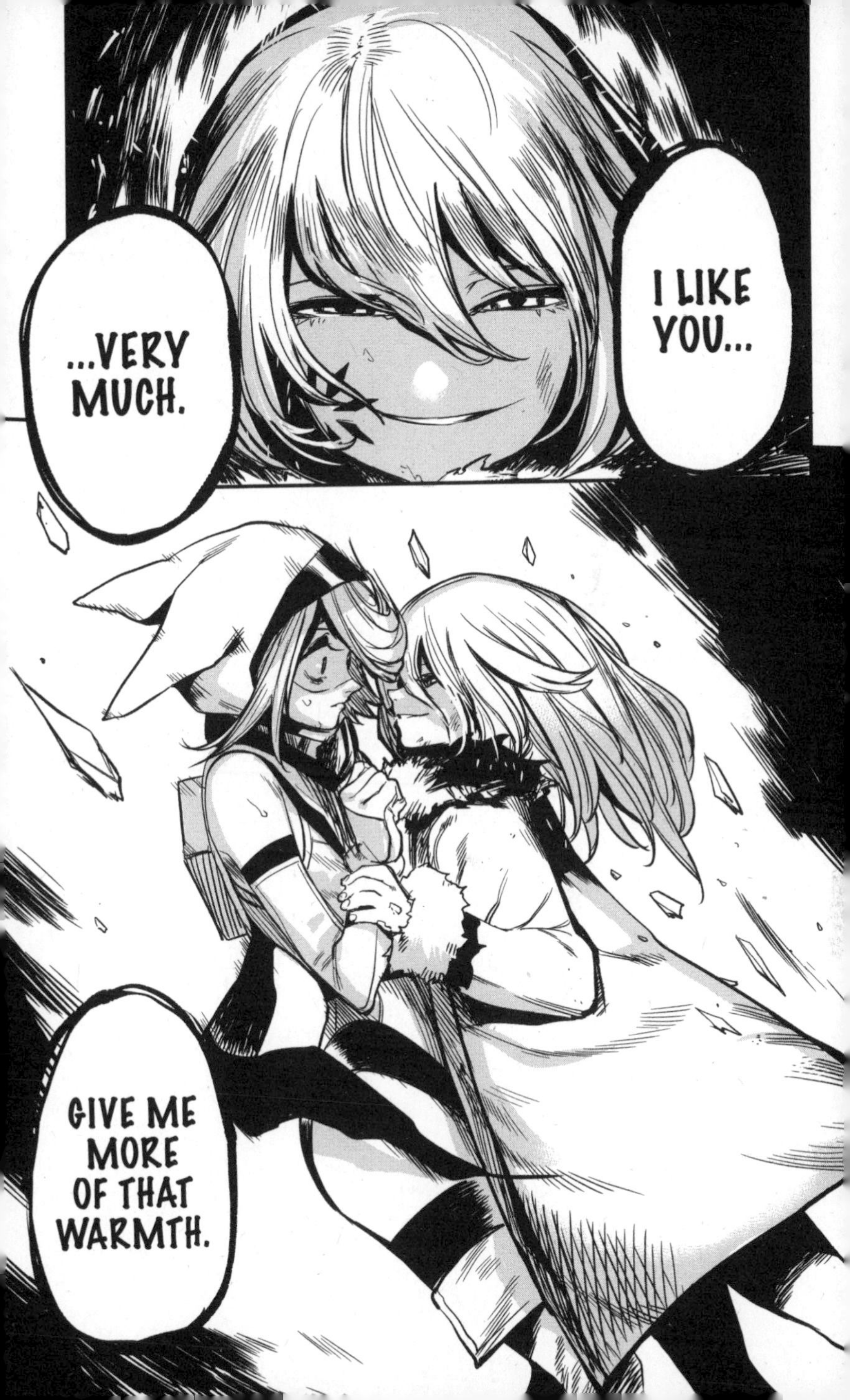
I LIKE YOU...
...VERY MUCH.
GIVE ME MORE OF THAT WARMTH.

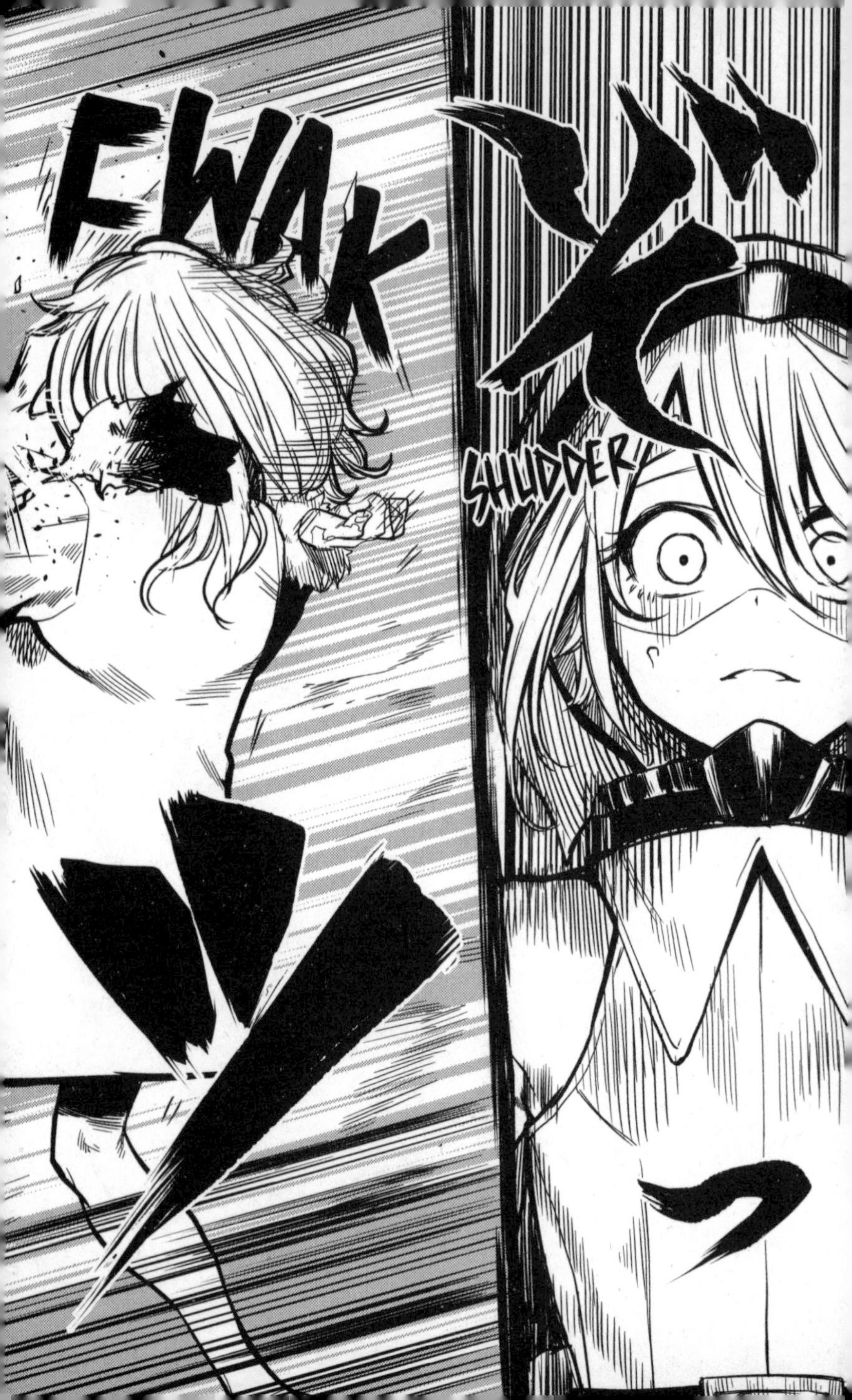
SHUDDER
FWAK

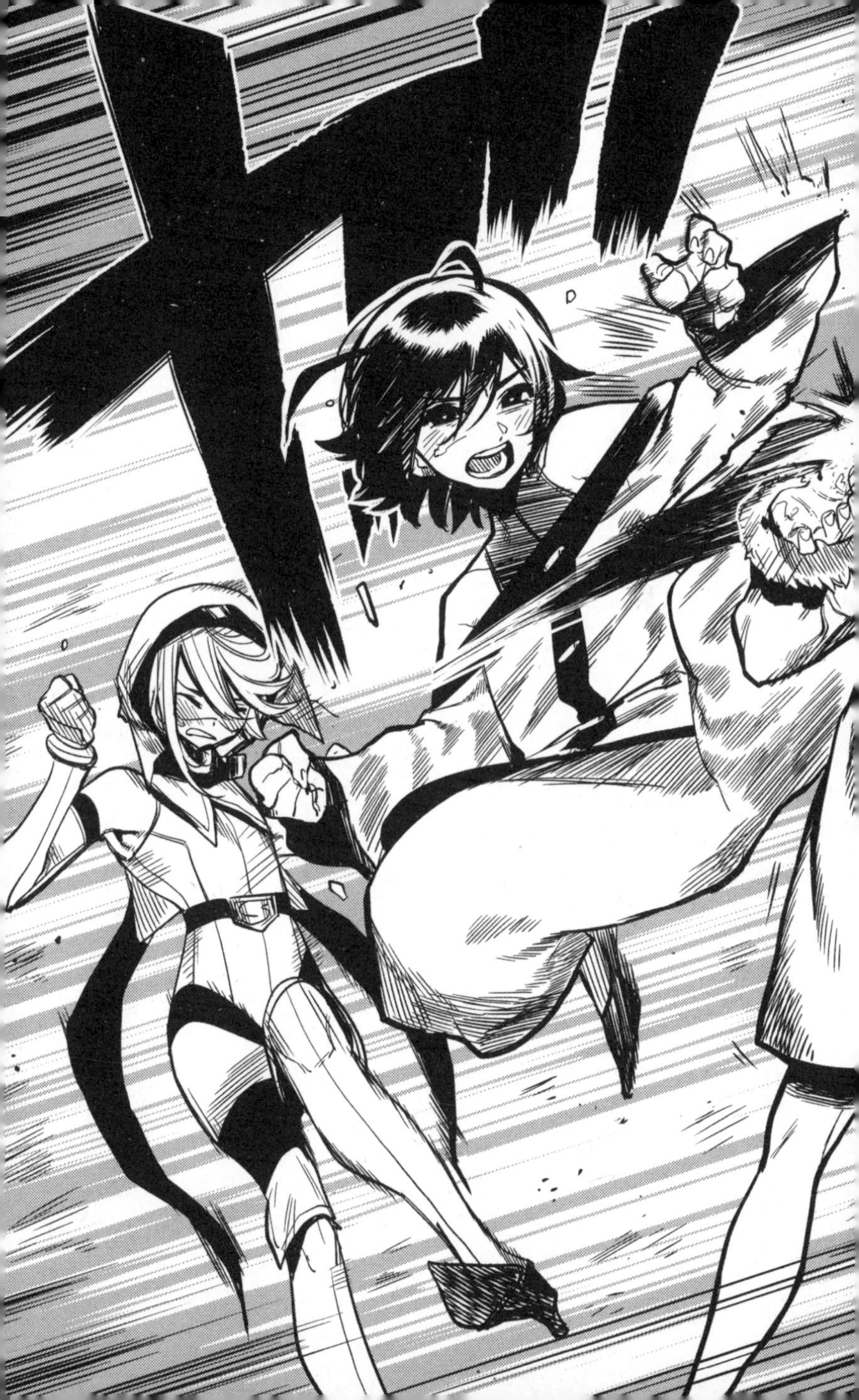

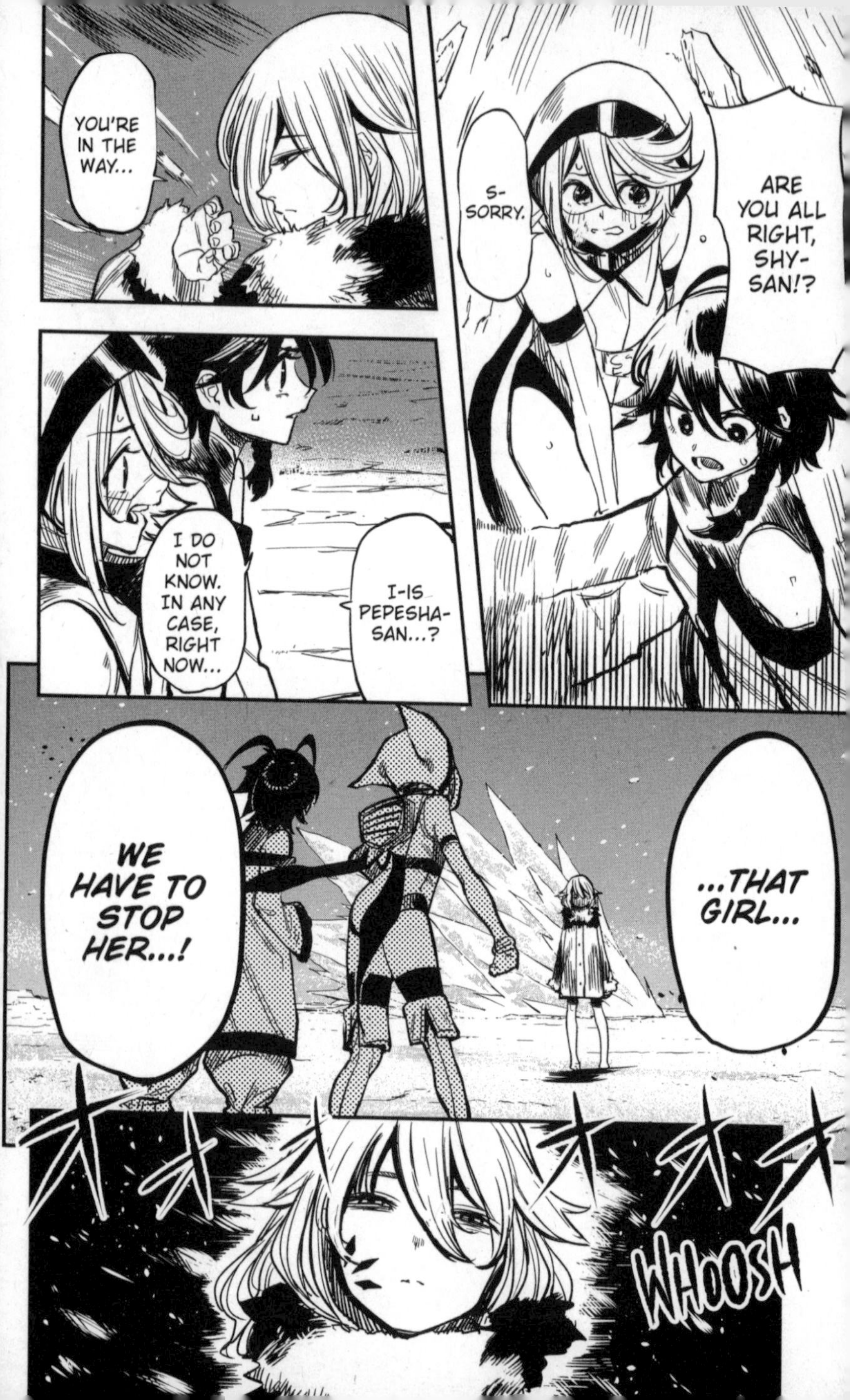
ARE YOU ALL RIGHT, SHY-SAN!?
S-SORRY.
YOU'RE IN THE WAY...
I-IS PEPESHA-SAN...?
I DO NOT KNOW. IN ANY CASE, RIGHT NOW...
...THAT GIRL...
WE HAVE TO STOP HER...!
WHOOSH

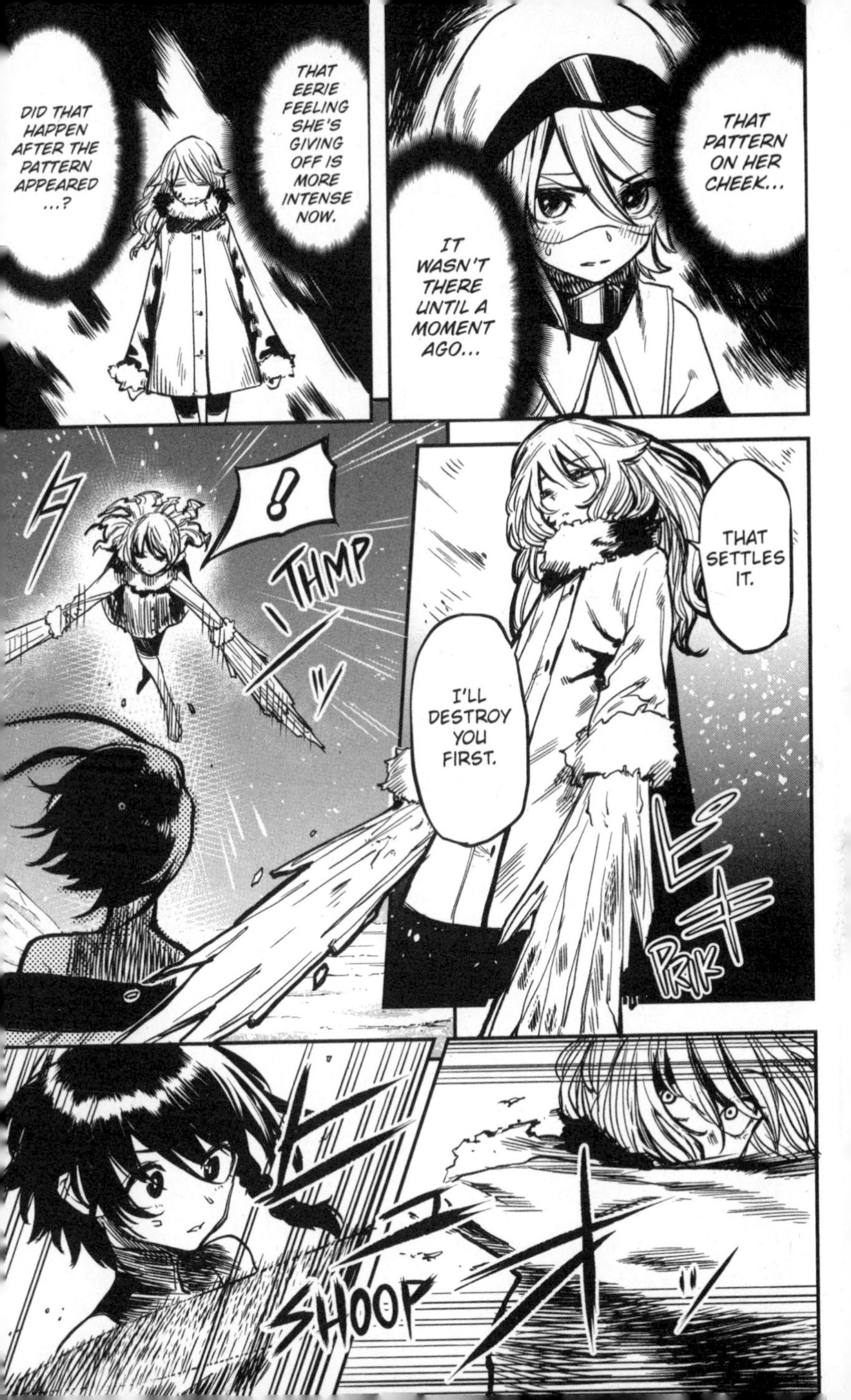
THAT PATTERN ON HER CHEEK...
IT WASN'T THERE UNTIL A MOMENT AGO...
THAT EERIE FEELING SHE'S GIVING OFF IS MORE INTENSE NOW.
DID THAT HAPPEN AFTER THE PATTERN APPEARED ...?
THAT SETTLES IT.
I'LL DESTROY YOU FIRST.
PRIK
!
THMP
SHOOP

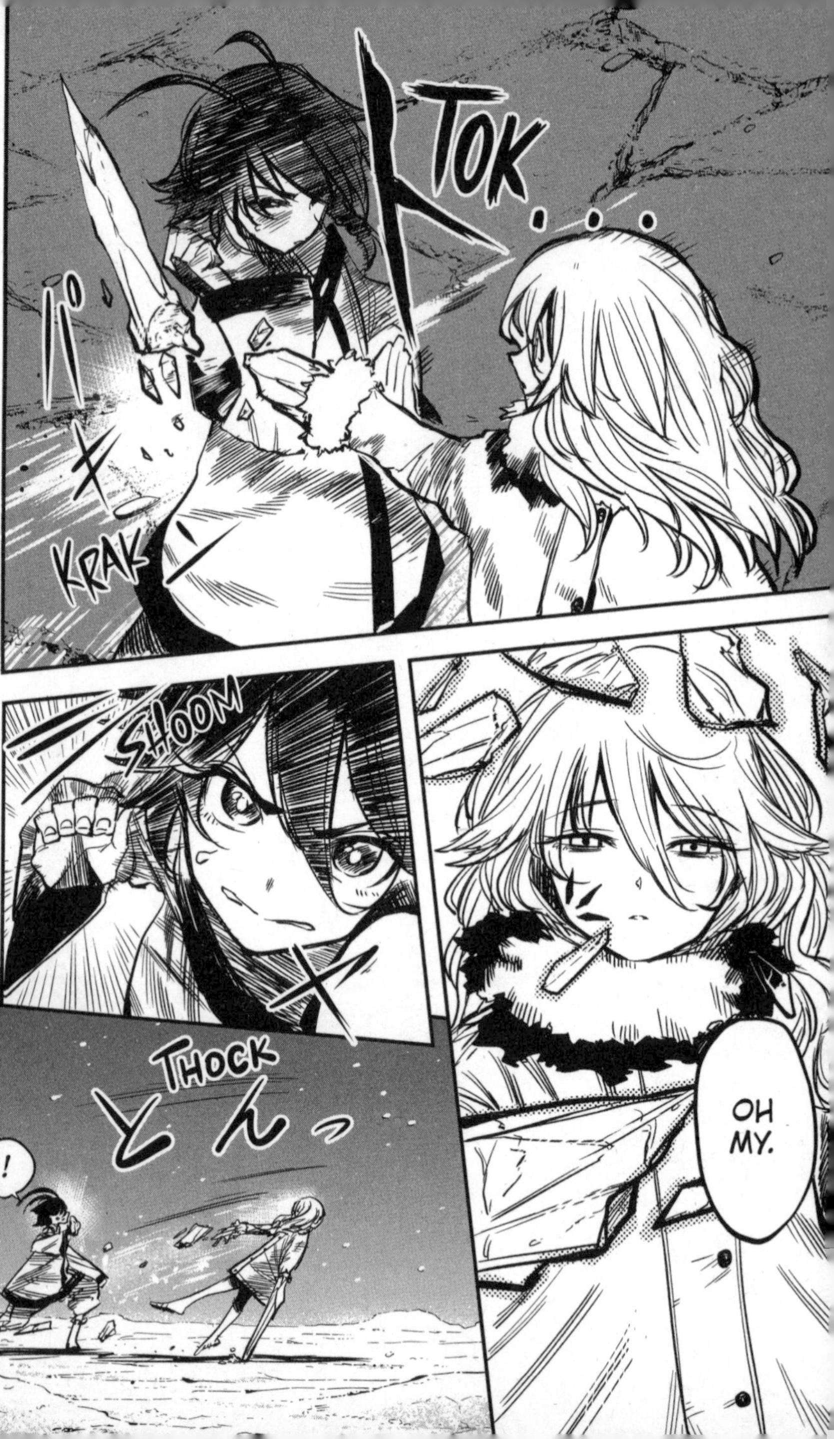
TOK
...
KRAK
OH MY.
SHOOM
THOCK
とんっ
!

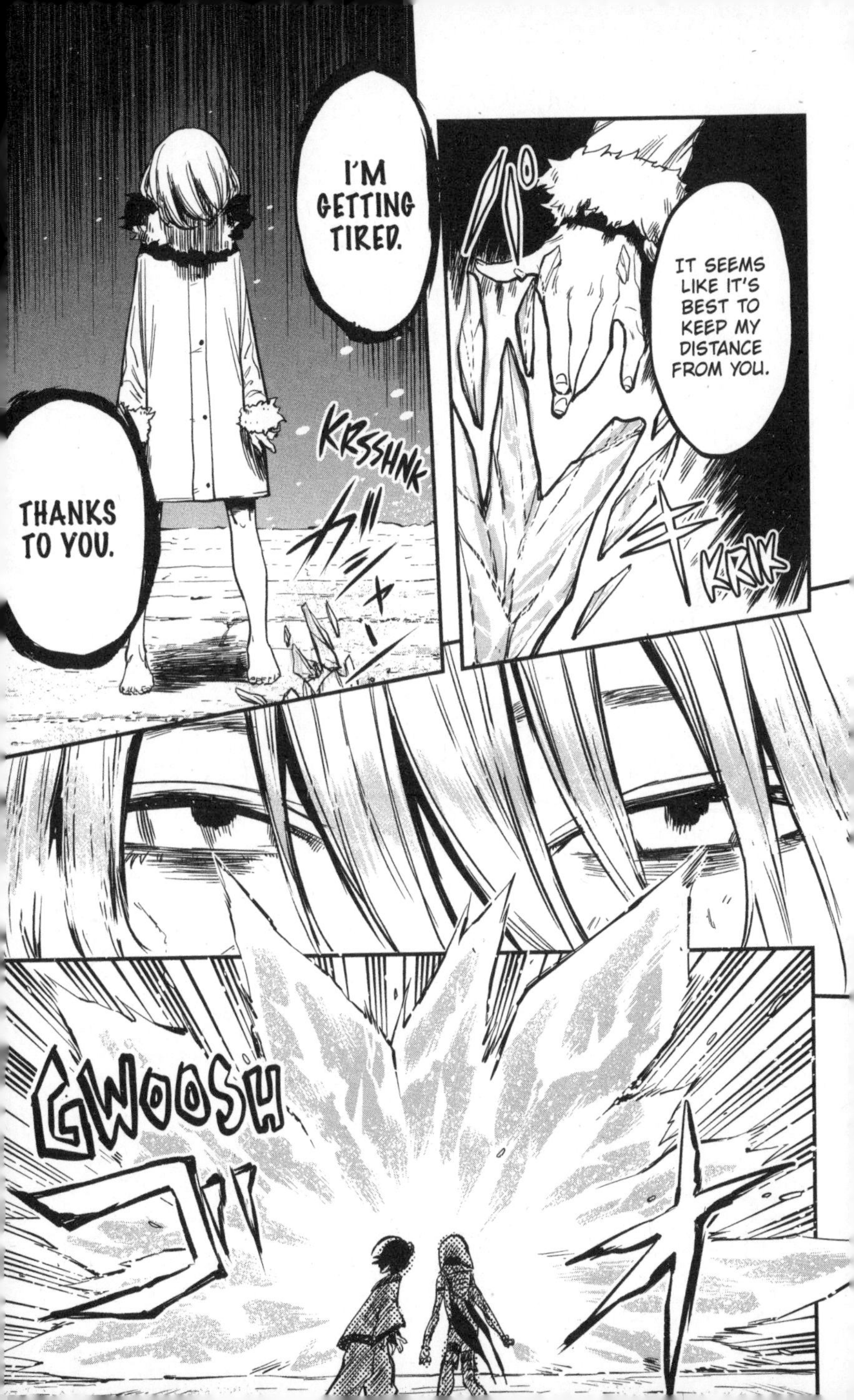
IT SEEMS LIKE IT'S BEST TO KEEP MY DISTANCE FROM YOU.
KRIK
I'M GETTING TIRED.
THANKS TO YOU.
KRSSHNK
GWOOSH

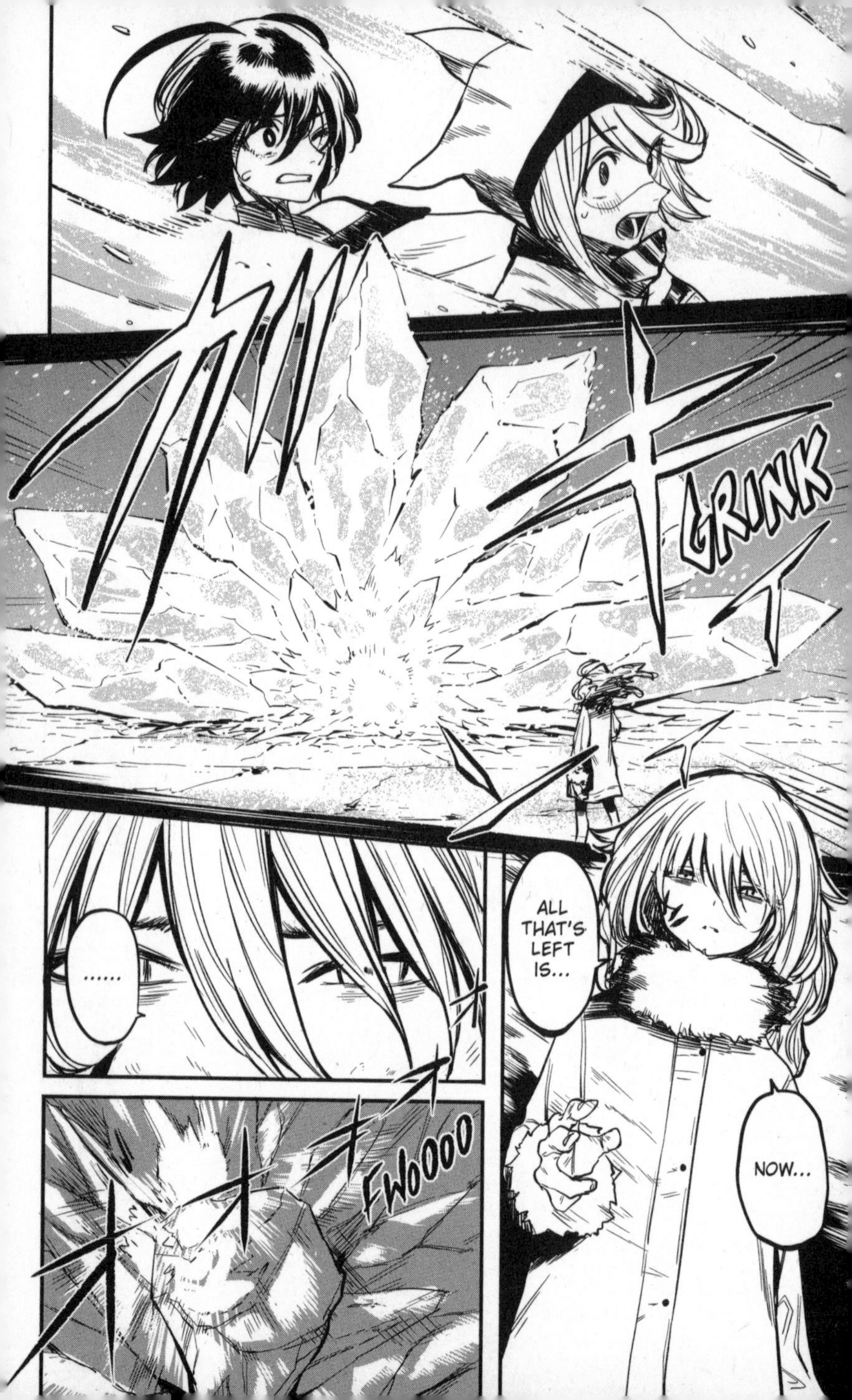
GRINK
ALL THAT'S LEFT IS...
NOW...
......
FWOOOO

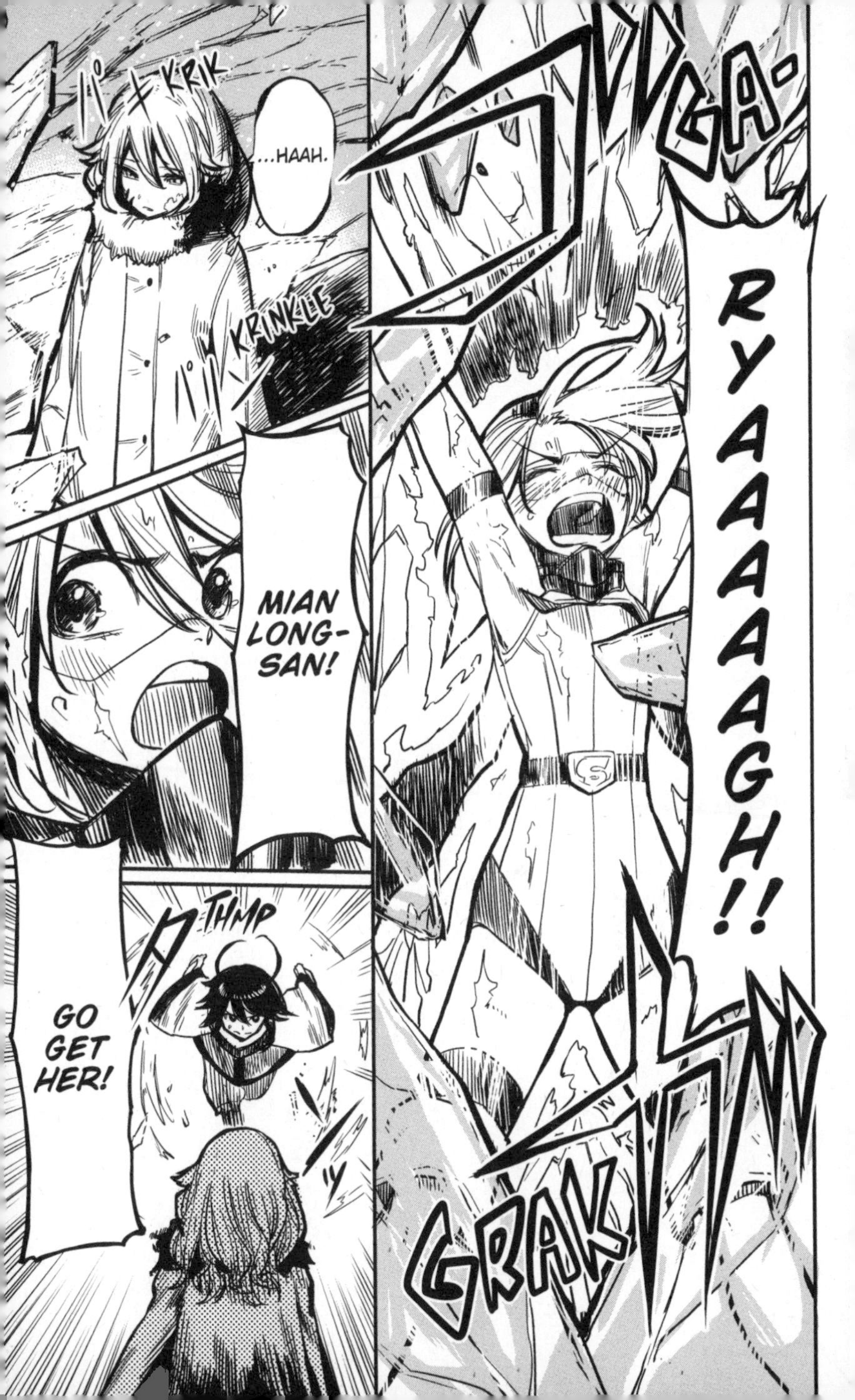
GA-
RYAAAAAAGH!!
GRAK
KRIK
...HAAH.
KRINKLE
MIAN LONG-SAN!
THMP
GO GET HER!

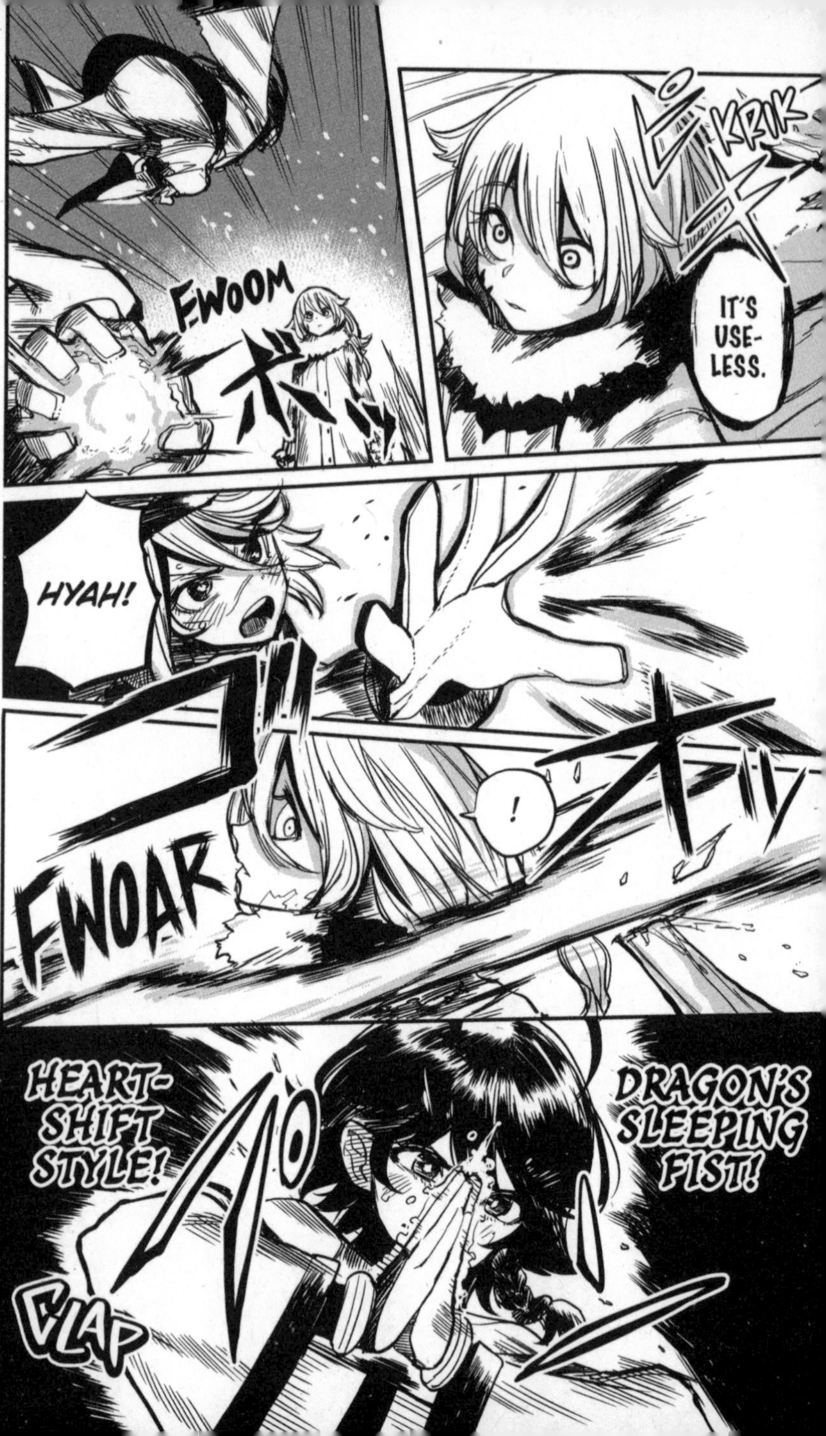
KRIK
IT'S USE-LESS.
FWOOM
HYAH!
!
FWOAR
DRAGON'S SLEEPING FIST!
HEART-SHIFT STYLE!
CLAP

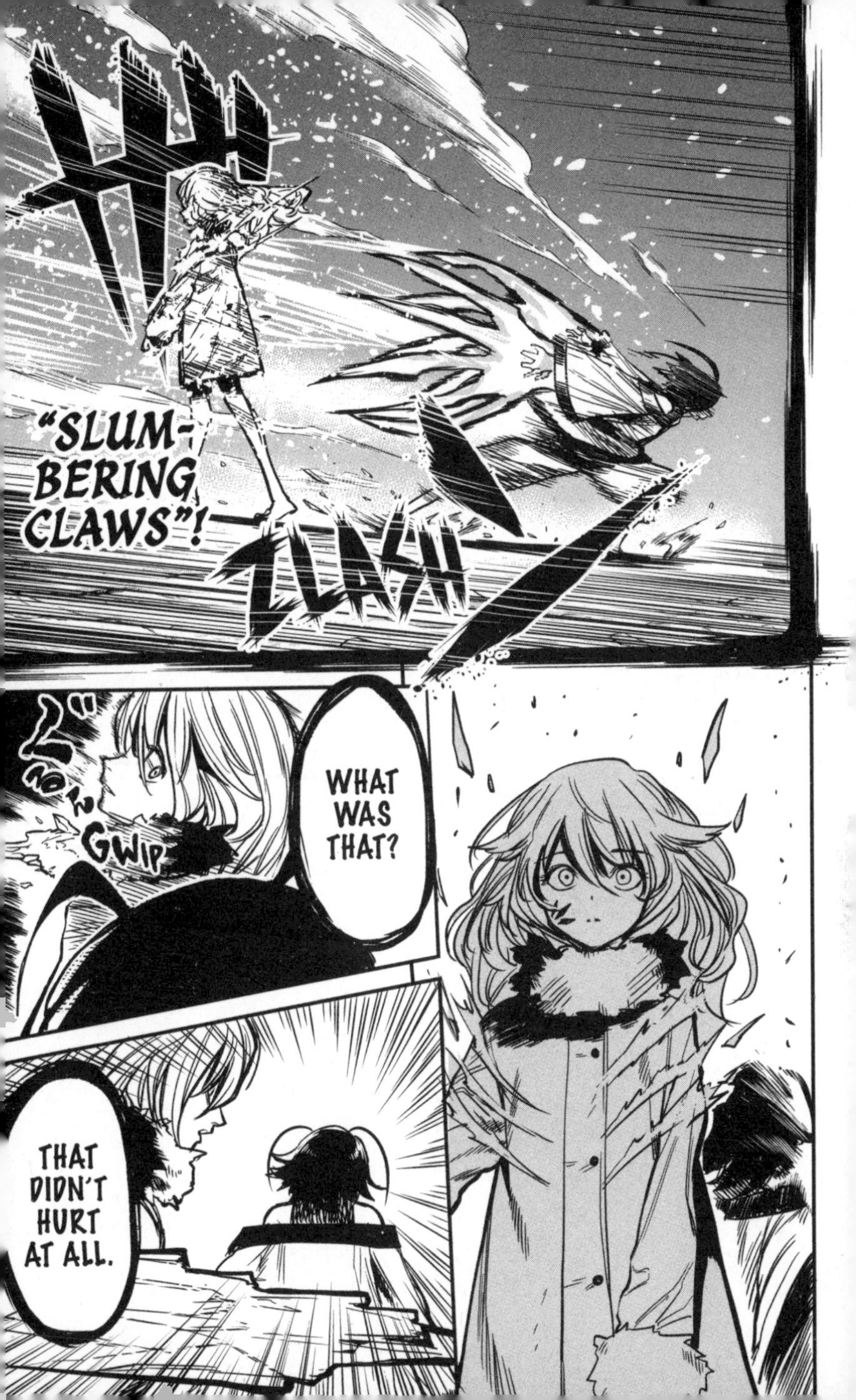
"SLUMBERING CLAWS"!
WHAT WAS THAT?
GWIP
THAT DIDN'T HURT AT ALL.

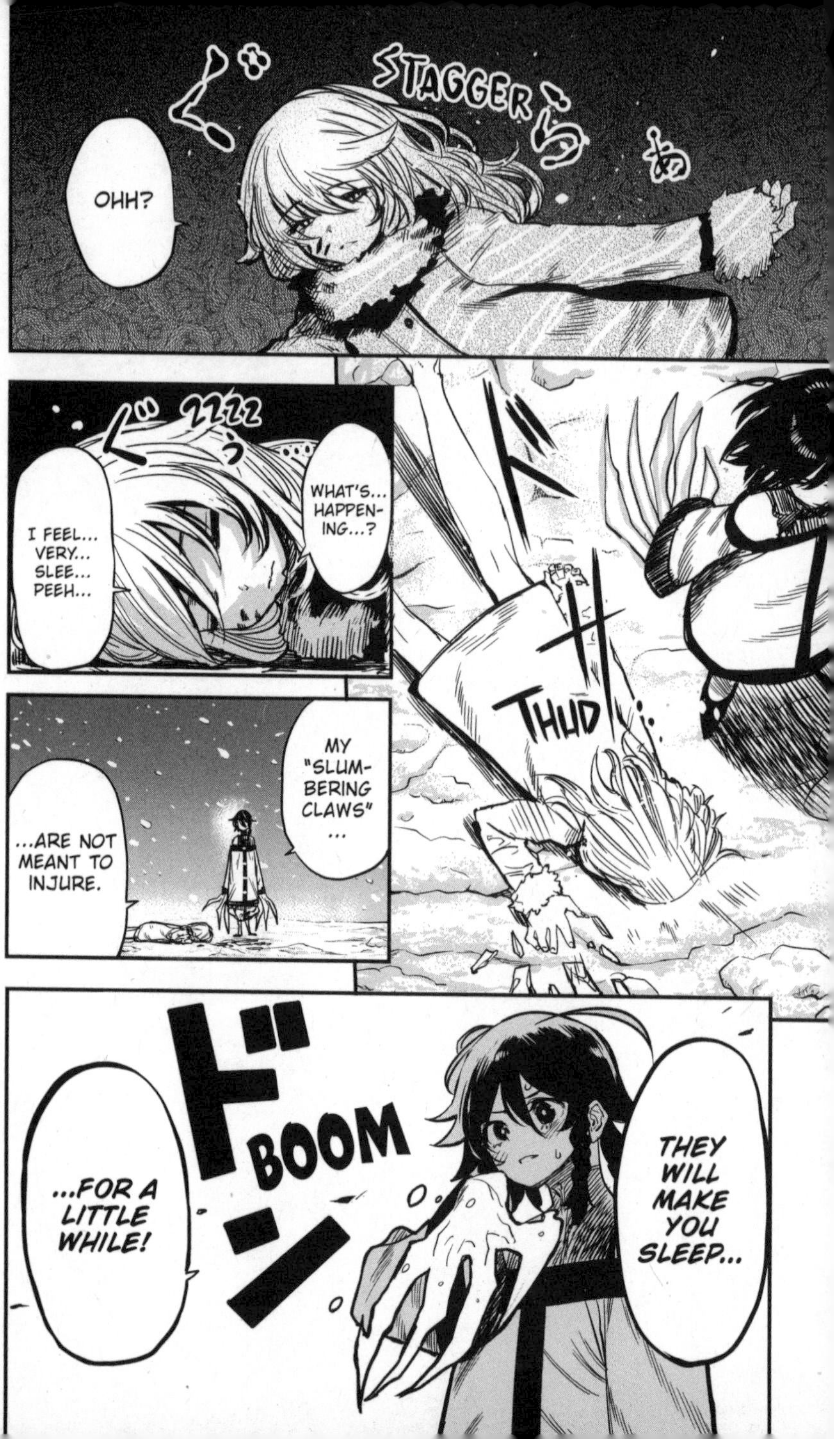
STAGGER
OHH?
THUD
ZZZZ
WHAT'S... HAPPEN-ING...?
I FEEL... VERY... SLEE... PEEH...
MY "SLUMBERING CLAWS"...
...ARE NOT MEANT TO INJURE.
BOOM
THEY WILL MAKE YOU SLEEP...
...FOR A LITTLE WHILE!

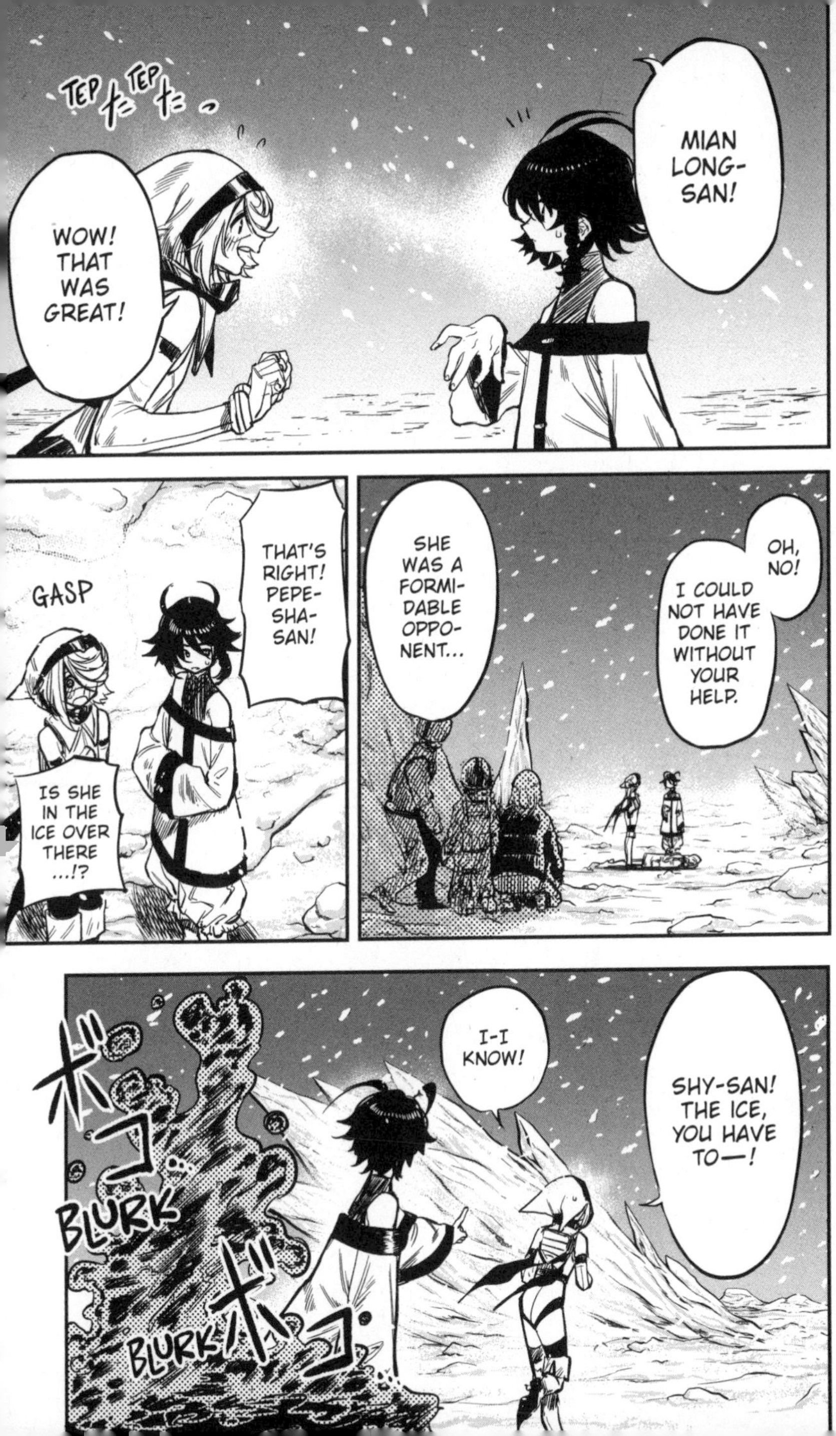
MIAN LONG-SAN!
TEP TEP
WOW! THAT WAS GREAT!
OH, NO!
I COULD NOT HAVE DONE IT WITHOUT YOUR HELP.
SHE WAS A FORMIDABLE OPPONENT...
THAT'S RIGHT! PEPE-SHA-SAN!
GASP
IS SHE IN THE ICE OVER THERE ...!?
SHY-SAN! THE ICE, YOU HAVE TO—!
I-I KNOW!
BLURK
BLURK

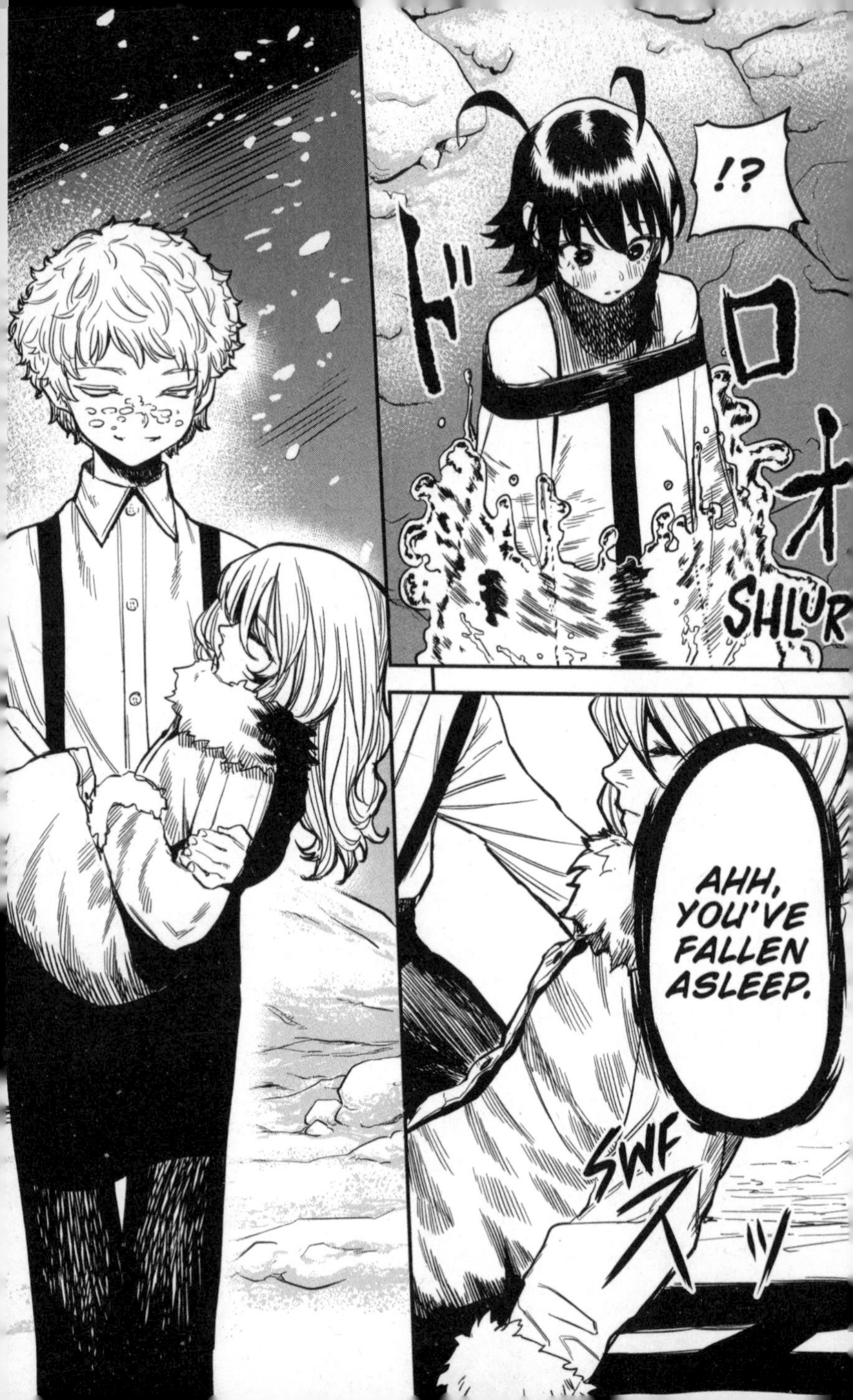
!?
ドロオ
SHLUR
AHH, YOU'VE FALLEN ASLEEP.
SWF
スッ

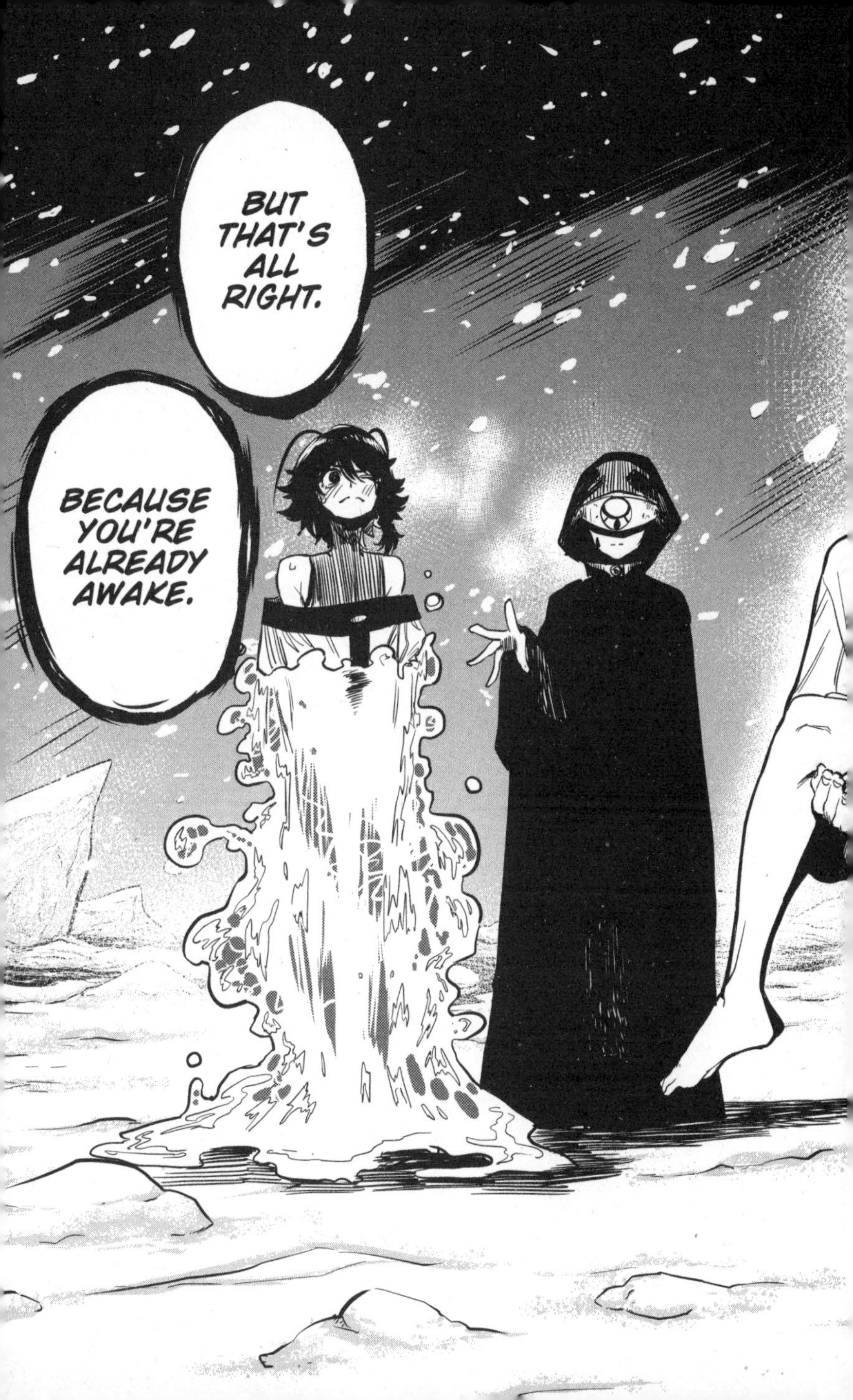
BUT THAT'S ALL RIGHT.
BECAUSE YOU'RE ALREADY AWAKE.

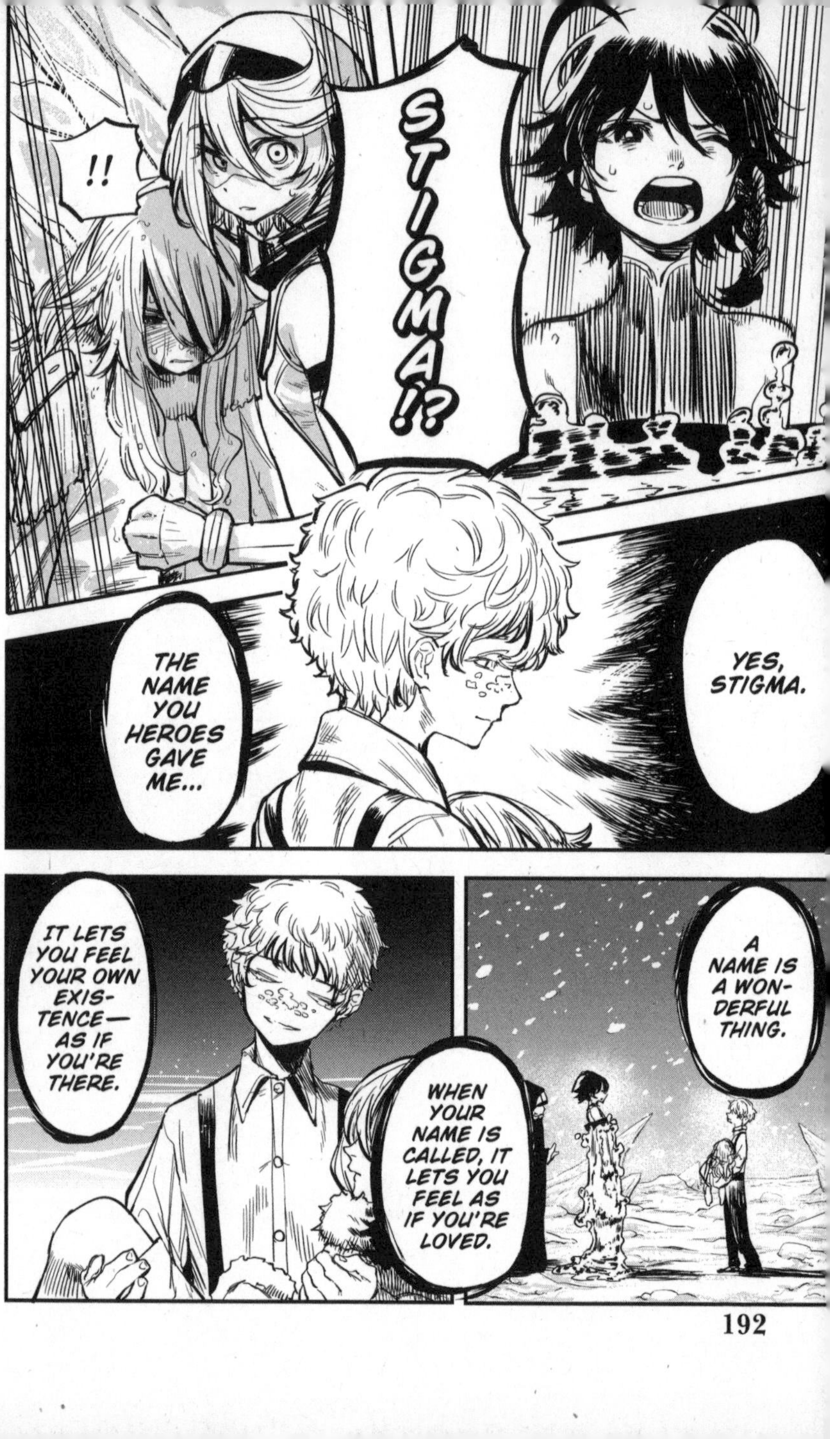
STIGMA!?
!!
YES, STIGMA.
THE NAME YOU HEROES GAVE ME...
A NAME IS A WONDERFUL THING.
IT LETS YOU FEEL YOUR OWN EXISTENCE—AS IF YOU'RE THERE.
WHEN YOUR NAME IS CALLED, IT LETS YOU FEEL AS IF YOU'RE LOVED.

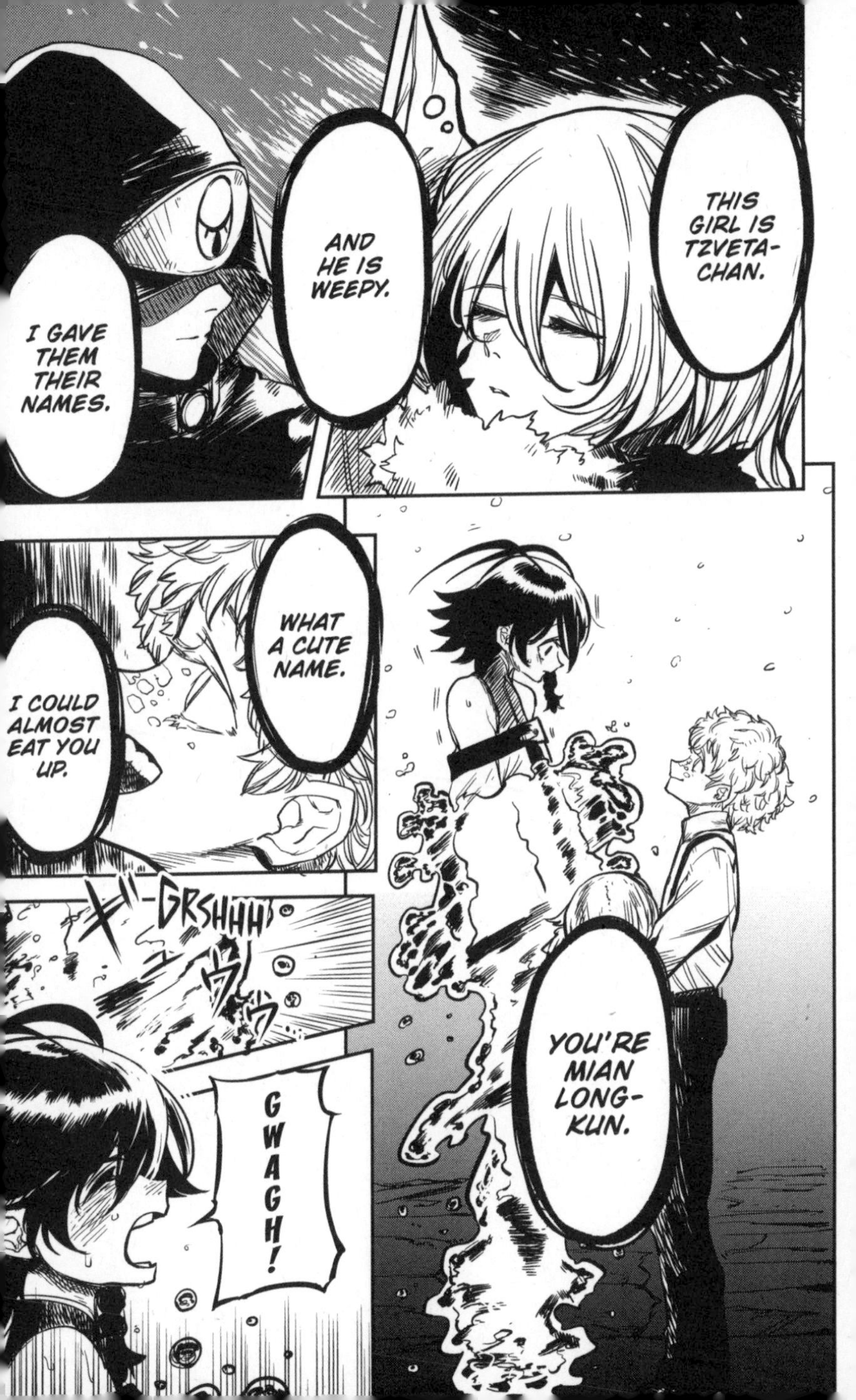
THIS GIRL IS TZVETA-CHAN.
AND HE IS WEEPY.
I GAVE THEM THEIR NAMES.
YOU'RE MIAN LONG-KUN.
WHAT A CUTE NAME.
I COULD ALMOST EAT YOU UP.
GRSHHH
GWAGH!

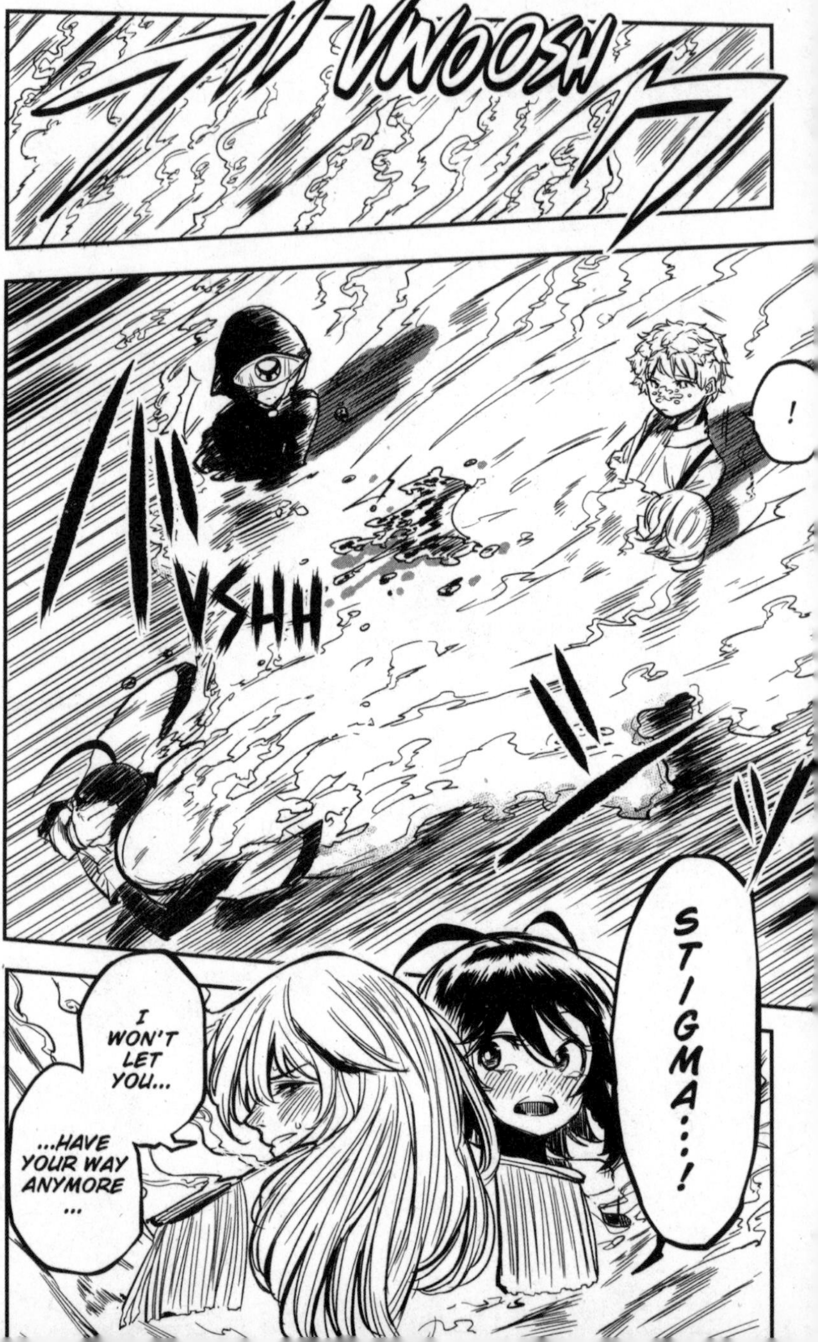
VWOOSH
!
VSHH
STIGMA...!
I WON'T LET YOU...
...HAVE YOUR WAY ANYMORE...

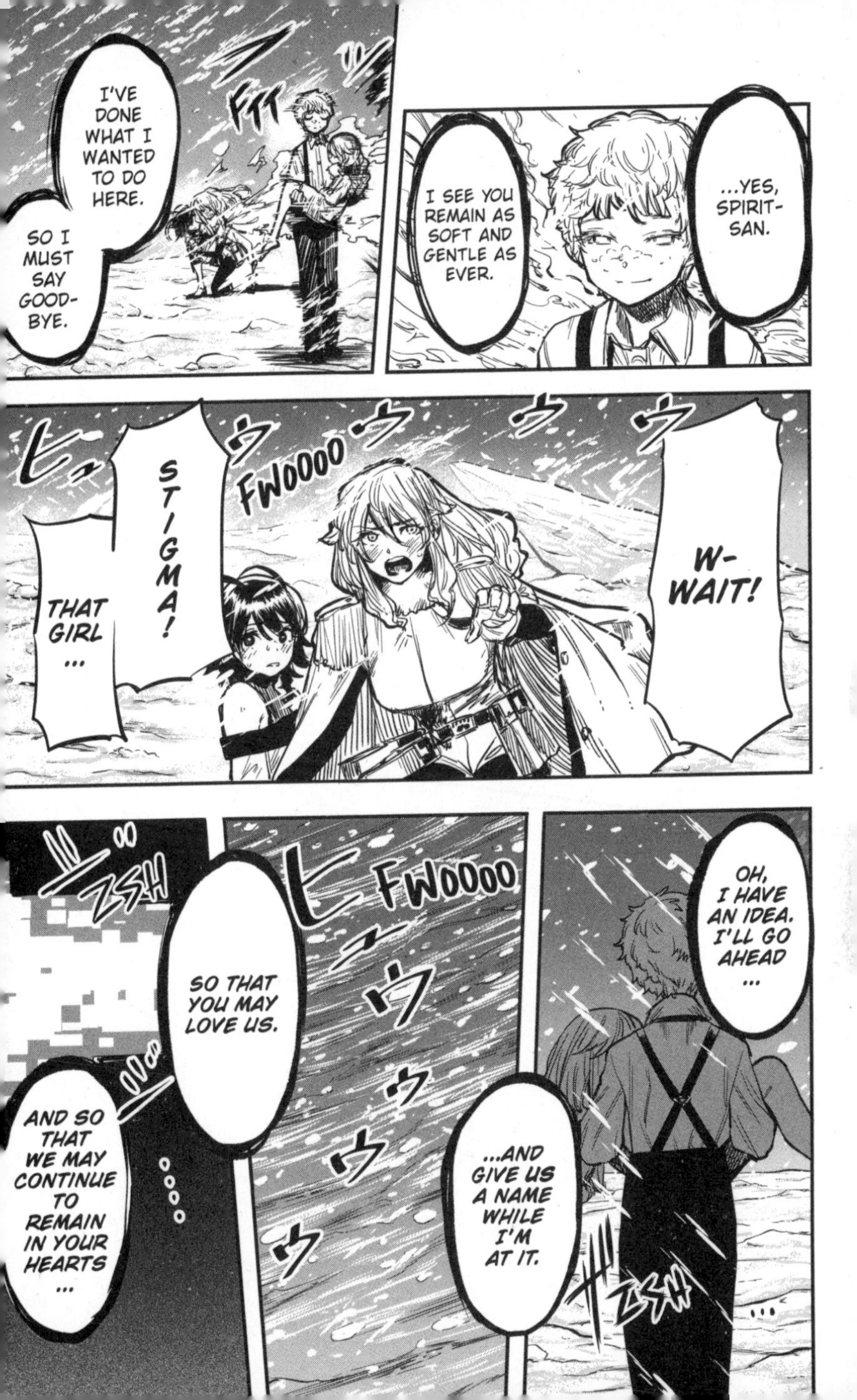
...YES, SPIRIT-SAN.
I SEE YOU REMAIN AS SOFT AND GENTLE AS EVER.
I'VE DONE WHAT I WANTED TO DO HERE.
SO I MUST SAY GOOD-BYE.
W-WAIT!
FWOOOO
STIGMA!
THAT GIRL...
OH, I HAVE AN IDEA. I'LL GO AHEAD...
...AND GIVE US A NAME WHILE I'M AT IT.
ZSH
...
FWOOOO
ZSH
SO THAT YOU MAY LOVE US.
AND SO THAT WE MAY CONTINUE TO REMAIN IN YOUR HEARTS...

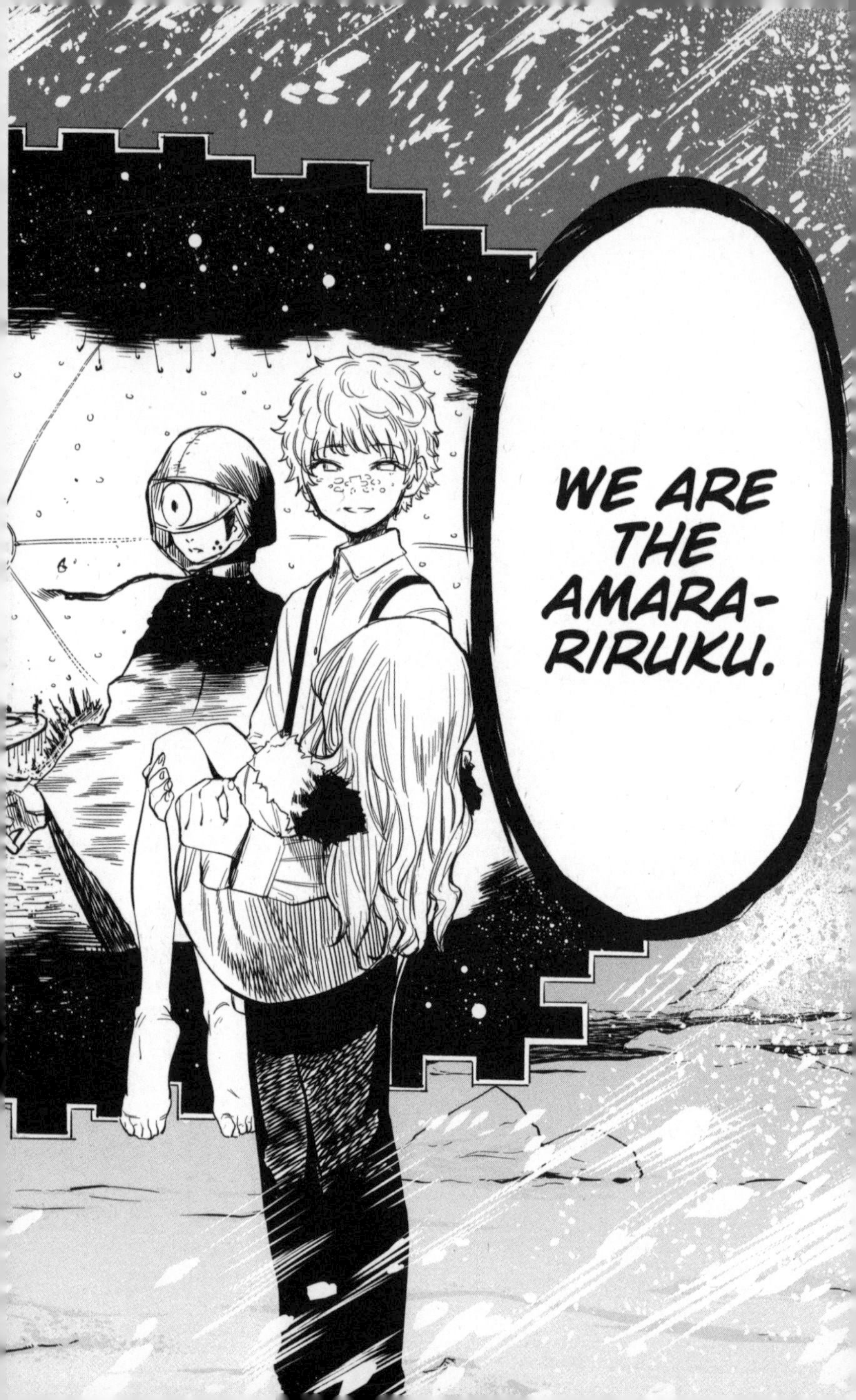
WE ARE THE AMARA-RIRUKU.

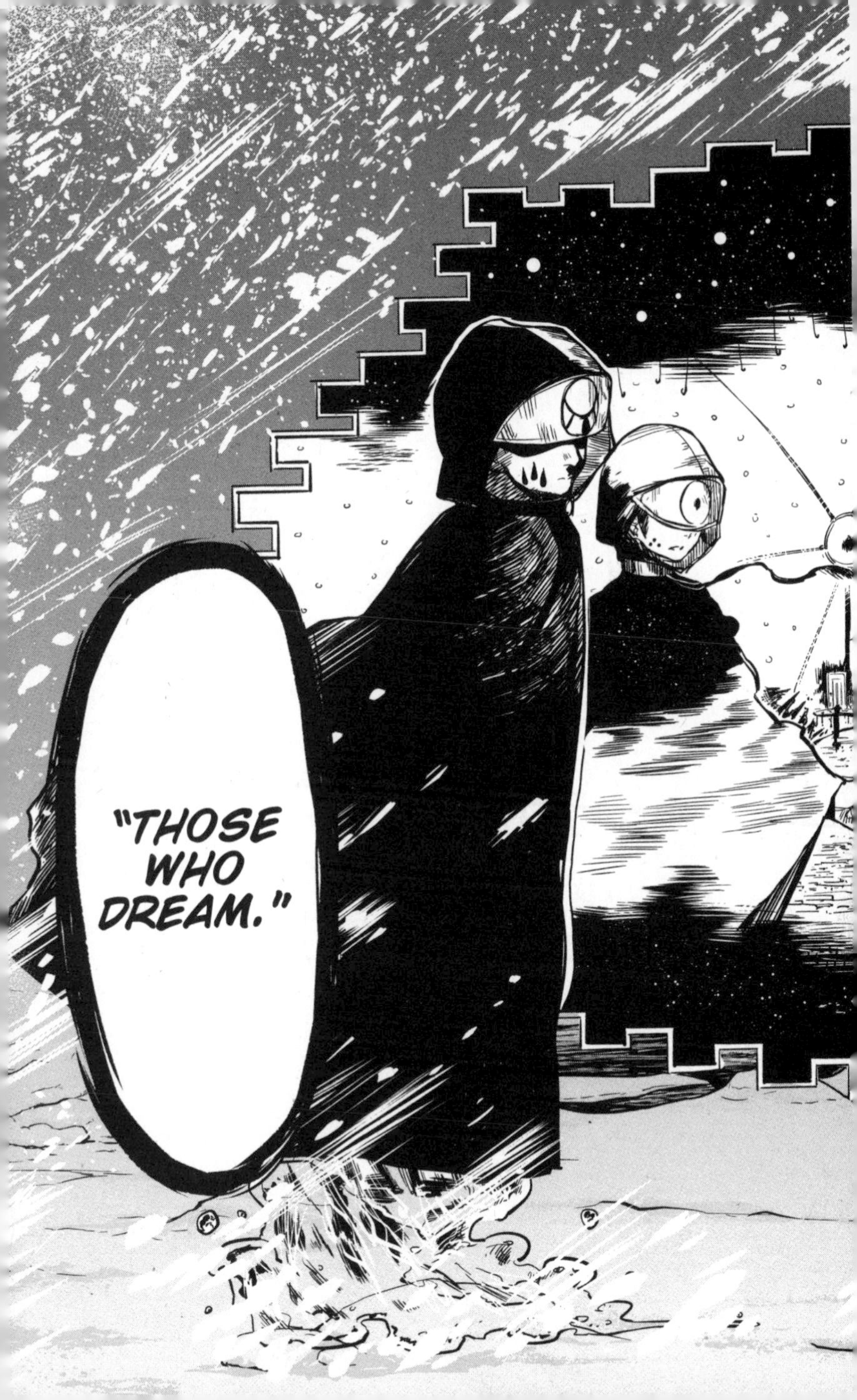
"THOSE WHO DREAM."

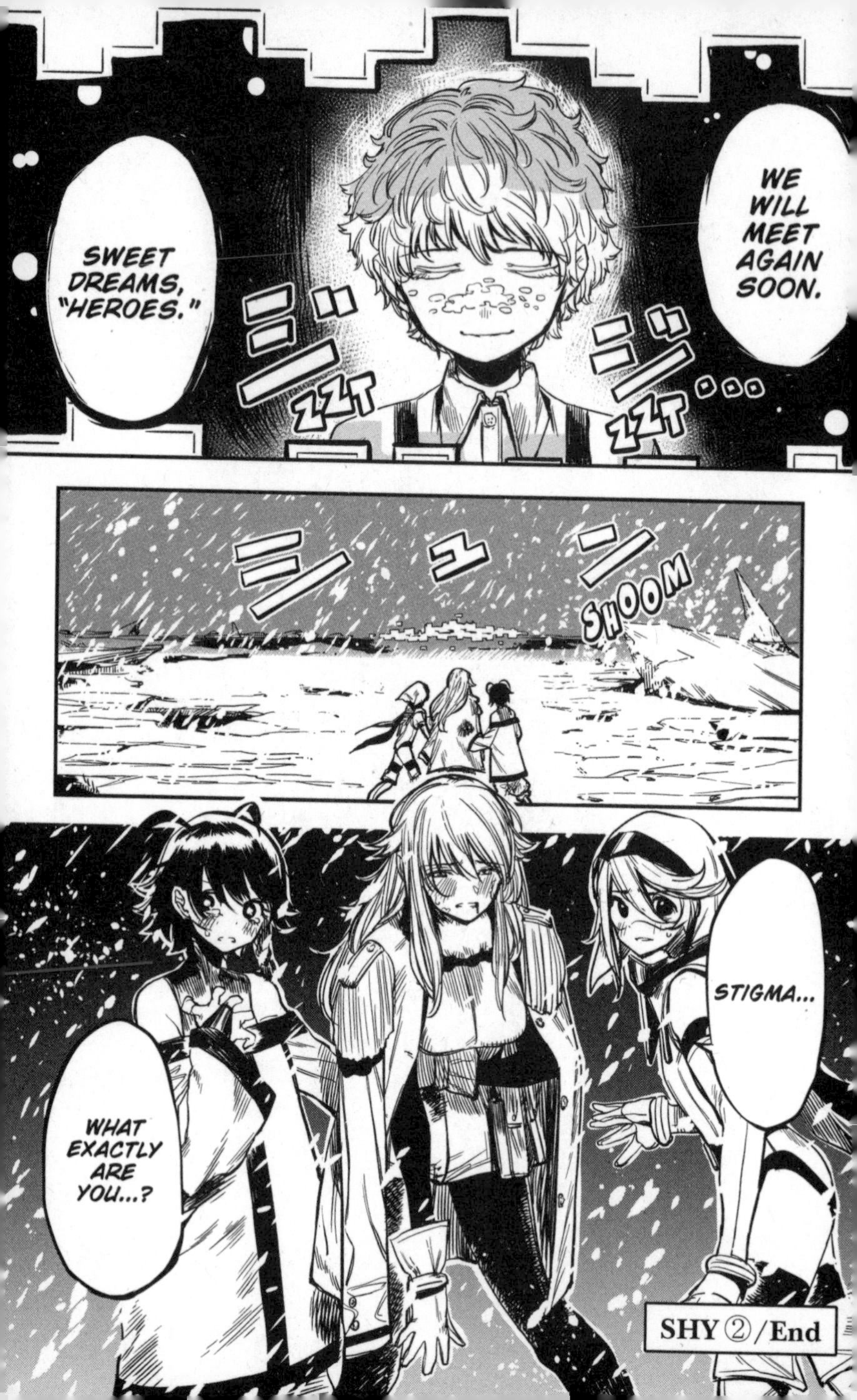
WE WILL MEET AGAIN SOON.
ZZZT...
SWEET DREAMS, "HEROES."
ZZZT
SHOOM
STIGMA...
WHAT EXACTLY ARE YOU...?

SHY ②/End

BONUS

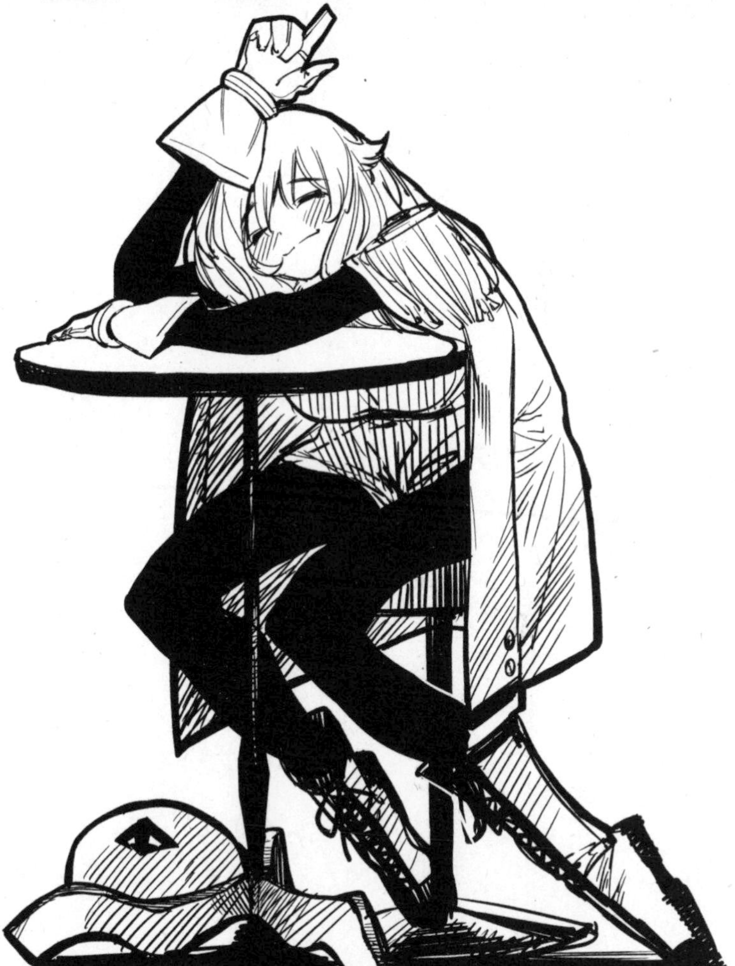

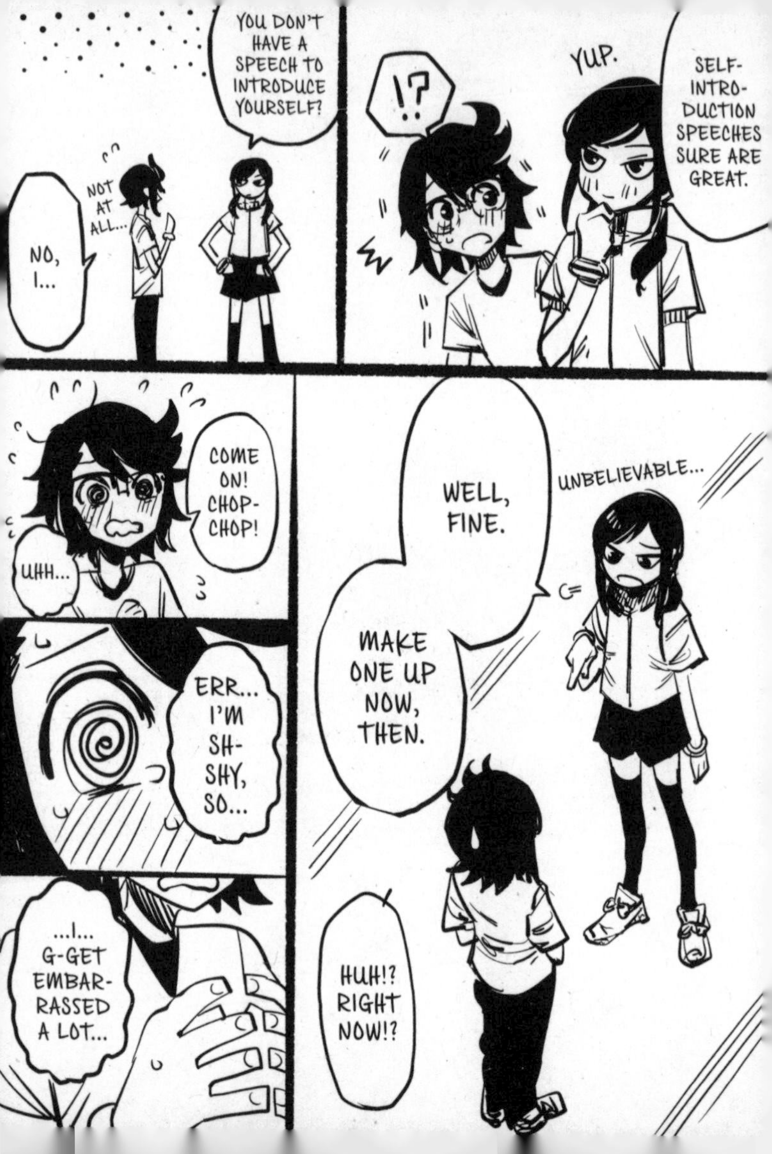
SELF-INTRODUCTION SPEECHES SURE ARE GREAT.
YUP.
!?
YOU DON'T HAVE A SPEECH TO INTRODUCE YOURSELF?
NOT AT ALL...
NO, I...
UNBELIEVABLE...
WELL, FINE.
MAKE ONE UP NOW, THEN.
HUH!? RIGHT NOW!?
COME ON! CHOP-CHOP!
UHH...
ERR... I'M SH-SHY, SO...
...I... G-GET EMBARRASSED A LOT...

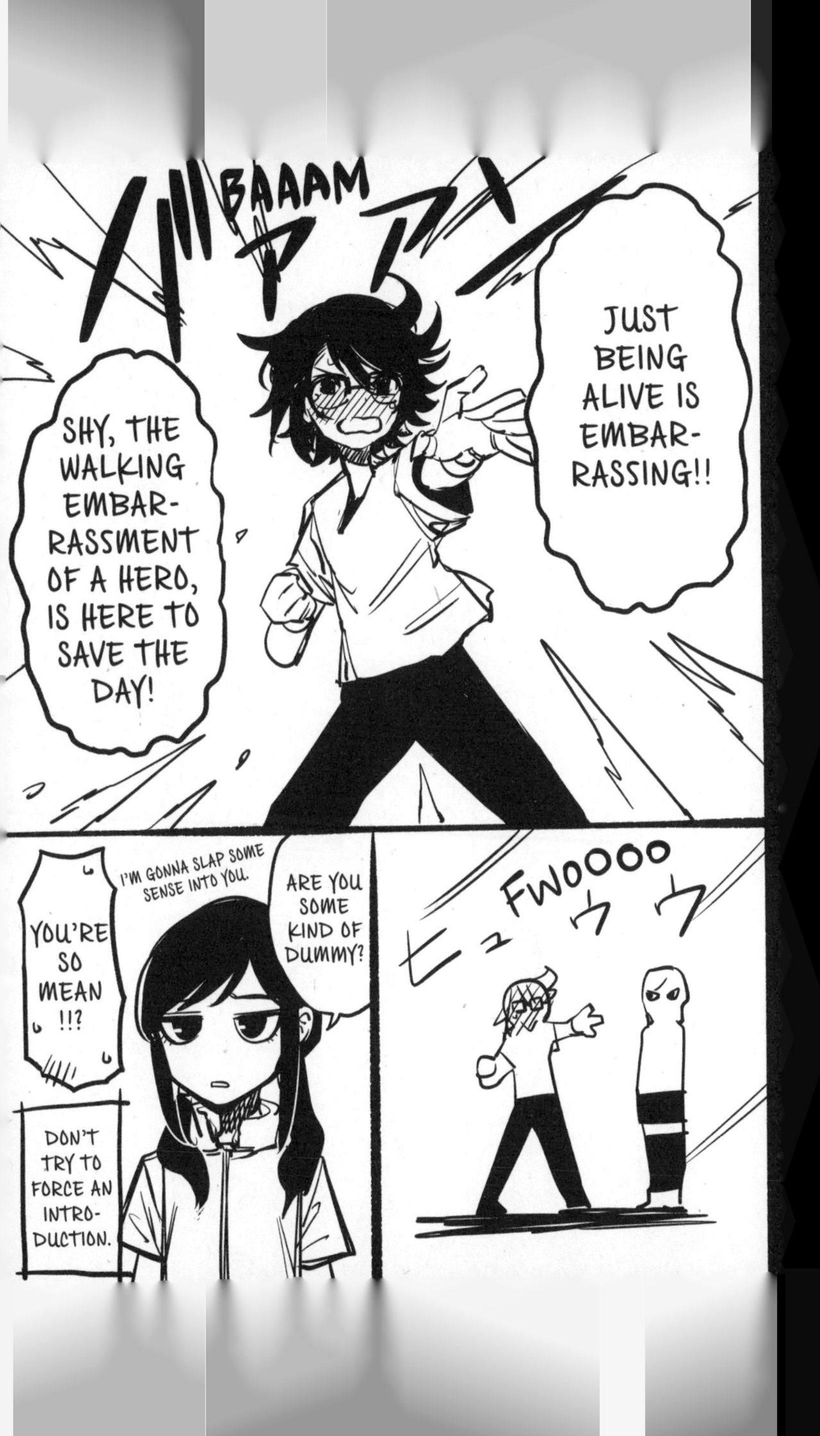
BAAAM
JUST BEING ALIVE IS EMBARRASSING!!
SHY, THE WALKING EMBARRASSMENT OF A HERO, IS HERE TO SAVE THE DAY!
FWOOOO
ARE YOU SOME KIND OF DUMMY?
I'M GONNA SLAP SOME SENSE INTO YOU.
YOU'RE SO MEAN !!?
DON'T TRY TO FORCE AN INTRODUCTION.

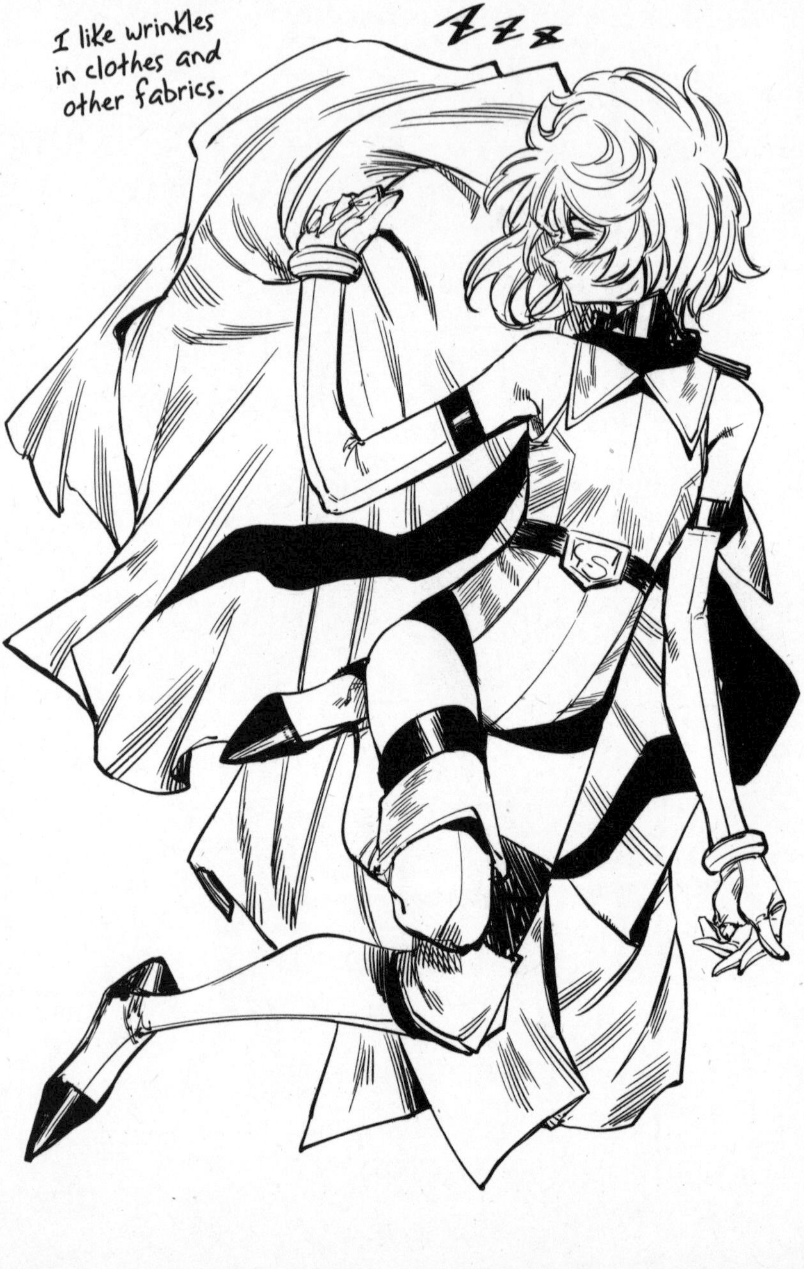
I like wrinkles in clothes and other fabrics.
Zzz

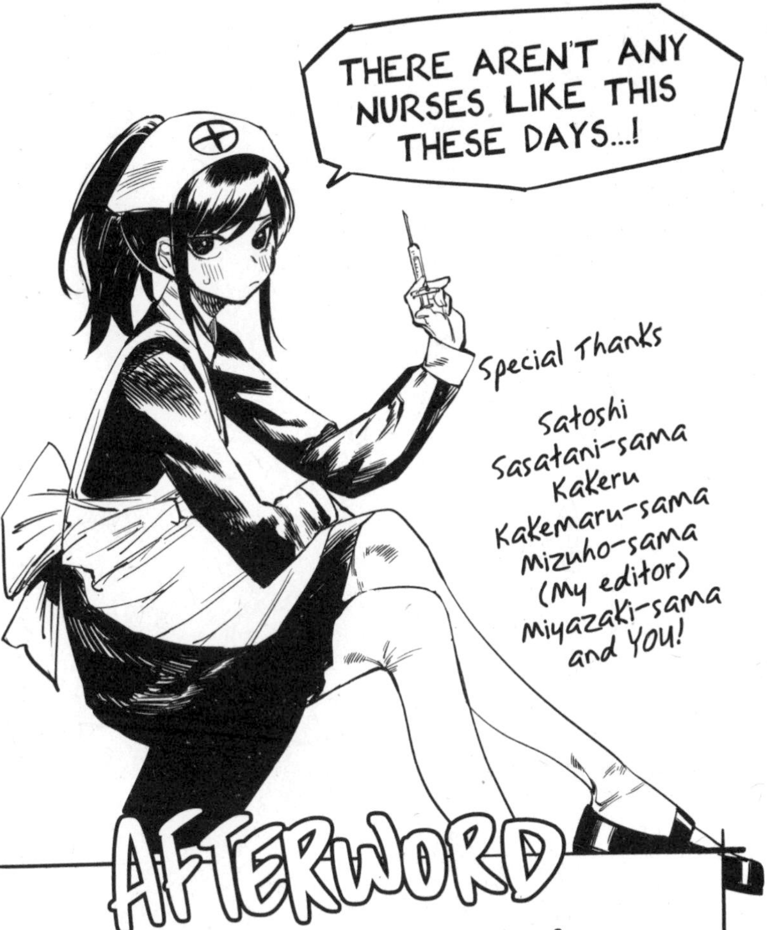
THERE AREN'T ANY NURSES LIKE THIS THESE DAYS...!

Special Thanks

Satoshi
Sasatani-sama
Kakeru
Kakemaru-sama
Mizuho-sama
(My editor)
Miyazaki-sama
and YOU!

AFTERWORD

Thank you for grabbing Volume 2. When life keeps marching on as we all stumble around through things, it can sometimes feel as if you don't even have time to breathe, but I hope you're able to get at least a little enjoyment out of this manga. I'll also do my best to make this enjoyable for myself.

Bukimi Miki

2020.01.13 OTNPK

NEXT
Volume Preview

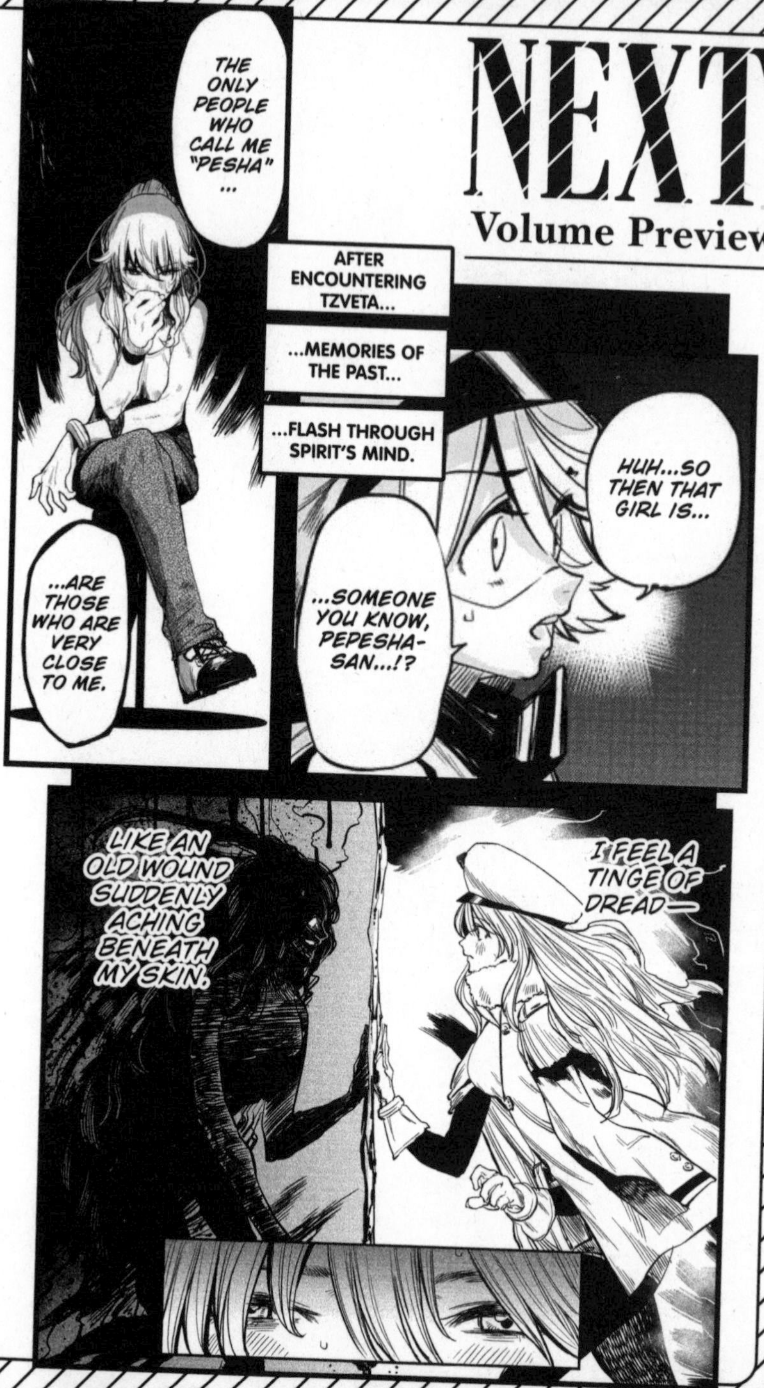
AFTER ENCOUNTERING TZVETA...
...MEMORIES OF THE PAST...
...FLASH THROUGH SPIRIT'S MIND.
HUH...SO THEN THAT GIRL IS...
...SOMEONE YOU KNOW, PEPESHA-SAN...!?
THE ONLY PEOPLE WHO CALL ME "PESHA"...
...ARE THOSE WHO ARE VERY CLOSE TO ME.
I FEEL A TINGE OF DREAD—
LIKE AN OLD WOUND SUDDENLY ACHING BENEATH MY SKIN.

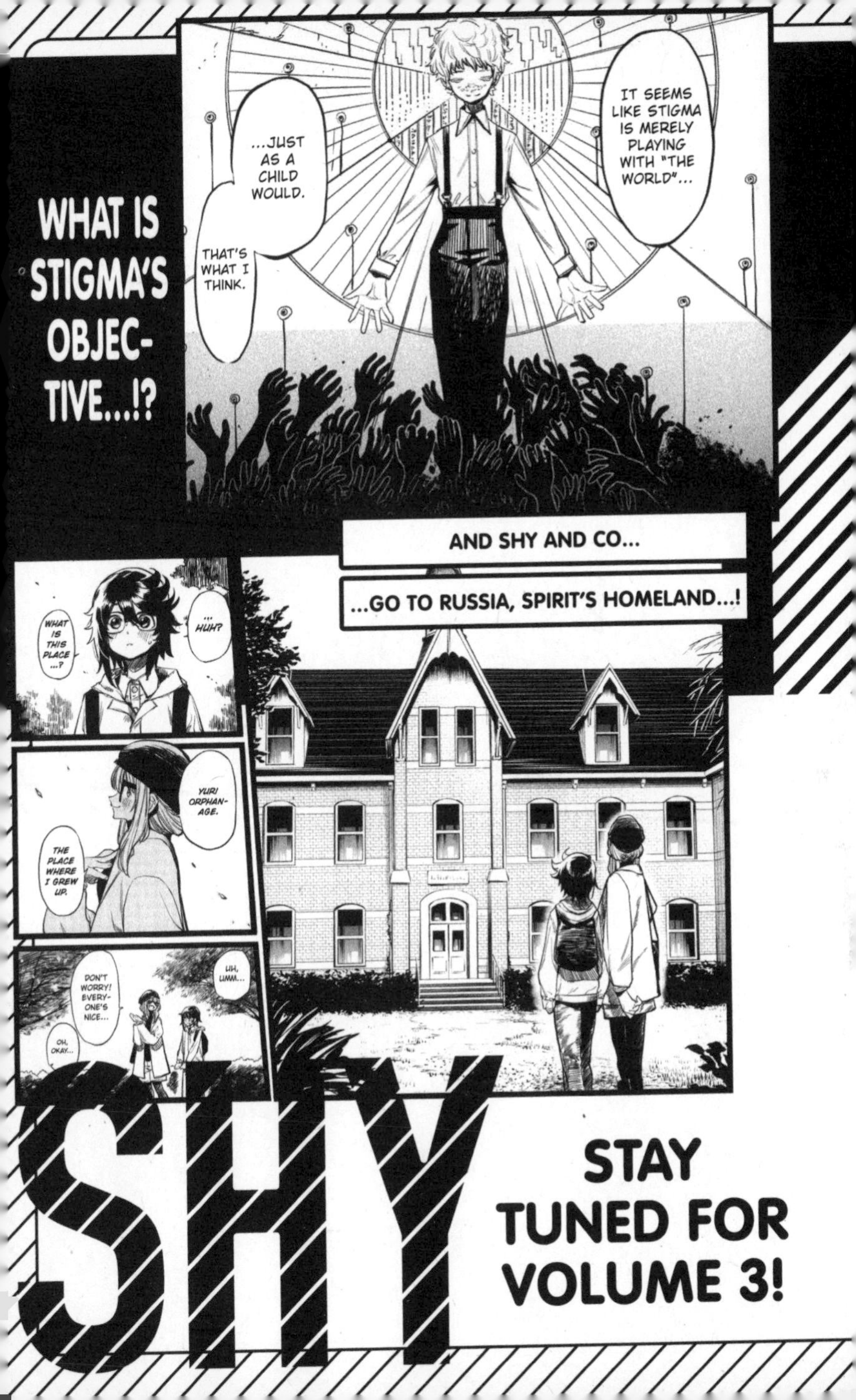
WHAT IS STIGMA'S OBJECTIVE...!?
IT SEEMS LIKE STIGMA IS MERELY PLAYING WITH "THE WORLD"...
...JUST AS A CHILD WOULD.
THAT'S WHAT I THINK.
AND SHY AND CO...
...GO TO RUSSIA, SPIRIT'S HOMELAND...!
... HUH?
WHAT IS THIS PLACE...?
YURI ORPHANAGE.
THE PLACE WHERE I GREW UP.
UH, UMM...
DON'T WORRY! EVERYONE'S NICE...
OH, OKAY...
SHY
STAY TUNED FOR VOLUME 3!

SHY

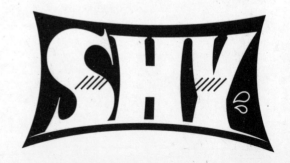

TRANSLATION NOTES ▬

GENERAL

-san: The Japanese equivalent of Mr./Mrs./Miss. If a situation calls for politeness, this is the fail-safe honorific.

-kun: Used most often when referring to boys, this indicates affection or familiarity. Occasionally used by older men among their peers, but it may also be used by anyone referring to a person of lower standing.

-chan: An affectionate honorific indicating familiarity used mostly in reference to girls; also used in reference to cute persons or animals of any gender.

Page 100

This spelling of **Kurou** is a reference to Kurou Hazama, the real name of the protagonist of *Black Jack*, the classic medical adventure manga, which was also published in *Weekly Shonen Champion*.

Tennouzu Isle is a classy Tokyo waterfront district with easy access to Odaiba and Tokyo Disneyland.

Champion is most likely a reference to *Weekly Shonen Champion*, the magazine *Shy* was originally published in.

Otsunpoko is Bukimi Miki's farewell phrase (usually abbreviated to "OTNPK" in English characters) and is a play on *otsukaresama*, meaning "good work" or "farewell." Look for it in the afterword!

Haruku Amami is most likely a reference to Haruka Amami, a main heroine in the *iDOLM@STER* game series.

Shihoshishi refers to a fan coupling of Shiho Kitagawa from *THE iDOLM@STER Million Live!* and the ninja dog Shishimaru from 1960's kids manga series *Ninja Hattori-kun*. Formed with the idea of matching normally cold and aloof Shiho's love of stuffed animals with the plushy-like cuteness of Shishimaru, Bukimi Miki created a *doujinshi* fan comic of the two prior to the publication of *Shy*.

Page 107

Though the calligraphy club members didn't notice it, Teru was writing her name when she wrote "**shine.**" The kanji character her name is written with is more typically read as *kagayaku* and is specifically used to describe a beautiful, brilliant light. "Teru" is a non-standard reading that comes from another word for "shine" with slightly different connotations—the illumination of the sun or moon. However, the kanji for *teru* is also used in *tereru*, which means "to be shy."

SHY 2

Bukimi Miki

Translation: Ajani Oloye ▼ Lettering: Arbash Mughal

SHY Volume 2
© 2020 Bukimi Miki
All rights reserved. First published in Japan in 2020 by Akita Publishing Co., Ltd., Tokyo
English translation rights arranged with Akita Publishing Co., Ltd. through Tuttle-Mori Agency, Inc., Tokyo

English translation © 2023 by Yen Press, LLC

Yen Press
150 West 30th Street, 19th Floor
New York, NY 10001

Visit us at yenpress.com ▼ facebook.com/yenpress ▼ twitter.com/yenpress
yenpress.tumblr.com ▼ instagram.com/yenpress

First Yen Press Edition: March 2023
Edited by Yen Press Editorial: Thomas McAlister, Carl Li
Designed by Yen Press Design: Madelaine Norman

Yen Press is an imprint of Yen Press, LLC.
The Yen Press name and logo are trademarks of Yen Press, LLC.

Library of Congress Control Number: 2022946494

ISBNs: 978-1-9753-5239-4 (paperback)
978-1-9753-5240-0 (ebook)

10 9 8 7 6 5 4 3 2 1

LSC-C

Printed in the United States of America